Power, Politics, and Organizational Change

Power, Politics, and Organizational Change

Winning the Turf Game

Second Edition

David A. Buchanan and Richard J. Badham

Cranfield University School of Management and
Macquarie University Graduate School of Management

Los Angeles | London | New Delhi
Singapore | Washington DC

First Published 2008 Reprinted 2010

SAGE Publications Ltd
1 Oliver's Yard
55 City Road
London EC1Y 1SP

SAGE Publications Inc.
2455 Teller Road
Thousand Oaks, California 91320

SAGE Publications India Pvt Ltd
B 1/I 1 Mohan Cooperative Industrial Area
Mathura Road
New Delhi 110 044

SAGE Publications Asia-Pacific Pte Ltd
33 Pekin Street #02-01
Far East Square
Singapore 048763

Library of Congress Control Number: 2007931450

British Library Cataloguing in Publication data

A catalogue record for this book is available from
the British Library

ISBN 978-1-4129-2833-5
ISBN 978-1-4129-2834-2 (pbk)

Typeset by CEPHA Imaging Pvt. Ltd., Bangalore, India
Printed in Great Britain by Ashford Colour Press Ltd, Gosport, Hampshire
Printed on paper from sustainable resources

For Lesley and Santiago, with love

Contents

Acknowledgements

Both editions of this book have benefited from the contributions, collegiality, advice, ideas, and criticisms of a significant number of managers, personal friends, and academic colleagues. These include Lawrence Ang, Hooman Attar, Helen Bevan, Lesley Buchanan, David Boddy, Richard Carter, Paul Chapman, Ian Clark, Richard Claydon, Tim Claydon, Stewart Clegg, Paul Couchman, Patrick Dawson, Simon Down, Elena Doldor, Mike Doyle, Dexter Dunphy, Pelle Ehn, Karin Garrety, Keith Grint, Gus Guzman, Norma Harrison, Maree Horne, Martin House, Andrzej Huczynski, Bill Johnson, Grant Jones, Hugo Kerr, Sven Kylén, Karen Legge, Stuart Macdonald, Ian McLoughlin, Amanda Mead, Brian Moran, John Neath, Paul Nesbit, Rosemary Nixon, Chris Provis, Andrew Sense, Val Singh, Derek Staniforth, Paul Steadman, Susan Vinnicombe, David Webster, Yehudi Webster, David Weir, Michael Zanko – and many others too numerous to mention, including the hundreds of managers who have taken part in analyses and discussions of their own political behaviour as participants on our management development programmes. For all their individual and collective inputs, we are extremely grateful, and indebted.

We would also like to thank the following for helping us to identify copyright holders and for arranging permission to reproduce the various images, cartoons, figures, and other materials that appear in this book, including in some cases their own work: Reagan Carmona at Universal Press Syndicate, Andre Gailani and Nick Roberts at Punch Limited, Sidney Harris at ScienceCartoonsPlus.com, Jennifer Hawdon at Edward Elgar Publishing Limited, Tony Husband and Amanda Alcock at Private Eye, Jennifer Jones at Elsevier Limited, Merrideth Miller at The Cartoon Bank (New Yorker Magazine), Jon Mirachi for the use of the cartoon drawn by his late father Joseph Mirachi, Simon Spicer at Kiss Me Kwik Ltd, Anne Taintor of Anne Taintor Inc., Charles Barsotti, Michelle Kacmar, Bruce McCall, Mike Shapiro, and Eran Vigoda-Gadot.

We would also like to offer special thanks to Kiren Shoman and Anne Summers at Sage Publications for all their encouragement and editorial support. The flaws and errors in this book, however, remain the responsibility of the authors.

We hope that you will find this book useful, interesting, and enjoyable. However, we welcome your feedback. We are particularly interested to hear from readers whose experiences of organizational politics are consistent with the argument set out here – and also from those who feel that we have misrepresented these issues. Our email addresses are:

David: David.Buchanan@Cranfield.ac.uk
Richard: Richard.Badham@Mgsm.edu.au

Illustrations

Figures

Tables

Preface to the Second edition

> Organization politics are a reality in most organizations, and while game-playing might outwardly appear to be wasted time, it is necessary in order to secure resources, progress ideas, achieve personal goals, and often to enhance one's standing. It is naive to realistically expect to be able to stand aloof from organizational politics. You may be respected for doing so, but your progress will be limited and you will be seen as an easy target.
>
> *middle manager, private sector manufacturing company, male.*

Welcome to the second edition of this text. Since the first edition (1999), further evidence and commentary have been published, and the subject of organization politics is now covered on a number of masters degrees and executive development courses. We have therefore developed this edition so that it can be used as a core teaching text for specialist courses on organization politics, as well as support reading for courses in organizational behaviour, change management, leadership, and innovation. We hope that the availability of this text will encourage more instructors to offer courses in organization politics, rather than confine the topic to a session or two in their organizational behaviour courses. Research suggests that most managers view organization politics as a routine part of their experience, and a key factor in career success. However, the evidence also reveals that most managers have had no training in how to deal with this dimension of their role. We hope that practising managers will also find useful the evidence, arguments, case materials, diagnostics, assessments, practical advice, and other material that we have incorporated in this new edition.

The aims of this new edition are to incorporate:

1 fresh and up-to-date evidence, argument, and examples
2 teaching materials for self-study, and for instructors to use and adapt as appropriate.

Organization politics is a controversial subject. Advising managers on how to become better organization politicians may not be widely regarded as a legitimate activity.

This book adopts a different stance, however, arguing that political behaviour is inevitable and desirable, as political exchanges generate the dynamic and drive the debate behind organization development and change initiatives. Most managers are likely to find the implementation of innovation and change challenging unless they possess political skill.

Current organizational trends have reinforced the significance of political skill. The stable, ordered, bounded, predictable, rule-based hierarchical organization today seems to be an anachronism. The so-called 'postmodern' organization is characterized by fluidity, uncertainty, ambiguity, and discontinuity. Organization boundaries are blurred with the development of partnerships and joint ventures, subcontracting and outsourcing, peripheral workforces and virtual teams, and social and technology-based collaborative networks. Hierarchy is replaced, in part, by reliance on expert power; in this context, those with the best understanding of the issues take the decisions. Many managers, and especially those with roles that include responsibility for innovation and change, have no direct line authority over those on whose cooperation they must rely. In this context, those with the best political skills attract more resources and support. In this (stereotyped) 'postmodern' organization, individuals are stripped of the luxury of a stable position, and are deprived of a predictable vision of their future. This fluid context implies an increased dependence on personal and interpersonal resources, and thus on political skills to advance personal and corporate agendas. There is clearly enhanced scope for political manoeuvring in a less well ordered and less disciplined organizational world, and hence the need for a critical understanding of the nature, shaping role, and consequences of political behaviour.

What's new?

Readers will find the following new material in this edition:

- New *research data* concerning the management experience and perceptions of organization politics. This shows that most managers regard political games as ethical, and identifies common and rare tactics.
- A further introduction to *research perspectives* in a field which is dominated by a positivist approach that struggles with the problem of finding a single undisputed definition of politics. That problem dissolves with a perspective that regards politics as a socially constructed phenomenon. What matters is not how researchers define politics, but how organizational members understand and define political behaviour.
- Additional discussion and illustration of *critical perspectives* on power and organization politics. These views bring into question common sense understandings of the nature of power and politics, and also what it means to be innovative and entrepreneurial. They address the personal (emotional) and social costs as well as benefits of Machiavellian management and political entrepreneurship.

- A new *antecedents – behaviours – consequences model* of organization politics, based on how practising managers understand these 'A–B–C' linkages. This model exposes the multiple triggers of political behaviour (which is not exclusively self-serving), the extraordinarily rich behaviour repertoire of the organization politician, and the 'dual effects' of politics concerning the range of individual and organizational benefits and costs flowing from the use of these tactics.
- Exploration of political skill, or rather *political expertise*. What is political skill? What does it mean to be an expert organization politician? How can political expertise be developed?
- An assessment of *women behaving badly*, exploring gender differences and gender effects in the understanding of, approaches to, and the use and consequences of political behaviour. Are women's attitudes to politics different from those of men? Are women affected differently? Do women play 'a different game'? What is the impact of making the distinction between 'men' and 'women' in this regard?
- A variety of *teaching materials*, which can be adapted for personal and instructional use, including incident reports, self-assessments, organization diagnostics, and analytical frameworks. Each chapter recommends a feature film (or DVD) which portrays aspects of organization politics. Dramatized fictional accounts offer valuable insights into the nature, practice, and implications of organization politics, for both skilled and unskilled players – issues that are difficult to demonstrate through other teaching vehicles. Film suggestions are intended mainly for home viewing. For classroom use, an appropriate licence is normally required. Before using film in the classroom, confirm with your local copyright administrator that you are operating within the law. In Britain, check the terms and conditions of two organizations which supply licences: Educational Recording Agency (www.era.org.uk) and Filmbank Distributors who provide Public Video Screening Licenses (www.pvsl.co.uk).

What's the point?

> My view is that organization politics are almost inevitable, but they can be constructive or destructive. The best management skills would seek to ensure that constructive uses, such as attraction of resources, or changed working practices, are delivered through using supportive political skills. The worst skills are tantamount to bullying and dishonesty, which should not be condoned.
>
> *middle manager, public sector hospital, female.*

The purpose and argument of this book remain the same. Our purpose is to offer a theoretical and practical guide to the politics of organizational change and innovation. The exercise of organization politics can be conceived as a game in which players compete for different kinds of territory – for turf. What kind of game is this? What are the rules? How is it played? What ethical issues – if any – are raised? Should one play this game to win, and how? The underpinning argument is that the change agent who is not able and willing to engage with the organization politics will fail in that role, sooner or later, and probably sooner.

Our focus lies primarily with the *internal* change agent. A lot of commentary focuses on external agents and consultants (Ginzberg and Abrahamson, 1991; Hartley et al., 1997). But change is often a significant element of the roles and responsibilities of most functional and general managers, as well as many other staff, at all levels.

Age and treachery

The American police chief, Bill Bratton, became known for his ability to 'turn around' problem police forces. In 1980, when he was a young lieutenant (age 34) in Boston's police department, he put up this sign in his office: '*Youth and skill will win out every time over age and treachery*'.

However, within a few months, he was shunted into a dead end position, through a combination of office politics and his own brashness. Bratton took down the sign, having learned the significance of the plots, intrigues, and politics driving organizational change.

Source: based on an anecdote reported by Kim and Mauborgne (2003).

Our purpose is based on four underpinning beliefs.

1 The reality of politics

Political behaviour plays a more significant role in organizational life than is often recognized, or openly admitted. We like to think of our social and organizational cultures as characterized by order, rationality, openness, collaboration and trust. The reality, however, is often different. Competition sits alongside cooperation. Informal 'backstaging' supports public action. We see self-interest, deceit, subterfuge, and cunning, as well as the pursuit of moral ideals and high aspirations. It is uncommon to hear decisions defended in terms of political motives and behaviours. Reason and logic must be seen and heard to prevail, and to suggest otherwise is to risk censure and ostracism. But initiatives are pursued, decisions are taken, and changes are introduced to preserve and extend the power bases and influence of individuals and groups, as well as to deliver corporate benefits. Major decisions and significant changes are particularly liable to heighten political activity. When observing outbreaks of either consensus or conflict, organizational behaviour cannot be understood fully without a knowledge of the role of political motives, agendas, and behaviour.

or not they have an official title recognizing that responsibility. (While concentrating on internal agents, much of the argument here applies to external change agents as well.) The simple notion of 'relevance' is not much help. Some of the more esoteric analyses of power shed useful light on the shaping role of politics. Some of the more readily accessible conceptualizations of power and politics tend to oversimplify the issues. We have therefore sought to survey the field from the standpoint of the change agent, exercising the authors' privileged politics of inclusion and exclusion. Academic readers familiar with the wider literature of this field will doubtless note major gaps.

This begs the question: who is this 'change agent' whose perspective is being adopted? We will first address this question in Chapter 1, but two comments may be helpful. First, the concept of *change agency* is of more value than the notion of the singular change agent (Buchanan and Storey, 1997; Denis et al., 2001). Change is typically driven by what Hutton (1994) describes as a 'cast of characters'. Our change agent is any member of that cast, formally appointed, or self-appointed, seeking to drive or subvert a change agenda. Second, the change agent is viewed here as a *political entrepreneur* (Laver, 1997), deploying political tactics when necessary to advance combinations of personal and organizational agendas, potentially in the face of opposition. This does not imply that change agency is an exclusively political activity, but political skill is a key element in the behaviour repertoire of the change agent.

The term *political entrepreneur* is chosen with care. The label 'political activist' is drawn from the domain of national party politics, implying a highly visible, ruthless and self-serving approach. The term 'political operator' is in more widespread use to describe the politically aware, astute and skilled manager. However, the term *political entrepreneur* has the advantage of emphasizing the risk-taking and creative dimensions of the role of the change agent, and also the personal commitment, extending on occasion to passion, towards the change agenda. The term political entrepreneur thus implies a behaviour repertoire, of political strategies and tactics, and a reflective, self-critical perspective on how those political behaviours should be deployed. As we see in Chapter 6, this extends to critical reflection on the personal costs as well as benefits of such an entrepreneurial approach.

We will also argue that the change agent who strives to be politically neutral or 'squeaky clean' faces double jeopardy.

Squeaky clean and outmanoeuvred

First, the 'squeaky clean' approach is likely to be ineffective in the face of self-interested and sophisticated resistance tactics, or 'counter-implementation' measures. The change agent who is not equipped, or not willing, to deal with political issues and power plays is thus likely to be outmanoeuvred. This argument is based on the presumption that organization politics are pervasive, and cannot be 'wished away' or managed away. It is necessary to confront circumstances as they are, and not as one would wish them to be. In colloquial terms, management in general, and change management in particular, is a 'contact sport'. Those who do not wish to get bruised should not play.

Squeaky clean and unprofessional

Second, the 'squeaky clean' approach which ignores, avoids, or otherwise denies the political realities of organizational life can be viewed as unskilled, incompetent, unprofessional and unethical. As we shall argue later, advocates of 'squeaky clean' management obscure the political dimensions and implications of that position. It may be more ethical and professional to deal effectively with the political aspects of change than simply to observe the political realities from a remote moral high ground. Change often stimulates both support and resistance. Some resistance may be self-serving, while some may be based on a sincere belief that change is misguided. A committed change agent inevitably becomes a 'guardian' of the change agenda. This can warrant a politically entrepreneurial approach to conducting that protective function in the face of public challenge and 'backstage' tactics. Again in colloquial terms, if you confront a 'bodyguard', you presumably know what to expect.

There is no simple contrast between a politically neutral or ethical stance on the one hand, and on the other an unprincipled approach in which 'anything goes' in the pursuit of change, although this is how the field of organization politics is often portrayed. The judgements that one may need to bring to this domain must be contingent and situational. The popular notion that 'power corrupts' must be balanced against the observation that power also helps in the pursuit and achievement of valuable social and organizational objectives. The politically entrepreneurial actions of the change agent will invariably be defensible, on some criteria and for some constituencies, while being wholly unacceptable on other grounds and for other players. We hope to demonstrate the integrity (personal, and organizational) of consciously undertaking political behaviour in an organizational change context.

The text is constructed in an accessible, if sometimes demanding, writing style, assuming a readership with practical organizational and managerial experience. Our aim is to make the text entertaining and engaging, and also to reflect the non-linear, untidy character of change, and the sometimes devious character of much of the subject matter.

Calvin and Hobbes

Calvin and Hobbes © 1990 Watterson. Distributed by Universal Press Syndicate. Reprinted with permission.

The structure of the book is as follows.

Chapter 1, **When necessity commands**, explores the nature of power and politics, the significance of political behaviour in organizational change, and the problems of finding and defining 'the change agent' (change driver, or change leader). New research offers insights into the management experience of organization politics, exposing the range of popular and rare tactics, and linking the antecedents of political behaviour to a range of individual and organizational consequences through a varied behaviour repertoire of political tactics.

Chapter 2, **The terminology game**, examines the literature of power and politics in search of competing definitions of these terms. Power can be conceived as a property of individuals, a property of interpersonal relationships, or as a property of social and organizational structures and procedures, although those three perspectives are intertwined rather than distinct. The problems of defining political behaviour are also examined. The ways in which we use conversation controls, influence tactics, and impression management methods are explored, illustrating that it is possible to conceive of every social interaction in political terms. This definition problem can be resolved by adopting a constructivist perspective; the ability to define behaviour as political, or to reject such a definition, is itself a political act.

Chapter 3, **Sit in judgement**, presents a series of incident reports from managers describing examples of political behaviour in their own experience. How should someone faced with political tactics respond? One answer to this question relies on an 'ethics test'. However, the problems of determining whether political behaviours are ethical or not are discussed, and an alternative, more practical approach is presented. This chapter introduces three central concepts concerning *warrant*, for political actions, *accounting* for those actions, and *reputation*, concerning how a change agent is perceived by other members of the organization. Case material at the end of the chapter illustrates this argument in practice, using actual instances of political exchanges.

Chapter 4, **Men behaving badly,** draws on historical and contemporary views of negative politics, contrasting 'thugs' and 'pragmatists'. These are not personality types, but rather loosely drawn perspectives on the use of power and politics in organizational settings. The politically incorrect chapter title reflects the fact that early writers in this genre (in the 1960s and 1970s) were mostly male, and were writing about men, for men. The stereotype of the Machiavellian thug has been well established, but this chapter argues that such a simplified view is unsustainable, and the alternative perspective of the Machiavellian pragmatist is presented. Deceit, manipulation, and coercion may be part of the pragmatist's behaviour repertoire, without being the sole or preferred approach to dealing with political issues. In contrast to the thug, the pragmatist uses such tactics with care and restraint, when they are warranted by the context (as argued in Chapter 3). This pragmatic, situational approach contributes to the profile of the *political entrepreneur*, explored in Chapters 7 and 9.

Chapter 5, **Women behaving badly**, considers evidence regarding gender differences and effects concerning organization power, politics, and influence. It was pointed out to us that this was also a politically incorrect (perhaps insulting) title, but one of our (female) reviewers commented sharply, 'So, only men get to behave badly, but not women?' Consequently, we have retained this heading, and hope that this does not cause offence. Do women approach organization politics differently from men? Do they play the same game? Is political skill equally central to the careers and reputations of male and female managers? While some research evidence tends to support the stereotypes of 'tough males' and 'tender females', other evidence and experience argues that women in management and change agency roles recognize the need for a broad repertoire of political skills, and act accordingly.

Chapter 6, **The entrepreneurial hero**, explores the contemporary stereotype of the creative, innovative, bureaucracy-busting entrepreneurial visionary, or what Kanter (1989) calls the 'post-entrepreneurial hero'. This stereotype now informs pervasive and dominant images of the goals, tactics, and ethics of organizational innovators. This chapter thus explores contemporary prescriptive models of risk-taking 'champions of innovation' and their distinctive approach to 'positive' politics, in contrast with the 'negative' thuggery described in Chapter 4. In so doing, the chapter considers the insights that such models provide for managing the politics of innovation. The chapter also opens up for critical discussion the sharp contrast often drawn between the 'positive' power tactics of innovative 'entrepreneurial heroes' and the 'negative' politics found in traditional bureaucracies.

Chapter 7, **The good, the bad, and the ugly**, subjects the image of the entrepreneurial hero and the Machiavellian manager to more critical analysis, exploring the 'ugly' dimension of 'good' entrepreneurial and 'bad' Machiavellian strategies. In particular, this chapter details how contemporary organizations encourage both entrepreneurial and Machiavellian behaviours, while imposing personal costs on those adopting such perspectives. At the risk of creating fresh labels and dichotomies, but in order to characterize more clearly the practical options in these conditions, a fresh contrast is drawn. The differences between Machiavellian 'thuggery' and 'pragmatism' are supplemented by a distinction between the dangerous and self-defeating attributes of 'entrepreneurial zealots', and more constructive and viable 'entrepreneurial creatives'. This chapter reinforces and develops the argument that a sharp distinction between 'positive' and 'negative' politics is far from clear, either in theory, or in practice.

Chapters 4 through 7 present the caricatures and stereotypes outlined in Table P.1. The 'thuggery' of the traditional Machiavellian stereotype (or 'street fighter') and the entrepreneurial heroism of contemporary 'zealots' is unsustainable. The pragmatic, situational use of Machiavellian tactics and the constructive aspects of entrepreneurial creatives belong to the profile of the political entrepreneur, as explained in Chapter 9.

Chapter 8, **Power assisted steering**, considers the array of practical advice available to change agents in the use of political strategies and tactics. Much of that advice is couched in 'simple recipe' terms, offering checklists in the style of 'do this', and 'don't do that'. Missing from this advice is any notion of the frame of reference, or perspective, required to translate such guidance into appropriate and effective action.

Table P.1 Caricatures and stereotypes

Machiavellian thuggery	traditional stereotype	not sustainable
Machiavellian pragmatism	part of traditional stereotype	component of political entrepreneurship
Entrepreneurial heroes	zealots	not sustainable
	creatives	component of political entrepreneurship

Practice in this domain cannot follow a recipe, but is creative, judgement-based and improvisatory. The change agent will thus typically deploy 'complicating strategies' which are multi-dimensional, multi-faceted, complex and evolving through time, based on the opportunities and resources available in a given context. This improvisational approach, based on 'intuitive artistry' involves *bricolage*; the change agent is a *bricoleur*.

Chapter 9, **Political expertise**, explores how organizational trends may have heightened the significance of political skill, and identifies the triggers and intensifiers of organization politics, concluding that political behaviour is a naturally occurring phenomenon. An overview of Michel Foucault's perspective on power is provided, emphasizing the pervasive and productive aspects of power. The concept of political skill and its dimensions is then considered. Skill and competence are narrow and fragmented concepts, and an argument is developed for the value of the alternative concept of *political expertise*, which also involves informed judgement, creative improvisation, and critical self-monitoring. Drawing together the discussion of thugs and street fighters, pragmatists, entrepreneurial heroes, zealots, and creatives, a profile of the political entrepreneur is drawn. It is important to recognize that this is not a personality type but a perspective, a way of approaching, a lens through which organizational issues and their political dimensions can be analysed to inform effective and sustainable action.

1 When necessity commands

Chapter objectives

1 To explore and challenge popular stereotypes of organization politics.
2 To introduce working definitions of power and politics.
3 To present research evidence concerning management experience of and attitudes towards organization politics.
4 To develop a model of the Antecedents (or triggers), Behaviours (or tactics), and Consequences (or outcomes) of organization politics (the 'A–B–C' of organization politics).

'You're an evil bastard, Gilroy. I like that.'

Reproduced by kind permission of *Private Eye and Tony Husband.*

Laughter and tears: popular images of politics

> **Researcher** But many managers argue that organizational politics are a distraction, it's not what they're paid for, not part of the job?
>
> **Manager** I would say bollocks to that. I would say that people who get to those jobs only get to that level because, first, they are reasonably good at playing these games, and second, actually enjoy playing them. The people who fail at that level are, by and large, people who aren't particularly good at playing and don't understand.

Does that interview response offer a cynical view of management, where only the 'wheeler–dealers' rise to the top through political gaming? Or does this present a realistic view of the links between organizational politics and management careers? We will argue for the latter perspective, adding that political behaviour can contribute to the effective implementation of change and innovation and to organizational effectiveness, as well as to individual success.

This argument confronts two components of the popular stereotype of organization politics, first as humorous, and second as damaging. We have used cartoons to illustrate this book. Television comedies from *Yes Minister* to *The Office* can attribute at least part of their success to the way in which they exploit stereotypes of cunning, underhand, Machiavellian behaviour. However, the perception that a subject is comical means that it is difficult to treat seriously, and organization politics has only recently become the focus of sustained academic research. Consequently, the evidence base is thin, and it is rare to find organization politics taught in business and management schools as a professional competence.

The popular perception of organization politics is also a negative one, focusing on the waste of time and energy, and the damage which such behaviour can cause. While also recognizing the potential benefits from political behaviour, Ferris and Kacmar (1992, p.113) observe that:

> A fundamental issue in work on organizational politics concerns its largely negative interpretation. Most people perceive only the dark side of politics, and indeed there is a dark side, characterized by destructive opportunism and dysfunctional game playing.

'Machiavellian' is an insult, not a compliment, and this perception is widely reflected in the language used to describe organization politics. Calhoon (1969) describes political tactics as 'unsavoury'. Keen (1981) observes that politics is equated with 'evil, corruption, and blasphemy'. Ferris and King (1991) describe politicized decision making as 'a walk on the dark side', echoed in Egan's (1994) book on the 'shadow side' of management.

Chanlat (1997) describes politics as a 'social disease'. It is not surprising that Jackall (1988) criticizes the 'emotional aridity' of managers who compromise a caring ethic by playing political games. This is a difficult topic to research, therefore, because the sensitivity of the issues inhibits research access and stifles candid responses. Madison et al. (1980) advise researchers to disguise their intentions by avoiding the word politics as this is 'too sensitive for use in direct investigations'. In feeding back to management her analysis of politically motivated and internally authored accounts of change, depicting the company's organization development unit in a pivotal light, O'Connor's (1995) management contact described her account as shocking, outrageous and unacceptable, and never met with her again.

  Researching organization politics presents unique challenges. Organization gate-keepers may dismiss requests to explore company politics; managers may not reveal tactics to strangers who want to publish their findings. These problems have been addressed using 'safe' research methods such as self-report questionnaires (Gandz and Murray, 1980; Vigoda, 2003), student respondents (Drory and Romm, 1988), and indirect studies of attitudes and stress in university employees (Ferris et al., 1996). Later in this chapter, we report a study of the management experience of organization politics based on a 'safe' survey approach. While this method has limitations, the pattern of findings is nevertheless interesting.

Politics as comedy: Office wisdom

These items are among hundreds of comments submitted to a British Broadcasting Corporation (BBC) website by fans of the television comedy series, *The Office*, starring Ricky Gervais who played David Brent, the office manager. While these remarks do not appear in the programme scripts, fans clearly felt that they reflected David Brent's idiosyncratic management style:

- There may be no 'I' in team, but there's a 'ME' if you look hard enough.
- Remember that age and treachery will always triumph over youth and ability.
- Every time you open your mouth you have this wonderful ability to continually confirm what I think.
- Show me a good loser and I'll show you a LOSER.
- Never do today that which will become someone else's responsibility tomorrow.
- If you treat the people around you with love and respect, they will never guess that you're trying to get them fired.
- If at first you don't succeed, remove all evidence you ever tried.
- You have to be 100 per cent behind someone before you can stab them in the back.

Continued

- Know your limitations and be content with them. Too much ambition results in promotion to a job you can't do.
- Quitters never win, winners never quit. But those who never win and never quit are idiots.
- Remember the three golden rules:
  - It was like that when I got here.
  - I didn't do it.
  - I like your style (to your boss).
- Avoid employing unlucky people – throw half of the pile of CVs in the bin without reading them.

Source: selected from www.bbc.co.uk/comedy/theoffice/wisdom

Academic commentary and research evidence reinforce the negative stereotype. Klein (1988, p.1) argues that the claim that organizations are political is, 'a myth propagated and entertained to address various needs of organizational members'; accepting this myth makes it self-perpetuating, and political behaviour should instead be eliminated. Eisenhardt and Bourgeois (1988) argue that politics in the top management team is linked with poor company performance, by creating inflexibilities and communication barriers, restricting information flows, and consuming time. Zaleznik (1997) distinguishes between 'psychopolitics' and 'real work', advising managers to ignore the former. Personnel decisions, such as selection and performance evaluation, should be depoliticized, according to Ferris and King (1991). Voyer's (1994, p.84) study of a computer company concluded that politics were 'mostly dysfunctional', and that management should, 'step in and reduce the level of politics'. For Stone (1997), eliminating politics is a management duty. Studies consistently associate the perception that levels of political behaviour in an organization are high with high levels of stress, depression, and other undesirable individual and corporate outcomes (Ferris et al., 2005). However, those findings depend on how 'politics' is defined and measured, and we will explore these issues in more detail in Chapter 2.

The negative view of politics has been widely challenged. Mangham (1979, p.16) observes that reasonable people often disagree, with regard both to ends and means, and can thus be expected, 'to fight for what they are convinced is right and, perhaps more significantly, against that which they are convinced is wrong'. Butcher and Clarke (1999) view politics as 'battles over just causes', in which debate sharpens the quality of decisions. Gandz and Murray (1980) found that organization politics were considered functional in terms of careers and power-building. For Keen (1981), organizational power and politics provide the dynamic for change. Harrison (1987) argues that political behaviour can be used to counter the use of legitimate tactics to achieve undesirable ends, and to help implement decisions reached by legitimate means. Frost and Egri (1991) argue that political struggles play a role in resolving competing perspectives and interests in the context of organizational changes. McClelland and

Burnham (1995) distinguish between institutional (socialized) and personal uses of power, the latter for personal gain, the former in the interests of group and corporate goals, potentially involving self-sacrifice. The history of conflicting interests, alignments, and negotiations, argue Bacharach and Lawler (1998), is the history of change.

Hardy (1996) also argues that political forces generate the energy for organizational change. To shut down the political action is to turn off this source of energy and creativity. This is a *social facilitation* argument, based on the observation that we change our behaviour in the presence of others. Just as tennis players will 'lift their game' when faced with someone whose level of skill is equivalent to or greater than their own, so the change agent preparing a business case is encouraged to gather more evidence, to develop more compelling arguments, to explore the views of critics, and to form a coalition to support the initiative. While arguing that the costs of eliminating politics are high (assuming that is possible), Pfeffer (1992a) also observes that the quality of debate in the 'politics-free' organization is likely to be poor.

For Provis (2004, p.233) the varied circumstances of political behaviour mean that the claim, 'politics is always bad', is 'an easy view that we can set aside'. Political behaviour creates both damage and benefit, and is not special in this regard. Most management actions have 'dual effects'. Will politics have a negative impact on morale? Possibly, but relocating or outsourcing parts of the business can have the same effect. Will organization politics reduce faith in top management? Maybe, but managers can damage their credibility in numerous other ways, should they wish to do so, without playing any political games. Is organization politics really a waste of time? Perhaps, but the use of political tactics can also speed up the implementation of critical decisions. With a hammer, we can fix your furniture, or splinter your skull. The consequences depend on the context, and on why and how the tool is used. Political behaviour is just another tool or, as we shall see, a rich and varied toolkit. But are the users of tools not also affected by that usage? As we will argue later, it may be prudent to use the toolkit of political behaviour with that possibility in mind.

Making things happen, getting things done

Those who are engaged in decision making and change must recognize that these are political processes, and must be able to intervene and to act accordingly. The American diplomat Henry Kissinger once wrote (cited in Pfeffer, 1992b, p.31):

Before I served as a consultant to Kennedy, I had believed, like most academics, that the process of decision-making was largely intellectual and all one had to do was to walk into the President's office and convince him of the correctness of one's view. This perspective I soon realized is as dangerously immature as it is widely held.

Why does political behaviour occur? Its roots lie in personal ambition, in organization structures that create roles and departments which compete with each other, and in decisions that cannot be resolved by evidence and reason alone but which rely on the values and preferences of those involved. A fourth and related trigger is organizational change that threatens to push people out of their comfort zones and challenge vested interests, which they may then struggle to preserve. Change is thus one of the key triggers and intensifiers of political behaviour. The reader who is content with a static role and a plateaued career in a stable organization will find this book of little relevance (until forced to defend that situation). In contrast, readers who are concerned with facilitating, supporting, driving, or implementing organizational changes, and who are also concerned with their own career progress, are more likely to find a lack of political awareness and skill a handicap.

Power, politics, and change are inextricably linked (Pettigrew, 1973; Frost and Egri, 1991; Dawson, 2003). Change creates uncertainty and ambiguity. People wonder how their jobs and their workload will be affected, how their relationships with colleagues may be altered. Change in one organizational dimension can have knock-on or 'ripple' effects in other areas. As organizations become more complex, the ripple effects become difficult to anticipate. Managing change can thus be a challenging and exhilarating activity, and the uncertainty generated by change can create room for manoeuvre. However, the role of politics in change agency is controversial. Voyer (1994) and Peled (1999) argue that the change agent must be involved, and Hardy (1996) argues that power provides the energy for change. On the other hand, Ferris and King (1991) and Stone (1997) argue that change agents should avoid politics. Cobb (1986) advocates a diagnostic approach to organization development interventions. While the 'correct' answer to the question, 'how much politics?' will always be 'it depends', we will argue that an understanding of politics, combined with a willingness and ability to engage with an organization's political processes, are indispensable attributes of the effective change agent. Recent research suggests that political skill (see Chapter 9) is a better predictor of managerial performance than other aspects of social effectiveness such as self-monitoring, leadership, and emotional intelligence (Semadar et al., 2006).

Frost and Egri (1991) argue that the interplay of power and politics at individual, intraorganizational, interorganizational, and social levels determines the success or failure of proposed innovations. Kumar and Thibodeaux (1990) argue that change agents have to adjust their political game according to the degree of change. First-level change involves improving effectiveness. Second-level change involves introducing new perspectives. Third-level change concerns organization-wide shifts in values and working practices. The more significant the change and its implications, the greater the political involvement required by the change agent. While first-level and second-level changes require political awareness and facilitation respectively, third-level change means political intervention; stimulating debate, gaining support from key groups, and covert manipulation. Kumar and Thibodeaux (1990, p.364) admit that such tactics may be 'ethically objectionable', in their defence pointing to the 'distasteful' reality of organizational politics.

We will use the term change agent (also described as change leader, champion, or driver) broadly, to include all those who are actively seeking to influence change, regardless of their formal role or job title. In most organizations, most employees are now change agents within this broad definition, and most managers combine their regular day job with change responsibilities. The literature of change agency advocates the need for what Schön (1963, pp.84–5), writing about radical military innovations, calls a 'champion of the idea':

> Essentially the champion must be a man [sic] willing to put himself on the line for an idea of doubtful success. He is willing to fail. But he is capable of using any and every means of informal sales and pressure to succeed. No ordinary involvement with a new idea provides the energy required to cope with the indifference and resistance that major technical change provokes. It is characteristic of champions of new developments that they identify with the idea as their own, and with its promotion as a cause, to a degree that goes far beyond the requirements of their job. In fact, many display persistence and courage of heroic quality. For a number of them the price of failure is professional suicide, and a few become martyrs to the championed ideas.

The importance of the single change champion, maverick innovator, or small band of enthusiasts, has been widely accepted. Maidique (1980, p.59) argues that, 'At all stages of development of the firm, highly enthusiastic and committed individuals who are willing to take risks play an important role in technological innovation'. However, major change is rarely dependent on the actions of single key figures, but is typically shaped by the actions and interactions of what Hutton (1994) calls 'the cast of characters'. Change agency today is often a distributed phenomenon, an issue to which we will return in Chapter 8.

Our interest lies not just with the small group of champions, but with all those involved in change, in making things happen, in getting things done. We also have to recognize that change agents – internal and external – often play a number of different roles, each role making different demands. Buchanan and Storey (1997) thus argue for the concept of 'change agency', identifying eight distinct roles; initiator, sponsor, driver, subversive, passenger, spectator, victim, and paramedic (Table 1.1). One individual can play more than one role at the same time. Some role combinations are straightforward, such as 'initiator–sponsor' or 'sponsor–driver'. Some combinations are awkward, such as 'driver–victim'. Also, individuals can move from one role (or role combination) to another as change unfolds.

Three points emerge from this analysis of change agency roles:

1 Different roles, different skills
   The behaviours and skills involved in each of these roles are different. The actions of the initiator concern inciting enthusiasm for new ideas and projects, infecting others with that enthusiasm, and stimulating the desire for change. This is quite

different from the sponsor, a formally identified and senior position in many organizations, who serves in a monitoring capacity. Sponsors often chair a steering or review group, and act as 'protector/guardians' for change, perhaps negotiating or fighting for additional resources when a project falters, and dealing with challenge and resistance from other senior players in the organization. The behaviour repertoire of the change agent concerns a combination of project management skills, interpersonal skills in negotiating, persuading and influencing, and political skills, combined possibly with knowledge of the substance of the change itself. The behaviours and competencies of the subversive mirror those of the change agent.

2 Positioning: role taking and role switching

Key components in the skill of the change agent lie with what Buchanan and Storey (1997) call 'role taking and role switching', involving calculated decisions concerning which of these positions to occupy and play at any given time, and also when to switch from one position or role combination to another. These positioning skills are discussed in Chapter 8. The position or location of the individual in relation to the change process is often a matter for personal choice and shaping, within the wider constraints of the organization's structure. While it may be advantageous to be an initiator in some settings, it may be more advantageous in other circumstances to be viewed as a driver, or as a paramedic, or even as a subversive. Whatever the skill demands of a particular change agency role, one of the key capabilities, therefore, is 'chameleonic flexibility' (Ferris and King, 1991).

3 The desirable subversive

Although this is a negative term, the subversive role can be a positive one, for at least two reasons. First, as suggested earlier, subversives keep the debate alive, maintain a challenge to the dominant arguments, and ensure that those who would be in the 'driving seat' for change are clear about their position, their arguments, their objectives, and their allies. Without challenge, criticism and debate, our thinking can become careless, and subversives discourage this tendency. Second, it is useful to be aware of the strategies and tactics of the subversive, so that these can be identified and countered. It may also be useful to use these behaviours to block and divert the potentially damaging changes being driven by others. To understand the political skills of the change agent is to be able to use those skills both to drive and to subvert change in the organization.

When decisions are unstructured, or unprogrammable, choices are typically resolved through political processes. Stakeholders have differing perceptions, goals, and values, rational arguments are often implausible where uncertainty is high, and reason and evidence alone are rarely compelling (Schilit, 1986; Drory, 1993; Fitzgerald et al., 1999). Those with clear personal visions, biases, prejudices, intuitions, and convictions are thus often able to influence decisions in their preferred direction. Decisions can be the

Table 1.1 Change agency roles

initiator	the ideas person, the heatseeker, the project or process 'champion'
sponsor	the main beneficiary, the focal person, the project or process 'guardian'
agent or driver	promotes, implements, delivers – often the process or 'project manager'
subversive	strives to divert, block, interfere, resist, disrupt
passenger	is carried along by the change
spectator	watches while others change
victim	suffers from changes introduced by others
paramedic	helps others through the traumas of change

result of a combination of rational argument supported by lobbying, trading, influencing, coalition formation, and other political tactics. Consequently, the change agent must be accomplished in this 'fixer–facilitator–wheeler–dealer' mode. Kakabadse and Parker (1984, p.182) note that:

> Change is not about one truth or an open sharing of views. Change is about renegotiating certain dominant values and attitudes in the organization in order to introduce new systems and subsystems. Under such circumstances, visions and values are not likely to be shared, with the likely result being a clash of wills. Successful change involves one person or group influencing the organization according to their values.

Researcher You think some managers enjoy playing the politics game?

Manager Absolutely, I think most do. I think if you took that out of management, then it would in effect become a very sterile kind of technocratic activity. That may reflect the fact that I enjoy it, and that I see it as being part of the natural state of things. People are naturally competitive. I suppose the thing about building a successful team is not about eradicating that competition but in being able to harness it and focus it, therefore the competitiveness can be a force of good. I think people argue that politics is a destructive process when they're losing. Normally, if you lose, you vow to get them next time, don't you? There's always a rematch.

Pfeffer (1992a, p.30) argues that, 'Unless we are willing to come to terms with organizational power and influence, and admit that the skills of getting things done are as important as the skills of figuring out what to do, our organizations will fall further and further behind'. This means abandoning the notion, popular in the field of organization development, that change agents are 'neutral facilitators' using appropriate techniques to encourage information sharing, joint problem solving and collaborative action planning among an organization's willing members. There may, of course, be occasions when a change agent can function effectively in this way, but this is only one dimension of a wider behaviour repertoire.

From experience of major change in health care, Wallace (1990, p.59) describes how his large-scale information systems project was 'characterized by rapid activity and forward thinking but, above all, by a series of activities associated with influencing the actions of others in order to achieve organizational objectives'. He describes how the uncertainties surrounding the project uncovered opportunities for politically skilled managers (Wallace, 1990, p.60):

> A significant issue appeared to be the considerable state of turbulence in the orga-
> nization as a whole. A large and very complex amalgamation was occurring. There
> were frequent changes of staff, staff responsibilities and reporting relationships. In
> some senses, these changes created information and power 'vacuums' resulting
> in people being unclear and confused about the events occurring about them.
> One effect of this was that people were distracted from concentrating on the
> project, which suggests that managers may well be able to take advantage of such
> circumstances in order to achieve change.

In our experience many managers are uncomfortable with the argument that change agents must be political. This runs counter to the values of open, caring, participative management. Playing organization politics inevitably means losing friends, and making enemies. However, as a (female) character in a recent television spy thriller replied, when criticized for exploiting a naive informant to subvert a terrorist plot (the informant having been killed in the action), 'If I wanted a job in which everybody loved me, I would have been a vet'.

Defining politics

How can we distinguish 'political' actions from 'non-political' ones? Without an agreed definition, it is difficult to construct measures of the amount of political behaviour taking place. The definition of politics from Mintzberg (1983) is the one most often cited, but not all commentators agree. Part of the problem lies with the observation that, to define a particular action or behaviour as 'political' is not a neutral theoretical task, but one which criticizes and stigmatizes those who behave in that manner. Who decides which behaviours are 'illegitimate', and which are not? In other words, offering a definition of political behaviour is a 'political' behaviour in its own right.

Organization politics defined

individual or group behaviour that is informal, ostensibly parochial, typically divisive, and above all, in the technical sense, illegitimate – sanctioned neither by formal authority, accepted ideology, nor certified expertise (Mintzberg, 1983, p.172)

acts of influence to enhance or protect the self-interest of individuals or groups (Allen et al., 1979, p.77)

the exercise of tactical influence which is strategically goal directed, rational, conscious and intended to promote self-interest, either at the expense of or in support of others' interests (Valle and Perrewé, 2000, p.361)

intra-organizational influence tactics used by organization members to promote self-interests or organizational goals in different ways (Vigoda, 2003, p.31)

the ability to effectively understand others at work, and to use such knowledge to influence others to act in ways that enhance one's personal and/or organizational objectives (Ferris et al., 2005, p.127)

The absence of a common definition of organization politics is a long-standing concern, and commentators continue to grumble about the lack of agreement (Drory and Romm, 1990; Ferris et al., 2002a). Kacmar and Carlson (1997, p.656) argue that, 'Only when consensus is reached about what organizational politics is and how it should be measured will the field be advanced'. Chapter 2 explores the further problems of defining power and politics, and why it is naive to seek one common definition. For now, we will use these working definitions:

- **power** the ability to get other people to do what you want them to do
- **politics** power in action, using a range of techniques and tactics

Power can be viewed as the ability 'to produce intended effects' in line with one's perceived interests (Pettigrew and McNulty, 1995), to 'overcome resistance on the part of other social actors in order to achieve desired objectives or results' (Astley and Sachdeva, 1984). While power has traditionally been defined in terms of changing others' behaviour, the concept of 'soft power' – the ability to get other people to think the way that you do – has become significant, particularly in a geopolitical context (Nye, 2002). Power is a latent capacity, a resource, while politics can be viewed as the practical exercise of power, as 'the observable, but often covert, actions by which executives enhance their power to influence decisions' (Eisenhardt and Bourgeois, 1988, p.737). Mintzberg (1983, p.25) argues: 'But having a basis for power is not enough. The individual must act'.

Table 1.2 The defining features of political behaviour

influence	the currency of organization politics is influence, getting others to do or to think as you want them to, and enhancing one's power to influence
self-interest	political behaviour is concerned with the goals of the individual, and not with organizational objectives, or with 'the greater good'
damage	acting against the organization, and against other people, and ignoring or reducing organizational effectiveness
backstage	out of sight, behind closed doors, in locker rooms, squash courts, golf courses, private dinners; anyone not engaged in those activities is excluded
conflict	disagreement, over the distribution of resources, or over goals and/or how to achieve them

With commentators adopting different approaches, a common strategy has been to identify recurring themes across their definitions (e.g., Drory and Romm, 1988 and 1990; Ferris et al., 2002a). This strategy produces the defining features summarized in Table 1.2. Following this approach, behaviour that displays those five attributes is categorically political. This does not mean, however, that behaviour lacking those attributes can be described as non-political. Organizational behaviour is rarely so tidy.

Influence? The evidence shows that the political behaviour repertoire extends far beyond what are commonly regarded as interpersonal influence tactics (direct request, reward, rational appeal, ingratiation, the exchange of favours). This can also involve blocking, undermining, delegitimating, delaying, subverting, sidelining, and out-manoeuvring others, preventing them from acting in certain ways, closing off their access to information and to decision-making forums, and constraining their options, in order to advance one's own ideas.

Self-interest? This has conventionally been seen as the single main defining feature of political behaviour (Burns, 1961). However, it is not difficult to identify situations in which self-interested acts can benefit the organization, either in the short term, or in the future. The fortunes of the individual are often bound closely to those of the organization, and it is unrealistic to claim that all self-interested acts must, by definition, run counter to organizational and wider social goals. Self-interest can be pursued either through the selfish pursuit of influence and power, or through a belief in so-called selfless motives and actions, on behalf of the individual or the group. Moreover, acting in pursuit of one's perceived self-interest may not always be in one's self-interest at all, and acting for what appears to be the common good may not always benefit others. One problem here is that what constitutes self-interest is a matter of interpretation. Another problem is, this dimension of political behaviour is often presented in 'either/or' terms; one is either acting for the organization, or for oneself. There is no reason why both sets of goals cannot be pursued simultaneously through the same actions. In addition, self-interested acts may be essential in preserving the credibility and 'voice' of the individual concerned. While one may not be contributing to the organization through short-term actions, maintaining one's reputation and influence may sustain or strengthen one's ability to shape events in positive ways in future.

Damage? As discussed earlier, organization politics can also be used in ways that bring personal and organizational benefit. The inappropriate use of political tactics can of course be damaging, and actions that may be judged to be effective, overall, may also have some negative consequences (i.e., dual effects). While this attribute cannot be denied, it would also be wrong to label all political behaviour as necessarily and only damaging.

Backstage? Political behaviour is often concealed, in private meetings and conversations, and in locations that are difficult for others to access. However, organization politics has a very public face, in the influence and other manipulation tactics of conversation control and impression management (see Chapter 2), and in the more blatant uses of autocratic power. While some of these behaviours are not hidden at all, it is often the intent, the purpose, the motivation that is backstage.

Researcher Is this an ethical issue, or are we simply talking about effective management?

Manager It's probably naive, but I believe that you can't be an effective manager unless you understand the politics and the processes that go on. If you don't believe that's going on, then you are operating almost in an ivory tower. And there are some managers who operate in an ivory tower, and wonder why they are never successful, why they don't get that extra quarter ... hundred thousand or whatever it is they want. Unless you can read that political situation, you are in the s***.

If you've got naive people at the top who believe that the facts alone will sell the idea, and you don't realize you need to wheel and deal, then you don't delegate and you end up wondering why you don't get what you want. In any organization, I mean, you have to know how to play the managing director, don't you? If you didn't know that, then somebody else usually walks all over you.

Conflict? This is perhaps the one aspect of political behaviour over which most commentators agree. Where there is consensus, around goals and how to achieve them, there may be little need for the use of political tactics to influence the outcomes. Only when we are in dispute, and when the parties to that dispute are locked in disagreement and unlikely ever to reach a satisfactory compromise, are we likely to see the use of political behaviours. However, political tactics can also be used to orchestrate collaboration by avoiding conflict (Hardy, 1996). Consensus can be achieved through influence, agenda manipulation, and other political tactics designed to encourage compliance. Moreover, such a consensus does not invariably mean that the following actions will be in the best interests of everyone concerned, and agreement today can turn into dispute tomorrow. In other words, consensus may be genuine or imposed, enduring or transient. Nevertheless, while perceived in negative terms and widely regarded as undesirable, conflict often has the positive result of forcing issues into the open, stimulating wider debate, leading to improved decision making.

While this combination of influence, self-interest, damage, backstage, and conflict offers an approximate working definition, it does not help us to distinguish clearly between 'political' and 'non-political' behaviour. Another problem is that, as all social exchanges involve mutual influence, every interaction can be interpreted as political (Mangham, 1979; Astley and Sachdeva, 1984), and the term loses much of its value. The boundary between what is political, and what is not, is blurred and controversial. Attribution theory suggests that it is important for managers to avoid having their actions linked with political intent, and it may often be desirable to create the impression that one's goals are selfless and non-political. Successful manipulation and influence attempts may be those which attract attributions of legitimate motivation (Allen et al., 1979, p.82). It is interesting that Ferris et al. (2000, p.30) capture these issues by defining political skill as:

> an interpersonal style construct that combines social astuteness with the ability to relate well, and otherwise demonstrate situationally appropriate behaviour in a disarmingly charming and engaging manner that inspires confidence, trust, sincerity, and genuineness.

From a qualitative study of an ongoing political exchange in a British computing company, Buchanan (1999) concludes that traditional theoretical concepts of organization politics are inaccurate and oversimplified, and suggests the contrasts summarized in Table 1.3.

Table 1.3 Concepts of politics – tradition versus practice

traditional concept of politics	characteristics revealed in practice
regarded by managers with ambivalence	can be tedious, but can be beneficial
characterized by covert means	behaviour reported is 'non-discussable'
undesirable	keeps discussion alive, reasonable in context
illegitimate, unsanctioned	managers do not visibly sanction all actions
devious, divisive, underhand	'sparring' has organization and team benefits
self-serving	mix of individual and corporate benefits
triggered by conflict and uncertainty	many personal and organizational triggers
unprofessional to play	unprofessional to ignore

Skilled organization politicians disguise their self-serving intentions, thus defeating an objective definition of their actions. We will consider in more depth in the following chapter the two main perspectives that have been brought to bear on the subject of organization politics, positivist and constructivist. In a constructivist perspective, the definitions that matter are those of organizational members, not outside researchers, and in this perspective the definition problem becomes an empirical question, not a theoretical debate.

The turf game

Our aim is to explore the nature of the turf game, and to expose its strategies and tactics in the context of shaping organizational change processes. Why have we chosen the label 'turf game'? Turf, from the phrase 'turf wars', is a colloquial term meaning territory, or any other resource of value to an individual or group. Also when we discuss politics, we tend to speak of winners and losers, players and tactics – the language of games. This terminology allows us to ask what kind of game this is, what the object (or objects) of the game is, and how it is played. Bardach (1977) discusses 'implementation games'. Riley (1983) found in her research that the game metaphor was a common feature of organization political imagery. At least some managers seem to enjoy playing this game; organization politics can be a motivator, and a factor in keeping individuals committed and energetic.

This is a game in which individuals and groups seek to defend and extend their turf, avoiding 'poor quality' turf where possible. Turf may concern power and influence, status and reputation, access to and control over resources; people, information, space, and money. Sometimes, the turf that matters may simply be individuals' desire to keep doing what they enjoy doing, to preserve their 'comfort zone'. Turf can be personal, and it can also be collective. In our first edition, we identified the main categories of turf game tactics (based on Gray and Starke, 1984), and Table 1.4 provides an updated summary.

Like any metaphor, this one collapses when pursued too far. There are at least three respects in which game imagery can be misleading. First, this is a 'long game', concerning exchanges between players over extended periods, and not one which is often resolved in 'single plays' around specific issues. Second, the action is not confined to a well-defined arena or pitch but is worked out on an undulating and unpredictable organizational terrain. Third, the metaphor implies 'playing hard to win', whereas in many situations one may deliberately decide to lose, in the interests of maintaining long-term relationships, or in the context of anticipated future events and favours. The concept of 'winning' is explored further in Chapter 8.

The turf game is not reserved for senior management, although some individuals and groups are better placed with regard to resources and power bases than others. Anyone, at any level in an organization, can be a player, and even low-skilled, low-status and ostensibly powerless individuals can bring an organization grinding to a halt

Table 1.4 Turf tactics

image building	we all know people who didn't get the job because they didn't look the part – appearance is a credibility issue
information games	withholding information to make others look foolish, bending the truth, white lies, massaging information, timed release
scapegoating	this is the fault of another department, external factors, my predecessor, a particular individual
alliances	doing secret deals with influential others to form a critical mass, a cabal, to win support for and to progress your proposals
networking	lunches, coffees, dinners, sporting events, to get your initiatives onto senior management agendas, to improve visibility
compromise	all right, you win this time, I won't put up a fight and embarrass you in public – if you will back me next time
rule games	I'm sorry, but you have used the wrong form, at the wrong time, with the wrong arguments; we can't set inconsistent precedents
positioning	switching and choosing roles where one is successful and visible; avoiding failing projects; position in the building, in the room
issue selling	packaging, presenting, and promoting plans and ideas in ways that make them more appealing to target audiences
dirty tricks	keeping dirt files for blackmail, spying on others, discrediting and undermining, spreading false rumours, corridor whispers

through determined collective action. Power and resources are important, but so are the skill and the timing with which those resources are deployed. Knowledge of strategies and tactics can compensate for weaker power bases. Brass and Burkhardt (1993, p.466) thus argue that:

> Strategic action can be used to compensate for relatively weak resources. Skilful political activity is one tool for overcoming a lack of resources or making less valuable resources more potent. Actors in powerful positions, who control ample resources, are less dependent on their capabilities to use resources strategically than are actors who lack ample resources.

For most managers, political behaviour is part of their 'recipe knowledge', acquired with experience. Schön's (1983) 'reflective practitioner', or 'practical theorist', has a repertoire of experience and theory which is deployed to meet changing circumstances as required. Reflective practitioners develop their own theories and interventions in a considered and self-critical manner. In this respect, management practice is experimental and *improvisatory*. This is not simply 'making it up as you go', but suggests that decisions and actions are skilfully informed by theoretical frameworks, past experiences, current judgements, and personal assumptions and values. Collin (1996, p.74) draws a useful analogy with jazz: a more appropriate metaphor might be that of playing jazz. Jazz players improvise, but are not anarchic. They are disciplined, skilled, creative and intuitive. They make music in relational, collaborative, and non-hierarchical ways.

Favours and dirt files: found only in fiction?

The reason for all the security at Allerdyce's home was not fear of assassination or kidnap, or simple paranoia, but because he kept his secrets there – his files on the great and good, information he might one day use. There were favours there that he could call in; there were videotapes and photographs which could destroy politicians and judges and the writers of Op-Ed pages. There were audio recordings, transcripts, scribbled notes, sheaves of clippings, and even more private information: copies of bank statements and bounced cheques, credit card billings, motel registration books, logs of telephone calls, police reports, medical examination results, blood tests, judicial reviews ... Then there were the rumours, filed away with everything else: rumours of affairs, homosexual love-ins, cocaine habits, stabbings, falsified court evidence, misappropriated court evidence, misappropriated funds, numbered accounts in Caribbean islands, Mafia connections, Cuban connections, Colombian connections, wrong connections ...

   Allerdyce had contacts at the highest levels. He knew officials in the FBI and CIA and NSA, he knew secret servicemen, he knew a couple of good people at the Pentagon. One person gained him access to another person, and the network grew. They knew they could come to him for a favour, and if the favour was something like covering up an affair or some sticky, sordid jam they'd gotten into – well, that gave Allerdyce just the hold he wanted. That went down in his book of favours. And all the time the information grew and grew.

Source: from *Blood Hunt*, Ian Rankin (1995, p.241).

As Pettigrew and McNulty (1995, p.870) observe, the social and political dynamics vary from one organization to another. Skilled players have to use the resources at hand:

> Awareness and perspective is necessary to know when to intervene and how. There is, therefore, a premium on matching a constellation of power sources to a particular issue, situation by situation, and then drawing upon the right mixture of analysis, persuasion, persistence, tact, timing, and charm to convert potential power into actual influence.

In practice, the turf game is not played with reference to a checklist of tactics. Each set of circumstances is unique, requiring a reflective combination of general knowledge, previous experience, and an appropriate conceptualization of the presenting problem.

Technical knowledge takes second place to workable knowledge, concerning actions that will be effective in these unique circumstances and that are socially acceptable.

You stab my back, I'll stab yours

What does it mean to be engaged in the organization politics of a change process? What are the common, and less common, strategies and tactics of the turf game? How far are you prepared to go to achieve your objectives? Here, we present the findings of a recent study of the management experience and perceptions of organization politics.

Researcher So in your experience, political behaviour is widespread, across sectors?

Manager I said this is a naturally occurring phenomenon, and you were saying this is difficult to sell to people. I think that's people being somewhat dishonest, but that is the conventional wisdom of the day. Or perhaps they haven't worked in organizations. I've worked across a number of private and public sector organizations, and in all of those experiences, it seems to me there's been the same competition of ideas. I've worked in a couple of management services departments in the private sector, usually led by somebody who believes that they knew better than most other people how the organization should be run. If only the other buggers would move out of the way, if the sales and production directors would only listen to the management services department, the whole thing would be more profitable – and what we needed was more people in management services to prove that point. It's the same set of conflicts about how to do things. Most people have a reasonably high degree of conviction about that.

The main argument of this book is that *the change agent who is not politically skilled will fail*. This means that it is necessary to be able and willing to intervene in the political processes of an organization, to push particular agendas, to influence decisions and decision makers, to cope with resistance, and to deal with, and if necessary silence, criticism and challenge. This also implies the ability to intervene in ways that enhance rather than damage one's personal reputation.

What is already known about the experience of organization politics? Gandz and Murray (1980) found from their survey of 400 American managers that 90 per cent regarded politics as commonplace, and felt that executives had to be skilled politicians. However, 55 per cent said that politics impeded efficiency, and 50 per cent argued that management should eliminate politics. Allen et al. (1979; Madison et al., 1980) interviewed 87 senior and middle managers from 30 Californian electronics companies. Political tactics mentioned most frequently were blaming others, selective information, creating a favourable image, developing support, ingratiation, creating obligations, rewards, coercion and threats, associating with influential individuals, and forming

powerful coalitions. In addition, 60 per cent of respondents said that political behaviour was either 'frequent' or 'very frequent'. While 60 per cent agreed that political behaviour can advance careers, respondents were unanimous that politics can harm individuals, through loss of job, power, strategic position, and credibility. However, 45 per cent claimed that politics impeded goal achievement, and a third claimed that politics resulted in the misuse of resources. Given this blend of outcomes, Madison et al. (1980, p.93) describe politics as a 'two-edged sword'.

Exploring links between organization politics and job attitudes, Drory (1993) surveyed 200 supervisors and employees in five Israeli organizations. Pilot interviews with 25 employees were used to develop a measure of 'political climate' based on key decisions affecting task and budget allocations, performance appraisals, and organization structure, and survey respondents were asked to indicate whether these decisions were influenced by political factors. The findings suggest that lower status employees, lacking the power and influence to benefit from 'the political game', view politics as frustrating, but higher status employees did not associate politics with job dissatisfaction. Drory argues that political behaviour is an entrenched organizational feature, that in some circumstances this may be an appropriate aspect of decision making, and that negative outcomes cannot always be avoided.

Ferris and Kacmar (1992) report two studies linking perceptions of politics to contextual and personal factors. The first involved 264 managers and employees from three organizations. A 'perception of politics' measure included the incidence of favouritism, keeping the boss happy, avoiding criticism, and forming 'in' groups. Those at lower levels perceived a higher degree of politics than those at higher levels, and the perception that the workplace was political was associated with job dissatisfaction. The second study involved 95 hospital nurses and their supervisors, who completed a questionnaire measuring organization politics, job satisfaction, work environment factors, and personal influences. Findings suggest that politics can have positive individual and organizational consequences. The authors argue that research should explore links between political skill and job and career-related rewards (Ferris and Kacmar, 1992, p.113). However, using a Machiavellian personality assessment (the 'Mach IV' from Christie and Geiss, 1970), Graham (1996) found that 'high Mach' managers did not have more successful careers (defined by salary) than 'low Machs'.

Ferris et al. (1996) explore the links between politics and dissatisfaction, anxiety, and stress, using a questionnaire returned by over 800 non-academic university employees. Perceptions were measured using a 40-item scale with items such as 'favouritism rather than merit determines who gets ahead around here', and 'I have seen changes made in policies that only serve the purposes of a few individuals'. Centralization (concentrating power at the top) was positively related to perceptions of politics, and formalization (reducing uncertainty and ambiguity) was negatively related. Those who saw their organization as highly political showed higher levels of anxiety and lower satisfaction with both job and supervision. Lower level employees, and those who rated their career opportunities as low, perceived higher levels of politics, and male respondents saw more political behaviour than female (gender differences and effects are discussed in Chapter 5).

Studies of the experience of organization politics in other countries and cultures seem to be rare. However, a survey based on responses from around 300 senior executives in private and public sector organizations in Sweden revealed that organization politics was a widely encountered phenomenon, especially during change (Wickenberg and Kylén, 2004). Tactics encountered included reaching decisions in private, using passive resistance to exhaust change advocates, saying one thing while doing the opposite, lobbying influential individuals, and using formal bureaucratic rules to block particular individuals or groups. These methods are not consistent with the open, honest, compassionate, participative, consensual, Swedish cultural stereotype, and the researchers advocate, 'educating managers in manoeuvring in the grey zone of realpolitik in order to increase innovation and effectiveness without creating losers, victims and enemies' (Wickenberg and Kylén, 2004, p.12).

Our understanding of how organization politics is perceived thus relies heavily on surveys of mixed occupational groups of American and Israeli employees and managers. In summary, the evidence suggests that, while the incidence of behaviours perceived to be political is high, and although political tactics are seen to generate both positive and negative individual and organizational outcomes, many (but not all) managers dislike this dimension of their role.

Antecedents, behaviours, consequences

In terms of both practice and theory, the interesting questions concern the triggers of political behaviour, the nature of such actions, and the outcomes:

antecedents why do people play political games; what triggers organization politics?

behaviours how is politics played; what tactics are used, and how common are they?

consequences what are the outcomes, positive and negative, and what impact does politics have on organizational change?

The negative stereotype of organization politics is neatly captured by Stone (1997, p.1; original emphasis) who observes that:

The term 'company politics' refers to all the game-playing, snide, 'them and us', aggressive, sabotaging, negative, blaming, 'win-lose', withholding, non-cooperative behaviour that goes on in hundreds of interactions every day in the organization. Those who indulge in company politics do so in order to achieve their *personal agendas* at the expense of others in the organization. In the process, they demoralize the motivated and sabotage the company's success. Given their limited numbers, like one or two bad apples souring the whole barrel, they are disproportionately powerful.

Here, then, is the popular view of the source, nature, and effects of organization politics:

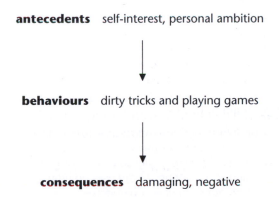

One of the most influential research-based models in this area suggests how a range of consequences (satisfaction, withdrawal, trust, performance, stress) depend on the perception of how political an organization is, a perception which in turn is influenced by individual and organizational factors (Ferris et al., 2002a). Ferris and colleagues have tried to identify a universal set of causal links between the components in their model. For example, does the perception that there is a lot of politicking in an organization invariably lead to lower job satisfaction? This mode of reasoning assumes that it is possible, in principle, to link organizational and individual characteristics with a measure of perceptions of politics, with outcomes such as stress levels, or decisions to leave the organization. In our view, those links will always depend on a range of contextual issues, which interact with each other in different ways in different settings, and the search for straightforward causal relationships is unhelpful. Instead, our approach seeks to understand how these links between triggers, political tactics, and a range of outcomes, are understood by organization managers, and in particular by those concerned with organizational change. (This alternative approach is described in Chapter 2 as a constructivist 'actor theory in use' perspective, which contrasts with the prevailing positivist approach in this field.)

What triggers organization politics? Most commentators focus on personal ambition and self-interest. However, as we shall see, other less personal motives and conditions can trigger political behaviours that can ultimately benefit the organization as well as the individual player (Chanlat, 1997). While we will focus for logistical reasons on a relatively small range of political tactics (Table 1.5), identifying which are perceived to be more or less common in use, it is clear from other evidence that the behaviour repertoire of the organization politician is creative and wide. We will also see that organization politics has consequences, both negative and positive, for individuals and for the organization.

Using a series of groups attending management development programmes, we surveyed over 250 British managers. These were mostly middle and senior managers,

Table 1.5 Common and rare tactics

more common tactics

- building a network of useful contacts
- using 'key players' to support initiatives
- making friends with power brokers
- bending the rules to fit the situation
- self-promotion, publicizing successes

less common tactics

- finding someone else to blame for mistakes
- claiming credit for the work of others
- conceding minor issues to win major goals
- using social settings to discover opinions
- using others to deliver bad news
- deliberately withholding useful information
- highlighting other people's errors and flaws
- using delaying tactics to block others
- breaking the rules to achieve objectives
- compromising now to win future favours

rare tactics

- using misinformation to confuse others
- spreading false rumours to undermine others
- keeping 'dirt files' to blackmail others

with experience of organizational change and politics. The questionnaire guaranteed anonymity and was designed for ease of completion, with four main sections. The first section asked respondents to rate 18 political tactics in terms of how often they had been experienced. Those items were not derived a priori on theoretical grounds or from literature (as, for example, the perception of organization politics scale devised by Kacmar and Ferris, 1991), but relied on tactics that managers themselves identified as examples of political behaviour (Buchanan and Badham, 1999a). Next, two sections contained items addressing general perceptions of organization politics. Finally, 15 items considered the consequences of political behaviour. For further details of the conduct and findings of this survey, see Buchanan (2007).

Of the 252 respondents, 68 per cent were employed by public sector organizations, 32 per cent by the private sector. However, there were no sectoral differences in responses. One explanation is that the experience of politics is not sector-dependent. Vigoda-Gadot and Kapun (2005) found that public sector employees view their organizations as more political, unfair, and unjust than private sector employees. The absence of sector differences may also be explained by the exchange of managers between sectors, and by responses based on general experience, rather than on one organization.

Five main themes emerged, concerning:

- the management experience
- opinions and beliefs
- organizational effectiveness and change
- performance, reputation, and career
- gender differences.

The management experience

The experience of politics seems to be frequent, visible, and sometimes painful. Only 12 per cent agreed that, 'my organization is relatively free of politics', and only 17 per cent agreed that, 'I don't see much political behaviour because it happens behind closed doors'. There were no job-level, gender, or sector differences in responses to those items. Political behaviour was not seen as a senior management preserve; 83 per cent agreed that, 'politics is played at all organizational levels'. It is not surprising, therefore, that 84 per cent agreed that, 'I am prepared to play politics when necessary', 87 per cent agreed that, 'politics is a natural part of the management job', and 93 per cent agreed that, 'most managers, if they want to succeed, have to play politics at least part of the time'. However, over 70 per cent said that they had been hurt by the tactics of others.

The survey sought to establish the perceived frequency of 18 political behaviours, leading to a ranking of more common, less common, and rare tactics (Table 1.5). At least 68 per cent of respondents said that they had experienced all but three of those 18 tactics at least 'sometimes'. This does not indicate the actual incidence of these tactics, but reflects management perceptions of how often such behaviours occur. Asked whether, 'my organization would benefit from a higher level of politics', only eight per cent agreed. Whatever the incidence of political behaviour, it appears that most managers consider that to be too high, confirming previous studies (Harrell-Cook et al., 1999, p.1095).

Opinions and beliefs

Respondents were asked to indicate which of four statements most accurately reflected their opinion of organization politics:

I don't want to be involved in organization politics, but it is necessary to understand what is going on.	63%
I believe it is necessary to play politics to achieve my objectives and enhance my reputation.	31%
I play politics because it is challenging and fun and is an important motivator for me.	3%
I ignore politics because it is unethical, demotivating, unacceptable and would damage my reputation.	3%

Almost two thirds saw politics as an aspect of their role which they had to understand, but which they preferred to avoid. There were no job-level differences in response to these items. However, women were more likely to choose 'understand but avoid' (69 per cent) than men (56 per cent), who were more likely to respond with 'necessary to play' (38 per cent compared with 24 per cent). Only 27 per cent agreed that, 'winning the political game is an intensely satisfying personal experience' (with no gender or job-level differences). Asked if 'political behaviour is unethical', only 12 per cent agreed, with 67 per cent in disagreement. Consequently, 88 per cent of respondents felt either that political behaviour was ethical, or were unsure. Nevertheless, two comments described politics as 'evil':

> Organization politics is a 'necessary evil' but need not be seen as a wholly negative concept. Often it is the informal route by which legitimate objectives are achieved. In my experience, organizational politics is a fact of life. (*senior manager, manufacturing, male*)

> I dislike it intensely, but recognize it as an evil others make me engage in. (*middle manager, public sector hospital, male*)

Around 80 per cent of respondents said that they were not prepared to hurt others, and over 80 per cent denied that they had hurt others in this way. However, there were gender differences in responses to these 'true–false' items. Reflecting traditional 'tough and tender' male and female stereotypes, a higher proportion of men said that they were prepared to hurt others to achieve personal and organizational goals, and men were more likely to admit that they had hurt others. However, women were more likely to agree that playing politics had contributed to their career (Table 1.6).

Not all political behaviour is a source of discomfort; 65 per cent agreed that, 'some managers play politics just for fun'. On the item, 'most managers dislike playing politics', the sample was divided, with only 17 per cent in agreement, 34 per cent unsure, and 50 per cent in disagreement (two per cent strongly). Asked whether, 'life without

Table 1.6 Gender differences in preparedness to hurt others

	male 'true' response %	female 'true' response %
My willingness to play organization politics has contributed to my career success	45	55
If necessary to achieve organizational goals, I am prepared to hurt others with political tactics	31	14
If necessary to achieve personal goals, I am prepared to hurt others with political tactics	31	11
I know that I have hurt others with my use of political tactics	26	14

organization politics would be boring', 38 per cent agreed (with 21 per cent unsure, 41 per cent in disagreement), and only 32 per cent agreed that, 'my ideal organization is one with no politics' (with 21 per cent unsure, and 48 per cent in disagreement). It thus appears that between one-third and a half of respondents held broadly positive views of organization politics.

With 81 per cent and 75 per cent agreement respectively that, 'I am prepared to play politics when necessary', and 'I engage in political behaviour when necessary to achieve my objectives', responses to two other items suggest a more calculating perspective. For example, 72 per cent agreed that, 'a manager has to be ruthless sometimes', and 89 per cent agreed that, 'those who use political tactics should expect to have similar tactics used against them' (with no gender differences). This consistent response pattern suggests that political tactics are considered justified in some contexts, that causing harm is less acceptable, and that 'ruthless reciprocity' is perceived as appropriate, implying an attitude of 'you stab my back, I'll stab yours'. How can willing ruthlessness be reconciled with the desire to avoid hurting others? This sentiment is perhaps captured by the following comment:

> While I 'agreed' with it, I don't feel comfortable with the word ruthless, as there is an element of vindictiveness implied by the word. (*senior manager, public sector hospital, male*)

One explanation is that ruthlessness is equated more with impersonal management actions (closing facilities, cutting budgets, declaring redundancies), while hurting another individual is personal, and is more difficult to do – or to admit to doing.

How do senior management actions influence political behaviour? It appears that senior management are believed to be more involved in political behaviour, with 87 per cent agreeing that, 'the higher you go in the organization, the more political the climate becomes'. Senior managers appear also to be regarded as role models, with 84 per cent agreeing that, 'when the top team play politics, other managers follow their example'. There were no job-level differences in responses to those items. However, while 23 per cent agreed that, 'senior management could stop the politics if they wanted to', senior managers appeared less confident than middle managers of their ability to do so, with 72 per cent of senior managers compared with 45 per cent of middle managers expressing disagreement.

Does the incidence of political behaviour vary? Only 21 per cent indicated that, 'the level of organization politics is constant', and 77 per cent agreed that, 'the degree of political behaviour varies over time'. Does organizational change intensify political activity? Only 20 per cent agreed that, 'you only see high levels of politics during periods of organizational change'. Respondents were asked to indicate whether, 'there is more organization politics today than five years ago'; 49 per cent agreed. However, more public sector respondents (52 per cent) agreed that there were 'more politics' than private sector managers (43 per cent).

Organizational effectiveness and change

Do managers regard politics as a useful tool, or as an impediment, with respect to implementing change and improving organizational effectiveness? The findings indicate that the answer is contingent on the way in which tactics are deployed. On the one hand, 85 per cent agreed (26 per cent strongly) that, 'I have seen organization politics damage organizational effectiveness'. But more than half of respondents (53 per cent) had experienced politics contributing to organizational effectiveness.

The great intimidators

Roderick Kramer (2006) challenges the view that managers must be nice and not tough, and should be humble and self-effacing rather than intimidating. Kramer argues that intimidation is an appropriate style when an organization has become rigid or unruly, stagnant or drifting, faces resistance or inertia, because abrasive leadership gets people moving. Intimidators are not bullies, but can use bullying tactics when time is short, and the stakes are high: 'They are not averse to causing a ruckus, nor are they above using a few public whippings and ceremonial hangings to get attention. They're rough, loud, and in your face' (p.90).

'In his mysterious way, God has given each of us different talents, Ridgeway. It just so happens that mine is intimidating people.'

Reproduced with permission.

Continued

Intimidators have 'political intelligence'. The socially intelligent manager focuses on leveraging the strengths of others, with empathy and soft power. The politically intelligent manager focuses on weaknesses and insecurities, using coercion, fear, and anxiety. Working for an intimidating leader can be a positive experience. Their sense of purpose can be inspirational, their forcefulness makes them a role model, and intimidators challenge others to think clearly about their objectives. Kramer quotes a journalist who said, 'Don't have a reputation for being a nice guy – that won't do you any good' (p.92). Intimidation tactics include:

Get up close and personal Intimidators work through direct confrontation, invading your personal space, using taunts and slurs to provoke and throw you off balance.

Get angry Called 'porcupine power', this involves the 'calculated loss of temper' (use it, don't lose it), using rage and anger to help the intimidator prevail.

Keep them guessing Intimidators preserve an air of mystery by maintaining deliberate distance. Transparency and trust are fashionable, but intimidators keep others guessing, which makes it easier to change direction without loss of credibility.

Know it all 'Informational intimidators' who appear to have mastery of the facts can be very intimidating indeed. It doesn't matter whether 'the facts' are correct, as long as they are presented with complete confidence at the right time.

Source: based on Kramer (2006).

The significance of political behaviour in change appears to be widely acknowledged:

- 60 per cent agreed that, 'politics become more important as organizational change becomes more complex'
- 79 per cent agreed that, 'politics can be used to initiate and drive useful change initiatives'
- 81 per cent agreed that, 'political tactics can be effective in dealing with resistance to change'
- 85 per cent agreed that, 'major changes need to be "steered" through the organization politics' and
- 93 per cent agreed (21 per cent strongly) that, 'politics can be used to slow down and block useful change initiatives'.

Only 24 per cent (four per cent strongly) felt that, 'major changes must be free from organization politics if they are to be effective'. In addition, only nine per cent agreed with the item, 'change agents who avoid organization politics are more likely to succeed in their roles'. As other studies have suggested (Ferris et al., 2000; Buchanan,

2003), the effectiveness of organizational change was perceived to be dependent, at least in part, on the political skill of change agents, catalysts or leaders.

Performance, reputation, and career

The view that political skill is central to personal reputation and career, as well as to aspects of management performance, also seems to be widely recognized. The findings suggest that managers who ignore organization politics may damage their reputations, their careers, and also the sections for which they are responsible. As noted earlier, over 90 per cent agreed (19 per cent strongly) with the item, 'most managers, if they want to succeed, have to play politics at least part of the time'. This is broadly consistent with the 72 per cent disagreement with the item, 'it is not possible to do a good job and play politics at the same time':

- 90 per cent agreed that, 'managers who play organization politics well can improve their career prospects'
- 81 per cent agreed that, 'personal reputations can be enhanced by appropriate political game playing'
- 75 per cent agreed that, 'the departments of skilled organization politicians attract higher levels of resource' and
- 60 per cent agreed that, 'managers who are not prepared to play politics see their careers suffer'.

There were no gender differences in responses to those four items. Responses to three other items indicate the potential risks in avoiding organization politics:

- 83 per cent agreed that, 'departments in my organization use politics to try and win the competition for resources'
- 71 per cent agreed that, 'managers who don't play politics are pushed aside by those who do' and
- 71 per cent agreed that, 'the departments of managers who are politically unskilled suffer in resource terms'.

There is a widespread perception, therefore, that managers unable or unwilling to engage in politics jeopardize the resourcing of their sections, as well as their careers.

Gender differences

Only 13 per cent agreed that, 'women are better at playing politics than men'; the modal response (47 per cent) was 'unsure'. A higher proportion of women (52 per cent) than men (41 per cent) disagreed with this item. Also, only 27 per cent agreed that, 'men play more political games than women'; the modal response (41 per cent) was again

The winner's commandments

Reggie Von Zugbach (1995) argues that winning the organization game is about overcoming the human and organizational barriers to gaining power with minimum effort and maximum rewards. While the term power can be used to describe wealth, status and influence, it also refers to the individual's ability to maintain control over their activities without interference from others. Power is about deciding what you want, and making sure that you get it:

1 Me first. Nobody else will put your interests before theirs.
2 There are no absolute rules. Other people's ideas of right and wrong do not apply to you.
3 The organization is there to serve your interests, not the other way round.
4 You are on your own. Nobody is going to help you become a winner.
5 Be paranoid. Watch out, the bastards are out to get you.
6 Suck up to those who matter and suck up well. Identify the key people in the system who will help you.
7 Say one thing and do another. You need to pay lip-service to the organization's cherished notions of how things should be done.
8 Be a team player, but make sure you beat your fellow team members.
9 Remember that the truth is not always to your advantage. Those who control your future do not necessarily want to hear the bad news.
10 Manipulate the facts to suit your interests. Even when things are bad you should come up smelling of roses.
11 Get your retaliation in first. When there is blood on the organization's carpet, make sure it's not yours.
12 Blow your own trumpet – or better still, get someone else to do it for you.
13 Dominate your environment or it will dominate you.

Source: from Von Zugbach (1995, pp.1–2 and 7).

'unsure'. However, more women (31 per cent) than men (18 per cent) agreed that men play more political games. These results are inconclusive. One possibility is that there are no gender differences; the motives, organizational infrastructures, and access to resources are equivalent for all players in the politics game. Another explanation is that the differences are too subtle and complex for a survey questionnaire to capture. Other responses indicate that, while women are as willing as men to engage in politics, women express more concern for potential interpersonal harm. Kanter (1979) and Mann (1995) argue that women are disadvantaged in the acquisition of organizational power, and Arroba and James (1988) argue that women need to be politically aware and 'wise', exploiting innate advantages such as intuition, sensitivity, observation, and a willingness to engage with feelings. Recent evidence, however, suggests that many women reject management roles because of their distaste for political behaviour (Arkin, 2004), an issue explored further in Chapter 5.

The A–B–C of organization politics

This evidence confirms that:

- organization politics can be triggered by numerous individual and organizational factors, other than (and as well as) individual self-interest
- the behaviour repertoire of the organization politician is rich and varied
- organization politics generates 'dual effects', and can be functional, in individual and organizational terms, as well as dysfunctional.

This study also confirms that the use of political tactics is widespread (Gandz and Murray, 1980; Ferris and Kacmar, 1992; Drory, 1993). Our 'A–B–C' model (Figure 1.1) combines what we know from previous studies with the findings of our survey.

Antecedents

Findings with regard to factors that trigger political behaviour reveal a mix of individual and contextual factors. These include fun, motivation, and reciprocity, as individual triggers, and change complexity, the political actions of others, managerial level, and senior management role modelling, as organizational triggers. Political behaviour seems to be widely perceived as a 'necessary evil', but ethical considerations appear to present no barrier to the deployment of such tactics for most managers. While most agreed that they were prepared to play politics to achieve objectives, around two-thirds (but a higher proportion of women than men) indicated that, although it was important to understand this aspect of organizational behaviour, they would prefer to avoid it. Most would like their organizations to be less political. Over two-thirds claimed that political tactics had caused them injury, and most indicated that they gained no satisfaction from winning a political exchange.

Women appear to engage in political tactics as readily as men, but seem less prepared to hurt others; a higher proportion of men admitted to injuring others through political tactics. Given the pervasive nature of organization politics, and the range of precipitating conditions, calls to depoliticize management behaviour (Klein, 1988; Stone, 1997) advocate an agenda which even senior managers would find challenging.

This evidence also suggests that previous studies may have underestimated the readiness of managers to overcome their ambivalence, and 'know how to do evil if that is necessary' (Machiavelli, 1514, p.101). The consistently high degrees of willingness to engage in politics, to act ruthlessly, and to reciprocate in kind when dealing with others who use political tactics suggest an attitude of, 'you stab my back, I'll stab yours'.

Antecedents (triggers)

individual

to achieve self-serving ends; self-interest
achieve role objectives
personal ambition
pursuit of concealed motives
desire to convey appearance of selflessness
desire to attract attributions of legitimacy
fun, motivating
ruthless reciprocity
necessary evil

contextual

to protect and achieve group interests
achieve organizational objectives
scale and significance of (third level) change
unstructured problems and decisions
structural differentiation
prompting by others
management level
senior management role models
complexity of organizational change

Behaviours (tactics)

general
informal influence
selective information
gaining and developing support
ingratiation
associating with influential individuals
favouritism
keeping your boss happy
avoiding criticism
blame others
creating a favourable image
creating obligations
rewards, coercion, threat
forming powerful coalitions
stimulating debate
covert manipulation
forming 'in-groups'

common
building a network of useful contacts
using key players to support initiatives
making friends with power brokers
bending the rules to fit the situation
self-promotion
less common
finding someone else to blame for mistakes
claiming credit for the work of others
conceding minor issues to win major goals
using social settings to discover opinions
using others to deliver bad news
deliberately withholding useful information
highlighting other people's errors and flaws
using delaying tactics to block others
breaking the rules to achieve objectives
compromising now to win future favours
rare
using misinformation to confuse others
spreading false rumours to undermine others
keeping dirt files to blackmail others

Consequences (outcomes)

functional

individual
succeed as a change agent
inspire confidence, trust, sincerity
increased self-confidence, reduced stress
power building
enhance personal reputation
career advancement

dysfunctional

individual
personal injury
frustration, anxiety, job dissatisfaction
individual harm through job loss
loss of strategic position and power
pushed aside by better players
damaged credibility

Figure 1.1   The A–B–C of organization politics.

Figure 1.1 Cont'd

organizational	*organizational*
enhance organizational effectiveness	reduce organizational effectiveness
support for desirable policies	departmental resourcing suffers
oppose undesirable policies	dysfunctional game-playing
win competition for resources	impede efficiency
improve quality of decision making	block goal attainment
counter legitimate tactics used for	block organizational change
illegitimate ends	delay organizational change
help implement legitimate decisions	misuse of resources
steer useful change initiatives	create inflexibilities
resolve conflict between competing views	raise communication barriers
deal with resistance to change	restrict information flows
create dynamic for strategic change	wasted time

That ambivalence may be diluted by the view that organization politics is necessary, ethical, and fun.

Behaviours

Previous studies have focused only on common political behaviours. This research addressed a much wider range, previously identified by practising managers as examples of political tactics – common and rare – in their experience. The evidence from this study confirms the richness of the behaviour repertoire, indicating the perceived prevalence of different tactics (Table 1.5). Five tactics were perceived to be common: building networks, using 'key players', befriending power brokers, bending rules, and self-promotion. Three tactics were seen as rare, but not unknown: using misinformation to confuse, spreading rumours to undermine, and keeping 'dirt files' to blackmail others. Interpersonal manipulation and impression management may be perceived as socially more acceptable and less hurtful than behaviours which involve dishonesty and coercion.

Consequences

Again confirming previous studies, organization politics is perceived to generate both functional and dysfunctional individual and organizational outcomes. The impact of politics on change and organizational effectiveness appears to be widely recognized, evident in blocking or driving initiatives, of value in handling resistance to change, and disrupting or contributing to effectiveness (itself an ambivalent and politically charged concept). Most managers appear to believe that change agents must be politically skilled. Extending the findings of Gandz and Murray (1980), most managers attribute success in reputation, career, and resourcing, at least in part, to the exercise of political skill.

Reproduced with permission, courtesy of www.kissmekwik.co.uk.

Graham's (1996) attempt to establish a link between political skill and career may have foundered on the narrow measures used to operationalize skill ('Mach IV' scores) and success (salary).

Implications

On this evidence, the political theory of organization held by most managers incorporates the following propositions:

- political behaviour is triggered by a combination of individual and contextual factors, and is not necessarily self-serving
- the behaviour repertoire of the organization politician is diverse, and while 'social' tactics may be perceived as more acceptable than covert manipulation, most managers see no ethical impediments to the use of political tactics

- political behaviour is not necessarily seen as damaging, but is perceived to generate both functional and dysfunctional individual and organizational consequences.

The Losing Manager

The price of failure in the organization game is losing it, and losers not only fail to attain power for themselves, they spend the rest of their careers concentrating on all those activities which are typically associated with losers. Here are just a few examples:

1 Attending meetings where there is no political decision to be made.
2 Caring about the task, the organization and its people.
3 Treating existing rules with sanctity rather than contempt.
4 Doing a task that could have been delegated.
5 Performing a task to a higher standard than is necessary.
6 Performing a task for which the team gets the credit.
7 Being available and allowing others to interrupt you.
8 Volunteering.
9 Reading every memo, letter, report and other type of document which lands in your in-tray.
10 Refusing to say 'no' when asked to do something.
11 Asking for permission to do something.

Source: from Von Zugbach (1995, p.14).

While the survey method has a number of advantages, it cannot capture the dynamics of political games which unfold through a series of overt and covert manipulations and influence attempts, involving shifting combinations of individuals and coalitions (Bacharach and Lawler, 1998). Survey methods can only sketch the outlines, revealing broad patterns and trends. Our sample was purposive and non-random, with a bias towards the public sector, and to well-qualified managers with experience of organizational change; statistical generalizations to a wider population cannot be confidently made. Nevertheless, it is reasonable to consider the relevance of these results to a wider management population. Confidence in that relevance is strengthened by the consistency of the response patterns, and by the extent to which the results broadly confirm those of previous studies, which also suggests a degree of shared experience across different cultural and organizational settings.

These findings leave a number of questions unanswered. Although we know which behaviours managers consider to be 'political', how do those behaviours come to be labelled and attributed with political intent? While political behaviour is perceived to vary in intensity, little is known about the intensifying and dampening mechanisms that cause that variation. Political skill is perceived to be central to the role of the change agent, and while Ferris et al. (1992) advocate a 'balance' between 'pure politician' and 'demonstrated ability', little is known about the development of that balance, presumably acquired as an individual's moral standards and ideals are tested and compromised by organizational realities (Jackall, 1988; Provis, 2004). Mainiero's (1994a and 1994b) study of female American senior managers, exploring the 'seasoning process' (see Chapter 5), is an exception in this regard. While reputation and career success are attributed to political skill, the conditions and processes through which political behaviours influence reputation are unclear. There appear to be no cross-cultural comparisons of management experience and perceptions of organization politics. Critically, little is understood concerning the combinations of circumstances in which the functional consequences of political behaviour, individual and organizational, are produced. While large-scale quantitative research may be appropriate in some settings, the more subtle aspects of the nature, processes, and implications of organization political behaviour may be more effectively revealed using small-scale qualitative methods.

The contemporary fashion for value-driven ethical leadership appears to have done little to reduce either the perceived incidence or significance of political behaviour. What are the main implications for management practice? Management selection, particularly for change-related roles, should consider candidates' political as well as professional competencies. Understanding politics, but without a willingness to become personally involved, may not be a good option for managers, particularly change agents, concerned with reputation and career. Those following Zaleznik (1997), focusing on 'real work', avoiding 'psychopolitics', may jeopardize the flow of resources to their sections, damage their reputations for 'getting things done', and limit their promotion prospects. Business schools and others engaged in management development may identify opportunity in the finding that, despite the significance of this component of management and change agency roles, almost 80 per cent of respondents said they had no training in dealing with organization politics.

Follow through

How political is your organization?

To what extent do the following statements describe your organization? Tick the appropriate box on the right:

		disagree	maybe	agree
1	who you know around here matters a lot more than what you know	❒	❒	❒
2	the most competent people in the business don't always get promoted	❒	❒	❒
3	decisions are often taken outside formal meetings or behind closed doors	❒	❒	❒
4	resource allocations between departments are a source of argument and conflict	❒	❒	❒
5	you have to be prepared to socialize to build effective networks and alliances	❒	❒	❒
6	information is jealously guarded and not shared openly between groups and departments	❒	❒	❒
7	people suspect that there are 'hidden agendas' behind management decisions	❒	❒	❒
8	some individuals always seem to be better informed than everyone else	❒	❒	❒
9	individuals are having their reputations damaged by 'whispers in the corridors'	❒	❒	❒
10	those who take the credit are not always those who made the biggest contribution	❒	❒	❒
11	you have to know how to 'play the rules' – breaking and bending them – to get things done	❒	❒	❒
12	when mistakes are made, people are quick to start putting the blame on others	❒	❒	❒
13	most people recognize that you're not going very far here unless you have the support of the key players	❒	❒	❒
14	being open and honest all the time can seriously damage your career	❒	❒	❒
15	people will criticize others' ideas merely to help win support for their own proposals	❒	❒	❒

Scoring

Give yourself:

- 1 point for each item where you ticked 'disagree'
- 3 points for each item where you ticked 'maybe'   Total ❒
- 5 points for each item where you ticked 'agree'.

This will give you a score between 15 and 75, which can be interpreted as follows.

The politics-free zone: if you score around 25 or lower. We are all coming to work with you. Your organization has a relatively low level of political behaviour. Either that, or you are just not aware of the degree of politics going on behind your back? In such a *politics-free zone*, are you concerned that:

- There is not enough discussion and debate before key decisions are taken?
- There is not enough constructive conflict and debate to stimulate creativity?

The free-fire zone: if you score around 65 or above. There is a high level of political behaviour in your organization. Either that, or you are reading too much into routine decisions and actions? In such a *free-fire zone*, are you concerned that:

- Too much time and energy is going into the politics game, and not enough into strategic thinking and performance improvement?
- The discussions and debates are motivated more by personal goals and are less related to the organization's strategies and goals?

The average behaviour zone: score between 30 and 60. Your organization is typical, middle-of-the-road in terms of the degree of political behaviour that you can expect to witness. In such an *average behaviour zone*, are you concerned that:

- There is still too much political behaviour diverting attention away from the day job?
- There is not enough political behaviour to stimulate the quality of discussion and debate around key issues and decisions?

On the basis of your scoring, what advice would you give to management about dealing with the politics in your organization?

Turf game tactics

This discussion works best using syndicate tables with three to five members each.

Briefing

The conduct of organizational politics can be described and analysed as a turf game. The object of this game is to defend your turf, enlarging your turf where possible, minimizing losses when necessary, and avoiding the 'poor quality' turf that others try to give you.

Turf comes in different varieties. It may concern power, influence and status in the organization, or in the wider community. Often, it concerns access to and control over resources such as people, space and budgets. Sometimes, it concerns nothing more than the individual desire to keep doing what you enjoy doing, to protect your 'comfort zone'.

Turf, of course, can be personal or collective. Individuals act to protect their own turf; groups act to protect their shared turf.

How is the Turf Game played?

Personal brief: five minutes

1 Identify *two examples* of political behaviour from your own experience, particularly in the context of organizational change.
2 Note the *motive or purpose* for this behaviour.
3 Note the *costs and benefits*, individual and organizational, of this behaviour.

Syndicate brief: 15 to 20 minutes

1 Share your personal examples around the group.
2 **Moves and tactics:** combining your personal examples, produce a 'master list' of the moves and tactics which illustrate, from your experience, how the turf game is played.
3 **Cost–benefit analysis:** using the group's examples as evidence, including motives or purposes, develop a cost–benefit analysis ('soft' as well as 'hard' costs), covering the individual and organizational advantages and disadvantages of political behaviour.
4 Nominate a spokesperson to present your conclusions in the plenary session.

Organization politics at the movies: *The Devil Wears Prada*

In *The Devil Wears Prada* (2006, director David Frankel), Miranda Priestly (played by Meryl Streep) is editor of the famous fashion magazine *Runway*. Miranda's management style is intimidating, ruthless, cruel and merciless, making challenging and unreasonable demands on those around her. However, the magazine is extremely successful, people clearly want to work for and to learn from her, and her confrontational approach encourages them to excel in their own roles. She is one of Kramer's (2006) 'great intimidators', and this style appears to be effective. Miranda also demonstrates her political skills through the manner in which she deals with the plot to replace her as *Runway*'s editor.

- Which of the following generic categories of political tactic does Miranda use?

image building	appearance, looking the part, credibility
information games	withholding and massaging information, bending truth, white lies
scapegoating	finding other people or departments to blame
alliances	secret deals with influential others
networking	lunches, coffees, dinners, to improve visibility
compromise	you win this time, but you'll support me next time
rule games	wrong form, wrong time, wrong arguments, can't set precedents
positioning	choosing roles which are successful; position in the room
dirty tricks	dirt files, undermining others, spreading rumours, corridor talk

- Which of Kramer's intimidation tactics does she use?

get up close and personal	direct confrontation, invading personal space, taunts and slurs to throw others off balance
get angry	calculated loss of temper, using rage and anger to prevail
keep them guessing	preserve air of mystery, maintain distance, keep others guessing
know it all	appear to have mastery of the facts

- What are the disadvantages, the limitations, the costs of maintaining this style?
- Would you like to work for someone like this (explain your answer)?
- Should other managers be advised to copy this style?

2 The terminology game: defining power and politics

Chapter objectives

1 To explain different ways of understanding power, conceptually, and in practice.
2 To explore different ways in which the concept and practice of organization politics has been understood and researched, and to argue for a contructivist–contextualist approach rather than a traditional positivist perspective.
3 For the change agent, to develop a practical approach to organization politics based on the development of personal reputation as a power base.

'Do I really want all this power? I think I do.'

Natural and desirable politics

This chapter explores contrasting perspectives on power and politics. The study of these issues has attracted more controversy than consensus. With the concept of power, we will argue, there are greater returns from combining perspectives, than from attempting to legislate on which is correct. With regard to organization politics, we will argue that the positivist approach that dominates this field has limitations, and that a constructivist perspective offers more promise, for theoretical understanding, and for guiding practice.

Change intensifies political behaviour. Schön (1963, p.82) argues that change 'champions' can expect to encounter resistance to new ideas. He also argues that resistance, often expressed in political behaviours, is beneficial:

> Resistance to change is not only normal but in some ways even desirable. An organization totally devoid of resistance to change would fly apart at the seams. It must be ambivalent about radical technical innovation. It must both seek it out and resist it. Because of commitments to existing technology and to forms of social organization associated with it, management must act against the eager acceptance of new technical ideas, even good ones. Otherwise the technical organization would be perpetually and fruitlessly shifting gears.

Our organizations are not always the happy, harmonious, collaborative communities that management texts imply. Decisions and organization structures are often the result of processes of influencing, trading, bargaining and compromise, to secure the best deals for the players involved in a series of 'competitive tactical encounters' (Bacharach and Lawler, 1981, p.7). The players may, of course, call on evidence and rational argument in support of their causes, but such appeals are rarely enough to make a particular case stick in the face of the competing demands of other players. Some managers regard those 'competitive encounters' as a waste of time and energy. Evidence and experience suggest, however, that these encounters can be fundamental to individual and organizational effectiveness.

Processual perspectives on change and innovation

Change and innovation are politicized processes. Frost and Egri (1991, p.231) argue that:

> [P]olitics is often the inevitable consequence of self-interested contests between and among actors which are engendered by the inherent ambiguity of issues, ideas and things. In that innovation at its core is about ambiguity and is replete with disputes caused by the differences in perspectives among those touched by an innovation and the changes it engenders, we believe that innovation often becomes a very political process. Rather than viewing these struggles for ascendancy in a negative

light, we propose that politics serves both a natural and necessary role in the course of human interaction. Judging political actions and outcomes as good or bad, right or wrong, is to a large extent a function of the perspective, the values and the interests of the evaluator.

This view of politics as 'natural and necessary' is reflected in theories of change which draw on processual–contextual perspectives. Pettigrew (1973; 1985; 1988) and Dawson (1994; 1996; 2003) argue that outcomes depend on the interactions between the substance, context (external and internal), and process of change. Those authors also note that change agents must be willing to intervene in the political system of the organization, to legitimate change in the face of competing proposals, and to discredit other views. This involves what Bennis (1984) describes as 'the management of meaning', through efforts to establish the validity of particular definitions of problems and solutions, and to gain the compliance and support of those involved. Change agents who are unwilling, or unable, to act in this way are likely to find that their ideas and initiatives are not welcomed, and that it is the suggestions and projects of others which win support.

Change is not only about politics, however. The external context often suggests or shapes the substance of change (new legislation, innovative competitors). Internal factors can also facilitate or constrain proposals (availability of expertise and technology, culture which supports risk-taking). In turn, the substance of change shapes both the form and possibilities of political activity. Consider the contrasting implications of change which is of marginal significance, on the one hand, and that which is central to the success of the organization, on the other – or change which is slow, and that which is rapid. Actors can draw upon evidence from the context and substance of change to legitimate proposals with the 'we must do this because' argument. It is therefore *interaction* between context, substance and political factors which shapes the process and outcomes of change.

You take the high road

Our understanding of how political factors interact with the substance, context, and process of change clearly depends on how the concepts of power and politics are defined. Unfortunately, there are no agreed definitions, and research reveals an ambivalence in attitudes towards organization politics. That ambivalence is shared by academic commentators, further compounding the definition problem.

More power to ya

A positive view of politics can be seen in popular titles such as 'more power to ya!' (Matejka et al., 1985), 'playing the game' (Conklin, 1993), 'politics: a key to personal success' (Coates, 1994), and 'navigating the waters of organizational politics'

(Buhler, 1994). The negative view is reflected in works such as 'the illegitimate discipline' (Thompkins, 1990), 'a walk on the dark side' (Ferris and King, 1991), and '*21 Dirty Tricks at Work*' (Phipps and Gautrey, 2005). Theoretical accounts often display this ambivalence in a neat and intriguing 'two-dimensional' manner, which allows commentators simultaneously to recognize, and to distance themselves from, politics as dirty tricks. For example, McClelland and Burnham (1995; McClelland, 1970) distinguish between 'institutional' and 'personal power' managers. The latter seek personal gain at the expense of others and 'are not disciplined enough to be good institution builders' (McClelland and Burnham, 1995, p.130):

> [They] exercise their power impulsively. They are more often rude to other people, they drink too much, they try to exploit others sexually, and they collect symbols of personal prestige such as fancy cars or big offices.

The institutional manager, in contrast, combines power motivation with self control, and represents 'the socialized face of power' (McClelland and Burnham, 1995, p.129):

> Above all, the good manager's power motivation is not oriented towards personal aggrandizement but toward the institution that he or she serves. [They] are more institution minded; they tend to get elected to more offices, to control their drinking, and have a desire to serve others.

Good 'institutional' managers have the following profile (McClelland and Burnham, 1995, p.133):

- feel responsible for developing the organizations to which they belong
- believe in the importance of centralized authority
- enjoy the discipline of work, and getting things done in an orderly way
- are willing to sacrifice self-interest for organizational welfare
- have a keen sense of justice, concerning reward for hard effort.

In other words, good managers use power in the interests of the organization, rather than in pursuit of self-interest. The use of power can therefore be acceptable, as long as it is subject to discipline, control and inhibition. However, this viewpoint does not admit the possibility that institution building and personal career enhancement can be pursued simultaneously.

Greiner and Schein (1988) contrast 'the high road', in which power brokers behave in ways that are 'open and above board', with 'the low road', where deceit, manipulation, and 'political games' are used to further self-interest. The low road, they argue, is not appropriate for the professional, ethical, organization development (OD) practitioner or change agent. Egan (1994) similarly bases his advice for 'working the shadow side' of the organization on a distinction between institution-building and empire-building politics.

The silver-tongued hustler

In their classic OD textbook, French and Bell (1999) review the concepts of power and politics, and argue that OD practitioners should understand the nature of power and politics, the strategy and tactics of influence, and the characteristics and behaviours of powerholders. However, they emphasize the 'normative–re-educative' and 'empirical–rational' bases of OD, and deny the relevance of 'power–coercive' strategies. They conclude that the change agent should not be a political activist or power broker, but a facilitator, catalyst, educator, and problem solver. Adopting the same stance, Ward (1994, p.143) argues that:

> To ignore organizational politics when managing change is to fail. What then is the alternative? Should one be political? The short answer is no. You should not be political. If you do become political, then professional integrity is sacrificed. You are just another silver-tongued hustler parading your wares while seeking to manipulate. This is the road to disaster. Politics does not add value.

The distinctions between socialized and uninhibited, institution-building and empire-building, high road and low road, establish a legitimate domain of the 'political', allowing commentators to claim that their perspectives address the realities of organizational life, while dismissing the legitimacy of political tactics used to further self-interest. What are the practical and moral implications of this view?

Practical implications

The main practical implications concern the personal and organizational risks of not engaging with organization politics. Assume that the change agent faces covert resistance and subversion from other players, concerning a change agenda which has widespread support. It may not always be possible or credible to deal with those threats through public, formal channels. A professional approach will often involve the use of political tactics to disarm such threats. To ignore the political tactics of others may have damaging consequences for the change initiative, for other members of the organization expecting to benefit from the change, and for the reputation of the change agent.

A further problem arises where those empire-building political players who seek only personal advantage and satisfaction establish control over an organization's change agenda. This can cause significant damage, sooner or later, unless other players have the will and skill to challenge and to stop them. To avoid the use of political tactics in such circumstances may lead not only to the abandonment of valuable initiatives, but to the pursuit of alternative projects of dubious long-term organizational advantage.

Moral implications

The moral implications are more subtle. We have a compelling voice which says, 'don't get involved, keep it clean, be open, honest, collaborative'. But this defence of the moral high ground sidelines challenge and protest, by appealing to a common purpose in the interests of harmony. This principled position stifles dissent, reducing opportunities to press an individual's or a group's ideas and counter-proposals through whatever creative, forceful, ongoing, and socially acceptable means appropriate. In short, this claim to a moral high ground can be seen as an authoritarian political act which silences other legitimate voices. Even worse, those who wish to promote other viewpoints are forced to criticize those who are advocating harmony and consensus – social values that are awkward to challenge.

The cost of maintaining the high road

It is interesting to note that 'the high road' incurs costs. One problem is that, as Egan (1994) observes, even though you may be unwilling to use political tactics, the evidence shows that most other managers are prepared to behave politically, and to take advantage of those holding principled positions. Pfeffer (1992a) summarizes strategies for avoiding political behaviour in decision making, but also identifies the costs of those strategies (Table 2.1).

The political process cannot be 'managed away'. From the standpoint of the change agent in particular, the political system of the organization has to be managed proactively, and the 'high road' is not a realistic long-term option. However, the process of managing politics is not a technical matter of 'pulling levers' and using the

Table 2.1 Controlling politics – strategies and costs

Strategies	Costs
introduce slack in budgets, and create extra posts, to reduce competition for resources	overhead, inventory, excess capacity, more staff, higher costs
build a strong culture, with shared beliefs, values and goals, to reduce conflict	fewer points of view, less information brought to decision making, poor decisions
make decisions appear less important to reduce levels of challenge and dispute	decision avoidance, critical analysis missing, important information not used
reduce complexity and uncertainty to discourage political gaming for personal gain	create rigid rules and procedures, reduce the organization's capacity for change

Source: based on Pfeffer (1992a).

'right techniques'. More contextual awareness, judgement, creativity, and risk-taking is involved than that.

Power: what is it, and how can I get more?

Bertrand Russell (1938, p.12) observed that, 'the fundamental concept in social science is power, in the same sense in which energy is the fundamental concept in physics'. Power appears to be a straightforward concept. We know what it is when we see it, and it is usually not difficult to distinguish between those who have it, and those who do not. Power is often regarded as a latent property of the individual, as a capability exercised through social and interpersonal skills. This resource-based view is useful, but offers an incomplete account.

Episodic and pervasive views of power

Power is both an episodic and a pervasive phenomenon. Episodic perspectives concern 'the ability of A to make B do something', which they may not otherwise have done. Here, the use of power as a resource is direct and visible. I offer to give you a reward, or a punishment, and consequently you do as I ask.

However, if we shift our focus to the ways in which behaviour is influenced and controlled by features of organization structures and processes that are taken for granted, routine aspects of 'the way things are', it becomes clear that power is also a pervasive phenomenon. You ask me for a promotion or a pay rise, and I reply that such requests (of course) must be dealt with at the scheduled time, by the properly constituted committee, who must be sent the relevant paperwork, completed correctly, using appropriate arguments and evidence. This is a roundabout way to delay or reject your request, and it leaves you without any other options (in this organization). Power that is embedded in social and cultural norms, and in routine practices, is potentially more effective because it is discreet, non-obvious, sometimes more difficult to observe, and therefore much harder to challenge. In practice, the episodic and pervasive dimensions of power operate in tandem, and are difficult to disentangle. Those embedded norms and routines can themselves be viewed and used as resources by those wishing to exert and to maintain non-obvious and covert modes of influence over others.

Defining the concept of power thus turns out to be more difficult than it may at first appear. Hardy (1995, pp.xx–xxi) summarizes the range of perspectives on power:

> Power has been both the *independent variable*, causing outcomes such as domination, and the *dependent variable*, usually the outcome of dependency or centrality. Power has been viewed as *functional* in the hands of managers who use it in the pursuit of organizational goals, and *dysfunctional* in the hands of those who challenge those goals and seek to promote self-interest. It has been viewed as the means by which *legitimacy* is created and as the incarnation of *illegitimate*

action. Power has been equated with *formal* organizational arrangements and as the *informal* actions that influence outcomes. It has been seen as *conditional on conflict* and as a means to *prevent conflict*. It has been defined as a resource that is *consciously* and deliberately mobilized in the pursuit of self-interest, and as a system of relations that knows no interest, but from which some groups *unconsciously* and inadvertently benefit. It has been seen as an *intentional* act to which causality can be clearly attributed and as an *unintentional*, unpredictable game of chance. The study of power has created a *behavioural* focus for some researchers and *attitudinal* and ideological factors for others. Power has been berated for being repressive and lauded for being productive. Small wonder, then, that there is little agreement.

In the absence of an agreed framework, our strategy is to set out broad perspectives. However, we will not attempt to determine which is correct. These contrasting views offer different ways of looking at power, different lenses through which we can see power being formed and activated. In other words, these contrasting perspectives are most valuable when used in combination.

Power as a personal property

The popular conception of power concerns the 'latent property' notion. Power is something you possess, a set of resources which you can accumulate. This leads to questions such as, how much power does an individual have, where did it come from, and how can an individual acquire more power? Pfeffer (1992a) lists a series of structural and individual sources of managerial power. Structural sources of power include:

- formal position and authority
- ability to cultivate allies and supporters
- access to and control over information and other resources
- physical and social position in the organization's communication network
- the centrality of your unit or section to the business
- role in resolving critical problems, in reducing uncertainty
- degree of unity of your section, lack of internal dissent
- being irreplaceable
- the pervasiveness of one's activities in the organization.

Although not all of these structural properties apply in every instance, Pfeffer's list explains why accountants tend to be more powerful than human resource managers, in most organizations. Individual sources of power include:

- energy, endurance, stamina
- ability to focus energy and avoid wasteful effort
- ability to read and understand others

- selecting flexible means to achieve goals
- personal toughness, willingness to engage in confrontation and conflict
- ability to play 'the subordinate' and 'the team member' to enlist the support of others.

The personal accumulation of power in this perspective thus involves strengthening, where possible, both structural and individual sources of power.

Power as a relational property

Power is typically considered from the viewpoint of the person exercising it. However, Crozier (1973, p.212) argues that it is necessary to look beyond this single standpoint and to see power, 'as a relationship between individuals or groups, as a process developing over time'. Crozier (1973, p.214) also points out that power relations are often reciprocal; 'if A can make B do something he would not have done otherwise, it is quite likely that B, for his part, is capable of making A do something he would not have done without B's intervention'. So, as Pettigrew and McNulty (1995, p.851) argue, 'Power is not an attribute possessed by someone in isolation. It is a relational phenomenon. Power is generated, maintained and lost in the context of relationships with others'. This perspective derives from the work of French and Raven (1958) who identified five power bases; reward, coercive, referent, legitimate, and expert (Table 2.2). The power bases identified by French and Raven have interesting features.

First, these power bases depend on the perceptions of others. Perceptions shape our behaviour as much as whatever constitutes reality. A change agent may be able to control rewards and penalties, and have superior knowledge, but if others do not believe that the change agent possesses these attributes, then they may be unwilling to comply with requests. Similarly, change agents may be able to persuade others that they do possess power which they do not have, and compliance may be forthcoming even though the

Table 2.2 Five power bases

reward power	is based on the belief of followers that the change agent has access to valued rewards which will be dispensed in return for compliance
coercive power	is based on the belief of followers that the change agent can administer penalties or sanctions that are unwelcome
referent power	is based on the belief of followers that the change agent has desirable abilities and personality traits that can and should be copied
legitimate power	is based on the belief of followers that the change agent has authority to give directions, within the boundaries of their position or rank
expert power	is based on the belief of followers that the change agent has superior knowledge relevant to the situation and the task in hand

Source: based on French and Raven (1958).

change agent does not have access to, say, rewards, sanctions, expertise, or friends in high places.

Second, these five power bases are interrelated. The exercise of one can affect your ability to use another. The change agent who uses coercive power, for example, may lose referent power, but one can deploy legitimate power to enhance both referent and expert power.

Third, the change agent can operate from multiple power bases. As the American gangster Al Capone is reputed to have said, 'You can get a lot more done with a kind word and a gun than with a kind word alone' (McCarty, 2004). The same person may be able to use different power bases, in different combinations, in different contexts, and at different times. This framework has been developed by Benfari et al. (1986), who identify eight power bases, adding information, affiliation, and group power (Table 2.3). These authors note that the exercise of power can be perceived by recipients as either positive ('P+') or negative ('P−'), depending on circumstances. Reward power and referent power are usually welcome, while coercion and information power are usually seen in negative terms. But perceptions of the other power bases depend on how they are exercised. The abuse of authority to bully others is scorned; the exercise of strong leadership in a crisis is praised. Allowing others access to the thinking of senior figures through affiliation power may be regarded favourably, while inflexible appeal to 'what senior management wants' may not.

Benfari and colleagues (1986, p.16) also argue that referent power is underutilized:

> Because of multiple programs and limited resources, conflict is an everyday occurrence. The key to conflict resolution is the ability to negotiate workable psychological contracts with colleagues who have no formal reporting obligations. The use of threats (coercive power) or appeals to upper authority can lead to long-term conflict. The party under siege can, at some time in the future, make use of affiliation power to retaliate. Acquiring and using referent power effectively is important not only to managers in matrix organizations but to all managers at any level in any organization.

They offer suggestions for building referent power, as a 'cheap and easy way to build a relationship', noting that this should be neither time-consuming nor costly:

- get to know the motives, preferences, values and interests of your colleagues
- build relationships using shared motives, goals and interests
- respect differences in interests and don't attack another person's style
- give 'positive strokes', use reward power, confirm others' competence
- invite reciprocal influence, show that you respect the opinions of others
- share information, give your expertise, particularly where you stand to benefit
- minimize concerns with status, put signs of office aside, people relate to equals
- develop communication skills, people value clear and consistent messages

Table 2.3 The effective use of power

power base	explanation	seen as
reward	positive strokes, remuneration, awards, compliments, other symbolic gestures of praise	P+
coercion	physical or psychological injury, verbal and non-verbal put-downs, slights, symbolic gestures of disdain, physical attack, demotion, unwanted transfer, withholding of needed resources	P–
authority	management right to control, obligation of others to obey, playing 'the boss' and abusing authority	P–
	exercise of leadership based on authority in times of crisis or need	P+
referent	identification based on personal characteristics, sometimes on perception of charisma; or reciprocal identification based on friendship, association, sharing personal information, providing something of value to the other, and on common interests, values, viewpoints and preferences; creation of reciprocal 'IOUs'	P+
expert	possession of specialized knowledge valued by others, used to help others, given freely when solicited	P+
	unsolicited expertise, seen as unwarranted intrusion; continual use can create barriers; expertise offered in a condescending manner can be seen as coercive; withholding expertise in times of need	P–
information	access to information that is not public knowledge, because of position or connections; can exist at all levels in the organization, not just at the top; those at the top may know less about what is going on; secretaries and personal assistants to senior executives often have information power, and can often control information flows to and from superiors	P–
affiliation	'borrowed' from an authority source with whom one is associated – executive secretaries and staff assistants act as surrogates for their superiors; acting on the wishes of the superior	P+
	acting on their own self-interest; using negative affiliation power by applying accounting and personnel policies rigidly	P–
group	collective problem solving, conflict resolution, creative brainstorming; group resolution greater than the individual contribution	P+
	a few individuals dominating the proceedings, 'groupthink'	P–

Source: based on Benfari et al. (1986, pp.12–16).

- get to know how people react to stress and crisis
- get to know the informal political structure of your organization.

There are at least two problems with 'property' and 'relational' concepts of power. First, they do not distinguish power-related tactics from other behaviour. As we saw earlier, one can see power and politics manifested in every nuance of social and organizational life, from clothing to motor car, from size of office to size of salary, from family name to job title, and in female–male relationships. Second, these perspectives offer a surface view of power, as something that can be neatly categorized, and confined to interpersonal relationships. These perspectives overlook the less visible, structural, or 'embedded' elements of power.

The 'distinctiveness' problem

Many commentators equate power with influence, with cause and effect, with A making B do something. While power can be seen as a potential to act, Dahl (1957) argues that unused potential cannot be regarded as power. In Dahl's view, power is exercised episodically, whenever one party influences and changes the behaviour of another.

There is a difficulty here. We ask you the time, you raise your wrist, you shift your gaze, you read your watch, you shift your gaze back to us, you tell us the time. We have manipulated your behaviour in this episode, albeit in a trivial way. Every social encounter involves ongoing mutual influence of this kind, affecting attitudes and behaviour. And many social encounters are characterized by power imbalances, in which one party has more skill and resources than the other, and is able to maintain a higher degree of control over the interaction and its outcomes. Astley and Sachdeva (1994, p.104) observe that:

> [I]t is possible to interpret every instance of interaction and every social relationship as involving an exercise of power, because actors clearly affect one another all the time they are interacting. But this very pervasiveness tends to make the concept of power elusive and redundant, for it begins to have no meaning apart from the ideas of social interaction and organization.

A term that does not help us to make distinctions between different categories of behaviour is not very useful. We are thus not able to tell when somebody is utilizing a power-based approach and when they are not, or when they are engaged in organization politics or not.

The 'embeddedness' issue

A second problem concerns the focus on visible aspects of power, and the neglect of 'hidden' dimensions, which are hidden only until one knows what to look for. Frost and

Egri (1991) discuss this in terms of the surface and deep structure of organization politics, noting that the latter are often difficult to detect, forgotten, unrecognized. But power is designed into organization structures and processes, giving some individuals greater access to information, decision making, budget responsibility, and other resources, for example. Formal position facilitates this access, but other organizational players can enjoy similar privileges.

Some of the power implications of organization structures are more visible than others. Hickson et al. (1971) argue that the power of a group or department depends on its centrality in the workflow of the organization, its relative independence from other sections, the uniqueness and non-substitutable nature of its expertise, and its ability to cope with uncertainty. The most powerful groups, therefore, are those which cope independently and effectively with the greatest uncertainty using expertise not available elsewhere. This 'strategic contingencies' explanation of relative power again helps to explain the different levels of influence of, say, finance and human resource management functions.

That which is hidden or latent is less easily detected, but is not necessarily less potent. Consider the promotions process in a university. These procedures are driven by a range of actors including staff seeking promotion, department heads, faculty deans, personnel officers, and committees populated with 'neutral' members drawn from around the organization. Where does the power reside in this process? One can look at the relative status of the key players and coalitions, and reach a judgement concerning their impact on decisions. Behind their interactions lies a set of paperwork, which requires completion, signature and counter-signature. There are also regulations concerning the timing of submissions, the hearing of cases, the style and nature of cases that are presented, and the timing and conduct of committee meetings. The regulations also address the nature of the arguments that are considered appropriate; are we evaluating the job, or are we assessing the individual, for example, where different considerations apply? To confuse matters further, there are subtly different procedures, paperwork, and committees for different categories of (professorial, other academic, academic-related, and non-academic) staff.

Players in the promotions game can call upon the rules and regulations surrounding the procedures to interfere with, delay or block a case. It may be possible to claim, for example, that while an individual merits recognition, the case has unfortunately been submitted in the incorrect format, at the wrong time, to the wrong committee, countersigned by the wrong person, using inappropriate arguments. The point at issue appears to concern the degree of rigidity or flexibility with which the regulations are applied. When formal regulations and unwritten rules converge in the notion of precedent, it is difficult to counter the argument that, 'we must apply our rules consistently', and to avoid accusations of making 'special cases' or bending the rules to suit particular circumstances. In this way, less powerful individuals (personnel staff, lay members of a committee) can exploit regulations to block or delay a case, while sounding supportive in public. Power does not just lie with individuals and relationships, but also with the way in which processes and procedures are designed. These properties of the organization can also become valuable resources in the hands of skilled political players seeking other more subtle forms of influence to achieve their ends.

Power as an embedded property

Moving beyond the formal rules and regulations, and the subtle ways in which they can be exploited, there are in most organizations a number of other unwritten rules (Scott-Morgan, 1995) concerning 'the ways things are done around here'. Here we enter the cloudy domain of organization culture, concerning values, standards, modes of behaviour, expectations, rituals, procedures, and goals, which combine to create a fabric of norms and expectations that not only shape attitudes and behaviour, but also influence the distribution of power across the organization's membership. It is important to recognize that this fabric, this power distribution, is fluid and not static, shifting with circumstances and rarely stable. However, those norms and expectations can be exploited in precisely the same way as written, formal procedures, to support an argument or a position, to advance a perspective, to challenge or block an initiative being driven by someone else.

Power, therefore, is woven into what we take for granted, the order of things, the social and organization structures in which we find ourselves, the rule systems that appear to constitute the 'natural' running of day-to-day procedures. It is difficult to challenge 'the way things are', or even to recognize in the first place that what one is presented with is an established pattern of power relations and not some immutable facet of social life. It is in the interest of those who can manipulate and exploit these taken for granted norms that the unequal distribution of power is accepted and not subject to challenge.

One aspect of this face of power is *non-decision making* (Bachrach and Baratz, 1962). This refers to the ways in which key figures work behind the scenes to ensure that processes, situations, and rules are constructed to prevent those with complaints or demands from expressing their views openly, and thus avoiding conflict. Agendas are restricted to 'safe' issues; controversial issues are excluded from informal conversations and from formal decision-making forums; procedures are invoked to exclude those in subordinate roles from debates. Power brokers decide outcomes backstage, in the corridor, before the meeting. Another mechanism, which Bachrach and Baratz call the *mobilization of bias*, can favour some individuals, groups, interests, and topics, over others. The norms and procedures of an organization, 'the rules of the game', can thus be designed to function systematically to the benefit of some, and the disadvantage of others. This can lead to a situation in which concerns are not raised because some problems are not recognized as such. Individuals and groups may thus be rendered politically passive because they accept the 'existing order', or because they lack the understanding or imagination to conceive of a different order, or because they anticipate that resistance will be ineffective. Non-decision making and the mobilization of bias may take three forms (Clegg, 1989, p.77):

1 the more powerful deal with the grievances of the less powerful by ignoring them, by dismissing them as minor, unsubstantiated, or irrelevant, or by subjecting them to endless and inconclusive consideration by committees and enquiries
2 anticipating the consequences, the less powerful may see that their grievances and demands will be ignored or dismissed, and do not raise them in the first place
3 the more powerful define which matters are legitimate and discussible, and the forums and procedures through which such issues are raised, thus stifling the articulation of some issues and demands, while encouraging 'acceptable' or 'safe' topics and themes

These quite different forms of power relationships can be deeply embedded in organization structures and procedures, such that they come to be taken for granted. Lukes (2006) calls this the 'third dimension' of power, whereby the potential demands of subordinate groups are not raised, not because channels are unavailable, but because they have been socialized into not recognizing these as problems. Embedded power relations can thus operate by influencing our basic understanding and perceptions (Hardy and O'Sullivan, 1988). However, as Clegg et al. (2006) observe, delving 'deeper' into the workings of power becomes a highly abstract exercise. The main point is that power and politics operate simultaneously at a number of different levels. Managers in general, and change agents in particular, need to understand how these are intertwined, their own scope for manoeuvre, and the modes of influence that are available to them and to others.

Valuing diversity

We have described three interrelated concepts of power:

1 power as *a property of individuals*, expressed in terms of power sources and bases, structural and individual
2 power as *a property of interpersonal relationships* between organization members, expressed in the perception that some individuals possess or lack particular power bases
3 power as *an embedded property* of the structures, procedures, and norms of the organization, perpetuating existing routines and power inequalities.

The notion of power as an embedded and pervasive construct, lacking a clear and distinctive definition, has three major consequences. First, this alerts us to the less tangible dimensions of power, carried in the taken for granted procedures and practices of the organization, and of society as a whole. This is important because intangibility is not equated with insignificance. On the contrary, these dimensions of power can be extremely potent in skilful hands. In addition, that which cannot be readily seen, described, or defined can be extremely difficult to challenge and resist.

Second, this alerts us to the wide range of methods and techniques available to the change agent, and also to the range of potential responses from the targets of political tactics. While the resource-based view regards power as 'one way', something which 'we use on you', the concepts of non-decision making and mobilization of bias suggest that power is a more fluid, dynamic, shifting, and malleable resource. Determining an appropriate strategy requires personal skill, knowledge of the context, judgement, and creativity. A broad understanding of the embedded nature of power relations, along with the property and (interpersonal) relational dimensions, exposes the scope for such creativity.

Third, this alerts us to the notion that what may be defined as 'power' in textbook terms may not be unambiguously so regarded, or so represented, in practice. Power in practice becomes a slippery concept when its users can credibly claim that they are applying custom and practice, or accepted norms, or 'the rules and regulations', or precedent in the interests of consistency. What may be defined as the exercise of power from one perspective may be defined as commonplace and routine from another. Suggesting how such ambiguities can be exploited, Ferris et al. (2002b) note that it is often useful for managers to avoid attributions of political intent; skilled political actors are those who can disguise such intentions.

We'll take the low road

Mangham (1979, p.15) observes that, 'each of us has the capacity consciously to *manipulate* our own behaviour and that of others and that many of us fully utilize that capacity, for good or ill'. Emphasizing cooperation and collaboration, organization theory 'chooses to ignore "the darker side of humanity", man's [*sic*] evident capacity, and occasional ardent desire, to screw his fellow man (or, in more polite terms, to achieve his ends at the expense of his colleagues)'. Selfless collaboration thus sits alongside political manoeuvring. While we probably do not like to consider ourselves as manipulative, most if not all social exchanges inevitably involve manipulation to some degree, and this accusation is difficult to avoid.

In spite of the stereotype of politics as 'dirty tricks', we have tried to defend political behaviour in at least some settings, as potentially pro-social, even if it is manipulative. We have not, however, attempted to define political behaviour with precision. What features distinguish political behaviour from non-political or apolitical behaviour?

Dimensions and elements politics

One widely cited approach to the terminology issue comes from the work of Mayes and Allen (1977) who base their definition of political behaviour on the means and ends of

Influence means	Influence ends	
	Organizationally sanctioned	**Not sanctioned**
Organizationally sanctioned	**I**: Non-political behaviour	**II**: Dysfunctional behaviour
Not sanctioned	**III**: Potentially functional behaviour	**IV**: Dysfunctional behaviour

Figure 2.1 Dimensions of organization politics. *Source*: based on Mayes and Allen (1977).

influence attempts (Figure 2.1). The means which one player uses to influence another, to achieve their preferred outcomes, can either be sanctioned by the organization, or not. Similarly, the outcomes sought may or may not be sanctioned. Behaviours where the goals and the tactics both enjoy organizational sanction are labelled 'non-political' (Cell I). Whether the tactics are sanctioned or not, and the ends or goals are not sanctioned (personal gain), the behaviour is labelled as both political and dysfunctional (Cells II and IV). Where ends are sanctioned but means are not, the behaviour is potentially functional for the organization (Cell III).

There are problems with this approach. Who decides what is sanctioned and what is not? Many organizations have codes of conduct which identify unacceptable behaviours; but these rules usually cover the obvious topics of theft of company property, disclosure of sensitive information, and health and safety regulations, for example. Such rules cannot cover every contingency that might arise in interpersonal and group behaviour across the organization over time. Different members of the organization, in different functions and at different levels, often have different views on these issues. Some players may describe as political behaviours which are in fact sanctioned in some form. It may not always be apparent which behaviours are sanctioned, and which are not. Behaviours defined as 'political' may also belong to other categories of action: revenge, returning a favour, incompetence, defending a colleague, lack of understanding, rigid rule following, and so on. A further difficulty concerns the narrow definition of the terms 'functional' and 'dysfunctional' which seem to concern contribution to 'the greater good'. That is often a source of dispute. And the concept of means and ends being functional or dysfunctional for the change agent, irrespective of organizational outcomes, is not admitted in this approach.

Supporting the negative view of political behaviour, Drory and Romm (1990) offer a definition based on the common elements across the different perspectives found in the literature and covering outcomes, means, and characteristics of the context or situation (Table 2.4). They first point out that politics is played, and can be analysed, at three levels: individual, group, and organization. We are not dealing just with individual actions, but also with collective leadership, establishing group consensus, and the formation of coalitions.

In this perspective, behaviour is defined as political if the motivation is self-serving, with regard to winning power and acquiring resources, in ways that are against the

Table 2.4 Elements of political behaviour

Outcomes	• are self-serving • act against the organization's effectiveness and goals • are concerned with the distribution of resources and advantage • usually involve behaviour linked with the attainment of power
Means	• involve influence attempts or tactics • concern the use of power tactics • include informal, covert, non-job-related behaviours • true motives are concealed
Situational characteristics	• there is conflict and resistance in the organization • there is uncertainty in the decision-making process

Source: based on Drory and Romm (1990).

interests of the organization. Such behaviour is further characterized by the informal use of power and influence to achieve hidden goals. Political behaviour is further encouraged by uncertainty, conflict, and resistance, and is therefore likely to be intensified by change.

This approach again denies that political behaviour may be deployed with corporate objectives in mind, instead of – or in some instances as well as – personal goals. While conflict and resistance may trigger political behaviour, particularly on the part of change agents and those who seek to challenge change initiatives, many change settings are also characterized by some degree of support for change (from senior management, from individuals and groups who will benefit). In other words, the 'situational characteristics' may be better represented by a continuum of coexisting views, from public welcoming acceptance of change, to covert challenge and subversion.

However, 'ethically objectionable' as this may seem, the exercise of power is pervasive in social interaction. Kakabadse and Parker (1984, p.62) observe that, 'social order rests on deceitfulness, evasiveness, secrecy, frontwork and basic social conflicts'. Shulman (2006, p.2) argues that lies and deceit are necessary as, 'people routinely use lies as a tool to navigate workplace expectations [and] acting deceptively is an important means of administrating work'. Shulman cites examples such as pretending to show deference, shirking work, crafting misleading reports, making false claims to customers and coworkers, and covering up transgressions. We may describe how we exercise power over others in more or less acceptable terms: 'normal interaction', 'influencing', 'persuading'. But the end results – shaping, affecting or manipulating others' behaviour – are the same. We achieve this, sometimes consciously, sometimes unwittingly, through three related mechanisms:

- conversation controls
- impression management
- influence tactics.

Conversation controls

We 'manage' our conversations through a range of conscious and unconscious verbal and non-verbal signals and questioning techniques which tell the parties, for example, when one has finished an utterance and when it is somebody else's turn to speak. These signals also reveal agreement, friendship, dispute, and dislike, emotions which in turn shape the further response of the listener. Normally, we send these signals unconsciously or habitually, but awareness of the methods being used allows us to bring them under conscious control. This can be advantageous in many social settings. Therapists and counsellors, for example, shape conversations in ways that allow their clients to articulate their problems and to work towards identifying solutions. Managers holding selection, appraisal and promotion interviews need to understand conversation control techniques to handle these interactions effectively.

We can also use conversation controls to achieve our preferred ends by shaping or steering the behaviour of others. For example, Huczynski (2003) describes the 'high power' and 'low power' strategies which signal to others how powerful we are, or how powerful we perceive ourselves to be (Table 2.5). As these strategies involve normal behaviours, it is possible to use powertalking and avoid low power indicators (Table 2.6)

Table 2.5   Powertalking strategies

positive talk	Respond positively, make commitments, have high expectations, optimistic, avoid conditional phrases, seek creative solutions, look for the benefits.
give credit	Alter or ignore shortcomings, describe achievements positively, neither apologize nor justify, praise others for their success.
learn from experience	Say, 'I learned' instead of 'I failed', seek the positive in the face of setbacks, think positive when feeling low, focus on options rather than regrets.
accept responsibility	Admit your feelings, accept responsibility for your actions, control your use of time.
persuade others	Emphasize benefits, keep options open, seek ways to improve relationships, focus on the positive, accept the ideas of others.
decisive speaking	Commit to specific duties and targets, get detailed information, set realistic goals, decide what to say and then say it.
tell the truth	Avoid suspicious and misleading phrases, say 'no' when you mean 'no', avoid self-criticism, respect those with whom you interact – remembering and using others' names.

Source: based on Huczynski (2003).

Table 2.6 Low power indicators

hedges and qualifiers	'Maybe it has some strengths': Qualifications means avoiding commitment, so you don't have to disagree with someone. You can change your view when you discover theirs.
irritators	'. . . you know', 'sort of', 'kinda': These suggest you lack confidence in what you are saying, that you feel the need to apologise, that you lack knowledge and ability.
intensifiers	Redundant adjectives, like 'really', 'awfully', 'horrendously'. These terms lack substance; use more powerful language such as 'remarkably', 'outstanding', 'excellent'.
tags	Tags are the bits at the end where you say, 'aren't they?', or 'didn't you?'. These turn a decisive statement into an unnecessary question, attempting to please, avoiding conflict.
hesitations	'Um, er, ah, uhh, well . . .': These suggest the need for time to think, or the fear of 'coming over too strong'. Can signal uncertainty, and encourage interruption.
excessive questions	A speech pattern that signals uncertainty and need for attention.
others	Unnecessary or excessive apologizing, giving irrelevant information, excessive personal disclosure, over-politeness.

Source: based on Huczynski (2003).

in order to signal the impression of power (other impression management techniques are discussed below).

Powerful individuals (female or male), or those seeking to give others the impression that they are powerful, tend to dominate conversations, offer less personal information and emotional display, and assert status by interrupting, speaking firmly and in detail, and by providing opinions, suggestions, information, and disagreement.

Impression management

Impression management is the process by which we control the image that others have of us. This concept is based on the work of Goffman (1959), and is now recognized as a key aspect of organizational behaviour. Rosenfeld et al. (1995, p.4) argue that:

> We impression manage in many different ways: what we do, how we do it, what we say, how we say it, the furnishings and arrangement of our offices, and our physical appearance – from the clothes and make-up we wear to non-verbal behaviours such as facial expressions or postures. All these behaviours in some way can help define who and what we are.

Effective impression management means being aware of and in control of the cues that we send to others through verbal and non-verbal channels. In these ways, we consciously manipulate the perceptions that others have of us, and therefore shape their behaviour, too. We do this, for example, by 'giving off' the impression that we are friendly, submissive, apologetic, angry, defensive, confident, intimidating, and so on. The more effectively we manage our impression, the greater the control we can achieve in social interaction, and the greater our ability to achieve our preferred outcomes. Noting that dramaturgical behaviours are used as influencing tools which often disguise ulterior motives, Gardner (1992) describes 'organizational life as drama', arguing that managers need 'stagecraft' skills in order to play their roles effectively. He discusses how the use of impression management methods in an organizational setting can be analysed according to its elements; actors, audience, stage, script, performance, and reviews (success when the actor creates the desired impression).

Creating a favourable self-image

ingratiation — Use flattery, agree with the opinions of others, do favours to encourage people with power and influence to befriend you.

intimidation — Convey the image of potential danger to those who could stand in the way of your advancement. Use veiled threats of exposure.

self promotion — Win respect and admiration of superiors through embellishing your accomplishments, overstating your abilities, displaying awards.

exemplification — Create an impression of selfless dedication and self-sacrifice, so those in positions of influence will feel guilty and offer reward or promotion.

accounting — Distance yourself from negative events, deny personal responsibility for problems, diminish the seriousness of difficulties.

supplication — Get those in positions of influence to be sympathetic and nurturing, for example, through requests for 'mentoring' and other support.

Source: based on Feldman and Klitch (1991).

Feldman and Klitch (1991) also argue that a 'careerist orientation' is based on beliefs which incorporate much practical impression management advice:

1 Merit alone is insufficient for career advance. Creating the appearance of being a winner, or looking 'promotable', is equally important.
2 To advance, it is critical to pursue social relationships with superiors and colleagues. On the surface, these relationships should appear to be social, but in reality they are used instrumentally for contacts and insider information.

3 Looking like a 'team player' is central to career progression. However, individuals should still pursue self-interest at work through 'antagonistic co-operation', appearing co-operative and helpful on the surface, while seeking information about how to overcome the competition.

4 In the long run, an individual's career goals will be inconsistent with the interests of any one organization. Therefore, in order to advance, individuals must appear to be loyal and committed to their current employers, while keeping their résumés circulating and keeping their options open.

One interesting aspect of impression management concerns the concept of the 'tell'. A 'tell' is a signal or cue which reveals something about us, and we may do this deliberately, or unwittingly. One important set of signals (Table 2.7) concerns 'power tells' (Collett, 2004).

Feldman and Klitch (1991) emphasize the need to maintain the illusion of success, collaboration, loyalty, integrity and power. This advice can be seen in either evaluative or descriptive terms. On the one hand, we may consider this guidance in the context of personal and social values and norms, and make a judgement with regard to how ethical and legitimate we consider this to be. On the other hand, we may simply note that this advice describes the realities of organizational life, in a way that may or may not

Table 2.7 Power tells

The power tells of dominant individuals include:

- sitting and standing with legs far apart (men)
- appropriating the territory around them by placing their hands on their hips
- using open postures
- using invasive hand gestures
- smiling less, because a smile is an appeasement gesture
- establishing visual dominance by looking away from the other person while speaking, implying that they do not need to be attentive
- speaking first, and dominating the conversation thereafter
- using a lower vocal register, and speaking more slowly
- more likely to interrupt others, more likely to resist interruption by others.

The power tells of submissive individuals include:

- modifying speech style to sound more like the person they are talking to
- more frequent hesitations, using lots of 'ums' and 'ers'
- adopting closed postures
- clasping hands, touching face and hair (self-comfort gestures).

'Leakage tells' which reveal stress and anxiety include blushing, coughing, dry mouth, heavy breathing, heavy swallowing, increased heart rate, lip biting, rapid blinking, and sweating.

Source: based on Collett (2004).

match with our personal values. But this argues that dishonest or unethical behaviour is sometimes necessary in order to get the promotions to which one feels entitled. One may not advocate or acknowledge the existence of such behaviours in public. Instead, one must become adept at inconsistency, and be able to hold public positions that are mutually inconsistent. Much of the 'real work' of management cannot be tangibly assessed, and it is helpful, perhaps necessary, to maintain the illusion of success and power symbolically, through dress, office design, and the ways in which one's actions and achievements are presented.

Symbols of organizational power

To what extent are you able to:

- intercede favourably on behalf of someone in trouble with the organization
- get a desirable placement for a talented subordinate
- get approval for expenditure beyond the budget
- get above-average salary increases for subordinates
- get items on the agenda at policy meetings
- get fast access to top decision makers
- get regular, frequent access to top decision makers
- get information about decisions and policy shifts

Source: based on Kanter (1979).

Change agents as compliance professionals

In addition to conversation controls and impression management, we use influence tactics to persuade others to do what we want them to do, sometimes against their will. This topic has attracted considerable research interest, and we will consider two influential perspectives. One is based on the work of Kipnis et al. (1984), who identified eight categories of influence tactic; assertiveness, ingratiation, rational appeal, sanctions, exchange, upward appeal, blocking, and coalition (Table 2.8). Kipnis and colleagues note that managers do not exercise influence for self-interest and enjoyment, but in order to promote new ideas, encourage others to work more effectively, or introduce new working practices, for example. Models such as this, focusing on individual tactics, imply that influence is episodic. However, influence attempts may be repeated following initial failure and resistance, especially where work-related resources are at stake (Maslyn et al., 1996). A tactic that fails to work on one occasion can be used again, or the same influence attempt may be repeated with other tactics.

Table 2.8 Influence tactics

assertiveness	Order the person to do it. Point out that the rules demand it. Keep reminding them about what is required.
ingratiation	Make the request politely and humbly. Act friendly and complimentary before asking. Sympathize with any hardships that may result for them.
rational appeal	Write a detailed justification. Present relevant information in support. Explain the reasoning behind your request.
sanctions	Threaten to get them fired. Threaten to block their promotion. Threaten them with a poor performance evaluation.
exchange	Offer an exchange of favours – mutual backscratching. Remind them of favours you have provided them in the past.
upward appeal	Get higher level management to intervene in your support. Send the person to speak to your boss.
blocking	Threaten to stop working with the person. Ignore the person and stop acting friendly. Withhold collaboration until they do what you want.
coalition	Get the support of colleagues to support your request. Make the request at a formal meeting where others will support you.

Source: based on Kipnis et al. (1984).

From their study of American, Australian, and British managers, Kipnis et al. (1984) identified four types of manager based on their patterns of use of these tactics:

- *Bystanders* rarely use any of these influence tactics, have low organizational power, have limited personal and organizational objectives, and are frequently dissatisfied.
- *Shotguns* use all of these influence tactics all the time, have unfulfilled goals, and are inexperienced in their job.
- *Captives* use one or two 'favourite' tactics, habitually, and with limited effectiveness.
- *Tacticians* use rational appeal frequently, make average use of other tactics, tend to achieve their objectives, have high organizational power, and are usually satisfied.

A recent study of roles in implementing major changes in health care showed that doctors in management positions (e.g., clinical directors) were 'captives' relying on rational appeal, while 'tactician' management colleagues used a range of methods, tailored to the influence target. Although holding senior positions in the organization, doctors felt outmanoeuvred in their discussions with managers concerning changes (Buchanan et al., 2005).

Robert Cialdini (2001; Cialdini and Sagarin, 2005) identifies six principles of influence by observing 'compliance professionals' who persuade for a living; salespeople, fund-raisers, advertisers, political lobbyists, cult recruiters, and con artists. He argues that we have learned a number of automatic responses to familiar social cues, and that compliance professionals exploit those socialized behaviours.

1 Reciprocity	we are more likely to comply with a request from someone who has given us a gift, favour, or concession

We have a socially trained sense of obligation, to give 'something in return', even when the gift is unsolicited. Survey researchers include small payments to increase questionnaire response rates; restaurant staff increase tips by giving customers sweets with their bills.

The door-in-the-face technique

The influencer begins with an extreme request (join a long-term blood donor programme), that is usually rejected, then makes the request which they intended (make a one-off donation). The influencer has made a concession, and expects a concession from the target. This is also known as the 'reciprocal concessions' tactic.

2 Social validation	we are more likely to comply with a request, or to adopt a behaviour, which is consistent with what similar others are thinking or doing

If other people think it is correct, then we tend to agree. If others are doing it (driving fast on a stretch of road), then we feel justified in doing the same. Bartenders 'salt' their jar of tips to indicate that tipping is 'appropriate' behaviour. Church ushers use the same method, and evangelical preachers use 'ringers' who are briefed to 'spontaneously' come forward at predetermined moments during the service.

The list technique

The influencer makes a request after the target has seen a list of others who have already complied (donated, purchased); the longer the list, the greater the effect.

3 Commitment/ Consistency	we are more likely to comply with a request which leads to actions consistent with our previous acts and commitments

Consistency is linked to intellect, rationality, honesty, and integrity, and tends to be valued; we like to appear to be consistent. If we can get you to commit to something, then it will be easier to persuade you to behave in ways that are consistent with that prior commitment.

The four walls technique

Doorstep salespeople use this technique to gain permission to enter, asking a series of questions to which the target's answer is likely to be yes. To be consistent with their earlier answers, the target then has to agree to the final – crucial – question. The encyclopaedia salesperson asks you:

1 do you feel that education is important for your children?
2 do you think that homework contributes to the quality of education?
3 don't you agree that a good set of reference books helps with homework?
4 well, you'll be interested in these encyclopaedias that we're now offering at a very good price. Can I come in and show you?

The foot-in-the-door technique
The influencer first asks for a small favour that is almost certain to be granted (wear a small pin to promote a charity), followed by a bigger related request (donate cash). Those who agree to the small request are more likely to agree to the larger one.

The bait-and-switch procedure
This is illustrated by retailers who advertise goods (e.g., furniture) at an especially low price, but when the customers show up, the products are either poor quality, or they are sold out. Customers have made a commitment to purchasing at that store, and are more likely to consider alternative products without going elsewhere.

The low-ball technique
The salesperson 'throws a low ball', by persuading the customer to buy (e.g., a car) at a low price, or by offering an inflated trade-in for their old vehicle. But then a calculation error is discovered, or an assessor disallows the trade-in valuation. Having already committed to the purchase, most customers will go ahead even at the higher price.

---

4 Friendship/ liking	we are more likely to comply with requests from friends, or from others who we like

---

Tupperware parties use friends and neighbours, rather than company sales staff, to persuade participants to purchase. Charities recruit volunteers to collect donations in their local area. Compliance professionals as strangers, however, have to find ways to get us to like them.

Physical attractiveness
Attractive individuals are generally more persuasive. Those whom we believe to be attractive are also attributed with traits such as talent, kindness, honesty and intelligence.

Similarity
We tend to like, and to be persuaded more readily, by those who are similar to us; opinions, background, lifestyle, personality, dress. In one study, a survey response rate was doubled by giving the person sending the questionnaire a name similar to that of

the respondent; Bob Gregar and Cindy Johanson sent survey questionnaires to Robert Greer and Cynthia Johnson.

Compliments
Praise encourages liking, unless it is obvious that the flatterer's intent is manipulative.

Cooperation
Cooperation enhances compliance. Salespeople often appear to 'do battle' on the customer's behalf with a remote 'villain' of a sales manager. This cooperation in a shared outcome leads to liking, which promotes sales.

---

5 Scarcity   we are more likely to comply with requests that will lead to the acquisition of opportunities that are scarce

---

Opportunities tend to be more highly valued when they are less available, and items that are difficult to possess are 'better' than items that can be easily acquired, including information.

The limited number tactic
Customers are told that products, services, membership opportunities are in short supply and will not last long. 'Hurry, buy now.'

The deadline technique
An official time limit is placed on the opportunity to purchase or acquire: 'offer available for one week only'. This may be accompanied by a statement indicating that the item will either be unavailable, or become more expensive, once the deadline has expired.

---

6 Authority   we are more likely to comply with requests from those in positions of legitimate authority

---

Position power can be extremely persuasive. The title 'doctor' often commands blind obedience to dangerous instructions, such as administering an unsafe level of a drug. People are more likely to comply with instructions from a security guard in uniform, and the expensive business suit can have a similar effect.

The bank examiner scheme
A man in a business suit comes to your house claiming to be a bank official investigating irregularities in transactions by a local teller. Will you help? All you have to do is withdraw your savings from that teller's window, so that they can be caught in the act. Then, pass your money to the uniformed security guard, who will return it to your account (allegedly).

The career value of political skills

Often requiring the cooperation of others over whom they have no direct management authority, change agents may thus have to become compliance professionals, practising what Cialdini calls 'the science of getting what you ask for'. And these are teachable, learnable techniques which do not rely on personality, charisma, or genius. Cialdini also argues that these methods are ethically acceptable when they are a natural part of the influence situation. The influencer does have more authority and expertise; this opportunity will not be available for long. However, these techniques can be abused when the conditions surrounding their use are fabricated to suit the influencer's purpose. An understanding of influence methods, however, is a critical component of political skill, central to the effectiveness of the change agent in organizational terms, and also in relation to reputation and career.

An understanding of conversation controls, impression management techniques, and influence tactics, is significant for the change agent for at least five reasons:

i. As already indicated, evidence and rational argument are rarely sufficient to establish unambiguous choices between significant organizational options.

ii. The change agent often has to work quickly to achieve results, to change behaviour, and does not always have time for protracted negotiation. It may be necessary in some circumstances to take shortcuts through the organization's political system.

iii. The change agent often has to deal with turbulent and uncertain situations, in which an array of different types of tactics, deployed in a creative manner to fit the circumstances, is more valuable than reliance on past habit.

iv. Change agents often have to work with people over whom they have no formal authority, but from whom they require compliance. Those individuals and groups can say 'no', and methods more subtle than demanding 'do what I tell you', are helpful.

v. Change agents have to use tactics which are effective, but which will also sustain or enhance their reputation. Approaches that are effective in one setting may be inappropriate elsewhere, and the change agent needs a broad behaviour repertoire of conventional and political tactics.

Every social interaction combines aspects of conversation control, impression management, and influence. This is how we shape the attitudes and behaviours of others. Some of us are more accomplished, although these skills can be developed with training and experience. Nevertheless, the use of conversation controls, impression management, and influence tactics, involves the exercise of power, and may be labelled as political behaviours.

The social construction of political behaviour

If everything that we say and do can be described in terms of power and politics, manipulation and control, then these concepts have limited value. However, political behaviour is a useful category if it is regarded as *socially constructed*. In other words, how do actors in a given setting come to describe or to label certain behaviours as political?

Researcher How do you mean – the soft side? Politics is usually covert, symbolic, rather than formal visible displays?

Manager I guess what I'm saying is, if you're asking people to . . . what's power, OK? Power is control, agree with that? If you're talking about fundamental changes which bring about pretty fundamental power shifts, what you're asking people to do is to either give up their control or change the nature of their control. I think that there's aggressive ways of doing that, but there's also ways of doing that which are 'nicer' ways of doing it. Methods of going about things that, because you're creating a context for people and because they have got a bigger picture and understand where they fit in and are part of the process of change, often people are willing to forego some of that control because of what they get back in exchange. And I've seen that happen a lot with doctors. When you go to doctors and say, we want to change your role and we're going to take all your nurses out of your outpatient clinics and swap them for unqualified workers 'cos you don't need a nurse – they go mad. But if you say, 'we've got a situation here, what do you think the key issues are, how do you think we should go about creating solutions?'. Approached in that way, people will change fundamentally, because they've bought into the problem, and also bought into the solution. And they will forego control.

Researcher But this is not politics. This is participative management.

Manager No, it's different. It's about . . . people talk about participative management, but I'm talking about a dimension on from that. How do I describe it? It involves specific techniques to bring about political changes, and I think this builds on participative management.

Researcher We maybe don't have a good enough language to deal with this – but it's about 'supportive manipulation'?

Manager Yes, that's exactly what it is. And participative management is not enough. It's about finding ways, at the individual level, of implementing the things you want to happen at the corporate level.

The notion of socially constructed meaning is easily illustrated. Let us assume that you are studying the incidence of aggression in nightclubs. Aggressive behaviour could be defined in terms of raised voices, angry language, physical contact, harm, pain, and damage to property. An operational definition of aggression, for use in field research, could be a checklist of such behaviours, which can then be counted as they are observed. Now let us imagine that on your first nightclub visit, armed with notepad, you witness an episode involving two young men at a table near the bar. Voices are raised. Insults are exchanged. One man punches the other on the arm. Wincing in pain, the other retaliates by pushing the first man away. A chair is knocked over. The table is shaken. Beer is spilled. Glasses shatter on the floor. You reach for your notepad and tick on the checklist all of the behaviours that you have observed; this looks like an incident with a 'high aggression score'.

However, let us now also imagine that, to complete the field notes, you interview the men to establish the cause of their aggressive outburst. They are shocked that you regard their behaviour as aggressive. They are best mates. What you saw was 'a bit of fun', a 'typical knockabout', a regular Friday night joke that got out of hand. The spilled beer and broken glasses were accidental. The episode you witnessed demonstrated the opposite of aggression. This was a display, in their view, of a close and continuing friendship. It would take an inflexible observer to insist, on this evidence, that what they saw was a display of aggression. Surely the definition of the episode that matters in terms of understanding this social drama must take into account the definition of the players? In other words, aggression is a socially constructed concept difficult to define, even in more extreme cases (crimes of passion, for example), without knowledge of the meaning attached to the behaviour by those involved (while accepting that, on occasion, they could be mistaken or confused).

What has this to do with politics? Research in this field is dominated, not by a constructivist perspective, but by a positivist social science tradition, with the following characteristics.

Definition

A positivist approach depends on an agreed definition of organization politics. A definition is required in order to develop measures of politics, and also serves to distinguish between political and non-political actions. However, as discussed earlier, no consensus has emerged, and most publications in this genre begin with a discussion of the definition problem. Most commentators rely on the 'definition elements' identified by Drory and Romm (1990) who conclude that political behaviour can be defined by the presence of influence, actions beyond the requirements of the formal job role, and conflict (see Chapter 1).

Measurement

This perspective is concerned with measuring politics, or rather with measuring employees' perceptions of how political their organization is. One popular measure is the Perception of Organization Politics Scale (POPS) (Table 2.9), based on the literature, theoretical considerations, and personal experience of the researchers. The number of items used in this scale varies from study to study, with most using a 12-item version (Vigoda, 2003), reflecting three dimensions labelled 'general political behaviour', 'going along to get along', and 'pay and promotion', although different studies have identified other dimensions (Ferris et al., 2002a). These items form the basis of a questionnaire that asks respondents to rate their agreement, generating a POPS score; a high score implies a high incidence of political behaviour.

Table 2.9   The Perception of Organization Politics Scale (POPS)

1 Favouritism rather than merit determines who gets ahead around here.
2 There is no place for yes-men around here: good ideas are desired even when it means disagreeing with superiors (reversed score).
3 Employees are encouraged to speak our frankly even when they are critical of well-established ideas (reversed score).
4 There has always been an influential group in this department that no one ever crosses.
5 People here usually don't speak up for fear of retaliation by others.
6 Rewards come only to those who work hard in this organization (reversed score).
7 Promotions in this department generally go to top performers (reversed score).
8 People in this organization attempt to build themselves up by tearing others down.
9 I have seen changes made in policies here that only serve the purposes of a few individuals, not the work unit or the organization.
10 There is a group of people in my department who always get things their way because no one wants to challenge them.
11 I can't remember when a person received a pay increase or a promotion that was inconsistent with the published policies (reversed score).
12 Since I have worked in this department, I have never seen the pay and promotion policies applied politically (reversed score).

Source: from Vigoda (2003, p.202); reproduced with permission; and see the 14-item scale in Kacmar and Carlson (1997, p.656).

This perspective makes a distinction between *perceptions* of politics and *actual* political behaviour (Valle and Perrewé, 2000; Ferris et al., 2002a; Vigoda, 2003). Studies based on this distinction regard the influence tactics identified by Kipnis et al. (1984) as actual political behaviours. This means, for example, that 'rational appeal' (providing information), 'assertiveness' (giving an order) and 'exchange' (swapping favours) are categorically actual political behaviours, even though the actors in a given organizational context may not always understand or describe those actions in that way. In contrast, providing information, or doing a favour for a colleague, may be seen simply as routine parts of the management role.

What is striking about this perspective is that, judging from published work on measurement and modelling, these researchers appear never to have spoken to managers about the subject, to discover how they view, use, and are affected by organization politics. We will meet this approach again in Chapter 9 in our discussion of political skill, where a four-dimensional skills inventory, based on a literature review, was initially tested and 'validated' using a group of over 200 American university undergraduate students (Ferris et al., 2005).

Modelling

With a measure of politics established, it has been assumed possible to identify the links to antecedents or triggers, and also to correlate the measure with outcomes. Do organizations with particular characteristics display higher levels of perception

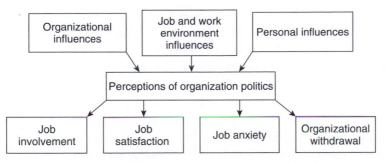

Figure 2.2 Modelling perceptions of organization politics. *Source*: based on Ferris et al. (2002a) and Vigoda (2003).

of organization politics (POPs) than contrasting settings? Do high POPs mean more damaging consequences than a low POP score? Quantifiable metrics are also sought for those organizational characteristics and consequences. One version of this model is outlined here; other studies have sought to elaborate this approach, identifying other combinations of independent, moderating, and dependent variables (Ferris et al., 2002a, p.181; Vigoda, 2003). Such models (Figure 2.2) aim to establish generalizable links between the measured variables of interest, and to show how those links vary in predictable ways across different contexts, and in different combinations.

Vigoda (2003, p.51) thus considers whether job dissatisfaction and low commitment to the organization result from the perception that the level of politics is high, or whether the causal arrows run in the opposite direction; in other words, the perception that there is little organization politics may result from high levels of satisfaction and commitment. The model itself suggests that this line of questioning is fruitless. Clearly there cannot be any stable, predictable, generalizable relationships between these variables, given the range of fluid individual and contextual factors, not to mention all the other issues (within and outside the organization) that influence satisfaction and commitment. The positivist response to this criticism is to control for other factors; age, gender, experience, personality, organizational size, sector, and so on. However this presumes that it is possible to identify and to measure those, and that their measures will also remain stable over time, and between different contexts.

The constructivist alternative: actor theory in use

A constructivist approach regards political behaviour as a socially constructed phenomenon; the definition that matters is the definition used by those who practice organization politics. The theoretical constructs of the researcher are less important than the interpretations of those who engage in turf games, or what is known as *actor theory in use*. The A–B–C model in Chapter 1 thus reflects how managers appear to understand the antecedents, behaviours, and consequences of organization politics.

A constructivist perspective is also sensitive to the influence of context. While some managers may experience dissatisfaction with a high level of politics, others may welcome the opportunities to develop and exercise their political skills, as well as to advance agendas and pursue goals in ways that may not be possible in a less turbulent setting. This perspective also regards organization politics as a fluid and unfolding process, and not as a series of discrete influence attempts.

How do managers respond when asked for examples of political tactics? We have put this question to numerous groups with whom we have worked. Table 2.10 sets out the response from a group of middle and senior Australian managers (from a state public sector organization) who were asked for examples during a management development programme. In our experience, this list of 'turf tactics' is typical.

This response has a number of interesting features. First, this is a long list of tactics; the behaviour repertoire of the organization politician appears to be rich and diverse, reaching far beyond the tactics included in the survey reported in the previous chapter. Second, this list of tactics perceived by middle and senior managers to be political bears little relation to the researcher-inspired items in the POP Scale, thus questioning the validity of a measure of perceptions that is not related to the perceptions of those being investigated. Third, this is clearly not a definitive list of tactics; such a listing can have no closure, as the domain of organization politics appears to be a highly creative one. These tactics are diverse and ingenious, from 'including a committee role on my CV without actually doing any work for the committee' to the 'whirlwind' tactic of arriving late and leaving early to avoid task allocations, from using 'car park talk' to 'outrageous deadlines'. Actions such as these, if they are to have the desired effect, need to be deployed according to circumstances, in multiple modes, degrees, and combinations. A stark list of tactics offers only a glimpse of the processes involved in ongoing organization political exchanges.

From a constructivist perspective it is not possible to define any particular behaviour, action, or tactic as categorically political. The attribution of political status or intent relies on those observing, assessing, and otherwise taking part in a given setting. The evidence indicates that political behaviours lie across the broad spectrum summarized in Figure 2.3.

At one end of this spectrum, we have conversation controls, impression management methods, and influence tactics. These behaviours tend to be routine, unexceptional, and visible. They are integrated with other conventional interpersonal behaviours, and are relatively harmless. At the other end of this spectrum sit 'dirty tricks' and illegal acts, which tend to be rare, exceptional, and concealed (but see the work of Punch, 1996, on *Dirty Business*, discussed in Chapter 4). These behaviours are quite distinct from conventional interpersonal skills and tactics, and are potentially harmful. However, while the end-markers of this spectrum of political behaviours are relatively clear and unambiguous, much political behaviour takes place in the middle ground, and is more difficult to label or define, unless we know how actors and observers understand those actions.

Table 2.10 Management turf tactics

Able to include committee role on CV, but not actually do things	Information control; withholding, timing, selective
Actively gathering group support	Information presentation verbal or non-verbal, exclusive or inclusive
Allocating and controlling budgets	Ignore deadlines
Appealing to egos and playing on fears	Influencing the classification of jobs
Ask 'how' questions	Intimidation
Ask, 'how may this benefit you?'	
Attending the right conference	Late arrival at meetings
Audience management	Links, relationships, partnerships
Avoidance; e.g., email rather than conversation	Lobbying behind the scenes
	Lobbying and strategic alliances (e.g., people, research)
Blocking	
Bullying	Making it personal; silence, bullying
	Membership of relevant groups; colluding
Car park talk	Minutes changed or none given
Chairing style (neutral chair, biased chair)	Moles and spies
Communication; setting up feedback loops	Most articulate listened to; others' opinions not heard – lack of inclusivity
Consequences; adverse	
Cultural and staff change	Networking
	Non-engagement
Decisions made prior to the meeting	
Delaying, avoidance, silence	Outrageous deadlines
Designing the consultation process to meet certain ends	
Developing relationships	Passive resistance
Distractive behaviours	Persistence
	Personal influence
Emotion, anger, tears, passive aggressive	'Politicizing' an issue
Engaging with people	Position power
Establishing a false camaraderie	Prepare yourself; do your homework, be confident
Excluding potential competitors; not invited	Pre-planning
Excuses; sorry, my network was down	Promotion; celebrating the culture
	Providing evidence
False consultation	Purposeful networking
Fear	
Focusing on one element to deflect criticism on others	Rehearsal, and put into performance at the meeting
Fostering influential friendships	Rewards and incentives; concrete, verbal, access
Gossip that divides and conquers	Role playing and impression management
Haven't received email; too many emails	
Hiding behind something that they have set up	

Continued

Table 2.10   Cont'd

Sabotaging contributions	Tailoring your argument for your audience
Selective praise	Taking on the work of other people
Selectively nominating to powerful groups	That's not my job
Setting the agenda and minutes	
Setting up structures	Using departmental hierarchy
Showing your personal side, empathy	Using the person who has the most influence
Sidestepping, then going to others who may be able to influence the situation	Using outside networks
Silence; say nothing	Voice credibility
Slamming the door	
Social interactions	Wet blanket
Sorry, I'm at the wrong meeting	Whirlwind; arrive late, leave early, don't get tasks to do
Stacking the decision-making process	
Stonewalling	Winging it
Strategic use of knowledge, research, statistics	Withholding information
Strategies not done by designated people	Yes at the meeting, but not followed through
Structured discussion, e.g., of protocols	Yes, but …
Sucking up	

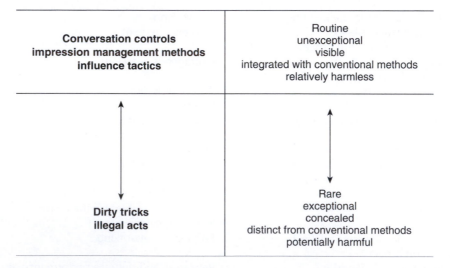

Figure 2.3   The spectrum of political behaviour.

While the positivist tradition has been valuable in stimulating and sustaining interest in this field, and in exposing some of its dimensions, it is not a wholly adequate platform on which to build either our theoretical understanding of organization politics, or to develop practice, for managers, change agents, and other organizational members. The constructivist perspective, based on the interpretations and understandings of those who live with and are engaged in these behaviours, offers a more useful standpoint from which to view and understand the rich and creative processes of organization politics in context.

Accounting for political behaviour: reputation as power base

This argument has a further and more fundamental step. This concerns the concept of the individual's reputation as a power base, not identified by either of the frameworks discussed so far in this chapter, but fundamental to the management role in general, and to the role of the change agent in particular. Reputation is defined not just in terms of the opinions of others, or the regard in which an individual is held. It is also defined by what one has done and achieved, on actions and outcomes. In other words, one does not simply have 'a reputation'; one has a reputation *for*. This dependence on outcomes means that reputation as a power base is related to, but distinct from, position, expert, and referent power, whose sources respectively lie not with achievements, but with title, knowledge, and personality.

In terms of our earlier discussion of power, reputation can be seen simultaneously as a personal, relational, and embedded property. Reputation is commonly considered to be the property of the individual, an attribute that one possesses, acquired and developed through one's actions over time. Reputation is also held in the opinions of others, based on their perceptions of those actions and their assessments of the outcomes, thus making this also a relational property; your reputation is what others believe your reputation to be. In reaching decisions on how to act in particular circumstances, individuals concerned with reputation must constantly ask themselves, 'how will this be seen and judged', and respond accordingly. Reputations also become institutionalized, expressed in terms of the anecdotes, jokes, stories, myths, and legends that surround key individuals and their contributions (negative and positive) either to a single organization, or to the various organizations in which they have worked. Reputations that have become embedded in this way are 'learned' by newcomers who consequently hold opinions of individuals who they have never met.

While reputations tend to be built gradually over time, they are fragile and can be reversed by a single act or a series of related incidents. This is seen most clearly in the careers of national politicians, where decades of commitment to party and cause are sidelined by the headline revealing some indiscretion such as a relationship, a habit, an expenses claim, or an offensive joke told at a private gathering but overheard by a journalist. While such actions may have no direct impact on the person's ability and work, their trustworthiness becomes suspect, their judgement is questioned, and their career can be terminated.

Reputations thus depend on how actions are perceived, understood, interpreted, and judged. While those judgements lie with the observer, one of the principal ways in which observers' perceptions can be influenced is through the manner in which behaviour is presented and described, through the accounts that change agents provide for their actions. The concept of labelling behaviour in the way that we have been discussing has interesting consequences. For example, let us say we 'catch you out' in some devious, underhand, cunning political power play, to discredit a colleague (for the sake of illustration). If we are able to make this accusation 'stick', then your reputation could be badly damaged, colleagues may be reluctant to trust you again, cooperation will be withheld, your promotion chances will be blighted, and we can make your life in this organization unpleasant for some time to come – should you decide to stay. However, if you are able to refute this accusation, then your reputation could not only be saved, but could be enhanced. Your counterclaim could run something like this:

Don't be ridiculous. This was not a power play. This was simply a routine attempt to persuade someone of the logic of the case, to bring someone round to my way of thinking which, by the way, has widespread agreement across the organization. And this individual was not only going to damage the change initiative, but also damage the futures of many colleagues who would benefit (through improved job security, quality of working life, and so on). In any case, this individual was acting against the change out of purely personal motives. I was just doing my job.

The essence of political behaviour lies not just in tactics and techniques, but in the ways in which such behaviour is accounted for and represented by the players in the game. Accounting involves the 'management of meaning', which is achieved through symbolic actions, through the judicious use of language, and through the stories or narratives that we use to explain ourselves. The manner in which we construct and present those accounts or narratives is another form of impression management. As Pettigrew (1977, p.85) argues:

> Politics concerns the creation of legitimacy for certain ideas, values and demands – not just action performed as a result of previously acquired legitimacy. The management of meaning refers to a process of symbol construction and value use designed both to create legitimacy for one's own demands and to 'de-legitimize' the demands of others.

What we are dealing with here, however, is not so much the legitimation of interests and demands, but the representation of those interests and the legitimation of the political tactics used in their pursuit. Power, in this perspective, is the ability to impose one's interpretation on events in competition with the meanings offered by others. The quintessential political behaviours thus lie in *labelling* actions as political, in *challenging* such classifications, and in *justifying* such actions when necessary and appropriate with a plausible *account* in the prevailing circumstances. Power thus belongs to the best story-tellers.

The conduct and justification of organizational politics is thus a language game, as well as a game of strategies, tactics and behaviours. Pfeffer (1992a, p.190) describes this activity as 'framing', which refers to the need to appear reasonable in context. Thus, 'what looks reasonable, or ridiculous, depends on the context – on how it is framed in terms of what has preceded it and the language that is used to present it'. In our culture, decisions must *appear* to be rational, even though the players involved typically know this is not a wholly accurate representation. As Pfeffer (1992a) observes:

> All organizations strive for the appearance of rationality and the use of proper procedures, which include using information and analysis to justify decisions, even if this information and analysis is mustered after the fact to ratify a decision that has been made for other reasons (p.248).

Thus, in many instances, individuals in organizations do not seek out information in order to make a decision, but rather, they amass information so that the decision will seem to have been made in the 'correct' fashion – i.e., on the basis of information rather than uninformed preferences or hunches (p.250).

Because of the need for the appearance, if not reality, of rational decision processes, analysis and information are important as strategic weapons in battles involving power and influence. In these contests, the ability to mobilize powerful outside experts, with credibility and the aura of objectivity, is an effective strategy (p.254).

This argument reinforces the role of accounts in justifying political action in organizational change. Does this reduce the political dimensions of the work of the change agent to appearances, to surface characteristics, play acting and illusion, to a devious combination of 'frontwork' and 'backstaging'? The significance given to accounting, to form over substance, illusion over reality, may appear to be a cosmetic stance, with negative implications for personal job and career satisfaction. Jackall (1988, p.198) observes that:

> In such a world, notions of fairness and equity that managers might privately hold, as measures of gauging the worth of their own work, become merely quaint. One fluctuates between a frustrated resentment at what seems to be a kind of institutionalized corruption and systematic attempts to make oneself a beneficiary of the system. Being a 'good soldier' may carry for some the private satisfactions of work well done, of bargains kept, or of organizational goals attained through one's best efforts. But one's dedication may also make one unfit for the manoeuvres that can bring organizational privilege and reward.

Despite the negative tone of Jackall's remarks, it is important to recall the substantive, unavoidable, and necessary shaping role of power and politics in change. We are dealing with skilful behaviour that can have positive as well as negative individual and organizational consequences. We are dealing with a range of political styles, from coercion at one extreme, to a variety of less aggressive methods. We are faced with the need to represent our goals and behaviours, and the goals and behaviours of others, in a manner that promotes the legitimacy of one and, where appropriate, the unacceptability of the other. We are playing a game of symbols and language in which what one says and how (and when and where and to whom) one says it, can be as significant as what one does, and how one does it. The change agent concerned with implementing an initiative, with making a mark, with making a difference, with career progression, with organizational success, can only escape from this game by pursuing some other career.

In the following chapter, we will invite you to sit in judgement with respect to a number of accounts of political behaviour. What kinds of behaviours and tactics are justifiable, and which are not, and why? Some commentators have approached these questions from a rather traditional ethics perspective. As we will demonstrate, however, abstract ethical guidelines are of limited use when applied to real settings. It is useful to remember that the majority of managers apparently do not regard the use of political tactics in an organizational context as unethical. It is necessary to find other criteria to bring to this domain, which is where the concepts of accounting and reputation become particularly significant.

Follow through

Personal power bases: assess and build

1 First, working alone, carry out a realistic assessment of your current managerial and/or professional power bases. Estimate your current power as high, medium, or low in each area. Then select two 'priority' bases where you feel that it would be personally valuable, and practically possible, to develop your power base.

power base	high, medium, low?	priorities for development
reward		
coercion		
authority		
referent		
expert		
information		
affiliation		
group		
reputation		

2 Second, in your table or syndicate group, share your assessments and priorities. As a group, identify one power base that all or most of you have prioritized, or in which you have a particular shared interest. Brainstorm the practical steps, as many as you can identify, that you could each take to develop power in that area.

3 Nominate a spokesperson to share your advice on strengthening that power base with the rest of the group.

This assessment and discussion should demonstrate that one does not have to take the strength, or weakness, of existing power bases as given. Combining the resource-based, relational, and embedded views of power, we can see how in practical ways power bases can be strengthened (and, of course, weakened) through particular actions, and also by events occurring in a given context. Power in any organizational setting is thus fluid, rather than static, depending on circumstances and actions over time. It is helpful to remember that the power bases of others are also fluid, for the same reasons.

Networking: how good are you?

Tick whether you agree, or disagree, with each of the following statements.

	agree	disagree	
I enjoy finding out what other people do	❐	❐	**1**
I feel embarrassed asking people for favours	❐	❐	**2**
I send Christmas cards to ex-colleagues and business contacts	❐	❐	**3**
I usually call or email former colleagues and contacts when I am struggling with a particularly difficult problem	❐	❐	**4**
I do not like to waste time going to conferences	❐	❐	**5**
I cannot remember the names and family details of all my team members	❐	❐	**6**
I cut out articles from the press that I think might interest colleagues	❐	❐	**7**
I prefer to write emails or letters to picking up the phone	❐	❐	**8**
I am quick to return phone calls	❐	❐	**9**
I pursue opportunities to work on committees, task forces, and projects	❐	❐	**10**
I like to solve problems on my own	❐	❐	**11**
I am happy to ask people for their business cards	❐	❐	**12**
I go to social events with people outside my team	❐	❐	**13**
I have lost touch with my ex-bosses	❐	❐	**14**
I use the internet to make contact with people in my field	❐	❐	**15**
I do not mix work and social life	❐	❐	**16**

Networking: how did you score?

Give yourself one point each if you *agreed* with these items, scoring up to 9:

1   3   4   7   9   10   12   13   15

Give yourself one point each if you *disagreed* with these items, scoring up to 7:

2   5   6   8   11   14   16

Add these two scores to produce your final total score out of 16:

❐

Score	Implications
0–5	You do not appear to do much networking, and you may need to be careful that you are not overlooked for promotion. What can you do to lift your profile, to make yourself more visible?
6–9	You network a little, but you could do more to develop relationships that would improve your career opportunities. Where are the gaps in your networking efforts, and how can you fill them?
10–13	You are a competent networker, but you could improve. What areas are you not covering? Do you need to do more external networking?
14–16	It looks like you are a natural networker. However, you may need to be careful not to overplay this aspect of your profile building, as there is a danger that this can annoy some people.

Reproduced with permission from *The Ultimate Career Success Workbook: Tests and Exercises to Assess Your Skills and Potential*, by Rob Yeung, first published in Great Britain by Kogan Page Limited in 2003 © Rob Yeung, 2003.

Organization politics at the movies: *Dirty Rotten Scoundrels*

The comedy film *Dirty Rotten Scoundrels* (1988, director Frank Oz) tells the story of Freddy Benson (played by Steve Martin) and Lawrence Jamieson (Michael Caine), two conmen working together on the French Riviera. The strapline for the movie is 'Nice guys finish last. Meet the winners'. In a short section, lasting about two minutes, near the beginning of the film (track 2 on DVD format), Freddy persuades a woman on a train, a stranger, to buy him an expensive meal. How does he achieve this?

- What influencing techniques does he use?
- What impression management methods does he use?
- How can his success in this brief episode be explained?
- What practical lessons can we learn from this episode?

Debrief

Freddy Benson uses the following influencing techniques:

- first, he carefully selects his target or victim, as well as the time and place
- appropriate time and place
- he has a good, interesting, believable story to tell
- gradual build-up of case, pulls target progressively into the story
- uses a story with which the target is likely to sympathize
- brings in irrelevant details to strengthen credibility
- self-disclosure and self-criticism to emphasize honesty
- unselfish legitimation; 'I'm doing it for my grandmother'
- checks once only with the target's compliance, then acts without hesitation.

Freddy Benson uses the following impression management methods:

- casual, crumpled, inexpensive appearance
- humble, unassuming demeanour, both hands on hat, bowing
- pleasant, slow, clear and friendly voice
- unhurried body movements, slowly eating bread roll
- resigned tone of voice
- 'prayer' hands gesture, appealing to 'higher values', suggesting piety
- self-critical self-disclosure, appearance of honesty and integrity
- positive non-verbal behaviour, full-on position, smiling, eye contact, nodding.

Freddy Benson does nothing extraordinary. The effectiveness of his technique relies on the mundane ordinariness of his behaviour. But he has carefully chosen the context, the timing and the target or victim, and these factors combined with his behaviour pattern lead to the desired outcome. He gets a free meal, and even 'buys' his victim a beer.

3

Sit in judgement

Chapter objectives

1 To consider the ethical issues raised by the use of organization political tactics.
2 To illustrate the ethical and practical issues and dilemmas through examples.
3 To develop a decision framework to guide the change agent's use of political tactics.

"Life isn't fair, Milford, and that's what makes it fun"

Do the ends justify the meanness?

The means to any end are merely mechanisms for accomplishing something. The something can be grand, grotesque, or, for most of us, I suspect, somewhere in between. The end may not always justify the means, but neither should it automatically be used to discredit the means. Power and political processes in organizations can be used to accomplish great things. They are not always used in this fashion, but that does not mean we should reject them out of hand. It is interesting that when we use power ourselves, we see it as a good force and wish we had more. When others use it against us, particularly when it is used to thwart our goals or ambitions, we see it as an evil. A more sophisticated and realistic view would see it for what it is – an important social process that is often required to get things accomplished in interdependent systems (Pfeffer, 1992a, p.35).

What ethical concerns are raised by the use, and advocacy, of political tactics? Some commentators regard organization politics as categorically unethical. One has only to turn to a typical list of tactics (see Chapter 2) to understand why. Bullying, fear, intimidation, information control, 'moles and spies', sabotage; how can these behaviours be considered ethical? Other tactics appear to be more socially acceptable; networking, developing relationships, carefully presenting information. However, if we understood the wider context in which they were used, would we reach a different judgement?

It is the context, not the terminology, that can make political behaviour justifiable. Consider lying, which is often cited as an example of a political tactic. Asked whether lying is ethical, most of us answer 'no', but it is not difficult to think of circumstances in which telling a lie benefits the other person, preserves our relationship, and contributes to social harmony and team performance (Shulman, 2006). If we were to go through life always telling others the truth as we saw it, we would find ourselves unemployed, unemployable, and without friends. That is why most (if not all) of us are liars (on occasion). We disguise our actions as 'not really lying', and with euphemisms such as 'little white lies' and 'bending the truth'.

The change agent who believes that political behaviour is unethical faces other problems. Our evidence suggests (Chapter 1) that most managers (around 80 per cent) do not regard politics as unethical, and will use political tactics to achieve their aims. Fritzsche et al. (1995) also found that 80 per cent of managers in their cross-cultural study saw no ethical issues in two of the cases they were asked to judge, one concerning the use of bribery to secure business, and the other involving a request to reveal sensitive technical information from a previous job to a new employer. Most respondents regarded the former issue as an economic one, and the latter as a question of loyalty. Provis (2004) argues that ethics and politics are distinct spheres of activity, and that it may be more appropriate to judge political tactics with considerations of practicality and prudence, rather than with reference to a code of moral conduct. Most managers seem to regard politics not as unethical, but simply as part of the job. This is illustrated by 'the tennis analogy'. It is not unethical for tennis players to attempt to beat their opponents. While an organization is not sport, the competition of ideas is pervasive. Resistance and challenge, overt and covert, are inevitable. The competition can be productive and fun, can stimulate debate, and can lead to better decisions and outcomes.

To resolve such tensions and dilemmas, one set of commentators designed a template to distinguish 'dirty politics' from 'responsible political action' (Cavanagh et al., 1981; Velasquez et al., 1983). This perspective is based on the normative ethical frameworks of utilitarianism, individual rights, and natural justice (Table 3.1). The authors argue that these criteria should be combined in reaching ethical judgements.

Table 3.1   Ethical frameworks

	strengths	weaknesses
utilitarianism	encourages efficiency	impossible to quantify variables
	parallels profit maximization	can lead to unjust resource allocation
	looks beyond the individual	individual rights may be violated to achieve greatest good
rights	protects the individual	may encourage selfish behaviour
	establishes standards of social behaviour independent of outcomes	individual rights may become obstacles to productivity and efficiency
justice	ensures fair allocation of resources	can encourage a sense of entitlement that discourages risk and innovation
	ensures democratic operation, independent of status or class	some individual rights may be violated to accommodate justice for majority
	protects the interests of the under-represented in the organization	

Source: based on Velasquez et al. (1983).

Utilitarian theory

A utilitarian perspective judges behaviour in terms of outcomes; this is the classic 'ends justifies means' argument. This approach considers the 'balance sheet' of benefits and costs to the population involved; behaviour is acceptable if it achieves 'the greatest good of the greatest number'. However, in even modestly complex settings, with a number of stakeholders and actions that will have a range of consequences, performing the utilitarian calculus of benefits and costs can be problematic.

Theory of rights

This perspective judges behaviour on the extent to which fundamental individual rights are respected. This includes the right of free consent, the right to privacy, the right to freedom of conscience, the right of free speech, the right to due process in the form of an impartial hearing. Performing the ethical calculus here is a relatively simple matter of establishing whether or not individual entitlements have been violated.

Theory of justice

This perspective judges behaviour on whether or not the benefits and burdens flowing from an action are fairly, equitably and impartially distributed. Distributive justice states that rules should be applied consistently, those in similar circumstances should be treated equally, and individuals should not be held responsible for matters beyond their control. As with the utilitarian calculus, these issues are awkward to resolve in practice, as judgements of consistency, similarity, and responsibility are subjective and vary from one setting to another.

This produces a 'decision tree' for deciding whether or not an action is ethical (Figure 3.1).

The first problem with this framework lies with the apparently straightforward opening advice; gather the facts. On whose version of 'the facts' are we going to rely? The facts surrounding most political actions are incomplete, and difficult if not impossible to establish beyond dispute. As we are dealing with political tactics (often backstage), many of the facts are unlikely to be evident even to close observers and participants.

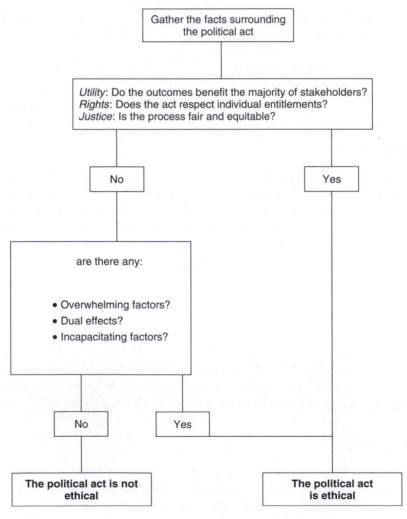

Figure 3.1 An ethical decision tree.
Source: based on Velasquez et al. (1983).

More significantly, however, as political behaviour is a socially constructed phenomenon (Chapter 2), there are no 'facts', but only our interpretations of circumstances and events, which are often presented in a manner that best suits the purpose of the narrator.

A second problem lies with the three overlapping sets of mitigating circumstances which potentially justify political actions. Overwhelming factors are issues that justify setting aside ethical criteria. Some actions may have dual effects, with positive and negative outcomes, and the latter may be acceptable if they are outweighed by the positives. Incapacitating factors are those which prevent the decision maker from applying ethical criteria. For example, managers can be constrained by the views and actions of colleagues, and may be pressured into behaviours that they would not choose independently, and individual managers may have inadequate information on which to reach a judgement. Finally, the individual may doubt the relevance of one or more ethical criteria to a given setting. The right to free speech, for example, may not apply if this were to lead to the dissemination of information that would be damaging to others.

Consequently, there are multiple escape routes or 'fudge factors' which permit actions that would be proscribed by a more basic reading of the framework. The urgency of the case, time pressures, resource constraints, penalties for inaction, and so on, can be called upon as overwhelming, dual, or incapacitating factors. Velasquez et al. (1983, pp.79–80) observe:

> The manager who is unable to use ethical criteria because of these incapacitating factors may justifiably give them a lesser weight in making decisions about what to do in a political situation. The underlying rationale for such systematic devaluation of ethical criteria is simple. A person cannot hold himself responsible for matters which he cannot control or for matters of which he is sincerely ignorant or sincerely in doubt. However, determining whether a manager's lack of freedom, lack of information, or lack of certitude is sufficient to abrogate moral responsibility requires one to make some very difficult judgements. In the end, these are hard questions that only the individuals involved can answer for themselves.

Cavanagh et al. (1981) illustrate this decision process with the following examples.

Lorna and her team

Lorna is a production manager with a 'noncohesive work group' which has a deadline requiring coordinated effort. To encourage the team to collaborate, Lorna leads them to believe that the sales department want them to fail to meet the deadline, so that sales will have an advantage over production in the next budget round. The authors argue that if the team meets the deadline, then from a utilitarian perspective Lorna's action is acceptable. However, they observe that 'leads them to believe' is a euphemism for lying, which is unethical. While no clear resolution is offered in this example, it highlights the problem of attempting to combine criteria in practice. One perspective (utilitarian) suggests acceptability, but others (rights and justice) argue that it is unethical. The authors seem to argue that behaviour has to pass all three tests before it can be considered ethical.

Sam and Bob

Sam and Bob are research scientists in the General Rubber product development laboratory (Cavanagh et al., 1981, p.369). Sam, who is introvert, quiet, and serious, is more technically proficient; his patents have earned the company around $6 million over the past ten years. Bob does not have the same expertise, his output is 'solid though unimaginative', and he is extrovert and demonstrative. The rumour is that Bob will be moved into an administrative role. The lab offers a $300,000 fund each year for the best new product idea. Sam and Bob both submit proposals, which are assessed as having equal merit. Sam takes no further action, but Bob conducts a publicity campaign, about which he tells Sam in advance, promoting the advantages of his proposal to those who might influence the final decision. Informal pressure builds to decide in Bob's favour.

The authors consider Bob's actions to be unjust. From a utilitarian perspective, the outcome is acceptable as both proposals had equal merit. From a rights perspective, Sam had the same opportunities as Bob, who was, he knew, conducting an informal campaign. By introducing 'irrelevant differences' between the two proposals based on personal lobbying, however, Bob's behaviour breached the principles of justice, and was therefore unethical. But ideas in most organizational settings do not make progress on merit alone. As Bob recognized, initiatives benefit from active publicity (Dutton et al., 2001), and we will explore 'issue-selling' tactics in Chapter 8. On one account, we should praise Sam for his ethical stance, and accuse Bob of unfair practice. Or, we can praise Bob for his enthusiasm, energy, and understanding of the context, and regard Sam as naive, careless, lazy, and unprofessional. In addition, Bob's actions were visible to all concerned, and they were effective in winning him the prize. For the company wishing to encourage innovation, Bob may be the better role model. The ethical decision framework offers contradictory assessments, and ultimately reaches a judgement that can be seen as at best contentious, if not inappropriate, in circumstances such as these.

Lee and Charlie

Lee is 61 and has been director of engineering for American Semiconductor for fourteen years. Intelligent and with a reputation as a good manager, he has not kept up to date with technological developments. The manufacturing process produces toxic waste, and Lee's casual approach to disposal has culminated in two court cases which could cost the company considerable sums in damages. The company's executive vice-president, Charlie, has tried for about three years to persuade Lee to prioritize the disposal problem, without success. Having decided that Lee should be removed from his position, Charlie is reluctant to fire him as that would demoralize other managers. He therefore tells colleagues, informally, that he is not satisfied with Lee's work, and exaggerates Lee's faults in these conversations. When he encounters a growing lack of support from colleagues, Lee decides to take early retirement.

While the utilitarian calculus renders this action acceptable, the authors argue that Charlie violated Lee's right to be treated honestly by damaging his reputation behind his back. Consequently, Charlie's actions were unethical. But Lee had not responded to Charlie's request to alter behaviour that was causing environmental damage; this can be read as a negation of Charlie's rights, as well ignoring the rights of shareholders and the community. Charlie's actions can also be seen as personally sensitive and organizationally prudent, given Lee's problematic behaviour, his proximity to retirement, his past excellent record, and the limited options open to Charlie to resolve the matter quickly. To discipline or to fire Lee would be humiliating at this point in his career, and those actions could damage his pension entitlement. Charlie instead informally creates the circumstances in which Lee reaches his own decision to quit.

This ethical decision framework promises to offer a structured approach for resolving difficult choices. Instead, the algorithm can produce outcomes which are contradictory, confusing, and in some cases perverse. Returning to our earlier discussion, would most managers regard the circumstances of Lorna, Sam, Bob, Lee, and Charlie as 'political' in the first place? There is a danger that 'ethical' in these examples is being used to describe behaviour that is careless, amateurish, naive, and insensitive, if not incompetent, while contextual awareness, prudence, astuteness, and professionalism are being labelled as 'unethical'. In those examples, it is not difficult to see how the politically expedient actions described as unethical can also be presented as generating desirable outcomes for most of the stakeholders.

This decision framework has another problem, with its focus on single incidents. However those issues are resolved, Lorna, Bob, and Charlie have to continue working for their organizations. The actions that they take, and the results they achieve, influence how they are regarded, which in turn affects how colleagues feel about and respond to them. Whether they get results, or avoid the difficult issues, affects their career prospects and the degree of influence that they can exert in the organization in future. In other words, the way in which they handle these issues affects their reputation beyond the single incident, and it may be more appropriate to adopt a broader time horizon in reaching such decisions.

Organizational codes of ethical conduct often mirror this kind of deterministic decision framework. For example, the *National Health Service Code of Conduct for Managers* in England expects managers to 'be honest and act with integrity and probity at all times', and to ensure that staff are 'valued as colleagues', are 'properly informed', and are 'given appropriate opportunities to take part in decision making' (Department of Health, 2002). Did Lorna, Bob, or Charlie breach this code? Was Lorna dishonest? (Her story about the sales department was a plausible one.) Did Bob devalue a colleague? (He actually promoted his own ideas.) Did Charlie misinform his colleagues? (His assessment of the problems that Lee was causing was accurate.) The point is not to argue in support of one interpretation or another, but to show how this line of reasoning can generate either interminable dispute with no closure, or dogmatic conclusions that permit no further discussion.

Who to influence

Manager I think political behaviour is being able to get your own agenda through, possibly by means that wouldn't normally work, or through routes that aren't direct. For example, when we originally set up the management development programme, that was driven by a small group of senior officers who wanted it to happen. I sat on the senior officers' working group, but the interesting thing was, out of that group, if you really wanted to get something done, you knew there were only two or three of them that you needed to influence. The political game for me was making sure that what I wanted and what they wanted actually lined up, and then we knew we could get it. But it was also watching the other alliances in that group. Politics to me in the organization is about knowing who's in with who and who's out of favour now, so that you don't back the wrong horse.

Given the difficulties with this ethical decision framework, we will propose an alternative, based on the concept of *reputation*. This approach has at least four advantages. First, by emphasizing issues that may need to be considered in a given context (including personal values and beliefs), judgements with regard to appropriate behaviours lie with the manager or change agent, and not with a mechanistic algorithm. Second, this perspective is more amenable to resolution, to closure. Third, a concern for reputation in particular involves choosing behaviours that are sustainable over time, in contrast to the focus on isolated incidents. Fourth, decisions reached by this route are more likely to be effective in achieving management objectives, and to be acceptable to the wider organization. We will introduce this approach through (real) examples based on our own research, and develop this into a more systematic framework in the 'Follow through' section at the end of the chapter.

The following incidents are based on interviews with managers who were asked to describe situations in which they became involved in political behaviour (see Buchanan and Badham, 1999b, for details of this study). Two of these accounts (incidents 1 and 3) are from commercial contexts, and the other two (incidents 2 and 4) are from public sector settings. In one case (incident 1), the narrator is female, and the narrators of the other three incidents are male. The first three accounts are based on individual internal change agents, and the fourth concerns an external consulting team. We each respond differently to circumstances such as these, and the intent is not to legislate on 'correct' answers. Our aim is to contrast the difficulties in basing judgements in such cases on ethical criteria, with the benefits of a context-sensitive approach based on the notions of warrant, account, and reputation.

Before reading these incidents in full, you may find it interesting first to consider the exercises in the 'Follow through' section at the end of the chapter. There, outline versions of each incident are reported (designed for use in management development settings), along with the options that the narrator was considering. You are asked to decide how you would act in those circumstances, and why. Having considered those decision-making accounts, and discussed these with colleagues, return to this point and read the full incident reports. As you read the first two incidents, ask yourself whether the behaviours described by the narrator are ethical, considering utilitarian, rights, and justice criteria. For the second two incidents, consider also the following issues:

1 Do you feel that the narrator had a reasonable *warrant* for the behaviours described, given what we know about the context?
2 Do you think that the narrator offers a plausible *account* to justify those behaviours in this context?
3 Do you think that the narrator's *reputation* would have been strengthened, unaffected, or damaged by those actions?

The first two incidents are reported without commentary, to encourage you to develop your own response to these circumstances. Our assessments with regard to ethical criteria, warrants, accounts, and reputations, are then offered for incidents 3 and 4. You do not have to agree with those commentaries. The aim is to encourage reflection and discussion.

Researcher How do you define the acceptable boundaries or the limits in this area?

Manager The unacceptability is not necessarily in the tactics but in the outcomes. If you accept that the political manager has a role to play, then it's quite difficult to set boundaries around the tactics they can use. I'm not sure we came across any tactics that were unacceptable. I think we came across a number that were disappointing in terms of the impact they had. For me, it was very disappointing that one of the members of our senior team chose to sit on the sidelines and not be involved in the process until it was much further down the road. I would say that was unacceptable.

I would find that unacceptable because what they chose to do was to undermine the impact of the whole process. If they had reservations and concerns, then I'd rather they openly discussed that at the beginning. And if those had shaped the terms of reference of what we were doing, I think that would have been more useful. One of the consequences of that was, perhaps we created more fear of the impact of change in the organization, because the proposals which we developed were dragged back towards something more moderate. I think that was unfair for those people who experienced the fear of change, redundancy, loss of job, or whatever. If we'd been more honest about the extent to which we were prepared

Continued

to accept change, then we wouldn't necessarily have had to put those people through that. So in terms of the impact, a number of people were living with a very stressful process of change, had more stress than necessary, that was slightly unacceptable.

I haven't got strong views about the unacceptability of the tactics. I think if you accept you're going to play the game, you might as well use all the abilities open to you to play it. The only rider to that is perhaps, that can become uncontrollable from the organization's point of view. It exists, but it's not talked about; if you're prepared to be more open about accepting it as a process, you're then going to create something that runs and runs and will be hard to control. If you're talking about this as a fairly difficult process to understand and work out why individuals have this ability, where they attract their influence from, to then say, you can use it but only within certain parameters, is naive.

Incident report 1: Buying into it

I was working for an organization, not this one, and the person I was working for was doing a management course. There was a change approach I really wanted this person to take, and I was trying to persuade him. So he had to do a piece of work, and because it was a practical management course, he had to relate it to his work situation. So, I wrote it for this person. Basically, a piece of work which was the change strategy I wanted this person to follow. So, I wrote it in his name. It was about why doing this change process was the best thing he could possibly do in the circumstances. And he handed it in. I would call this devious because I wanted … it was highly manipulative, because I wanted that person to listen and do this thing I wanted him to do. So the way I persuaded him to do it was to write a piece of work which set out the thing which I wanted him to do. I wrote it in his name – and he did it.

The assignment got a very, very good grade. And he did all of it. It was very successful. That worked. I had built up the case for doing this thing I wanted him to do, bit by bit, step by step. He bought into it in a way that he wouldn't have if I had just tried to persuade him in other ways. But he owned this piece of work, which is what I wanted him to do.

Incident report 2: Keeping him out of it

As a 'traditional' university, we had never had to face any kind of systematic audit of our teaching quality. So mounting a response to this meant putting in place a lot of new procedures and documentation that we never had before, and also tidying up processes that had decayed somewhat. It also meant changing staff behaviour, with regard to teaching preparation and keeping records and files, and standardizing student handout material on courses, and also with lecture theatre – and tutorial room – behaviour. But we were also facing a research assessment exercise the following year. Putting effort and resource into teaching quality inevitably meant reducing the time and energy available for research.

Well, the senior staff in the department, mostly the professors, looked at the options. We could do nothing, concentrate on improving our research rating, we were one of the top ten in the UK, and accept a lousy teaching rating. Or we could concentrate on research while doing just enough to get a 'satisfactory' rating on teaching, not too damaging. Or we could push the boat out and go for teaching excellence. I reached my conclusion on these options pretty quickly, and most of the rest of the top team agreed. It would reflect badly on the university as a whole if we got a lousy rating. No other department had at that time been rated excellent on teaching. It would reflect badly on the department within the university if we went down. People could use that to block and snipe at all sorts of initiatives we wanted to put in place. How would it affect staff morale, retention and recruitment if we got a poor rating? And I didn't want to be known as the department head that botched this one, on the campus or off.

However, there were a couple of voices, one in particular, in the senior group who disagreed with this, felt we should do little or nothing to change our teaching activity, and concentrate on research output instead. A reasonable view, which we did consider, but which the majority decided was unrealistic. We reasoned with these guys, at length, and they saw they were outnumbered at an early stage. I thought, naively, they would accept the decision and pull along with it. Not a chance. One guy in particular wouldn't let it go, kept bringing the issue to committee meetings, kept getting the junior staff agitated about this – were they doing the right thing, should they be thinking of promotion and publishing instead? At first this was just annoying and time wasting. But it soon became damaging, in terms of the arguments other staff were getting into, in terms of the credibility of the top team and the approach we had decided on collectively. The rest of the team wanted something done about this.

So I kept up a pattern of spoiling tactics to keep this voice down. We had pre-meetings without him, to decide how decisions would go so that he would have less opportunity to argue an opposing case. My secretary put any issue that he wanted added to a meeting agenda at the end of the list, so we would have no time to discuss it properly. We just made some decisions in his absence, didn't tell him about a meeting. I spent a bit of time with a small number of the 'opinion leaders' among the junior staff, making sure they knew what was happening and why, that they accepted we needed to go for this teaching quality rating at this time, and hoping they would spread the message along to the others. We also had full department briefings about the exercise, which were led mainly from the front. And I hate to admit that it wasn't difficult to spread a little innuendo here and there, with academic and secretarial staff, to damage the guy's credibility, make him look less than competent on certain issues. Colleagues helped with this without prompting from me.

I don't see how I could have acted much differently in the circumstances, without accepting damage to my own reputation, as well as that of my department and perhaps the institution. And I think he knew that a lot of this was going on anyway. I don't regard any of this as unethical. On the contrary, to have ignored the issue, or to have just walked away from it, would have been difficult for me to defend. We got the 'excellent' rating.

Incident report 3: Sparring partners

This incident was reported by a senior manager working for a computing company in the British Midlands. As the computing industry became more competitive in the late 1990s, profit margins on hardware fell, and profitability became dependent on sales volume and efficient distribution. Profit margins on advisory or consulting services, however, remained extremely attractive. Our manager was recruited to develop 'professional services', but found himself in conflict with the company's most successful hardware salesman, Simon. Simon was recruited to deal with problems concerning a major customer. He established a good relationship with the customer, generating significant business for the company, and substantial commission payments for himself. The fact that one major account is now controlled by one salesman is recognized as a company problem.

When I came along, that was a threat to him. When I arrived, he was – is – a salesman, and he holds the largest account that we have. In fact, 75 per cent of my business comes through that one account, and 40 per cent of the company's turnover comes through that account. So he's quite an influential man, a key player.

He got off on the wrong foot. The very first day I met him . . . first of all he called me 'Mr Project Manager', which I don't take offence to. The second line he came out with was, 'you realize that when I want to get rid of you, I'll get rid of you?' Now, I'd been in the company for all of three days when this line came out. I'm not somebody that backs down. I take that as a threat, I really did. I didn't enjoy that at all. Once he had said that, he'd got trouble on his hands. So I guess that I've been a little rough – a little abrasive in my approach towards him on occasion.

But you have to look at the background. The relationship with the client is actually between himself and one other person. And that other person just happens to be in the position where he can spend a lot of money. Whether it's wisely spent or not, is neither here nor there. The organization for which he works is huge, very poorly organized internally, especially in IT (information technology). So you have a very personal relationship, to the point of best man at each other's wedding, so it's not a professional relationship.

Of course, I came along and I looked at the situation and, somewhat unwisely I probably expressed my opinion about the whole thing. I said, OK, well, we've got a lot of good business there, but it's not the way that we want to go forward, this isn't what our group of people does, it isn't going to work that way. Well, that immediately put him on the defensive.

The task of the professional services manager was to amalgamate four separate departments, to create a professional services section and to develop that aspect of the business. This meant absorbing two of Simon's staff, and also changing the way services would be provided – and charged – to Simon's main customer, as well as to other customers.

I challenged his authority. Simple as that. He wants adulation. That's the sort of personality he has. He's a very insecure man. My figures didn't convince him, but unfortunately they convinced others. So he was at that time on the management team. There was myself, the financial director and the general manager. Simon was on the management team but he didn't contribute a lot. He used to do a stand-up act on the whiteboard, show all his figures for the next month. He has this wonderful talent of changing between foreign currencies, so you're never quite sure what's on the board. You don't know whether it's a million in one currency or a million in another, which can be a huge difference. I think that's one of the things he does on purpose. And Simon feels he is able to manipulate in the background, to challenge you through the back door. He has various means of doing this.

The first one, which is the most common, is he has a way of capturing all your emails. I also think I know who it is that does it for him, which unfortunately is somebody in my team, so I have a double problem here. I know that he keeps it on the general manager, he keeps it on the finance director, he certainly keeps it on the guy who used to run field services because he's publicized it twice. I know that all of my messages are captured. Simple answer to that is, you don't put anything in there that can be incriminating – I do things like that by phone. I assume that he can't record the phone. I'm told that he holds a personal file on everybody, and I must have one so thick, and I don't know what he's got in there. A twist in the tail is that Simon refuses to use email, because he doesn't believe it's safe.

The second thing that he does, because of his very good relationship with the customer, he can keep me out of there. That has come unstuck because I got involved in something – same client, separate department – and I got involved personally, by default, not planned on my behalf. As time has gone on, I have got more involved, and my position, my power in that part of the organization, has become stronger. This is very worrying for my friend Simon, because he doesn't have any friends in that side. So I've sort of closed that door off too.

His next thing was, through the management team … you'd be stunned at how childish some of the things are that affect him. We were due to have the Christmas party a few weeks back. Just before it, I had to stay at home for a few days, and I sent a message out advising that something was happening. In fact it was a job had started in Taiwan, and I sent out the details and I copied Simon, it's his account, let's be open about it. And I sent these details out. Unfortunately Simon didn't know anything about this at all, until I sent them. And he took that as a big offence. Why was he not involved in the sales process? Why hadn't he been informed? With that, as I would term it, the toys came out of the pram. 'I'm no longer going to the Christmas party if he's going there. And I'm resigning from the management team.' Well, he didn't go to the party. And the management team haven't missed him.

We went out to Poland, and that was my manager being devious, because I was sat in a conference call and Simon was on the call. This was before what is potentially the largest single project that the company, globally, has ever had. This is the one that I'm programme managing at the moment, which Simon can't get his fingers on, which is a huge problem for him. The first country we're working on is Poland. Simon said, we're going out there to meet some suppliers and so on, during this conference call. My director in London said, 'I think you should be with Simon on that one, we'll make the arrangements from here'. And I sat there on the other end of the conference call thinking, do I want to go? I had no interest in going at all, but he said, 'Just get yourself there and see what he's doing'.

So he put me out there just to keep tabs on him. And while I was there, in the hotel, it turned out that Simon had made no appointments. We arrived on the Sunday night, there was nothing to do on the Monday, so I made all the arrangements and managed to see several suppliers and parts of our organization out there as well. On the Monday evening, we arranged to meet for dinner, and I had a phone call about half an hour before. 'This is Denise, from such and such escort agency, I understand that you like blondes, we can't make it for quarter past but we'll have somebody to you at quarter to seven; would you like me to send them up to your room?' And I said, terribly sorry, I think that somebody's been playing a rather unpleasant game with you here and – this is Simon trying to trap me. I don't know how he would do it, but he would have photographs or whatever.

I have a long-term strategy here. I know that in order to either get him to change, or to get rid of him, my department has to take a controlling hand in his account. That is where all of his power comes from. It's not his personality, it's not his background, he doesn't have friends in high places. It comes purely from that account. So, I have to take control of that. And I do that through selecting and motivating and encouraging my team to go in there with a certain agenda. Number one is do the job properly. I would never put that second. I think that would reflect badly on me. So it would work against me if I said, make the job go badly. The second thing is that you're in there to sell. Consultative selling; look for opportunities, look for areas where we can spread further in there, stay clear of the internal politics because they're not going to do you any favours. Their political situation is far worse than the one that I deal with. And just make yourself very important in there. Make it so that the business is coming through you. Keep Simon in copy of everything you do. But if you are developing the order yourself, if you're bringing that order out, and then you inform Simon, what's Simon's purpose in there any more? He's no longer required. His power is getting less, to the point where I think he'll know that he no longer has any influence and on he'll move from that. So the politics, my fighting against him, is working on behalf of the organization.

So, bit by bit, I squeeze him tighter and tighter. I think another six months to a year and I'll have him out. Which is nasty, I know. I consider that to be a professional approach. I consider that because I don't believe that his attitude and his motivators are for the good of the organization. Whereas I consider mine to be.

You have to have sparring partners. You have to have people you can bounce ideas off, and in some ways politics can be used as that sounding board. Fighting against people, yes, but there are good things coming out of that. The new experiences that are being learned which are good for the individual. My sparring with Simon is beneficial to the organization, because they know they cannot rely on one person, especially somebody as temperamental as that, to run with one contract which has such a large percentage of the revenue. Putting somebody like me in there who is abrasive, who will not lie down and surrender, somebody who will fight against it, is working on behalf of the organization, and the fights that I have with Simon will actually give me insight into the next move – how do I go on to the next stage, I've done this to him, kicked the pedestal away and he's now the same level as everybody else – his role is diminishing, what's the next stage in that. How do you actually learn what the next move is within that arena?

What will be the consequences of this political strategy for Simon and his career?

Yes it can be damaging and time consuming. We've had a number of situations recently where Simon has threatened to resign. I very nearly had enough of it. Just couldn't be bothered with the fighting any more. So there are times when it becomes a very negative thing. But I believe the outcome will be positive for the organization. I've not sat and worked it out on paper, but there is a cost–benefit there.

The fact that Simon might be thrown on the streets at the end of this, the fact that he's 37 years old and possibly is going to struggle to get another job, recently married, hoping

for children . . . actually doesn't come into it at all. In my perception, he is damaging to
the company, and he is certainly damaging to me, so he's got to go. Or change. I'll give
him the choice. He can do one or the other.

I think that Simon will probably leave. I think that the days of the cowboy box-selling
salesman are limited. We're developing professional services. Simon will be in a world
which I don't believe he understands. I don't think he can thrive in that world. And I
think he will have a lot of difficulty in gaining credibility elsewhere. He may move into
another organization, but he'll be the new boy on the block. Unless he gets results very
quickly, he's not going to regain his old position. And I think that his career will go
backwards. You play with fire, you get burned.

Commentary

First, is the initiator's behaviour towards the target *ethical*?

From this account, the utilitarian calculus appears to be in favour of the organization as
a whole, considering the medium to long term development of the business. However,
individual rights are clearly damaged in the process, and justice is not being done
in relation to the target, Simon, who is systematically excluded from key business
developments. The 'overwhelming factors' which could be cited here relate to the
radically changing nature of the business in this sector. The initiator's actions clearly
have a 'double effect' in developing the business while damaging the target's career
prospects. The initiator faces 'incapacitating factors' in applying ethical rules to the extent
that his own corporate responsibilities and personal reputation are being put at risk by
the target's actions. Unless we deploy those 'fudge factors', the initiator's actions fail the
ethics tests on two counts, rights and justice.

Second, did the initiator have a reasonable *warrant* for the behaviour described?

The initiator has a corporate warrant to develop the professional services dimension of
the business. The initiator is also concerned with the achievement of personal goals, the
enhancement of personal reputation, with 'doing a good job', and with ensuring that
colleagues act professionally and effectively. A further warrant for the initiator's actions
can be seen to lie with the target's own actions (using personal friendship to enhance
company and personal income; capturing confidential email; threats of withdrawal;
entrapment) which are themselves ethically questionable.

Third, can a plausible *account* be constructed to justify the behaviour described?

While acknowledging almost certain and serious damage to the target's future prospects,
at a potentially critical stage in his career, the initiator develops a compelling justification for comparatively extreme actions. The warrant for those actions is extensive,
strengthening the plausibility of this account.

Finally, is the initiator's *reputation* left intact, strengthened, or weakened?

Whatever the views of the outside reader, the initiator's reputation in the organization seems likely to be strengthened considerably. The target is a 'known problem'. The strategy for handling this problem appears to be effective. The initiator is also enhancing his reputation through the effective development of his part of the business.

Incident report 4: Here come the sandwiches

This incident was reported by one member of an external consulting team working for a local authority in East Central Scotland. The assignment was to introduce structural and cultural change to an organization that had operated in much the same style since the early 1970s. A new chief executive had recently been appointed with this remit. The leader of the consulting team was a long-standing personal friend of the new chief executive.

The annoying thing was, we got this assignment against stiff competition, because we didn't want to sell any one particular solution. They were impressed by our flexibility. Local council, they wanted a review of their twenty-year-old officer and member organization structures. In fact they wanted us to present options, maybe simple, maybe radical, from which they could choose, within the constraint of a no-redundancy policy. We won the assignment in a presentation to [a policy and resources] sub-committee, mainly councillors, with a couple of senior officers present. The leader of our consulting team was an ex-colleague and friend of the council's new chief executive.

The following week, we were invited to a meeting with the chief executive, to launch the project, agree our liaison mechanisms, find a room to work in, and so on. We spent a couple of hours discussing the logistics, then he asked us if we would have some lunch, and sandwiches and stuff were trayed in. However, as we were hoovering this lot up, he produced a seven-page document, and gave the four of us copies. He worked through this, line by line for about an hour. This set out what he wanted to see in our final report. Some of this had been in the original brief for the assignment, set out in general terms, and here it was again with some specific recommendations and markers for action, concerning parts of the organization structure and named individuals in specific posts, which were not expected to survive the review. We didn't have as much such flexibility as we had thought.

The project rolled out over that year, and our recommendations got firmed up as we collected more information. Basically, this was an autocratically managed, hierarchical, rigid, bureaucratic organization, with lots of time and money wasted on unnecessary procedures and rule following, and with poor staff morale. So our recommendations were going to be about cutting hierarchy, empowering people, changing the management style, making procedures more flexible, getting decisions taken more quickly, and the chief executive was behind all this. The main client was the sub-committee to which we reported, about every quarter. But not before the chief executive had at his request seen an advance copy of the report, commented on it and suggested changes. Quite reasonable, as he would be directly affected by any recommendations about the structure, and also saw himself as a client for our services. This put us in an awkward position. We knew his thinking, and other managers would ask us about that, and we had to fudge answers like, 'that's one of the issues still under consideration'. This also meant we had to build his ideas into our reports, finding some rationale for supporting them, which was important because if questions came up in committee, we would have to explain and defend the point, although he might chip in and voice some agreement with and sympathy for our view from time to time.

Then we started getting bother from one of the councillors, who saw himself as an expert in organization theory. He came up with a proposal for a matrix structure with multidisciplinary team working. The team working was our idea too, partly to address some communications problems. But the matrix wasn't going to fit their business. We got nowhere with the guy in the full committee, so two of us asked him if we could meet him the next day, maybe over lunch, to kick this around. Turned out his concern was not with a matrix at all, but with the way the new director roles would be specified, that they would be like the previous management group (which he didn't trust), just with new titles. So we built the teamworking ('great idea, thanks for that') and a revised role spec into the report, and he bought that.

The chief executive even sub-edited our final report, making changes to the recommendations which we then had to justify. What if we hadn't been able to roll with these pressures? We would have upset the chief executive, who saw our ability to incorporate his thinking as a reflection of our consulting expertise, and we would probably get no more work with this client. If we hadn't handled these individuals, and others, in this sort of way, the whole project could have been at risk, and the time and contributions of a lot of other staff would have been wasted.

Commentary

First, is the initiator's behaviour *ethical*?

From this account, the utilitarian calculus appears to be in favour of the organization as a whole. Changing the traditional structure and culture will benefit most employees, particularly in the context of a no-redundancy policy. However, some senior managers are not expected to 'survive' the review, and their prospects will depend on prior judgements, not on evidence collected in the course of the consulting assignment. Some managers are excluded from key decisions; rights and justice are being violated. Relationships with the new chief executive can be regarded as 'overwhelming' and 'incapacitating' in this respect, effectively preventing the consulting team from acting otherwise, but nevertheless the team's actions fail the basic ethics test.

Second, did the initiator have a *warrant* for the behaviour described?

The initiator has a warrant from the client organization to facilitate structural and cultural changes which by the late 1990s were commonplace in British local government.

The initiator is also concerned with the reputation of the consulting team in the eyes of their clients, particularly the chief executive (who is a potential source of more future consulting business). Further warrant for the initiator's actions can be seen to lie with the disruptive actions (complaints based on personal concerns) of one council member.

Third, can a plausible *account* be constructed to justify the behaviour described?

Plausibility involves subjective judgement. Exploiting a personal relationship in this manner, to win the consulting assignment, may attract criticism. However, the small number of 'losers' in this instance (in terms of their jobs not surviving this review) are going to be in that category despite any actions of the consulting team. The credibility and professionalism of the consulting team, and the prospects for future work here, and recommendations to other organizations, lies partly in achieving the assignment goals, and partly in working with the chief executive to achieve them.

Finally, is the initiator's *reputation* left intact, strengthened, or weakened?

The initiator's reputation in the eyes of the clients (chief executive and the committee to which the team reports) will be enhanced if the assignment is successful in meeting the strategic aims of helping to create a more flexible, empowered, responsive organization, reducing costs, and improving effectiveness and staff morale. A reputation for coping with politically sensitive issues will also be enhanced, in the eyes of the chief executive.

Powerlessness corrupts

Rather than connoting only dominance, control, and oppression, *power* can mean efficacy and capacity – something managers and executives need to move the organization towards its goals. Power in organizations is analogous in simple terms to physical power: it is the ability to mobilize resources (human and material) to get things done. The true sign of power, then, is accomplishment – not fear, terror, or tyranny. Where the power is 'on', the system can be productive; where the power is 'off', the system bogs down.

Powerlessness, in contrast, tends to breed bossiness rather than true leadership. In large organizations, at least, it is powerlessness that often creates ineffective, desultory management and petty, dictatorial, rules-minded managerial styles. Accountability without power – responsibility for results without the resources to get them – creates frustration and failure. People who see themselves as weak and powerless and find their subordinates resisting or discounting them tend to use more punishing forms of influence. If organizational power can 'enoble', then, recent research shows, organizational powerlessness can 'corrupt'.

Source: from Kanter (1979, pp.65–6).

Dirty hands: warrants, accounts, reputations

It is clear from these examples that no simple set of principles or rules, code of conduct, or decision framework, will enable us easily to make 'correct' decisions in such circumstances. Indeed, rigid adherence to a set of principles or rules is likely to lead to perverse or damaging consequences, or to prevent us from acting in ways that would benefit others and the wider organization. Does effective political action then require us to set aside ethical principles?

Provis (2004, p.16) refers to this as 'the dirty hands problem'; those who practice politics inevitably violate moral standards. Managers may have to use methods and tactics that they find distasteful, but which are effective in achieving personal and organizational goals. Provis also notes that the considerations we may take into account (relationships, ideals, organizational authority) are not always helpful, as the implied obligations, to friends, colleagues, and employers, often conflict with each other in ways that cannot readily be reconciled. Provis (2005) notes that tensions between what is ethical and what is political are common, and that we need to use different criteria to make ethical and political judgements. What is ethical is not always prudent, or in our self-interest, which is why Machiavelli (1514) saw ethics as a barrier to the achievement of political goals. Provis also observes that, when conflicts of obligation arise, our information is often incomplete, and there is usually more than one reasonable conclusion, depending on which considerations are brought into play, and on how those are balanced. Effectively justifying one's own conclusion to such a conflict, therefore, puts a premium on the ability to offer a credible explanation, or account.

This argues for a situational ethics, in which rules and principles inform our decisions and actions, but where our judgement also takes other factors into consideration, including context, warrants, accounts, and reputations. This framework is set out in Figure 3.2. Unlike the decision tree described earlier, this is simply a map of the terrain on which reasonable judgements concerning the use of political tactics can be explored. While the map is described here in linear terms, the arrows indicate that this is a cyclical process; adding every interconnection between the components would make this unreadable.

Ethics and judgement

For all of us, constantly, in organizational politics, one of our most recurring difficulties is to come to conclusions on the basis of ambiguous, shifting and conflicting pieces of evidence, in circumstances where some people may be trying to mislead us, others have an erroneous or half-correct view they put to us, and some of the facts about others' intentions and expectations are not yet even fully determinate.

Source: Provis (2004, p.123).

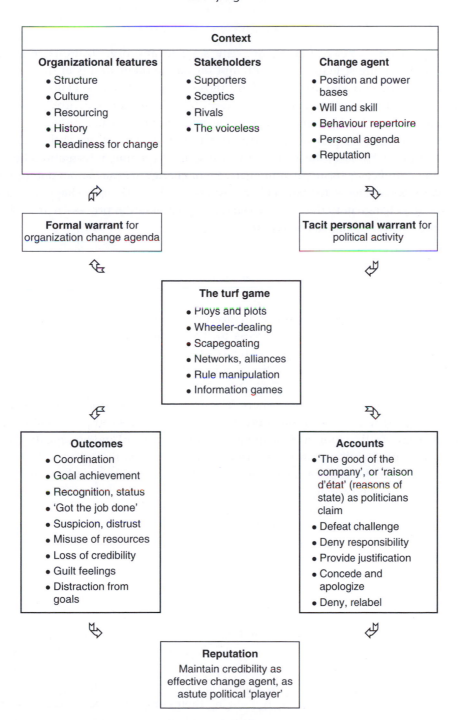

Figure 3.2 Context, warrants, accounts, and reputation.

Context

The change agent is not a 'free agent'. Any actor in any organizational role has to work within existing structures, and attempt to change them, and is at the same time influenced, facilitated and constrained by those structures. The sociologist Giddens captures this reflexive relationship in the term 'the duality of structure'. The actions of the change agent thus have to be seen in the context of the formal authority structure of the organization, the prevailing culture in terms of norms, values and expectations with respect to behaviour, the availability of resources (people, information, budgets), and past experiences – positive and negative – of change. These factors determine the organization's 'readiness for change' (Pettigrew et al., 1992), can shape the ease or difficulty of a change initiative, and can shape implementation processes including the degree and forms of political behaviour.

Change agent

The framework also has to consider the attributes and resources of the change agent. Formal position has a determining influence on factors such as perceived authority, access to senior management, and access to information and other resources. These factors and individual personality influence the change agent's power bases, their behaviour repertoire, and their expertise or 'will and skill' (Mintzberg, 1983) with respect to change implementation.

There are two other critical factors here. The first concerns *agenda*; what is the change agent attempting to achieve in this context? This is typically a complex combination of personal desires (satisfaction, achievement, career progression) and organizational goals (cost cutting, profitability, customer service). The second is *reputation* – the measure of esteem which the change agent enjoys in the assessment of other members of the organization. The change agent with a strong reputation generally carries more weight and influence than one held in low regard. Reputation is both an 'input' to this framework, and also one of the main 'outputs'. While some political tactics may damage the change agent's reputation, thus acting as a restraint on behaviour, other tactics will strengthen it.

Stakeholders

The other players in the game, the stakeholders in change, are elements in the context, but deserve separate attention. It has become commonplace to advocate stakeholder analysis when planning change. This involves identifying key stakeholders, clarifying their needs and interest, and establishing appropriate strategies for winning their support, accommodating their desires, or marginalizing their complaints. The change agent can expect to meet supporters, sceptics, 'subversives' and rivals, along with those who lack power and other resource to establish a voice. However, as Egan (1994) argues, 'the voiceless' also require active management, because they can be recruited by rivals and turned into challengers.

I'm on your side

Manager What's the most devious thing I have done? This is not self-effacing modesty that's causing me to think for a moment, because I'm as capable or as willing to do it as the next person. Well, if I can answer in a generic way, one of the skills of playing this game is to some extent being able to present yourself to other people in a way which, while not agreeing with things with which you don't agree, somehow also not disagreeing, if disagreeing is going to cause alienation and therefore put hurdles in the way to achieving the goal that you want to achieve. I mean, my wife would say that, in that sense, I am unprincipled because I will ask what gain or disadvantage it might cause me in the circumstances. And I would apply that in organizational terms. I am quite happy to let people think that I agree with them and I'm on their side, if that suits my purpose at the time. And I think I've got the skills of doing that, without blatantly lying.

If somebody is being run down in the organization, somebody that I'm opposed to, if I thought they were unfairly being run down, and it suited my purposes that they would continue to be denigrated, then I wouldn't step in and stop it, and say, well, look, in the interests of fair play and so on. I'll quite happily sit to one side. I suppose I would only stand up for people if I thought there was an advantage to be gained.

Warrants

Is the action that one is about to take justified; is it warranted by the context? The concept of warrant has two related dimensions. The first concerns *formal sanction* for particular change initiatives. The second concerns *personal conviction* that one's actions, political and otherwise, are appropriate. The fortunate change agent has a clear senior management remit and adequate resources to drive a particular initiative. However, life for the change agent is not always thus charmed. An initiative may be based on a mix of personal commitment and some limited managerial support, and senior management sponsorship and resources may need to be obtained as the initiative unfolds. In other words, the change agent may have to act (politically) without a formal warrant in order to obtain one.

The change agent will never receive a formal written warrant to act politically. That judgement will always rely on personal conviction and circumstances. A warrant to act politically can be based on a number of interacting factors; the benefits to be derived from change; personal career goals; reactions to past changes; the past, current, and anticipated responses of other stakeholders, particularly those seeking to block, disrupt, or subvert all or part of the agenda. Personal and organizational agendas are not as clearly distinguishable as these remarks imply. The perceived success or failure of a change initiative can influence the perceived effectiveness of the change agent responsible.

The turf game

The change agent may thus feel mandated not only to adopt a conventional change implementation posture (open, participative, supporting, joint problem solving), but also to engage in political tactics; recruiting support, forming alliances, anticipating and immobilizing resistance. This is what Kanter (1983a) calls the 'change architect', deploying 'power skills' and 'coalition forming'. Here are the wheeler-dealing, image-building and impression management, scapegoating, networking, coalition building, rule manipulation (and rule breaking), the 'tactical' use (and misuse) of information, and other tactics.

Outcomes

We saw in Chapter 1 how the use of political tactics can have both damaging and constructive consequences, a view now widely accepted (Kumar and Ghadially, 1989; Provis, 2004). The positive consequences may include improved coordination of effort behind change, the achievement of organizational goals or objectives, recognition, status and career enhancement for the change agent, feelings of personal achievement, and increased influence and power. Possible negative consequences include the creation of an organizational climate of suspicion and distrust, distraction from organizational goals, the unproductive allocation of resources (skilled management time as well as money), feelings of personal guilt, faltering change implementation, and a loss of credibility.

Accounts

Change agents may often be required to justify their actions. If so challenged, a satisfactory defence may require appeals to 'the greater good of the organization', or to the damaging actions of other stakeholders. But 'accounting' has other dimensions (McLaughlin et al., 1992). When faced with accusations of 'playing politics', the change agent can offer some other justification, concede the point and apologize, or simply deny that the behaviour was 'political'. Change agents who can 'tell a good story', and who are able to account effectively for their actions, can enhance their reputation. Although accounts and political ploys are distinguished here, accounting is a special, and critical, aspect of political skill. Accounts can also be regarded as the 'public' face of the change agent's warrant. The warrant to act politically is based in part on the question, 'am *I* doing the right thing?'; a satisfactory account has to persuade *others* that those actions were justified.

The need to be seen to be successful is often now equated with success itself. Form and substance, reality and illusion, become confused. As in national party politics, virtuosity in 'spin', or in presentation (of people, policies, actions, events, and outcomes) has become increasingly significant. Management 'skill' becomes the ability to simulate appropriate attitudes, values, beliefs, and emotions in an opportunistic manner to suit the circumstances. The perceived need to manufacture appearances at the expense of substantive change is what Ferris and King (1991) refer to as 'the dark side' of politics.

Reputation

This approach asks the change agent to consider; what do I want to develop a reputation *for*? Kotter (1985) argues that the change agent who combines personal credibility with an established track record obtains resources more readily. Laver (1997) defines reputation as a 'socially defined asset', dependent on one's behaviour, and on the observations, interpretations and memories of others. Reputation is part of the 'stock-in-trade' of the change agent. Will you do what you say? Have you done that before? Are your threats and promises reliable? Do you have a reputation for fair dealing, for keeping your word, for sidelining the opposition, for the careful and sophisticated building of support for initiatives and ideas, for the tactful removal of opponents? With what initiatives, policies, ideas and styles do you wish to be associated? Laver (1997, p.26) points out that reputation is tediously and painstakingly constructed, while desperately fragile:

> [I]t can take a very long time to build a reputation that can be effectively destroyed in seconds. A reputation for utter ruthlessness with the spiky club, for example, may be built painstakingly, even painfully, over the years on the basis of relentless repetition of ruthless acts. A reputation for honourable behaviour may take years of honourable behaviour to develop. But a single act of pointless mercy when utter ruthlessness was expected, a single dastardly deed when 'doing the right thing' was anticipated, can destroy these carefully crafted reputations at a stroke. Such reputations, viewed in these terms, represent huge but very fragile instrumental investments for the people who own them.

In an acceptable way

Manager But for the people in the competitive group, you don't have any particular duty of loyalty to, so their success or failure is an instrumental thing as far as I am concerned. Fair game. There must have been occasions where I've been prepared to lie, on the facts as I saw them, to gain a particular end. I just can't think that I wouldn't have done that. It's a bit like . . . goes back to what we said earlier about

Continued

---

what people admit to doing and what they actually do. Nobody ever admits to fiddling their expenses; although because everybody fiddles their expenses, you'd be a very foolish person to ever admit to fiddling yours, because that would be something which people would never forget you'd said. However honest you'd been, you'd be dead in the water. The reality is, we have all fiddled our expenses to some degree, at some time, for whatever reason. Just happened to need a few quid at that time. But you just wouldn't say that in public, would you. That would be a career threatening admission to make. What you learn as you go through your career, and get more experienced, is how to present these things, and rationalize these things, in an acceptable way.

This is not a simple 'ends justify the means' argument. The change agent who uses political tactics and emerges with their reputation in tatters (even if change is regarded as successful) will face future career difficulties. Means must be judged in relation to the context, in relation to a diverse agenda of personal and organizational goals and outcomes, and with respect to the effect that the change agent's actions will have on reputation, now and into the future. Reputation is thus a critical 'output' from this process, but it is also a critical 'input'. The change agent with a weakened reputation will have problems launching and moving any further significant change initiatives.

The fact that there are difficulties in applying clear ethical guidelines to political behaviour is not a conclusion of despair. Any 'ethics test' is artificial, and the penalties flowing from 'incorrect' choices are often insubstantial. But where the change agent initiating political tactics has no warrant for such actions, has limited creative accounting skills, where claims for personal and organizational damages can be upheld, and where a strong challenge is forthcoming, the social and organizational penalties can be powerful. The penalties for 'losing' the turf game include censure, ostracism and ridicule, curtailed future prospects, and perhaps even loss of job and career. The social and organizational controls which come into play carry significantly more weight in practice than the clinical, textbook-based results of an ethical decision tree analysis.

Follow through

Playing politics for real

Here are some real examples of managers dealing with organization political behaviour. These cases are all based on real situations. The behavioural options in each case are based on what the manager was considering, or being advised to consider by colleagues, at the time.

In each case, imagine yourself in this situation. How would you judge this situation? Is this example typical or rare in your experience? Are the behaviours described acceptable and commonplace, or disreputable and abhorrent? Which option would you choose, and why?

Playing politics (1): Buying into it

You are deputy product manager (female) in a 150-employee business unit in a manufacturing plant. You have established that a moderately complex reorganization would significantly improve employee motivation and performance, cutting production costs as well as increasing capacity and improving product quality. The product manager (male) seems to have other goals, and does not want to be diverted into a major change programme at this time. You believe these changes would benefit the company, as well as enhancing the careers of the managers associated with them. You have spent a lot of time and effort trying to convince him, without success.

What will you do, and why?

1 Give up. Life is too short. As product manager, he is accountable for the unit's performance. Let him damage his own career prospects.
2 Get tough. Get angry. Threaten to resign if he does not take your proposals seriously and agrees to their implementation soon. Give him a deadline.
3 Go over his head. Sell the change to his boss, the managing director (male). Persuade the managing director to have the product manager implement your proposals.
4 He has to write a change management assignment for his Masters degree. Write this for him, based on your proposals, and present it to him, identifying him as the author.
5 Be persistent. Keep up the pressure. Show him the figures again. Present the logic of your case in another format. Try to explain the benefits more clearly.

Playing politics: How to decide

Now that we have looked at an example, let's consider the criteria that can be used to guide behaviour in these cases. In this framework, two criteria are particularly important:

1 Probability of success
Will it work? Will this action lead to the outcomes you want? This may involve getting the job done, implementing the change initiative, dealing with 'difficult' colleagues, and so on, depending on the context. We can rate options on this criterion as having a *high*, *medium*, or *low* probability of success.

2 Impact on reputation
How will your choice affect your image? Will you be seen as someone who 'gets things done', or who 'avoids difficult problems'? We can rate options on this criterion as having a *positive* or *neutral* impact, or as putting your reputation *at risk*.

	low	medium	high
probability of success			

	risk	neutral	positive
impact on reputation			

These are judgement calls. There are no safe or certain ways to approach these situations. Management in general, and organization politics in particular, are not risk-free activities.

Two other criteria may be important:

3 Principles, values, and beliefs

You have to decide where to draw your own lines and limits concerning political behaviour. However, rigid adherence to those limits may damage your reputation, and may prevent you from acting in ways that would benefit colleagues and the organization as a whole.

4 If first choice fails

If one option fails, your other options may remain open. However, that is not always the case. You may wish to avoid, or to consider very carefully, those actions which, if they fail, leave you with no further options, other than perhaps to leave the organization.

These four criteria are presented in this sequence for presentational purposes only. In some circumstances, and for some individuals, principles, values, and beliefs may be of overriding significance, while in other settings what matters are outcomes and reputations. The numbering of these criteria, therefore, is not meant to imply a hierarchy of importance.

Playing politics (2): Keeping him out of it

You are director of a leading business school with 80 employees. In three months, you will experience your first external assessment of teaching quality. This will produce a ranking of 'poor', 'satisfactory', or 'excellent'. To achieve excellence requires major changes in systems and procedures, and in staff attitudes and behaviour. Implementing these changes will divert staff time away from research, which is also externally assessed. You have debated the options with the other seven members of the school's senior management team, and reached a majority decision to go for teaching excellence. Anything less would damage the reputation of the school and its parent university. One of your senior team disagrees strongly. This is not the first time that he has taken an opposing position on a major issue. Instead of accepting the majority decision, he is telling junior staff that you are wrong, that they should focus on research instead, and that they should ignore changes designed to improve teaching quality.

What will you do, and why?

1 Bring the senior management team together again and repeat the debate. Try to persuade him. Try to get him to accept the majority decision.
2 Ask university management to discipline him, with a view to termination, or forcing him to accept the majority decision. His behaviour is professionally unacceptable.
3 Marginalize him. Hold meetings without informing him. Put his agenda items at the bottom so there is no time for discussion. Spread rumours to damage his credibility.
4 Approach him one-on-one. Use a cascade of influencing techniques, starting with the reasoned case. If that fails again, try negotiation, horse-trading, and compromise.
5 Do nothing. Let him spread his rumours. Hope that the junior staff will see that he is wrong in trying to persuade them to focus on research and ignore teaching quality.

Playing politics (3): Sparring partners

You are appointed to the new post of professional services manager for a computer company. Margins on hardware have fallen. Revenue growth will come from selling business solutions and consulting services. Growth in your new section will take staff away from the traditional sales area. On your third day in the new job, the company's most successful sales manager approaches you, unprovoked, insults you, and threatens to have you removed from the company whenever he wants. He is the same management grade as you. You both report to the same company director. He generates 40 per cent of the company's turnover, and high levels of commission, from one customer whose buyer is a close personal friend of his. Senior managers are aware of the problems of dependency on one customer. The sales manager is in his mid-30s, recently married, and about to start a family. He consistently tries to block your contacts with this major customer. You discover that he is capturing your email traffic, and that of other managers. He is undermining your credibility with your staff with rumours and innuendo. You also know that he incurs high expenses on overseas trips that generate no new sales. On a joint business development trip to Poland, he arranges for two call-girls to come to your hotel room, apparently planning to take photographs with which to discredit you.

What will you do, and why?

1 Report his unacceptable behaviour to your director. Ask the director to speak to him, and to solve this problem for you, in the interests of morale and performance.
2 Force him out slowly. Develop your own business with that key customer. Make contacts and friends that choose to come to you, not to him. Reduce their dependence on him. Ensure that senior managers know about his mistakes and failures.

3 Ask the sales manager for a meeting. Share and explore your genuine differences. Jointly negotiate a compromise arrangement. Shake hands, and establish a friendly and effective working relationship.
4 Do not get involved in his devious games. Concentrate on your team. Ignore his tactics. Get on with your own job as best you can.
5 Put your new role to one side. Play by his rules. Copy his methods. Capture his emails. Spread unpleasant rumours about him. Damage his credibility with his own staff. Engineer some embarrassing incidents for him.

Playing politics (4): Here come the sandwiches

Your four-person consulting team has bid successfully for a project to review the organization structure and culture of a Borough Council (a local government body) in England, to include the professional (paid) management structure, and committee structures for elected Council members. Your remit is to recommend change for an organization that has been operating in the same way for over twenty years. This is an autocratic, hierarchical, rigid, bureaucratic organization, with lots of time and money wasted on unnecessary procedures and rule following, and with poor staff morale. Recommendations will concern cutting hierarchy, empowering people, changing management style, making procedures more flexible, and getting decisions taken more quickly (but there is a no-redundancy policy). The assignment was won against stiff competition. Your team appears to have been chosen because you were not offering a 'prepackaged' solution. Following the review, there may be further consulting work with this organization in change implementation and management development.

The Council recently appointed a new Chief Executive. The leader of your consulting team is a long-standing personal friend of this senior manager. You are invited to a meeting with the Chief Executive, to launch the project, agree liaison mechanisms, find a room to work in, and so on. The logistics completed, the Chief Executive asks you to join him for lunch. As the sandwiches are brought in, the Chief Executive produces a seven page document and works through this with your team, line by line, for about an hour. This sets out what he wants to see in your final report, including specific recommendations concerning parts of the organization structure, and named individuals not expected to survive the review. He will want to see and, if he thinks it necessary, edit your final report before it is made public.

What will you do, and why?

1 Reject the assignment if it is going to be conducted on such a dishonest and unethical basis.
2 Do nothing. When you report in three months time, circumstances may have changed, and the Chief Executive may have forgotten these initial recommendations.
3 Report the conduct of the Chief Executive to the (elected) Leader of the Council, advising disciplinary action.

4 Reason with the Chief Executive. His recommendations are premature. Your review must be independent and objective. Your recommendations will be based on the evidence which you collect.

5 Proceed with the assignment, ensuring that the Chief Executive's recommendations appear in your report and are supported with appropriate evidence and reasoning.

Playing politics: The options

In each case the italicized option is the one chosen and judged retrospectively to have been appropriate and effective by the change agent or agents involved.

1 Buying into it
 a   avoidance
 b   tantrum
 c   run to daddy
 d   *cheat*
 e   keep banging your head

2 Keeping him out of it
 a   keep banging your head
 b   run to daddy
 c   *neutralize*
 d   let's be friends
 e   avoidance

3 Sparring partners
 a   run to daddy
 b   *neutralize*
 c   let's be friends
 d   avoidance
 e   copycat

4 Here come the sandwiches
 a   walk away
 b   denial
 c   run to daddy
 d   argue
 e   *go with the flow*

Organization politics at the movies: *Kingdom of Heaven*

Set in twelfth-century Jerusalem, *Kingdom of Heaven* (2005, director Ridley Scott) tells the story of the blacksmith Balian (played by Orlando Bloom) who inherits his father's title of Baron of Ibelin. Jerusalem in 1184 is a place where Christians and Muslims live in peace. However, Guy de Lusignan (Martin Csokas), a Templar Knight, is a religious fanatic who wants to provoke a war with Saladin, the Arab King. Guy is married to

Princess Sibylla (Eva Green) who is the sister of King Baldwin of Jerusalem (Edward Norton). Baldwin is dying of leprosy, and Guy is next in line. But Sibylla's is an arranged marriage, and an unhappy one, and she has a romantic relationship with Balian. Balian finds himself caught between Baldwin's vision of coexistence (the kingdom of heaven) and the Templars' desire for war.

In an attempt to preserve the peace, Baldwin and Tiberias, Marshall of Jerusalem (Jeremy Irons) ask Balian if he would marry Sibylla and assume command of the army if Guy and the knights who support him were to be executed. Balian refuses to be the cause of Guy's death on principle, declaring that, 'It is a kingdom of conscience, or nothing'. Guy is successful in provoking war, Saladin's army lays siege to Jerusalem, thousands of soldiers on both sides are slaughtered in the ensuing battle for the city, the Christian forces are overcome, and Jerusalem is lost. Balian's conscience, however, is clear. The authors of the ethical decision framework described in this chapter would probably agree with his decision, as they argue that, 'When it comes to the ethics of organizational politics, respect for justice and human rights should prevail for its own sake' (Cavanagh et al., 1981, p.372). However, before the battle, and knowing that he could prevent this war, Sibylla tells Balian that: '*There will be a day when you will wish you had done a little evil to do a greater good.*'

- Assess Balian's choices using the 'ethical decision tree' framework (Figure 3.1) described in this chapter. How would that approach guide his actions?
- Now assess Balian's choices using the 'context, warrants, accounts, and reputation' approach (Figure 3.2). How would that approach guide his actions differently?
- How would you act if you were in Balian's position, and why?
- To what extent do you agree with Sibylla's argument that having her husband Guy and his friends executed (the 'little evil') in this context would have been warranted?
- In your eyes, what impact has his decision and the outcomes had on Balian's reputation, and why?

One of the arguments of this chapter is that rigid adherence to a code of conduct, ethical principles, or personal beliefs and values, will ultimately prevent the change agent from acting in ways that benefit colleagues and the organization. Balian's position is perhaps an extreme illustration of this. In your judgement, does this argument translate into management practice? Before the final movie credits start to roll, this observation appears on the screen: '*Nearly a thousand years later, peace in the Kingdom of Heaven remains elusive.*'

For more ideas on how organizational ethical issues are presented in movies, see Shaw (2004). Shaw discusses the ethical behaviour issues portrayed in movies such as *Glengarry Glen Ross*, *Philadelphia*, *Death of a Salesman*, *Barbarians at the Gate*, and *Wall Street*, suggesting how these can be used in a teaching context.

4   Men behaving badly

Chapter objectives

1 To argue for the inevitability and value of a Machiavellian political perspective.
2 To introduce thuggery and pragmatism as alternative political strategies, underpinned by different ethical perspectives.
3 To explore 'Theory M' as a perspective on human nature.
4 To provide a deeper understanding of how the 'rules of the turf game' are constructed, dealing with the stigma of 'dirty hands', and playing on a field that is not level.

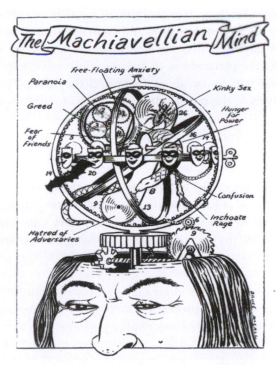

You have to play the game

> **A:** I don't become involved in politics. I don't play games at work.
>
> **B:** Ah, so you play the 'I don't play games at work' game.
>
> *Source*: Billi Lee (The Savvy Institute).

As we noted earlier (in Chapter 1), you are being insulted if someone describes you as Machiavellian. The popular stereotype concerns someone who is ruthlessly self-interested. This stereotype, however, is exaggerated and misleading, and this chapter argues that Machiavelli was probably advocating a more pragmatic and contextually sensitive approach to the effective use of power and politics.

Is it necessary to become involved in the power game, even if one does not want to? Can a manager not just get on with the job, and let others play these games? Are talent and hard work not enough to be successful? No. The choice lies between denial and acknowledgement, not whether or not to play. The interrelated factors that trigger organization politics are explored in Chapter 9. However, organization politics is sometimes blamed on the Machiavellian stereotype, that is, someone who brings politics into an apolitical setting. If organizations are already infused with power, then that blame is falsely attributed. Contacts and connections, relationships and alliances, are required to get anything done in organizations made up of complex webs of interdependency. As the platitude says, it is not only what you know, but also who you know, and what you know about them and they about you. Recognizing and participating effectively in the power plays are central to managerial success, to 'doing a good job'.

As most managers will confirm, organizational life is often one of pressure, insecurity, and a feeling (often well founded) of not being in control:

> It's the sheer frustration of not being able to get things done fast enough. Being constrained by, 'We've always done it this way'; having to justify everything 'n' times. Everyone's sitting there saying, 'We know you're right but … '
> (Watson, 1994, p.72, quoting a business development manager at the company ZTC Ryland.)

While pressures may have increased for many managers 'caught in the middle', this is a general rather than a specific problem. The practice gap, between what orders and rules prescribe, and what the situation requires, means that more resources are often required in order to 'get the job done'. In part, this is a technical matter – running operations, creating innovations, implementing change. These all create unexpected problems, produce unintended consequences, or have unwanted outcomes. To address these problems, managers require extra time, knowledge, skills, creativity, flexibility, and other resources. In seeking to promote their own ideas and to secure resources, managers thus inevitably involve themselves in the power game. It is not only the narrowly focused, self-interested, power-hungry organization politician that becomes involved in the struggle of ideas and resources. The agenda may be a corporate one, the manager principled and professional, and the lack of adequate resources recognized as a legitimate concern. However, the presence of actual or potential conflict over scarce resources is a feature of most organizations, and the turf game is one of the main avenues through which decisions concerning their distribution are reached.

Thugs and pragmatists: what is a Machiavellian player?

savvy shrewdness, to know or understand, knowledgeable

nous practical intelligence

Source: *Oxford English Dictionary.*

If playing the power game is inevitable, what is a good player? One answer to this question lies with the practice and ethics of Machiavellianism. The term, Machiavellian, is more than just an academic one. It is used as an insult. And Machiavelli's writings (and interpretations of his work) are often used as a source of advice and reflection, as both toolkit and warning. How then are we to understand Machiavellianism?

This issue is complex, because Machiavelli's ideas are disputed. However it is also significant in shaping our understanding of organization politics and politicians. Our understanding of Machiavelli determines whether organization politics is seen as a complex artform, a game to be played with skill and elegance, or whether it is regarded as a world of dirty tricks, to be condemned as an illegitimate and unethical distraction from real work – one which also damages collaborative relationships. Here we see alternative images of the organization politician. On the one hand celebrated, courageous, flexible and savvy, with principles, integrity, and nous; on the other hand harshly criticized, perhaps pitied, as a self-interested, ruthless, dishonest and scheming 'prince of darkness'. Or is there a third way?

Machiavellian thuggery

'When I am good, I'm good. But when I'm bad, I'm better' (Mae West).

Machiavelli has been responsible for the stereotype that we will call 'Machiavellian thuggery'. This is a negative strategy in which politics is seen as pervasive, and winning is equated with self-interest and personal power. This strategy involves using coercion, deceit, or 'whatever it takes' to achieve those personal goals. The standpoint of Machiavellian thuggery offers a bleak outlook on the cut and thrust of organization politics. Rather than viewing the competition for scarce organizational resources as healthy, Machiavellian thuggery sees a seamier or darker side. Organization politics becomes an overt conflict, each party seeking to dominate and control the other. It is therefore important in such a setting to follow what Bernard Shaw regarded as the true principle of business: 'Do others, for they would do you.' Those who display a preference for Machiavellian thuggery are often seen as 'power freaks' who believe that 'the end justifies the meanness' (Bing, 2002).

Thuggery

The term 'thug' comes from the name of a thirteenth-century Indian sect, and is derived from the Hindi word *thag* meaning swindler or thief. Thugs had a reputation for befriending unsuspecting travellers, winning their trust, and then robbing and strangling them, before concealing their bodies. The sect was apparently difficult to eliminate as members left neither witnesses nor evidence for their crimes, and made no confessions when captured. The term here is used to capture the association with brutality, manipulation, and deceit.

Machiavellian thuggery is thus condemned by private ethics, public morality, and civic codes alike. In the sphere of personal ethics, dishonesty, manipulation and aggression are usually regarded as evil. In relation to the public morality of organizations, Machiavellian thuggery betrays the trust and reciprocity that are essential if individuals are to cooperate in order to achieve shared goals. Machiavellian thuggery is thus an illegitimate and non-rational political intruder in the formally rational organizational domain. Emotive persuasion, deceit, and bullying are used in pursuit of the non-technical goals of enhancing self-interest and personal power. In organizational settings where efficiency and success are formally attributed to practical means–ends calculations, Machiavellian thuggery is counterproductive, the actions of a subversive schemer and a charlatan. Machiavellian thuggery is also castigated by the civic morality adhered to by many management advisers. From McClelland's (1970) distinction between personal and socialized uses of power (see Chapter 2) to Kotter's (1985) condemnation of the self-defeating cycle of negative politics, the self-interested organization politician is seen as a deviant, destructive, and anachronistic force. Table 4.1 summarizes the attributes of the stereotyped Machiavellian thug.

Table 4.1 The Machiavellian thug

power is the ultimate goal	Classic Machiavelli: the goal is the stability and glory of the organization (state) and a recognition of your own part in this. Popular Machiavellian: someone with narrow self-interested power motives
the ends justify the means	To achieve this goal, you have to perform unethical acts, but they are morally justified by the results
no holds barred; whatever it takes	There are no limits on what you are prepared to do
do not adhere to conventional morality, but use it to advantage	It is necessary to dispense with conventional morality because this is something that inhibits people from acting effectively
honest and loyalty are luxuries, not ideals or constraints	To retain power, it is not possible to be honest and loyal, so these should not be given any significance
self interest is the prime motivator, not morality or communal good	It is safe to assume that most people are motivated by short-term self-interest
fear is more important than love as a means of influence	Coercion, threat and fear are more effective techniques of power than participation, morality and love
ruthlessness and strength are to be admired	Many leaders fail because of not adhering to these principles; the ability to be strong and ruthless in doing 'whatever it takes' is to be admired

Machiavelli on Machiavelli

[It] has to be noted that men must either be pampered or crushed, because they can get revenge for small injuries but not for grievous ones. So any injury a Prince does a man should be of such a kind that there is no fear of revenge (Machiavelli, 1514, pp.37–8).

So it should be noted that when he seizes a state the new ruler must determine all the injuries that he will need to inflict. He must inflict them once for all, and not have to renew them every day, and in that way he will be able to set men's minds at rest and win them over to him when he confers benefits. Whoever acts otherwise, either through timidity or bad advice, is always forced to have the knife ready in his hand and he can never depend on his subjects because they, suffering fresh and continuous

Continued

violence, can never feel secure with regard to him. Violence must be inflicted once for all; people will then forget what it tastes like and so be less resentful. Benefits must be conferred gradually; and in that way they will taste better (1514, p.66).

So a Prince has of necessity to be so prudent that he knows how to escape the evil reputation attached to those vices which are not so dangerous, if he possibly can; but, if he cannot, he need not worry so much about the latter. And then, he must not flinch from being blamed for vices which are necessary for safeguarding the state. This is because, taking everything into account, he will find that some of the things that appear to be virtues will, if he practices them, ruin him, and some of the things that appear to be vices will bring him security and prosperity (1514, p.92).

Machiavellian pragmatism

But to discuss this subject thoroughly we must distinguish between innovators who stand alone and those who depend on others, that is, between those who to achieve their purposes can force the issue and those who must use persuasion. In the second case, they always come to grief, having achieved nothing; when, however, they depend on their own resources and can force the issue, then they are seldom endangered. That is why all armed prophets have conquered, and unarmed prophets have come to grief. Besides what I have already said, the populace is by nature fickle; it is easy to persuade them of something, but difficult to confirm them in that persuasion. Therefore one must urgently arrange matters so that when they no longer believe they can be made to believe by force (Machiavelli, 1514, pp.51–2).

If Machiavelli sought only to justify thuggery, he would be of little interest, and would not have endured so long or exerted such influence. His insights penetrate deeper. His characterization of an effective politician, the strategy of Machiavellian pragmatism, reveals a world of politicking and power plays that is often unacknowledged, uncomfortable, and brutally realistic, but is far from simple and deceitful thuggery. As far as Machiavelli was concerned, as Falco (2004, p.7) observes, the end which justified the use of dubious means:

was not evil for evil's sake, nor even self-interest or the attainment or maintenance of power exclusively, but the 'common good'. Nor was this evil to be exercised indiscriminately, but through necessity only, and never in so extreme a fashion as to arouse the hatred of the people. And always, the appearance of goodness, or virtue in its Christian sense, was to be maintained. At least that was the strategy Machiavelli believed most successful Princes pursued, no matter what their stated purpose.

Pragmatism

The term 'pragmatist', like 'thug', has both a popular and a more precise usage. First, popular usage emphasizes the compromise and flexibility that are required to be practical, and to achieve things in a particular context. Second, pragmatism refers to a school of philosophy that insists on consequences, utility and practicality as components of truth. Pragmatism is opposed to formal and rational schools of philosophy which seek to ground knowledge and ethics in universal truths.

Machiavelli recognized that thuggery existed, and that those who adopted this approach had to be taken into account when one was planning one's own strategies and forming alliances. However, Machiavelli's approach was not traditional and moralistic, but realistic:

> [The] gulf between how one should live and how one does live is so wide that a man who neglects what is actually done for what should be done learns the way to self-destruction rather than self-preservation. The fact is that a man who wants to act virtuously in every way necessarily comes to grief among so many who are not virtuous. Therefore if a Prince wants to maintain his rule he must learn how not to be virtuous, and to make use of this or not according to need (Machiavelli, 1514, p.91).

Machiavelli on Machiavelli

Everyone realizes how praiseworthy it is for a Prince to honour his word and to be straightforward rather than crafty in his dealings; nonetheless contemporary experience shows that Princes who have achieved great things have been those who have given their word lightly, who have known how to trick me with their cunning, and who, in the end, have overcome those abiding by honest principles (Machiavelli, 1514, p.99).

You must realize this: that a Prince, and especially a new Prince, cannot observe all those things which give men a reputation for virtue, because in order to maintain his state he is often forced to act in defiance of good faith, of charity, of kindness, of religion. And so he should have a flexible disposition, varying as fortune and circumstances dictate. As I said above, he should not deviate from what is good, if that is possible, but he should know how to do evil, if that is necessary (1514, p.101).

Men are so simple, and so much creatures of circumstance, that the deceiver will always find someone ready to be deceived (1514, p.100).

Table 4.2   The Machiavellian pragmatist

power is a means to an end	Achievement and recognition are what counts
the means do not justify the ends	Adherence to ethical codes of conduct does not justify failure to achieve desirable results
don't do whatever it takes, but take only what you can do	Use coercion, manipulation, and deceit with care, and only when necessary to achieve results
morality is not personal ethics while doing the job; it is how you do the job	Conventional morality should be adhered to when possible, and where not possible, its betrayal should be pragmatically considered, yet legitimated as conventionally moral
honesty is not always the best policy	Honesty and loyalty are ideals that may be possible and adhered to, but should be effectively dispensed with when necessary
don't over-estimate other people's intelligence or morality	Morality and desire to pursue communal good inspire many people, but they should not be relied upon, particularly when people are under personal threat
it is better to be loved than feared, but don't rely on it	It is best to influence through inspiration, love and respect, and to avoid stimulating hatred; but fear may often be necessary in difficult and threatening times
admire great achievements	We should admire the character, intelligence and strength to achieve outcomes by dealing with the fickleness of people and circumstances

In other words, Machiavelli the pragmatist felt that it was more appropriate to confront other people as they were, and not as they should be. This perspective is summarized in Table 4.2.

The two Machiavellis: reputation, flexibility, and ethics

Reputation

> 'The secret of success in business is honesty and fair trading. If you can fake that, you've got it made' (Groucho Marx).

Used consistently over time, the strategy of Machiavellian thuggery can give its user a reputation as a schemer, a factor that Machiavelli recognized can severely undermine political effectiveness. A good reputation and an appropriate 'legend' (Lee, 1992) are seen by many political actors and analysts as central to political success. As Kotter (1985) argues, those with a reputation for achievement and for forging good personal relationships, can gain cooperation, obtain resources and form alliances much more rapidly. The negative reputation attached to Machiavellian thuggery is a severe liability. A central component of political success is effectively bartering, negotiating, and making deals, and a reputation for unfair trading and dishonesty can be disastrous. The most effective organizational politician may well be one who is seen as not playing 'political games' and as being 'above politics', the person who crafts inclusive agendas and coalitions. As one Research Institute Director in an Australian university replied when challenged by a younger member of staff about how he would address the problems of internecine tribal department politics, 'That was what I meant earlier when I talked about creating good working relationships'.

However, as Lee (1992) observes, a reputation for political naivety is also damaging. In her analysis of what she calls the 'but' problem, Lee points to the dangers that attend those who are regarded as being 'technically competent, but' who are seen as lacking social and political sensitivity. Machiavellian pragmatiom recognizes the need to cultivate a reputation for social and political sensitivity and effectiveness.

Reputation, as Machiavelli emphasized, is significant in any attempt to gain or preserve power. Machiavelli's infamous remark about how it is better to be feared than loved is frequently cited. However, he also argued that it was important for a Prince to avoid being hated. To achieve this, he stressed the importance of stability, and fostering well-being and security, using coercive tactics only when necessary. To avoid being hated, therefore, a Prince should develop a reputation for fair dealing and honesty, for personal courage, for hiring and supporting credible colleagues and advisers, minimizing the threat to others, and avoiding conspiracy and deception where possible. However, Machiavelli realized that it was not always possible for a Prince to behave in these ways, and that the use of betrayal, fear, and punishment would occasionally be required. He argued that such actions should be performed quickly and effectively without hesitation, causing minimum short-term disruption, and cementing the Prince's reputation for decisiveness and strength.

Flexibility

Machiavellian thuggery is an inflexible, one-dimensional strategy, involving one behavioural style, whatever the situation, and with only one outcome. But Machiavelli advocates a more flexible, pragmatic approach. The main task of Machiavellian pragmatism is to 'read' situations, determine what is necessary in that context, and act accordingly. In other words, the Prince must not stray from 'good', if possible, but should know how to enter into evil when necessity commands. The concept of behavioural flexibility, dependent on the nature of the setting, is widely recognized.

Machiavelli on Machiavelli

A Prince, therefore, need not necessarily have all the good qualities I mentioned above, but he should certainly appear to have them. I would even go so far as to say that if he has these qualities and always behaves accordingly he will find them harmful; if he only appears to have them they will render him service. He should also appear to be compassionate, faithful to his word, kind, guileless, and devout. And indeed he should be so. But his disposition should be such that, if he needs to be the opposite, he knows how (Machiavelli, 1514, p.100).

[A Prince] must learn from the fox and the lion; because the lion is defenceless against traps and a fox is defenceless against wolves. Therefore one must be a fox in order to recognize traps, and a lion to frighten off wolves. Those who simply act like lions are stupid. So it follows that a prudent ruler cannot, and must not, honour his word when it places him at a disadvantage and when the reasons for which he made his promise no longer exist. If all men were good, this precept would not be good; but because men are wretched creatures who would not keep their word to you, you need not keep your word to them. And no Prince ever lacked good excuses to colour his bad faith (1514, pp.99–100).

[P]rinces should delegate to others the enactment of unpopular measures and keep in their own hands the distribution of favours (1514, p.106).

[T]he Prince should restrain himself from inflicting grave injury on anyone in his service who he has close to him in his affairs of state (1514, p.111).

There is no doubt that a Prince's greatness depends on his triumphing over difficulties and opposition. So fortune, especially when she wants to build up the greatness of a new Prince, whose need to acquire standing is more pressing than for that of a hereditary ruler, finds enemies for him and encourages them to take the field against him, so that he may have cause to triumph over them and ascend higher on the ladder his foes have provided. Many, therefore, believe that when he has the chance an able Prince should cunningly foster some opposition to himself so that by overcoming it he can enhance his own stature (1514, pp.116–17).

he who has but the few as his enemies, can easily and without much scandal make himself secure, but he who has the public as a whole for his enemy can never make himself secure; and the greater his cruelty, the weaker does his regime become. In such a case the best remedy he can adopt is to make the populace his friend (1531, p.155).

Organization politics also involves behaving appropriately in different contexts, in relation to different individuals and groups.

It is necessary to understand the perceptions, personalities, motives and interests of the cast of characters on whom one's effectiveness and success often depends. A pragmatic perspective works with those differences, rather than complaining about

Table 4.3 Types of game

the insurgency game	refuse to do something, rally people's insecurities and fears about losing the status quo and their security, find technical bureaucratic reasons
the blame game	weaken others' positions by blaming them or their unit for failures
the counter-insurgency game	tighten controls through force, fear and new rules; agree to changes but from strength and ensuring they increase your power; make deals if necessary but not in ways that gives them control; play off one group against another
the sponsorship game	attach yourself and your interests to a powerful sponsor; build relations with them; build other power bases in case your sponsor leaves
the alliances game	create a power base among your peers; form around single issues, personalities, or multiple issues; can be useful for sponsorship or insurgency
the budget game	build arguments and suppress counter-arguments; request less and exaggerate benefits; under-promise and over-deliver; use 'invisible' resources
the expert information game	obtain 'inside' and 'outside' information that is crucial; obtain one's own, and control what others have

Source: based on Griffin (1991).

the inappropriate behaviour of others, complaining about not being understood, and adopting the role of victim. This means diagnosing or reading the context, participating in the organization's political games, and changing strategy and behaviour according to circumstances (see Table 4.3).

An organization's political games are not neatly circumscribed. The 'rules of the game' are often unclear (Clegg, 1989). Kanter (1989) compares political games to the Queen's croquet game in *Alice in Wonderland*. The goals move (the playing-card servants acting as hoops stand up and stretch), the outcomes shift (the hedgehog balls unravel and wander off), and technologies change in unanticipated ways (the flamingo mallets move their heads as they are about to strike the ball). Managers are also likely to find themselves playing a number of related games simultaneously, to get the job done, to win resources, to advance ideas and initiatives, and to acquire and protect turf. Like many games, the turf game is uncertain and risky.

While Machiavellian pragmatism involves flexibility and contextually appropriate responses, the deceit and coercion of Machiavellian thuggery may be necessary and appropriate for some situations, where cooperation and mutual advantage are problematic. However, there may be longer-term costs attached to such actions; the situation may alter, the possibilities for collaboration may change. The ability to recognize and respond to the fickleness of others, alongside our own understanding of 'what is going on', is a key component of action under uncertainty, and there are very few situations more complex, uncertain and shifting than politicized contexts. Effective Machiavellian pragmatism is able quickly and decisively to read situations and understand what is required, and also to tailor actions and strategies, whether participative or coercive, in a way that achieves results.

Anxiety and insecurity are inevitable in the face of such uncertainties. As one senior manager at Covenant Corporation was reported in Jackall (1988, p.69) as saying, 'Anxiety is endemic to anyone who works in a corporation. By the time you get to be middle management, it's difficult to make friends because the normal requirement for friendship – that is, loyalty – doesn't fit in this context. You have to look out for number one more than anything else'. Christie and Geiss (1970) in their classic study sought to discover how Machiavellians (with high scores on their assessment; see Chapter 9) played the game. They found, as predicted, that Machiavellians were more flexible and adaptive in the negotiations surrounding competitive and collaborative games.... Unexpectedly, however, they also found that Machiavellians were seen by others as attractive and charming in their lack of rigidity, their openness, and their focus on getting things done. The ability to deal with 'the changeability of affairs' was a central theme in Machiavelli's thinking. The desire for certainty, stability, and predictability reflects Latour's (1988) *Scrabble* player who loses the game while waiting for the chance to lay down a word using all of their letters.

Machiavelli on Machiavelli

From this arises the following question: whether it is better to be loved than feared, or the reverse. The answer is that one would like to be both the one and the other; but because it is difficult to combine them, it is far better to be feared than loved if you cannot be both (Machiavelli, 1514, p.96).

One can make this generalization about men: they are ungrateful, fickle, liars, and deceivers, they shun danger and are greedy for profit; while you treat them well, they are yours. They would shed their blood for you, risk their property, their lives, their children, so long, as I said above, as danger is remote; but when you are in danger they turn against you (1514, p.96).

Men worry less about doing an injury to one who makes himself loved than to one who makes himself feared. The bond of love is one which men, wretched creatures that they are, break when it is to their advantage to do so; but fear is strengthened by a dread of punishment which is always effective (1514, pp.96–7).

Ethics

In spite of the arguments of Chapter 3, most observers will probably regard Machiavellian thuggery, as described here, as unethical in its use of lies and force to achieve personal ends. Machiavellian pragmatism, in contrast, incorporates a principled situational ethic. This is a stance that is not only central to the organizational politician's sense of direction and self-worth, but also one that influences political reputation and the ability to influence others.

Many managers acknowledge, if grudgingly, that Machiavelli dared to give voice to unspoken, publicly condemned, yet privately acknowledged organizational realities. The need for a degree of insincerity and deceit, a level of manipulation and coercion, and an awareness of the personal and political dimensions of practical tasks, is part of management folklore and common sense. It is quite normal and understandable to overhear comments about how a newly appointed manager 'is not Machiavellian enough', or 'needs to be more Machiavellian'. Associated with this is an understanding that those who claim to be 'above politics', are often misleading themselves as well as others, or they have not yet experienced the complex trade offs and moral dilemmas that are typically involved in getting things done. As Joe Wilson's ex-colleagues in US Corporation X put it: 'Sunday school ethics – the public espousal of lofty principles – do not help managers cut the sometimes unpleasant deals necessary to make the world work' (Jackall, 1988, p.118). Machiavelli was simply being honest and realistic, observing that one has to play power and political games if one wants to get things done, and advocating contextual sensitivity and flexibility, while rejecting the stereotyped views 'anything goes', 'whatever it takes', and 'my way or the highway'.

In other words, the Machiavellian pragmatist is aware of the fuzziness and complexity of organizational conditions and issues, rather than being someone who sets their moral barrier too low. The end does not justify the means in every instance, and the trade-offs between those ends and means have to be considered. But it is necessary to play politics to get things done, and this inevitably involves a degree of competition, manipulation, coercion, and deceit. We asked in Chapter 3 if playing organization politics should even be considered to fall within the scope of ethical considerations. Studies using the Machiavellian personality assessment show that those with 'high Mach' scores are neither immoral nor amoral, but adopt a situational code of ethics (Leary et al., 1986).

While *The Prince* was written for political leaders who wished to obtain and retain power, this has a specific place in Machiavelli's overall works. While writing *The Prince*, he also wrote *The Discourses* (1531), which makes a different argument concerning how to establish and run a republic. What unites these works is Machiavelli's interpretation of the doctrine of *raison d'état* (for the good of the state). This doctrine holds that state security is paramount, and that normal moral standards do not apply when acting to ensure that security. The popular image of Machiavellian thuggery is one of *raison d'état* where, in the words of the French Sun King Louis XVI, *L'état, c'est moi* (I am the state). In contrast, for Machiavelli, it was the glory achieved by successfully establishing and defending the state, a public honour and a private aspiration, that was valued, and not self-interest and aggrandisement. In achieving this glory, Machiavelli believed that the Prince and other political figures had to deal with the world as it was, and not with the world as it should be. As Skinner (1981) observes, Machiavelli was writing at a time when several 'humanistic handbooks' were also circulating, advising Princes to adhere to the classic civic virtues of ancient Rome. In the sixteenth century, Machiavelli's work was so shocking that it was added to the *Index Librorum Prohibitorum*, the Papal index of prohibited books. However, his work did not advocate an ethical vacuum, but rather an alternative, realistic, and pragmatic view of what it was to be 'ethical' in public life.

In his study of *Politics as a Vocation*, Weber (1919) contrasts what he calls 'the ethics of conviction' with 'the ethics of responsibility'. The ethics of conviction, or 'the ethics of ultimate ends', holds that dishonesty, insincerity, cruelty, and the pursuit of self-interest and power are inherently immoral. There is no room here for calculations of costs and benefits concerning means and ends. To act ethically, one must conform unconditionally to moral standards, regardless of the consequences. The ethics of responsibility, in contrast, is the domain of the practising politician. This is a pluralist perspective, based on the observation that we live in a world in which 'ends collide', a world characterized by competing values and interests, creating tensions between our ideals and the means by which we realize them. With Machiavelli, Weber thus argues that 'good ends' may require the use of morally dubious means, including the use of 'power backed up by violence' (Brubaker, 1984, p.70).

In an ideal world, would we all have the resources to carry out the job, and would we rationally pursue shared aims for the common good, social recognition flowing to those who acted honestly and sincerely? While in Chapter 9 we will argue that such a viewpoint is misguided and dangerous, we can observe with confidence that we do not live in such a world, anyway. Resources are scarce, legitimate interests compete, and individuals act in irrational and self-interested ways. Organizations often have multiple, vague, and morally dubious goals. Rewards frequently flow to those apparently least deserving. Weber argued that, in such a context, a responsibility ethic is more appropriate, given the inevitable tension between ends and means, observing that good can be produced by evil, and vice versa. In other words, allowing for the human deficiencies which Machiavelli also noted (men [sic] can be ungrateful, fickle, liars, and deceivers), effective politicians must anticipate the consequences of their actions, and must be prepared (in Weber's terms) to endanger the salvation of their souls (Brubaker, 1984, p.126). (One of our contacts, Gary, a senior manager in an Australian factory, observed that, 'they need to get into the mud pit and start wrestling'.)

Men on a mission

In the film *The Mission* (1986, director Roland Joffé), a Jesuit convert tries to convince his priest that he must fight the armed forces that are seeking to take over his mission. When the priest decides not to fight, the convert argues, 'This is the way of the world. You have to fight to save what you believe in'. The priest replies, 'I fear you may be right. But if that is the case, it is not a world I want to live in'.

In *Man on Fire* (2004, director Tony Scott), an ex-drunk bodyguard to a small girl conducts a personal vendetta against her kidnappers, using the brutality, violence and confrontations that 'legitimate' law enforcement officers cannot employ. He succeeds in getting her back, at the cost of his own life. Is this heroism justifiable or irresponsible, successful or tragic?

From this perspective, an effective strategy for addressing organization politics concerns a liberal moral pluralism, and not the one-dimensional stereotype of Machiavellian thuggery. This is the pragmatic situational ethic which Christie and Geiss (1970) found so attractive in their Machiavellians with their elegant political skills and realistic ideas of the 'fair deal'. At a deeper philosophical level, Machiavellian pragmatism inherits the 'brutal honesty' of the Marquis de Sade and Friedrich Nietzsche, without advocating the former's perversion or the latter's obsession with the 'Superman' (Badham, 1986). These three authors shared a commitment to reason and rationality, contrary to what they saw as the humanistic hypocrisy of their respective times. Where others sought to hide the moral problems facing practising politicians, they dared to observe that actors often have no effective moral clothing to guide their use of power. If Machiavellian pragmatism has an additional moral orientation, to accompany a public ethic of responsibility, it is this debunking, an antipathy to complacency, and a commitment to facing up to the often discomforting realities of self and others.

Organizations have multiple and contradictory goals, constituencies, ideologies, and processes, and are thus inherently hypocritical (Brunsson, 2002). Observers from Dalton (1959) to Burns (1961) have noted the dual moral and linguistic codes which managers use. March and Olsen (1983) thus describe the contrast between what they call the public 'rhetoric of administration' and a private, backstage 'rhetoric of realpolitik' (the implications of this dual code for the change agent are discussed further in Chapter 9). In public settings, there is an expectation that motives and decision criteria are articulated in technical terms, assuming shared goals, equity, and rationality. However self-interested one's motives may be, whatever the suspicions of others, and whatever the scepticism surrounding the public performance, the explicit acknowledgement of personal interest and gain can be disastrous. As Argyris (1985) notes in his discussion of defensive routines, such issues are 'undiscussable', and the fact that they are undiscussable is also undiscussable.

In private settings, however, the opposite is often the case. In the informal arenas of corporate gossip, the rhetoric of realpolitik is strong. Who is 'in' and who is 'out'? What are the leaders' career aims, and how are these reflected in the policies and programmes that they are espousing and on which you are required to work? What are your own 'real' interests in undertaking tasks or displaying commitment? To avoid speaking in these terms is to risk ostracism, suspicion, and exclusion from the give and take of informal relationships. As Hochschild (1979) observed, a shared 'ironic distance' from the corporate ethos, duties, and demands can create a deeper level of solidarity than more formal rituals and ideologies. The dividing line between 'public' and 'private' can, however, be a fine one. Drawing on Turner's (1987) notion that every ritual has 'liminal spaces' (i.e. boundaries) within which participants comment on the formal performance, Kunda (1992) observes how managers in the company that he studied developed a fine art of balancing public acknowledgement and private criticism of the company culture at different times during such rituals.

The balancing act, however, is complex and potentially dangerous. To be effective, organization politicians who overlook institutional hypocrisy and the distinction between those twin codes or rhetorics do so at their peril. In some public settings, directly addressing one's own interests, and those of others, may be significant in overcoming distrust, and building collaborative relations. On the other hand, all such actions can be career threatening. 'Calling the game', where established defensive routines prevent effective dialogue and decision making, can be either career enhancing or career threatening, depending on circumstances. Machiavellian pragmatism, considering such actions, is not deceived by formal statements of organizational goals or unilateral commitment to one of the 'dual codes'. It involves adroitly and flexibly moving from one discursive situation to another, and in so doing building a reputation for 'savvy' corporate citizenship. As we have seen, this entails 'brutal honesty' in reading the social dynamics, and also involves adopting a stance and presenting a self that is not solely driven by internal logic and preferences, but also takes into account what is acceptable in that context.

It is no accident, therefore, that Machiavelli devotes considerable discussion to the need for effective politicians to be seen to be ethical, honest, and good. Honesty and ethics are complex issues for Machiavellian pragmatism.

Theory M: Machiavellian politics and human nature

As McGregor (1960) argued in his classic analysis of Theory X and Theory Y, ideas about how to manage are largely a reflection of management views of the nature of those being managed. Does such a management perspective underpin Machiavellian pragmatism? Griffin (1991, p.102) argues for a benign Theory M:

The Theory M manager is not Machiavellian in the popular sense of the word, the evil sense, and he [sic] is certainly never cruel in his actions. Indeed, he is caring and concerned about his employees and uses those Machiavellian principles that are necessary to accomplish the tasks of the organization and assist him in reaching his goals.

While this separates the Theory M manager from Machiavellian thuggery, it does not point us to the key challenges and dilemmas facing a more pragmatic Machiavellian strategy. In order to capture some of the finer points of Theory M, therefore, the appropriate contrast is not with McGregor's categories, but with the classic statements of Thomas Hobbes and Jean Jacques Rousseau – humanity as either essentially self-interested, or cooperative.

Theory H, Theory R, and Theory M

For Hobbes (1651), human beings are primarily self-interested. In the absence of strong, central, coercive state control, unregulated competition and conflict will result, and life becomes 'nasty, brutish and short'. For Rousseau, on the other hand, people have a natural sympathy for their fellow humans, and are as interested in the development of others as they are of themselves. People are selfish and competitive as a consequence of badly designed social arrangements, leading Rousseau (1762, p.49) to observe that, 'Man was born free, and he is everywhere in chains'. Applying a Hobbesian perspective, the effective Theory H manager would enforce tight controls over self-interested and disruptive employees. In contrast, the effective Theory R manager would seek to facilitate and support the collaborative development of employees.

For Machiavelli, however, both of these perspectives are naive and simplistic. People are not simply either, on the one hand, externally motivated, short term focused and self-interested or, on the other hand, internally motivated, developmentally oriented, and cooperative. The Theory M view of human nature is one of a more fickle, changeable, and contradictory character. At times, Machiavelli appears to present a view that is similar to Theory H, viewing people as ungrateful, cowardly, greedy, and false. In this light, as he argued, if one relies on being 'loved', people will abandon you when it is to their advantage. In contrast, if one is feared, they will always keep this fear in mind. This argument implies a need for a strong and coercive Hobbesian leader.

Machiavelli does not, however, provide us with a simple Theory H. He argues that people are both 'man' [sic] and 'beast': that they may be inspired to be selfless, cooperative and virtuous or, if scared or left to their own devices, to be petty, narrow minded, self-centred and vindictive. One is reminded of Sam Goldwyn's cynical remark about American cinema-goers, 'No-one ever went broke underestimating the intelligence of the American public'. In this context, leaders should seek to retain and develop loyalty whenever possible, for to do so increases stability and the amenability of the population. Leaders should avoid acts that unnecessarily deprive people of their basic conditions of life or leave them in a state of fear and insecurity, for to do so would stimulate a dangerous level of hatred. Leaders should strive to be loved, but should not naively rely on this.

Machiavellian intelligence

Recent discussion in evolutionary biology concerning the development of the brain have added an interesting twist to classic philosophical discussions of our human 'state of nature'. Traditionally, the development of the human brain was attributed to the use of tools. The more recent 'social intelligence' hypothesis relates that development to the need to handle complex and nuanced social relationships. Byrne and Whiten (1988) and Byrne (1996) explicitly link this to the ability of our ancestors to be underhand and guileful enough to further their own interests without getting kicked out of the tribe; in other words, to handle effectively the inherent tensions between what they term as exploitative and pro-social behaviours. It was this 'evolutionary arms race', as individuals had to cooperate with others, yet secure and increase their personal standing and resources, that Byrne and Whitten saw as contributing to rapid increases in intelligence. 'Machiavellian intelligence' is not simply authoritarian or exploitative. As Byrne is reported as stating (Paul, 1999, p.2), 'Machiavelli seems to me to have been a realist, who accepted that self-interest was ultimately what drove people, and emphasized that the best way to achieve one's personal ends was usually through social, cooperative and generous behaviour – provided that the costs are never allowed to outweigh the ultimate benefits to oneself'. Consequently, it is this ability to 'play the game', balancing self-interest and social contribution, that has embedded a 'Machiavellian intelligence' in our genetic profile.

There has been an understandable backlash in biology against this version of the 'selfish gene' argument. This has emphasized the fact that some environmental conditions reward inherently cooperative behaviour. Another problem concerns the lack of precision surrounding the character of such 'intelligence' and its strictly 'Machiavellian' nature. The main debate, however, concerns the relationship between effectiveness and survival, on the one hand, and how well we combine cooperation and self-interest in different contexts on the other.

When love and loyalty clash with individual self-interest, when rumours and gossip undermine a leader's credibility and perceived benevolence, when people's emotions are whipped up by changing fortunes or hostile demagogues, then previous affection and commitment are often not enough to ensure loyalty. At such times, counter-manipulation of people's affections and the use of coercion to threaten or scare are regarded by Machiavelli as situationally appropriate tactics that not only be in a leader's arsenal, but be ones that leaders are prepared to use when conditions require them.

However, in contrast to McGregor (1960), Machiavelli is not concerned with work, or with whether people are inherently lazy and instrumental, or intrinsically creative and industrious. He is concerned instead with political order and security, and with the willingness of others to submit to authority. In this regard, his solution is neither the coercive totalitarian Theory H, nor the participative libertarian Theory R, but a more contingent and situational approach towards an inherently fickle and fluctuating set of moods and motives. Theory M, therefore, is neither a simple positive nor a negative view of human nature, but a more pragmatic and sociological view of how we perceive ourselves differently, and act in different ways as contexts and circumstances change. From the pragmatic point of view, human nature is held to be one of general self interest, although sympathy, benevolence and affection for others can be won or lost. In general, people are seen as relatively content and quiescent if things are going their way, if conditions are stable, a degree of prosperity is present, and they are not subjected to highly objectionable or tyrannical forms of rule. If conditions change, however, they may quickly turn into something else, revealing more selfish, deceitful and vindictive forms of behaviour. While people admire virtues of courage, honesty, honour and generosity in principle, they can betray these in practice. Loyalty and obligation may be relatively natural emotions, particularly after receiving benefits and favours, but these ties can be won or lost, and betrayed when situations alter.

From a sociological perspective, therefore, Machiavelli's situationalism embodies a realistic understanding of the impact of culture and social context on behaviour. An awareness of how people's actions are shaped by group dynamics and social rules, obligations, and expectations, and how these can be manipulated, is central to all influencing strategies.

We do as we have been socialized to do

Cognitive miser theory argues that we perceive our environment selectively, sacrificing accuracy and detail for speed and efficiency (Provis, 2004). We thus use social norms or 'scripts', concerning what we expect people to say and do, to filter our perceptions of social situations. We judge how we and other people ought to act on the basis of these scripts, but they are not unambiguous. Situations are often characterized by different and conflicting 'definitions of the situation' and what is appropriate. Our expectations are often 'primed' by recent experiences, conversations and interpretations, which then lead us to interpret new situations in specific ways. If we accept the notion that people are self-interested, this viewpoint shapes how we deal with others, often stimulating behaviours that in turn confirm our original viewpoint. In other words, the view that people are self-interested becomes a self-fulfilling prophecy. The more 'social' model that emerges from this line of reasoning is more one of frailty than of cynical egoism or self-interest. As evidenced

Continued

in studies of group dynamics, for example, in-group and out-group perspectives begin to form, bolstering our self-esteem by encouraging us to believe that we and our group are better than others. Cialdini (2001) and Cialdini and Sagarin (2005) identify several automatic socialized principles, which can be used as influence mechanisms (as described in Chapter 2). The image that emerges from such analyses of social cognition, and how it is influenced, serves to strengthen the Machiavellian pragmatist's view of human frailty and fickleness more than the Machiavellian thug view of a self-interested and cynical brute.

Behaviour cannot always be predicted confidently from a knowledge of attitudes and beliefs, as many psychological and sociological studies in organizational behaviour have found. We often behave in ways that do not conform to our self-image, to our actual or perceived interests, or to our conscious goals and priorities. As anyone who has ever been caught up in a crowd will recognize, social processes tend often to have a dynamic of their own. An awareness of those dynamics, and of the insidious as well as overt ways in which behaviour can be conditioned, is a component of the Theory M view of human fickleness.

For Berger (1991, p.173), the influence of such social processes opens up the spectre of what he calls 'sociological Machiavellianism': 'Only he who understands the rules of the game is in a position to cheat. The secret of winning is insincerity'. The subtle, and often not so subtle, use of influencing strategies and techniques is the stock-in-trade of sales, marketing and consulting programmes. However, awareness of this phenomenon, and of the manner in which it influences our own actions, does not in itself constitute unethical or immoral behaviour. It is how we come to terms with, justify and address issues of 'manipulation' that determines our ethical position. For adherents to Theory R (and romantic supporters of participatory leadership invoking Theory Y), Theory M appears as a negative view of human behaviour, leading to manipulative, and even authoritarian, forms of leadership. This should not, however, be allowed to cloud our perceptions of organizational realities, and mistakenly lead either to advocacy of a superficially ethically presentable Theory R view of Theory M, or relapse into the one-dimensional Theory H view of Theory M as a crude coercive model of leadership. It is a brutal honesty about the tensions and ambiguities in the human condition, with oneself as well as others, that lies at the foundation of Theory M.

Machiavelli beneath the surface

Early studies of what managers do, on the job, with their time, by Mintzberg (1977) and others (e.g. Stewart, 1963; and Kotter, 1999) did not reveal cool and rational planners basing their decisions on comprehensive and carefully collected information. On the contrary, it seemed that managers were hardly in control of their own work activities,

---

Aggression, manipulation, exploitation

The difference between administrative behaviour in Machiavelli's time and today is largely one of degree. Rules of the game are more complicated and restricted (killing off or putting the opposition on the rack is replaced by discharge, and even this modern 'industrial capital punishment' has become difficult). Behaviour today is smoother, less blatant, more subtle. However feelings, needs for power, and actions to control the behaviour of others follow remarkably similar paths.

A definition of the twentieth-century Machiavellian administrator is one who employs aggressive, manipulative, exploiting, and devious moves in order to achieve personal and organizational objectives. These moves are undertaken according to perceived feasibility with secondary consideration (what is necessary under the circumstances) to the feelings, needs, and/or 'rights' of others. Not that Machiavellianism is 'right' or even particularly 'bright', but it exists in today's leadership and needs to be recognized as such.

Source: from Calhoon, 1969, pp.210–11.

---

never mind the work of others. The picture that emerged was of an occupational group whose members were constantly on the move, bargaining, compromising, gossiping, working on hunches, persuading, and influencing. The view of managers as planners, controllers, and coordinators was replaced by the concept of the Machiavellian 'fixer' (Reed, 1989, p.13). This view of the manager as fixer, however, can be seen to have both surface and deep dimensions, intertwined in ways that are important to an understanding of Machiavellian pragmatism.

On the surface, Machiavellianism is about being an effective individual player in the organization politics game, knowing the rules, having the will and skill to play, winning in the cut and thrust of interest group rivalry. Here is a perspective made potentially more attractive with its focus on how to be a winner, rather than a victim, on the corporate battlefield. However, as we have indicated, this does not necessarily imply Machiavellian thuggery, as the cause may be a desirable one, the methods inclusive, and the politics not an end in itself, but rather a taken-for-granted aspect of organizational life. Butcher and Clarke (2003), for example, define organization politics as 'battles over just causes'.

At a deeper level, however, Machiavellianism concerns looking beyond and behind this 'game'. Where did the rules of the game come from? How is the playing field sloped or skewed? Who wins and who loses from the way in which the game is currently conducted? Why is this game discussed with military metaphors, and what are the implications of so doing? Where am 'I' or 'we' coming from? What leads us to define the territory, the prize, the winners, the losers, and the end zone in a particular way? And most importantly, what do we do with such knowledge? If, as Berger (1991) observes, we need to understand the rules so that we can cheat, does Machiavellian pragmatism involve accepting the roles one is given and playing within the rules, or attempting to cheat by shifting the game, or switching roles (Buchanan and Storey, 1997; see Chapter 8)? It is arguable that effective Machiavellian pragmatism involves understanding, implicitly if not explicitly, these background 'rules of the game': how to work within them, but also how to bend, break or work around them when necessary. We will discuss this issue in relation to two matters: first, the 'dirty hands' problem; and second, the 'skewed playing field' problem.

Dirty tricks, dirty hands, dirty work

The central Machiavellian dilemma is often described as the 'dirty hands' problem (Hampshire, 1989; Provis, 2005; see Chapter 3). To achieve desirable outcomes, it may sometimes be necessary to betray the principles and ethics that underpin the ideal towards which one may be striving. In other words, deceit, violence, treachery, and manipulation may sometimes be required. Faced with this dilemma, how should an ethical individual respond?

Superficially, this is a question of individual morality. The 'good' person may not succumb to the temptation to use lies and coercion, where the 'bad' person does. Consequently, an increasing number of manuals, mostly (but not all) American, offer advice on how to play organization politics in a 'positive' way (Wolfe, 1997; Salmon and Salmon, 1999; Dobson and Dobson, 2001; MacGregor Serven, 2002; Brandon and Seldman, 2004). Here we are warned of the dangers of office gossip, of backstabbing, of ignoring rules, and of indulging in parochial political behaviour. Instead, we are offered guidance on how to create common purpose, to forge productive win–win alliances, and to deal with the backstabbers.

However, Provis (2004, p.102) points out that contrasts between positive, democratic, supportive politics and negative, competitive, backstabbing, 'dirty tricks' politics are oversimplified, partial, and misleading:

> Well, fine, but what tricks are dirty? What is the difference between 'situational manipulation' and 'organizing'. If I report your adverse comments to the boss, is that backstabbing? What if I report threats you have made, threats perhaps against me, as well as others? It is not only with such prima facie questionable tactics like 'attacking or blaming others', 'selective use of information', and the like, that this point arises. [It is possible to regard] 'developing others' and 'training and orienting others' both to be strategies of organizational politics [because] they are the most effective tactics used with subordinates to get them to behave in desired ways.

In addition to such ambiguities, there are embedded tensions and contradictions concerning how to act morally in a world where, as observed earlier in this chapter, 'ends collide'. We can expect conflicts to occur between those who believe that they are pursuing legitimate and desired goals. What if organizational profitability conflicts with the continued employment of loyal employees dedicated to a previous way of working? What if encouraging the development, loyalty, and commitment of staff to the organization imposes unsustainable stresses on their domestic relationships? What if a commitment to open and honest communication demands that known opponents and dissenters are first silenced? Dilemmas such as these are not merely a matter for individual decision, but are socially and systematically constructed. For Machiavelli, the effective pragmatist is well aware of those tensions, and acts accordingly.

Deviant practice and dirty business

In his book, *Dirty Business*, Punch (1996) describes 'deviant' activities that have become informally institutionalized, including bribery, secrecy, deception, falsification, industrial espionage, black markets, intimidation, conspiracy, price-fixing, and the deliberate avoidance of regulation. Other institutionalized practices include:

- *informal rewards* perks, fiddles, discounts, presents
- *work avoidance and manipulation* arriving late, seeking 'cushy numbers'
- *individual and group deviance against the organization* stealing, absenteeism, neglect, sabotage, embezzlement
- *individual and group deviance for the organization* bending rules, avoiding safety regulations
- *organizational deviance for the organization* serious, deliberate and systematic practices designed to undermine internal and external formal regulations.

In the world of 'dirty business', Punch argues 'managers appear as amoral chameleons, buffeted by moral ambiguity and organizational uncertainty. They survive this "messy, not to say dirty" environment by engaging in Machiavellian micro-politics' (Punch, 1996, p.5).

An insight into what this means may be gained by reflecting on the social conditions that underlie the 'dirty hands' problem. Hughes (1958), a member of the Chicago school of sociology, observed how societies characterize and stigmatize 'dirty work'. All societies have beliefs, values, and ideals that celebrate some activities, and denigrate others. Depending on their respective occupations, while some individuals are regarded as attractive, morally upright, and hygienic, others are seen as repellent, reprehensible, and dirty. It is not only that activities that are physically unattractive (various forms of waste disposal, for example) are characterized as 'dirty work'; those who perform such tasks can also be stigmatized as morally degraded, as their work 'runs counter to the more heroic of our moral conceptions' (Hughes, 1958, p.50). In other words, it is a short step from allocating people to 'dirty work' that involves 'dirty methods', to stigmatizing those who carry out such activities as themselves socially deviant outsiders.

Why is 'dirty hands' part of managerial work? Four well-established trends seem to underlie this concern. First, the free market economy has long relied on variants of Adam Smith's (1776) concept of 'the hidden hand of the market' for goods and services. This 'hidden hand' ensures that competitive markets function in the best interests of society as a whole. However, this celebration of the pursuit of self-interest has always been a matter of social concern, leading to various forms of regulation and control. The idea that the unchecked pursuit of self-interest may lead to antisocial practices and consequences is deeply ingrained.

Second, some observers have expressed concern over what Chandler (1993) calls the 'visible hand' of management, exacerbated by the development of large corporations. As managers exert greater control over their environments, and over the lives of their employees, the potential to exploit or abuse that influence also increases. Are managers using their power in a humane and socially responsible manner, or are they abusing their position in a way that sacrifices principles and people to personal whims and self-interest? Third, participation in trade and business, in whatever form, has been regarded by many societies as a 'lower' form of activity, and one that should not distract from 'higher' religious, political, or social enterprise. The notion that a 'means' for existence should become elevated by those involved in it to become the 'end' of that existence is an established and ongoing concern. Fourth, western culture has consistently elevated the intellect over the hand, design over manufacture, invention over implementation. Consequently, design engineers enjoy higher pay and better working conditions than manufacturing engineers, and finance managers tend to have greater power and stronger reputations than human resource managers, for example. For managers, 'getting things done' is typically regarded as a less important and skilful activity, and given less recognition and reward, than 'deciding what to do' in the first place (Pfeffer, 1992a).

In combination, these four sets of cultural conditions, imprecise and over-generalized as they are, reflect the context in which many managers work. There is an attitude, and a degree of concern, that what they are doing is degrading and even dangerous, a stigma surrounding the 'dirty work' that managers may have to do. They are required to operate in a 'lowly' and 'crass' world of material gain, self-interest and authoritarian control, and do everything necessary to 'get things done' and produce the desired economic outcomes. Yet they must not be tainted by such work, or become self-interested and authoritarian in a way that offends social norms, or undermines the economic benefits that are expected from them.

How do managers handle the potential stigma attached to what they do? Do you do whatever it takes? Does it matter if you overstep the mark? Do the ends always justify the means, particularly in complex and ambiguous settings in which different stakeholders have different views of action and outcomes? How do managers cope with these challenges? Van Maanen (1980) and Dick (2005) provide useful insights into coping mechanisms from their studies of the 'dirty work' of police officers. Society, they argue, gives police the right to use violence against the violent, and criminal. However, ambiguity surrounds the question of how much violence is justifiable. Which rules can be set aside in order to achieve desirable outcomes? It is rarely clear, for example, whether the degree of violence employed is justified or not; but the violence that police use remains a matter of social concern. Van Maanen and Dick show how police officers present different narratives and use different 'vocabularies of motives', depending on the audience to which they are speaking. Van Maanen shows how police officers make different presentations to the public, to fellow officers, and to themselves. Dick describes the different accounts that are given 'frontstage' and 'backstage'. The dirty work of violence is often legitimated backstage by denigrating the villains while celebrating the (masculine) heroism of the cop. We will explore in more detail in Chapter 9 how telling a good story and providing a legitimate narrative are part of the 'accounting' skill of the organization politician.

Machiavellian pragmatism requires an understanding of, and skill in, such narrative or accounting practices. Like organization politics, this is unavoidable. Individual managers must grapple with their own sense of self-worth and their personal convictions; the stories that we tell others help us also to explain and justify our behaviour to ourselves. However, to be organizationally effective, the backstage and frontstage stories must be carefully presented. It may on occasion be helpful, for example, for the cop to argue frontstage that the blame for the use of coercive tactics actually lies with the morally retrograde character of the deviant and disruptive criminal, implying that one is truly heroic in one's own skill and will in the application of the necessary 'dirty tactics' (which are as a result socially benign and economically beneficial) to pacify the criminal. In contrast, it may on occasion be appropriate to reveal a greater degree of ambiguity and self-doubt, if not regret, in the canteen, backstage. To achieve the desired effect, the account which one provides, of course, depends on context and audience. It is not difficult to think of circumstances in which it may be more appropriate to use the 'doubt and regret' story in public, and tell the 'heroic victory' story backstage.

This interpretation of Machiavellian pragmatism and ethics is significant for the practising manager as organization politician. The problem cannot be articulated as a simple personal problem of 'morally grappling' with 'dirty tricks'. We must consider instead the intertwined individual and social issues involved in accounting for and legitimating ambiguously defined 'dirty work'. An understanding of these 'rules of the dirt game' is important for effective play, both in terms of personal comfort and career, and also for influencing others.

Skewed playing fields

The 'rules of the dirt game' can be regarded as one expression of the general rules of the political game of which Machiavellian managers are required to be aware. What are taken to be the interests of individuals and groups, determined by career paths, institutional boundaries, and group loyalties, are not just givens that the manager must address, but are outcomes of social and political processes. As Bachrach and Baratz (1970, p.43) observe, in their analysis of the 'mobilization of bias', many institutions possess, 'a set of predominant values, beliefs, rituals and institutional procedures (rules of the game) that operate systematically and consistently to the benefit of certain persons and groups at the expense of others'. Overt conflict, grasping and deploying whatever strategic resources are at your disposal, is only one expression of a Machiavellian strategy. Also significant is the recognition and manipulation of unobtrusive methods and tactics. In other words, if organization politics is a game, the playing field is systematically skewed in favour of some players, and to the disadvantage of others. This feature of the game was explored in Chapter 2 in terms of 'non-decision-making' and 'the mobilization of bias', subtle processes which discourage or prevent less powerful individuals and groups from voicing their concerns and challenges.

Several commentators have explored such covert aspects of power, including Lukes (2006), Hardy (1985; 1996) and Hardy and O'Sullivan (1988). For Hardy (1996) these include:

- the manipulation of organizational *processes*, such that the grievances and concerns of those who are unwanted, undesirable, or simply competing, are never allowed access to policy making or decision making forums or implementation situations;
- the management of *meaning*, as conflict between one's own agenda and that of others is avoided by manipulating perceptions, cognitions, preferences and emotions such that others believe that there is no alternative, or that your initiative is either a desirable or an inconsequential one, and thus beyond dispute; and
- the use of *systemic* power, exploiting the web of relationships and discourses that construct our sense of who we are (perceptions, interests, identities) and the organizational contexts in which we function.

Viewing such facets of power as a series of levels taking us 'deeper' into the workings of power can appear static and artificial (Clegg et al., 2006). For Machiavellian pragmatism, the central issue concerns the complex and multi-layered nature of power as a set of intertwined resources, identities, and relations. The practice of organization politics is thus highly dependent on the situation or context (Fleming and Spicer, 2005). Situational tactics include the prevention or exclusion of 'unwanted' individuals, by withholding information about meeting dates and times; or wording carefully the terms of reference of a committee to exclude discussion of particular topics; or defining how members are to be appointed to a committee to ensure that some individuals cannot be nominated. The rules determining the appointment of a chair, the meeting procedures, and the framing and sequencing of agendas can also be manipulated to achieve similar results.

Runaway Jury

The covert tactics used by specialist consultants who manipulate trial outcomes are shown in the movie *Runaway Jury* (2003, director Gary Fleder). Gene Hackman stars as Rankin Fitch, a ruthless jury consultant who observes that, 'trials are too important to be decided by juries'. The movie is fiction, but it offers a realistic portrayal of current practice. Jury selection has become a professionalized and knowledge intensive issue. The aim, of course, is to select a jury that is predisposed to display a particular bias. Once a trial is under way, each juror's current job, marital status, education, mannerisms, and even their nervous tics, are observed in the courtroom by trained observers, who assess the progress of a trial as it unfolds. Knowing how well, or how badly, a jury has responded to a line of questioning or the presentation of evidence, can result in the use of fresh tactics the following day, to swing their perceptions and the resultant decision back to what the lawyers want.

Covert tactics can also include counter-measures, and challenging decision-making rules, disputing the processes and procedures that prevent one's issues from being considered. For example, meetings can be arranged at times that do not prevent the attendance of working mothers, and the regulations governing consultation procedures can be altered. More threatening tactics include those which rely on 'anticipated reactions', which lead opponents to believe either that raising an issue will be futile, or will result in consequences that are damaging to them. Language, symbols, and rituals can be manipulated such that particular issues are ruled out, while others are ruled in. For example, in an Australian white goods company, the manufacturing manager insisted on labelling a radical reorganization as a minor step in an existing programme, in order to disarm opposition to the change. In a steel company, the loss of jobs due to reorganization was attributed instead to the changes in technology happening around the same time, because the trade union had agreed to technological redundancies (but not to redundancies due to restructuring). Machiavelli would have supported the use of these tactics, in defending management authority and influence, while avoiding the stimulation of hatred and discontent. Machiavelli also pointed to the value of symbolic actions, to direct discontent away from the Prince, and to deny wrongdoing.

It is important to recognize and adapt to the deeper and more complex relations of power in embedded inequalities and organizational controls. As Chapter 2 argued, these embedded properties are less visible, and can thus be more resistant to challenge, and are effective in maintaining power for those who can exploit them to their own desired ends. Clearly, these properties can also be manipulated in ways that enfranchise those who were previously disempowered. However, as Alvesson and Willmott (2002) argue, behind many organization culture change programmes, purported 'empower' employees, lie systematic and intrusive systems of 'identity regulation'. Broad structural inequalities of power and control typically underpin these empowerment initiatives, which can have the appearance of delegating responsibility, without actually giving those involved any additional autonomy or authority to act. In other words, surface initiatives that appear to offer greater freedom, even redistributing resources to that end, may be restricted in their effect by deeper power relations.

The rhetoric of empowerment, legitimated by changing competitive conditions (which demand committed and creative staff), can, however, create opportunities for management and employees to pursue agendas that were previously made problematic by embedded inequalities and practices. A senior human resource manager at an Australian bank, asked about the attitude of the company's board of directors to employee engagement, replied:

> No, it does not mean that they have become more interested in people issues. They remain concerned with the share price, takeovers, and shareholders. But nowadays, stock market analysts are attempting to estimate future as well as current corporate value. And employee engagement levels are taken as a sign of future corporate value, and therefore have an influence on the share price. Directors are concerned with that.

Deeply embedded structural power bases and inequalities may generate significant constraints on attempts to change structural conditions through 'surface' Machiavellian office politics. Yet, once understood, those constraints can at least be considered. The perspective of the Machiavellian pragmatist is to consider the multiple layers and relationships of power in the organization, and establish realistic options. Can objectives be achieved by working within the rules, or do the rules need to be bent or broken in a particular context?

Bringing the user back in

After years of advocating increased attention to the user in information technology (IT) projects, Clegg (1993) identified the profound cultural and structural barriers to achieving this objective. He claimed that he was tired of going to conference after conference where speakers presented new methodologies for improving user involvement in IT development and implementation; companies did not use these techniques, or they didn't work anyway. Clegg argues that these techniques overlooked the social, institutional, and political position of the users of new IT systems; consequently, appeals to rational and human considerations were unlikely to be successful. Communications between system designers and users are problematic in any case, due to the division in the education system between technical subjects and the humanities, to the differential rewards and status flowing to technical disciplines and occupations, and to the power of professional and managerial staff over the users and operators of the technology. Clegg's point is that if we want to shift the balance of concern towards the users of technological innovation, it is necessary to adopt a broader view of the complex webs of organizational power, and to address these.

In a study of an Australian steel mill, we found that users were never given time by engineers to become involved in shaping new technology projects. The presenting problem appeared to be the attitudes of the engineers. However, the capital budgeting cycle was so protracted that, by the time that the engineers were allocated the project funding, they only had a few months in which to spend it, leaving little or no time for staff involvement. The problem thus lay not with attitudes, but with the strategic process of capital funding, which was wrapped up in its own complex web of power relations, which local politics could never influence.

The Machiavellian pragmatist uses a spectrum of tactics, from the use of force, to subtle deception and intrigue. This involves identifying, assessing, and where necessary and possible influencing the rules of the game within which power is being exercised at a particular time, and in a given context. The Machiavellian pragmatist is not merely a ruthless competitor, but a reflective actor, who does not just play *by* the rules, but also plays *with* the rules. In this process, it is essential to understand what these rules are, whether the playing field is skewed against you, and whether it is possible to shift the rules of engagement if necessary. It requires the ability to shift from one organizational terrain, or from one level or set of power relations to another, to diagnose the situation in its particularity, and to create a workable solution. As Gabriel (2002, p.147) observes, citing Sun Tzu, 'The wise general is one who knows under what conditions to use specific instructions and does not seek to repeat a winning formula. When I have won a victory, I do not repeat my tactics, but respond to circumstance in an infinite variety of ways'.

Every manager has to play the turf game in order to get things done; a good player has to be Machiavellian. The effective manager is a pragmatic Machiavellian. However, it is often important to distance oneself from the label and from the stereotyped 'thuggery' commonly associated with it. The truly effective Machiavellian manager, therefore, is one who is not seen to be Machiavellian at all, as we argued in Chapter 1. One of the interesting features of the turf game is that 'it is the game that dares not call its name' (Knights and Murray, 1994). It is often inevitable, and indeed necessary, that the political dimension of one's actions is ignored, overlooked, actively repressed, or explicitly denied. While being involved in what many would take to be the real work of getting a job done – the intrusion of politics, spending time on managing impressions, lobbying for resources, persuading others – many view this as getting in the way. Consequently, when politics involves the use of stigmatised tactics and behaviours such as manipulation and deceit, moral compromise, ruthlessness, or the pursuit of self-interest, then discussion of actual political conditions is driven underground.

As we have seen, however, what is taken to be immoral manipulation, deceit, and self-interest, is context dependent, a matter of interpretation, and a discussion that is itself part of the politics game. There is no moral high ground on which to stand that is above politics, although we may want to stake our claim to such a stance. Machiavellian pragmatism involves recognition of this conclusion, challenging the hypocrisy of those who claim (or believe) themselves to be high-minded moralists, but who compete in the moral marketplace in a manner that is authoritarian, inflexible and unreflexive.

In this chapter, we have distinguished between the popular stereotype of ruthless Machiavellian thuggery, and Machiavellian pragmatism, which is probably closer to Machiavelli's own position. In practice, this distinction is less clearly drawn, and is open to challenge. For example, the accusation of thuggery is one that many would want to apply to others, because they dislike their actions, personality, and ethics. In other words, it is not just a label, but a politically motivated accusation, and one which we would doubtless ourselves wish to escape. Some would seek to apply such a label to the pragmatic Machiavellian use of deceit, manipulation and force, even when viewed as a necessary, rather than as a preferred (or only), strategy. However, it is our argument that the manager who is unable, or unwilling, to adopt such a contextual approach (and the challenges that it presents) is less likely to succeed as a manager, and will almost certainly fail as a change agent.

This argument does not mean that being Machiavellian carries no penalties. On the contrary, as Chapter 7 demonstrates, focusing energy and attention on 'winning' comes at a cost. Effectiveness is not the only moral standard, or the only meaningful personal quest. But contemporary trends appear to support, if not further encourage, Machiavellian behaviour (see Chapter 9). In this context, and in recognition of these costs, how far should a political entrepreneur adopting a pragmatic Machiavellian strategy be prepared to go?

Follow through

Organization politics at the movies: *Thank You For Smoking*

'Colonel Sanders of Nicotine' or 'Nice Guy'?

'I don't have an MD or law degree. I have a Bachelor in kicking butt and taking names. Michael Jordan plays ball. Charles Manson kills people. I talk. Everyone has a talent.'

In *Thank You For Smoking* (2005, director Jason Reitman), Nick Naylor (played by Aaron Eckhart) is head of the Academy for Tobacco Studies, an organization funded by cigarette companies to conduct research on the alleged links between smoking and health. As Nick explains, the tobacco companies have a team defending their interests; scientists to disprove the links to cancer and other diseases, lawyers to initiate and defend lawsuits, and those in charge of 'spin control' (including himself). The movie provides us with a clever and at times uncomfortably 'balanced' portrait of a manipulative player of corporate games, diabolical but charming. Is he a cold-hearted exploiter to be pitied or despised, or an energetic and fun realist who is also attractive and creative?

An unscrupulous reporter and girlfriend labels Nick 'the yuppie Mephistopheles' (fiendish, a devil). In what ways does Nick demonstrate the ethics, tactics, and skills of the Machiavellian pragmatist?

But I'm not after you, I'm after them

What rhetorical techniques does Nick use to undermine the credibility of his opponents and bolster his own reputation? In particular, how does he point out and use the moral hypocrisy of others and make his own 'brutal honesty' appear attractive? These tactics appear in the following DVD tracks:

Track 2: 'Meet Nick Naylor' (on the *Joan London Show* and at his son's school).
Track 5: 'Poison Challenge' (TV show on new cigarette hearings).
Track 10: 'Moral Flexibility' (Hollywood producer Geoff and talk with son Joey).
Track 11: 'The Original Marlboro Man'.
Track 18: 'The Sultan of Spin' (at the Senate Committee Hearing).

The yuppie Nuremberg defence; just obeying orders

In addition to voiceovers at the beginning and end of the movie, there are various points at which Nick explains why he does what he does, particularly in:

Track 6: 'The Captain'.
Track 8: 'Where the Devil Sleeps'.
Track 11: 'The Original Marlboro Man'.

How does Nick use openness about technical, financial, and egotistic motives as part of effective persuasion and influence?

You seem like a nice guy

The movie attempts to strike an ironic balance between the attractive and unattractive sides of Nick's character. Do we 'read' these attractive qualities from his actions, from the weaknesses of his opponents, from the voiceover narratives, or from the attitude of attractive and 'moral' others towards him? How does the movie's director manipulate these readings, and how are such readings manipulated in organizations with which you are familiar?

You really gave it to them

Appearing on the *Joan London Show*, Nick has the odds stacked against him. In terms of an established 'game' in a particular 'theatre', dealing with corporate engendered health hazards on a television programme, Nick is at a severe disadvantage, yet manages to turn the tables. How has he diagnosed this situation, and what is he able to achieve? What tactics does he use, and what personal skills and qualities are required in order to apply those effectively?

The Merchants of Death ('the MOD Squad')

What role does the MOD Squad play in helping Nick to cope with the stigma and criticism that he gets from his job? In what ways is the MOD Squad presented as an attractive group, and how does this affect our perceptions of Nick's personality and actions? In what ways do the MOD Squad provide different accounts of their activities to each other and to the public? How does Nick separate and intertwine his private and public accounts to gain legitimacy in public forums?

The Washington Post reporter

In what ways does Nick continue with or stop his pragmatic Machiavellianism in his relations with the reporter, and in his private and public responses to being exposed?

A tale of two bank(er)s

Tale 1: The Bank

> 'At the end of the day it is really quite simple. I just hate banks.'

In the Australian movie *The Bank* (2001, director Robert Connolly), the self-proclaimed macho and sexist 'Princes' of the banking industry come up against a motivated and scheming opponent. The opposition takes the form of the brilliant mathematician Jim Doyle (played by David Wenham) who claims he can make them a fortune through his computer modelling of chaotic market dynamics. In reality, however, he is concerned with revenge for his father's suicide, brought about by the bank foreclosing on his property.

In the course of pursuing his agenda, Jim Doyle distrusts and deceives his girlfriend and systematically lies and deceives senior management at the bank. He is also ready, as a test of his loyalty, to lie in court for the bank to destroy a case made against them by a mother and father who had lost all their money and their son as a result of the bank's incompetence and ruthlessness. 'Whatever it takes' is his response to the bank's chief executive Simon O'Reilly (played by Anthony Lapaglia) when offered the challenge. In the end, he succeeds in his goal to use the greed and corruptibility of the chief executive to bankrupt the bank. He asks his girlfriend Michelle Roberts (played by Sibylla Budd), who is also strongly critical of banks and unpragmatically outspoken in her political views, to join him in fleeing the country. She refuses, shocked at his ruthlessness in pursuing his agenda.

The corporate 'Princes' and the anti-corporate 'contender' are both ready to lie, deceive and act outside the bounds of legality and conventional morality in order to achieve their aims. The chief executive legitimates what he does in terms of 'winning' the game, overcoming 'weakness', and serving the 'society' for which he is responsible, including the shareholders. The contender is seeking revenge for what the bank did to his father, but also because he 'hates banks'. He also recompenses the father and mother that he lied to in court by transferring a vast amount of money to their bank account. The contempt that his girlfriend has for him, in both his early apparent role as a lackey of the bank and his later role as a ruthless 'guerrilla', brings his morality sharply into focus.

Tale 2: Jane, a senior female banker's career reflections

'Women often leave large organizations because they don't like the politics. Those who stay are more authentic. Men are more covert.'

Jane stated at the outset of her talk about her banking career that there were only two types of leaders: 'dreammakers' or 'dreambreakers'. The dreambreakers are those who say things won't work, won't listen to you, and put up barriers. The dreammakers work with their people, and coach them into becoming leaders in their own right rather than followers. They often have strong personal values and high integrity. They are ready to make mistakes; in fact, if they are not making mistakes, they feel they are not striving, but are ready to admit to them and, most importantly, to say they are sorry.

Jane observed that many women hide their light under a bushel. Reflecting on her first job, she said she nearly didn't get it, because she didn't push herself forward. In the end, she overcame this, and let her superiors know why she was being reserved. It was her big break.

As her career went from strength to strength, she emphasized the importance of internal and external networks, the contacts and resources she required. All of this came at the cost of her personal time. There is, as she said, a 'price for success', and we need to carefully balance the 'prize' and the 'price'. She emphasized that in doing so, one should not try to emulate others, for that would be too stressful; recognize and play to your own strengths. Also, she stressed the importance of hiring and mentoring a set of divergent and diverse thinkers to work with you. Another emphasis was the importance of leaders staying close to the customers and the front line; communication here is crucial to your success and development. Leaders are often insulated from the consequences of their actions, and good news is passed on up but bad news doesn't get there, so it is important to create good lines of communication.

Later on in her career Jane was offered a number of unfavourable job opportunities, offers she had to handle. The first one she negotiated was a six-month trial that allowed her to return quickly. The second was a difficult and challenging job that took her away from her partner and friends. She accepted this role, but negotiated favourable living and education deals (a three-month advanced programme at an American business school), and a return to head office in three years. The job was stressful. Working six days a week and for long hours, running a 'war room' with her colleagues, meant little personal free time. It is important, she emphasized, to keep a personal life, and to keep fit.

Her reflections on this career led her to emphasize the importance of balance, on a number of different dimensions. Examining and balancing the 'prize' and the 'price' of job decisions, balancing short term bottom line market considerations with longer term strategic goals, balancing commercial and compliance considerations, and analysis and intuition. Most organizations, and managers, she believes 'over-analyse', where gut feel is important.

She drew out a number of principles from her experience:

- Don't hide your light.
- Seize opportunities.
- Get noticed by decision makers, and this often involves extra work.
- Take risks but stick to personal values.
- Office politics; go over, under and around it, and understand the dominant coalition and informal networks.
- Don't become too obsessed with minor issues.
- Achieve an optimal level of chaos; you need to juggle given the pace of change.
- Value family and personal life, and keep friendships and create passions outside work.
- Business is the survival of the fittest, so go to the gym, practice your table conversation and manners, and go to the bookshop not just the business magazines.
- Recognize the importance of one-on-one conversations.
- You will never be successful if you don't have enthusiasm, energy and have fun.

In discussing politics and decision making, Jane said how much she had liked the second stressful job opportunity, where the catastrophe was so significant that there was no play of 'office politics' because of the imperative for survival. She also emphasized that her framework for decision making was: is it legal?; is it fair?; and is it moral? – applying the test of, 'if this were made public in the business press, and your family read about it, how would you feel?' She stressed repeatedly that the key roles of leadership were in mentoring and coaching others, attracting and developing energetic and enterprising people (and, for her, placing a priority on women). She kept returning to her own values of integrity, and owning up to making mistakes.

Discussion questions

These two tales provide us with four major characters. The two men are the ruthless banking Prince, Simon, and the anti-bank guerrilla, Jim. The two women are the morally outraged Michelle, and successful banker, Jane. The following questions can be put to all of these characters, and comparisons can be made within this group.

- How would you classify their approaches to organization politics? Do they represent different types of Machiavellian or anti-Machiavellian political styles?
- Which political style do you believe is (a) the most effective, and (b) most ethical to adopt for those working in the banking sector? Are there any tensions between what you see to be effective and what is ethical?
- How valuable do you find Jane's decision making guide, 'is it legal?; is it fair?; and is it moral?', as a way of dealing with managerial 'dirty work', in banks or elsewhere? If you apply this test to controversial decisions that you have made, how do those decisions stand up? What decision guidelines or test do you use?
- After reading Chapter 5, *Women behaving badly*, to what extent do you see the contrasting political styles between the two men, Simon and Jim, and the two women, Michelle and Jane, as symptomatic of general sexual stereotypes? Do you see Jane effectively deploying the political skills at which women tend to be better? Does this provide a role model for men?

5   Women behaving badly

Chapter objectives

1 To explore the nature and degree of gender differences in perceptions, use, and impact of organization politics.
2 To consider the practical implications for women in change agency roles.

"That's an excellent suggestion, Miss Triggs. Perhaps one of the men here would like to make it."

It is different for women

In her autobiography, reporting instances of humiliating sexual discrimination, harassment, and abuse from senior male management colleagues, Carly Fiorina (2006, p.70) concludes that, 'Life isn't always fair, and it is different for women than for men'. Anyone who believes that sex–role stereotyping, the systematic underestimation of women, and the resultant hostility are not part of the routine experience of senior female managers in large corporations may find Fiorina's account unsettling. There is little reason to suspect that her experience is idiosyncratic. On the contrary, the evidence suggests that such behaviour is widespread. Women are as likely as men to be exposed to organization politics, raising questions concerning whether women perceive, use, and are affected differently by such behaviour.

One feature of the commentary on the nature and use of power and political tactics is that much of it has been male dominated, or gender blind. This is especially noticeable in work on Machiavellianism and related themes, using perspectives and language that are today seen as biased and politically incorrect. This has created the impression that interest should focus on 'men behaving badly' (Chapter 4). In this chapter, we consider 'women behaving badly'; gender-blind advice on the nature and development of political skill, relevant to both sexes, is set out in Chapter 8.

The danger in segregating women and men for separate treatment lies with the implication that observed differences in attitudes and behaviours are attributable to sex. Some commentators note, for example, that men are more willing to engage in organization politics than women. Numerous studies suggest that, *on average*, this observation is correct. Nevertheless, many men report that they are uncomfortable playing politics, while many female managers feel that this is a natural component of their role. Numerous factors can explain differences in attitudes and behaviours, including innate personality traits and predispositions, socialization, other experience, and organizational role, as well as gender. However, research indicates that, in general, women and men view and use organization politics in different ways, and with potentially different consequences.

The study reported in Chapter 1 found almost no differences between women and men in their experiences of and attitudes towards organization politics. One contrast of interest concerned the higher proportion of men reporting that they were both prepared to, and had indeed, hurt others in order to achieve personal and organizational goals. The proportion of men answering 'yes' to those questions was around 30 per cent, compared with around 10 per cent of women, reinforcing 'tough and tender' stereotypes. However, a slightly higher proportion of women than men (55 per cent versus 45 per cent) said that their willingness to play organization politics had contributed to their career success. A tickbox questionnaire is not a sensitive measure of complex attitudes, and those results need to be interpreted in that context. Taking those findings at face value, it seems that the differences between the sexes in this domain are real but subtle, and that women are just as likely to experience and to use organization politics as are their male colleagues, if in different ways.

The lack of women in senior management roles is widely recognized (Singh and Vinnicombe, 2005). Oakley (2000) rehearses the reasons; leadership and gender stereotypes, limited access to line management roles in early career, lack of operational and budgetary responsibility, secretive promotion and reward systems, unequal organizational power distribution, power relationships between the sexes, and the 'good old boys network'. Discrimination appears to depend heavily on the durable and global stereotype that associates management with masculinity; 'think manager – think male' (Ryan and Haslam, 2007, p.550). While accepting those constraints, Perrewé and Nelson (2004) also argue that women are more likely to suffer from 'political skill deficiency'. As political competence is more significant in senior ranks, women either struggle in the competition for those roles, or struggle when they get there.

Gender effects: the evidence

Gender differences in the use of political tactics may have causes beyond work, and several commentators suggest that women are socialized to be more passive and accommodating than men. Tannen (1990, 1995) argues that boys and girls acquire different linguistic styles in childhood, with differential effects on working styles and career prospects. Girls learn conversation rituals that focus on rapport, while boys focus on status. Men thus tend to think more in hierarchical terms, and of being 'one up', and are more likely to jockey for position by putting others down, and by appearing confident and knowledgeable. Women are more likely to avoid putting others down, or to use behaviours that are face-saving. Women can also appear to lack self-confidence, according to Tannen, by playing down their certainty and expressing doubt more openly. Women adopting a 'masculine' linguistic style can be regarded as aggressive, and attract criticism accordingly. In negotiations, women are more likely to focus on what is fair, while men concentrate on winning.

Women don't ask

A survey carried out by the retail chain Woolworths over Christmas 2005 revealed that, on average, parents in England spend about £100 more on presents for their sons than for their daughters. When asked to explain, parents said that boys asked for more items, and what they asked for was more expensive. Boys also complained more loudly if they were disappointed. The most expensive toy in the top five best-sellers

---

for girls was the Amazing Amanda doll (£69.99), compared with the boys' Playstation Portable (£179.99).

The unwritten rule that says, 'if you don't ask, you don't get', also seems to apply to adults. Research in America (Babcock and Laschever, 2003) suggests that women after graduating from university are more likely to accept the starting salary that they are offered, while men are more likely to ask for, and to get, more. This may explain why women in Britain are paid 18 per cent less than men (the differential for part-time workers is greater). But does the explanation for inequality also lie with the fact that women tend to leave employment to look after children? Not entirely, because the difference in salary between equally educated men and women is 15 per cent, five years after graduation, long before those women begin to start families (according to Equal Opportunities Commission figures).

Why should women be less demanding? One explanation is that men do not need to feel that they are liked by their colleagues, and are less embarrassed about complaining and asking for more money. Women, in contrast, tend to be more concerned with maintaining relationships, and assume that if they were worth a higher salary, then their boss would pay them more.

Source: based on Webb (2006).

Reviewing the literature on the use of influence tactics, Ferris et al. (2002b, p.101) argue that there is evidence suggesting that men are more likely than women to use aggressive influence tactics, including threats, assertiveness, and drawing on their expertise. Women in contrast are more likely than men to use coalition-forming tactics, presumably through a greater perceived need for social support and a higher level of comfort with working in groups. One study found that men rated female speakers as more trustworthy and influential when they behaved in a tentative manner. However, many other studies have found no differences between the sexes in propensity to use influence tactics. Summarizing the broad findings of the available evidence, Ferris et al. (2002b, p.103) make the following observations:

1 women tend to use fewer influence behaviours than do men
2 those tactics that women use most often tend to be consistent with female stereotypes
3 organizational norms reward those who use traditional 'masculine' influence tactics
4 women who use 'male' tactics may attract organizational rewards (promotion, pay rises), but may get less social support from colleagues.

If there is a political skills deficit, and a higher degree of distaste for political behaviour among women, then these kinds of explanations rely on individual differences, on personality traits. Other commentators have argued that women's access to power and organization politics games is also constrained by structural factors. Kanter (1979), for example, argues that women are rendered 'structurally powerless' in being restricted to routine, low-profile jobs, as well as facing male discrimination in promotion decisions. Arroba and James (1988) also argue that women tend to lack confidence and (perceived) competence in organization politics, as well as finding political activity distasteful. However, they also argue that women have innate attributes that can be exploited to political advantage, including intuition, sensitivity, observation, and a willingness to engage with feelings. Women, they argue, should put aside their distaste for politics. Getting involved in the politics game, they note, is tough, but not getting involved means staying put.

Mann (1995) argues that women are less successful in acquiring organizational power, and that it is easier for men to acquire power. Organizations which encourage long working hours disadvantage women who have family responsibilities. Failure to participate socially (the late evening drinks) can also lead to exclusion. Inadequate child care facilities reduce flexibility for women. Meetings can be scheduled at times inaccessible for women (the early working breakfast), who can also be excluded from informal male meetings in inaccessible locations (golf course, locker room at the gym). Male conversations are often dominated by topics (cars, sport, particular types of jokes) in which women may not share an interest:

> The under-representation of women in top management is due in large part to the fact that they are less likely to acquire power than their male counterparts. This may be the result of the male-dominated culture of organizations that bias power in favour of men. Because they have access to less power, women are less likely to engage in, or make use of, organizational politics, preferring instead to rely on formal means to advance up the executive ladder. This political incompetence can lead to stunted career progression. The implications of this for change lie not only in relying on men to recognize the economic reasons for eliminating sources of power prejudice against women, but in women themselves who, by recognizing the important role of politics within organizations can help to redress the balance (Mann, 1995, p.14).

Mann (1995, p.9) also argues that many women are deterred by the 'politicking and power-mongering' that tends to be an inevitable feature of management life. In this way, Mann argues, women lose out not only through failing to acquire power, but also by denying or ignoring the importance of organization politics. The power imbalance accompanied by this attitude encourages women to adopt what Mann (1995, p.12) calls 'innocent' behaviours:

> The innocent politician is blind to power and organizational issues, placing emphasis on rationality and the formal organization. She sees politics as unpleasant. She assumes that she can mobilize resources through formal channels and believes

that promotion is gained by working hard without the need to influence others. The innocent politician believes that politics simply interfere with the processes of getting the job done.

Our token bimbo

In the 1980s, following a lawsuit, AT&T, the American telecommunications company, signed a 'consent decree' with the federal government which committed the company to hiring and promoting more women. Carly Fiorina describes her first management appointment:

> The district manager, my new boss, knew he was born to lead and seemed unusually proud of his monogram – RWP – which he put on everything. He knew he was about to be promoted at any moment to something much bigger and better. He knew all about the consent decree and why AT&T had to hire women. The numbers had to look good. That was just the way it was.
>
> He decided we should visit customers together so he could introduce his newest sales manager. At our first meeting he opened up by saying: 'I'd like you to meet Carly. She's our token bimbo'. The he laughed and said, 'Actually, she's your new sales manager'. I laughed too, and did my best to dazzle the client with my knowledge of their mission. After the meeting I took my boss aside and said, 'You will never do that to me again'. My anger outweighed my fear of speaking to him like that. He looked me up and down and replied, 'Okay. Sorry. Tell me, were you ever a cheerleader?'

Source: from Fiorina (2006, p.39).

But are women more 'politically innocent' than men? Reinforcing some of the findings reviewed above, Mann cites several studies suggesting that women tend to exhibit 'political *naïveté*'. For example, women appear to be less aware of the importance of organization politics, and prefer formal systems to informal networks and sources of information. Women are also less likely than men to use informal relationships, ties of loyalty, favours granted and owed, and mutual benefit and protection. Men in contrast have been found to be more proactive and successful than women in getting early information about decisions and policy shifts, and men tend to report using a wider informal network of contacts than women.

Singh et al. (2002) report two studies of how women use impression management tactics. One involved a survey of around 260 managers, male and female, and the second was based on interviews with 19 female and 15 male management consultants. Networking, ingratiation tactics, and self-promotion were reportedly used more by men than by women. Women were more likely to present a 'work-focused image' (avoiding family topics in conversations at work), a difference particularly significant among women in senior positions. Differences in the use of impression management tactics were stronger among junior and younger managers, and Singh et al. (2002) predict that young women adopting this approach were more likely to fall behind their male peers in promotion. They observe that female managers who said they used impression management tactics also said that, 'they only started to do so after they noticed men with equivalent experience and qualifications getting more promotions' (p.82). This effect was more pronounced among women over 30 years of age.

Although career planning systems are presented as rational approaches based on skills, knowledge and experience, Singh et al. (2002, p.78) note that, 'Employees accepting this view may however become confused when, having done all that seemed to be required, they do not achieve the anticipated career rewards'. Women seem more likely to believe that 'doing a good job' is enough, and that political tactics should not be required in order to achieve. Despite those apparent gender differences, it was clear from their interview study that women understood as well as men the need to 'read' the organization and to 'play the game' in order to be recognized and to increase their promotion chances. However, while most (not all) men took this for granted, many (not all) women said that they were uncomfortable with having to behave in a self-promoting manner. Men saw networking as a key and necessary activity, for building visibility and reputation. While women expressed the same views, some felt that networking was not a natural female behaviour, recognizing that a failure to network could limit their career progression. In other words, the women in this study understood 'the rules of the game', but some deliberately chose not to play.

Feminists for Machiavelli

I conclude, therefore, that as fortune is changeable whereas men are obstinate in their ways, men prosper so long as fortune and policy are in accord, and when there is a clash they fail. I hold strongly to this: that it is better to be impetuous than circumspect; because fortune is a woman and if she is to be submissive it is necessary to beat and coerce her. Experience shows that she is more often subdued by men who do this than by those who act coldly. Always, being a woman, she favours young men, because they are less circumspect and more ardent, and because they command her with greater audacity. (Machiavelli, 1514, p.133)

Following that famous quote from Chapter XXV of *The Prince*, Machiavelli has traditionally been seen as an arch misogynist. Machiavellian politics is often depicted as a masculine world of combat and domination, contrasted with a feminine world that is more cooperative, nurturing and constructive (Pitkin, 1984). In both of his books, *The Prince* and *The Discourses*, Machiavelli uses the term 'effeminate' as an insult, and on several occasions discusses the problems that women cause in politics. He contrasts Princes as, 'one man effeminate and cowardly, another fierce and courageous' (Machiavelli, 1514, p.91). He then argues that a Prince, 'will be despised if he has a reputation for being fickle, frivolous, effeminate, cowardly, irresolute; a Prince should avoid this like the plague and strive to demonstrate in his actions grandeur, courage, sobriety, strength' (Machiavelli, 1514, p.102). The titles of two of his chapters in *The Discourses* have failed to endear him to feminist writers: 'How a state is ruined because of women', and 'The reason why the French have been, and still are, considered braver than men at the outset of a battle, and less than women afterward' (Chapters 26 and 36, in Bondanella and Musa, 1979, pp.402 and 408).

More recently, however, a more nuanced account of Machiavelli's views on women has emerged. Drawing on Machiavelli's plays *Le Mandragola* and *Clizia*, Falco (2004) notes that he presents powerful female role models, who operate effectively 'behind the scenes'. Machiavelli also praises the 'feminine' values of prudence, and service to the greater good. He was not a sixteenth-century protofeminist, but his more subtle and complex views on women and politics have been overlooked.

A similar argument may apply to realist views of politics which claim that, in order to attain what one might regard as a noble cause, there is a need for ruthlessness, manipulation, and deceit. If one adopts a stereotyped view of femininity as cooperative, open, and caring, then this appears to be a non-female or even anti-female code of conduct. However, an alternative picture emerges if one focuses on the practical responsibility of such an ethic, the challenge of dealing with the difficult decisions involved in protecting a precious public good, the value of the cunning use of persuasion, influence, and generosity – contrasted with a one-dimensional domineering political style. Recognizing these tensions and trade-offs, Machiavellian politics can be seen as honest and sincere attempts to wrestle with the intellectual paradoxes and moral dilemmas raised by practical problems. To this end, as Falco (2004, p.28) observes, Machiavelli leaves us with thoughts, 'that are not only chilling and depressing in their pessimism about human nature, but also optimistic and inspiring in their ultimate unwillingness to yield totally to the consequences of this condition'.

Source: based on Falco (2004) and Pitkin (1984).

Observing that, 'the millennium of equal access to leadership roles has not yet arrived', Eagly (2005) argues that women still confront the 'take charge, dominant male' stereotype of leadership. Women adopting that approach, she claims, prompt others to ask, 'should a woman behave like that?' (aggressive, assertive, competitive, clear, intense).

Those values and behaviours are reserved for men, and 'tough female managers are often labelled with epithets such as *battle axe*, *dragon lady*, *bitch*, and *bully broad*':

> If a leadership role requires highly authoritative or competitive behaviour that is perceived as masculine, the mere fact that a woman occupies the role can yield disapproval.... The more confidently a woman conveys these values, the less effective she may become because of her challenge to traditional gender norms and her overturning of the expected gender hierarchy (Eagly, 2005, p.464).

Women who moderate their display of femininity, and who model confident, authoritative masculine behaviours, are thus more likely to feel that they are inauthentic, unnatural, and play-acting. They are also more likely to meet with disapproval from others for failing to conform to expectations concerning appropriate female behaviour, and can also be seen as unacceptably pushy (Ryan and Haslam, 2007).

It is helpful in this discussion to distinguish between commentary that *describes* gender differences, and *explanations* for those differences. As we have seen, explanations have been primarily based on individual differences (inherited personality), on socialization (upbringing and cultural norms), and on structural factors (systematic barriers preventing women from accumulating power). Another line of explanation lies with gender differences in perceptions of ethics. Gilligan (1982) argues that women are more predisposed than men to view certain organizational behaviours as unethical. However, Harris (1990) reports similarities between male and female ethical values, and attributes this to occupational socialization. The research findings reported in Chapter 1 identified no significant gender differences in this regard.

The evidence is summarized in Table 5.1, which contrasts female and male stereotypes concerning attitudes towards organization politics. This appears to confirm the cliché that 'men are bad but bold and women are wonderful but weak' (Glick et al., 2004). These contrasts must be treated with caution, as broad patterns, as predispositions, or as general tendencies. Although based on research evidence, it is necessary to take into account the social desirability bias in measures of political behaviour. As some political tactics may be regarded as reprehensible, according to gendered norms, women might be less prepared to admit to using such behaviours, even though they do. And as noted above, we know many women who are skilled organization politicians, and we often meet men for whom political behaviour is abhorrent. Differences between the sexes must not be confused with individual differences, and we must recognize the danger that presenting these differences in this way may simply reinforce inaccurate or over-generalized stereotypes.

Cliffs, ceilings, and seasoning

Commentary on senior managers and top leaders traditionally assumed that leaders were men. Most of the research has thus been conducted by men whose subjects

Table 5.1   Gender stereotypes in approach to organization politics

wonderful but weak female stereotype	bad but bold male stereotype
socialized to be passive and accommodating	socialized to be proactive and competitive
politically innocent, naive	politically aware, skilled
emphasize rapport; 'we'	emphasize status; 'me'
strive for equity	seek to win
want to be liked	want to be one up
are less prepared to hurt others	are more prepared to hurt others
organizational power is difficult to acquire	organizational power is readily acquired
freely express doubt and uncertainty	freely express confidence and certainty
use passive or 'soft' influence tactics such as coalition forming	use aggressive or 'hard' influence tactics such as threats and assertiveness
use fewer influence tactics	use a wide range of influence tactics
use fewer impression management tactics	use many impression management tactics
use formal systems to get information	use informal systems to get information
narrow network of friends and colleagues	wide network of friends and colleagues
political behaviour is unnecessary	political behaviour is necessary
political behaviour is distasteful	political behaviour is routine
career depends on doing a good job	career depends on self-promotion
uncomfortable with self-promoting behaviour	self-promotion taken for granted
politics interferes with the job	politics necessary to get the job done

were men. Not only have women been poorly represented in management roles, but women were also largely ignored in leadership and change management research until the 1990s. Wilson (2002) argues that we are now witnessing a 'feminization of management', as flatter structures require skills and qualities often associated with women, such as communication, collaboration, consensus decision making, teamwork, networking, and developing others. The degree of feminization can be measured, as in America where all of the Fortune 100 (i.e., largest) companies have female board members in executive roles. In Britain, 78 of the top 100 companies have women on their boards, but in only 11 of those companies do women have executive roles (Singh and Vinnicombe, 2005). The feminization process appears to be in its early stages in Britain, and the evidence suggests that this process creates other problems for women.

Rees (2004) identifies three categories of women in management roles:

- *corporate high-flyers* motivated by influence and power, have pursued management careers and achieved senior roles to 'break the glass ceiling', and serve as role models for other women seeking similar career profiles.

If you don't play, you can't win

What are the implications for women seeking to develop and to use political skill to pursue a combination of personal career and organizational objectives?

Mann (1995) argues that many women, to their cost, fail to recognize the significance of political competence, and deny its value and relevance. The resulting 'innocent' behaviour can simply be read as political naïveté. The problem is that 'passive strategies' are not as effective as self-promotion in terms of career progression. She therefore advocates assertiveness training to overcome negative socialization with respect to political behaviour, and the careful planning of image or impression management, in terms of dress and actions; 'It is possible to be a woman and to mean business' (Mann, 1995, p.13). The development and infiltration of informal networks (including male networks) is another useful strategy.

To address the political skills deficit, Perrewé and Nelson (2004) advocate for aspiring female senior managers a combination of mentoring and executive coaching. Mentors, they suggest, can offer advice, open up access to new networks, influence promotion decisions, and 'run interference' to help their apprentices overcome obstacles. These relationships can be mutually beneficial as both parties increase their visibility and reputations. They note, however, that the literature on corporate mentoring rarely mentions the development of political skill. At senior levels, as political skills become more important, executive coaching by external and internal consultants and advisers may be particularly valuable. In these settings, political skill is often a key focus, and individually tailored executive coaching can be a valuable approach. The main point is that, while the acquisition and use of political skill may be related to personality, and perhaps also gender, we are dealing with approaches, behaviours, tactics, methods that are relatively well-understood and which can be learned and developed with appropriate training and experience.

Supporting the use of mentoring, in an 'executive commentary' on Mainiero (1994b, p.65), Addie Perkins Williamson comments that, 'One challenge many women face is spending sufficient time with their mentor yet making sure the mentor relationship is not misinterpreted as something more intimate'. She continues: 'It is also critical for women [in senior executive positions] to ask for and receive "no quarter". In other words don't expect any breaks. The competition is fierce at this level and no excuses are acceptable.... Most men sincerely feel that they are making tremendous sacrifices to get to the top and bitterly resent anyone, particularly a woman, who seems to move ahead as quickly without having to do so.'

In addition to Wilson (2002), whose 'feminization' argument was cited earlier, a number of other commentators have predicted that women will increasingly assume more leadership positions because they score higher on transformational leadership attributes involving motivation and support. Men tend to score higher on transactional leadership characteristics with an emphasis on traditional 'command and control'. What do men think of this argument? Hite (2000) advocates a new 'emotional–psychological landscape', based on the familiar argument that it is sexual politics that prevent women reaching senior management positions. Her research shows that male executives often admire female managers for:

- relative indifference to status symbols
- not playing office politics
- innovative ways of thinking
- understanding of service industries
- higher intellectual achievements
- greater productivity
- soft skills such as communication and networking.

However, Hite also claims that women attract male criticism for taking time off work to have children, for not fighting hard enough for power, for not making themselves visible, and for disliking the cut and thrust of the competition that drives organization politics. Singh et al. (2002) suggest that, if women were to copy their male colleagues, they would perhaps consider making more use of impression management tactics such as:

- ingratiation, building your relationships with superiors
- window dressing, displaying your competence
- taking credit for achievements beyond your contribution
- keen, ready and attentive body language
- adopting the style and mannerisms of the next management level up
- the instrumental use of networking, including women's networks
- good organization citizenship behaviour such as conscientiousness and courtesy
- actively repair damage to your image
- volunteer for extra responsibility.

Singh et al. (2002) do not necessarily approve of, or recommend, these tactics. This list is based simply on women's observations of male colleagues' behaviour. For example, women may be more prepared to take credit for their team's success, but only where the credit is shared with team members. These authors avoid the term 'ingratiation' in their recommendations, and suggest that 'building better relationships with superiors' is a better description of appropriate female behaviour. However, this leaves open the question; these tactics work for men, so why should women not use them?

Rubin (1997) in *Princessa: Machiavelli for Women*, argues that women should not rely on 'feminine' tactics such as nurturing, compromise, and negotiation, but should welcome and use conflict to establish their authority and make an impact in pursuit of their goals.

First, playing politics, as we have argued, is a contact sport. It needs a degree of energy, courage and persistence. It also requires creativity, poise and confidence. One does not have to exaggerate the role of the individual to note that the power to get things done is at least in part dependent on the will and skill of individuals and groups to realize what some would characterize as their 'potential' power. In realistic terms, initiative and enterprise *are* significant components of getting things done, and an awareness of the simplicity of overly heroic narratives should not blind us to this fact. Energy and creativity are important elements in the proactive stance of what we call the *political entrepreneur*.

Second, the culture of modernity, at least in its globalized Western form, celebrates individuality, initiative and enterprise. On the one hand, as Bell (1996) and others have pointed out (Gergen, 2000), our individualistic cultures frequently challenge and condemn business and politics for the ways in which they often restrict and distort individual creativity and self-development. On the other hand, they promote the idea that, in the right conditions, individuals and groups can achieve self-expression by aligning themselves with the institutions in which they work. As explored further in Chapter 7, the dominant form in which this occurs in contemporary organizations is what Du Gay (2004) and others (Salaman and Storey, 2006) call the discourse or culture of 'enterprise', the alignment of enterprising individuals with increasingly entrepreneurial organizational cultures and structures.

In such a context, the legitimation of a change initiative has to have at least a component of this individualistic, and frequently entrepreneurial, rhetoric. At an organizational level, it is necessary to 'sell' the positive and dynamic nature of the change. At an individual level, this can be an important source of motivation. A narrative that involves stories of individual and collective heroism provides much needed inspiration and support for people going through the effort and stress of bringing about substantial change. The realistic change agent must recognize, shape, and use such cultural conditions and narratives as support for the changes that they wish to introduce. As Pettigrew (1987) aptly observes, it is at this juncture of legitimacy that issues of organizational culture and politics are most closely intertwined. And as we argued in Chapter 3, the role of accounting in organizational change is a key political skill of change agents.

A difficult line, therefore, has to be taken in examining the contribution of the tradition of entrepreneurial heroism to our understanding of organization politics. On the one hand, the strategies and tactics of its more sophisticated exponents are of interest and value in their own right, and the ethos that they promote is an important component of a discussion of political ethics. To ignore or to underplay the value of this contribution is restrictive and dangerous. On the other hand, the crude contrasts, simplistic understanding of contexts, and crass evangelism of many commentators in this tradition are misleading and off-putting. Their failure to recognize and give voice to the everyday manager's ambivalence towards organization politics and the range of tactics, as outlined in Chapter 1, is unlikely to endear them to managers involved in the turf game.

The way in which we have sought to address this issue is to focus this chapter on capturing some of the central features of this tradition, the 'entrepreneurial agenda'. This consists of the central unifying themes underlying the discourse of advocates of an entrepreneurial approach to politics, from the most reflective and liberal to the most simplistic and evangelical. Similar to the treatment of Machiavellianism in Chapter 4, we focus on the lessons that the creative political entrepreneur can take from this tradition when shorn of the excesses of its more extreme supporters. We leave until the following chapter a more critical discussion of some of the costs and dangers of this stance.

The entrepreneurial agenda

Surviving in the change zoo

Change can be a zoo. That is, leaders might be dancing with grizzly bears that won't let them stop; they can sometimes feel like a canary in a coal mine, sent to sniff out danger even if it expires in the process; and they must be wary of being trampled by a herd of sacred cows.

Source: Kanter (2004) p.328.

Entrepreneurial heroes

In economies, sectors, and organizations that rely on innovation and change, it is not surprising that initiative, enterprise and enterprising individuals are celebrated. Throughout the twentieth century, different groups were given this mantle. In the first half of the century, the dynamism was first vested in entrepreneurial capitalists, subsequently with the new executive managerial class, and then in innovative engineers and technostructures (Berle and Means, 1935; Veblen, 1958; Schumpeter, 1968; Galbraith, 1974). In the last two decades of the century, there was more focus on those staffing organizational 'adhocracies', challenging corporate bureaucracy and making 'giants dance'; these were the change masters, the hero entrepreneurs, the intrapreneurs, the change leaders, the corporate rebels, and the post-entrepreneurial heroes (Pinchot, 1985; Pettigrew, 1987; Kanter, 1989; Nadler et al., 1995; Hamel, 2000). As 'champions of innovation' (Schön, 1963), these hero innovators were expected to work in new lateral forms of organization, lead with vision and commitment rather than by command and control, mobilize the collective intelligence of the workforce (Nonaka and Takeuchi, 1995), and be committed to 'doing things right' rather than 'doing the right things' (Bennis and Nanus, 1985).

In the twenty-first century, the mantle has shifted, albeit not fundamentally. There is greater attention to the politics of networks (Swan and Scarbrough, 2005) and the intertwine power, politics, and innovation. While including insights from numerous explorations of both innovation and office politics, it draws on the way in which these have been integrated in the view of the 'positive politics' of change provided by Kotter and Kanter. Their work provides the most substantial, comprehensive, and contemporary body of applied research on the entrepreneurial dimension of politics and change. The agenda is not restricted to their work, however, as it incorporates how the Schumpeterian imagination has been treated in the most recent analyses of strategic innovation. The agenda items that constitute the focus for this chapter thus include:

- making up the 'power gap'
- overcoming powerlessness
- working the bureaucracy
- playing positive politics
- framebreaker, framemaker.

Agenda items

Making up the power gap

Down in the mud and the blood and the beer

It beat any Indiana Jones movie! It started out with a real nice beginning. Then suddenly we got one disaster after another. The boulder just missed us, and we got the snake in the cockpit of the airplane – that's what it is all about! You've got to be down in the mud and the blood and the beer' (CEO, major American airline, late 1980s).

Source: Nadler (1998, p.72).

In large and complex organizations, whether the innovation appears large or small, incremental or radical, it is nearly always difficult to implement. A good idea is one thing, getting it implemented is another. Kotter (1985) traces the problem to what he describes as the 'power gap', which is a discrepancy between the resources and authority attached to formal positions, and the power needed to obtain cooperation and support from the different groups on which a successful innovation depends. This gap leads to frustration from managers who see superiors, colleagues and subordinates obstructing change. The consequence is that entrepreneurial heroes have to increase and deploy their power.

This becomes particularly important in matrix organization structures, where cross-functional collaboration is necessary, and where managers have to use interpersonal influence rather than direct line authority to win cooperation and support. 'Organizational genius', Kanter (1983, p.216) notes, 'is 10 percent inspiration and 90 percent acquisition – acquisition of power to move beyond a formal job charter and to influence others'. The first step in making up the 'power gap' is being aware of its existence, and the need to understand and manipulate the informal nature of the organization in order to overcome the problems that it creates. This begins with recognizing how much power others exert over you, and the need to address this. It requires a sophisticated knowledge of the working of bureaucracy.

Awareness of the power gap has a number of important enabling implications. It means that, in taking on or preparing for a particular job or position, the political entrepreneur can deliberate on what will, in practice, be required to be successful. This involves considering the form and degree of the power gap, the time and energy required to mobilize the required formal and informal sources of power, and the personal costs and benefits of the identified 'rules of engagement'. On the one hand, this perspective supports a more mature and strategic approach to identifying and creating the conditions necessary to 'get things done'. On the other hand, it provides the basis for personal reflection on one's own interests and capabilities. If 90 per cent of your job is going to be 'playing politics', are you ready to make the necessary commitments? Have you the time, energy, capabilities and interest required to do this? Are you ready to commit to a life of 'zero drag' (Hochschild, 1997, p.233)?

Clearly, tasks, jobs and positions differ in the form and degree of power gap. At a general level, in complex, uncertain and contested situations, the power gap is likely to be more substantial than in simpler and more routine contexts. As one becomes involved in higher level strategic decisions, operating in changing organizational conditions, one can anticipate more substantial, complex and shifting power gaps. However, the diagnosis is rarely a simple one. It is not simply a matter of having a 'power gap checklist' and planning one's career appropriately. What is required will be uncertain, circumstances will alter, initial ideas and hypotheses will need to be revised. An awareness of the power gap is an initial sensitivity to the issues that have to be addressed, but also an ongoing mindfulness of how things change, new contingencies that have to be addressed, and the need to revise one's ideas. The map, in other words, is not the territory.

Overcoming powerlessness

Choice?

'The world is full of choices. But I don't get any!' (Charlie Brown, in *Peanuts*).

In the presence of a 'power gap', managers may feel themselves more or less 'powerless' to get things done. The daily unfulfilled expectations, unintended consequences and frustrations often lead to 'lives of quiet desperation', with managers feeling like they are banging their heads 'against a brick wall'. If this is happening to you, then colleagues are probably experiencing similar symptoms. In the face of opposition to change and innovation, there is a natural tendency to attribute resistance to deliberate obstruction, and to the active pursuit by others of their own agendas, in conflict with yours. At one level, this is an understandable and appropriate acknowledgement of the surface dimension of politics, the cut and thrust of self-interest and organizational turf wars. However, below this lies another reality; the more or less widespread experience of powerlessness.

A key dimension of this phenomenon is captured by Kanter (2006) who points to the generation of powerlessness by the conditions that confront everyone working in bureaucratic organizations. An indication of the conditions that restrict our ability to make up the 'power gap' is shown in Table 6.1.

For many supporters of 'principled leadership', such conditions represent a personal challenge. One of the Covey Institute's prominent commentators on power and politics, Lee (1997, p.37) argues that the danger for individual managers is that in response to such conditions, they fall into a 'spiral of powerlessness'. As a consequence, Kanter argues that it is often not power but 'organizational powerlessness' that corrupts (Kanter, 1997, p.136). Why? Kanter argues that powerful leaders are more likely to delegate, to reward talent, to support their subordinates. Powerlessness, in contrast, 'breeds bossiness',

Table 6.1   Organizational conditions affecting power and powerlessness

Can you identify factors contributing to powerlessness in your organization? How can you generate more power for yourself and others?

rules inherent in the job	few	many
predecessors in the job	few	many
established routines	few	many
task variety	high	low
rewards for reliability/predictability	few	many
rewards for unusual performance/innovation	many	few
flexibility around use of people	high	low
approvals needed for non-routine decisions	few	many
physical location	central	distant
publicity about job activities	high	low
relation of tasks to current problem areas	central	peripheral
focus of tasks in the work unit	inside	outside
interpersonal contact in the job	high	low
contact with senior officials	high	low
participation in programmes, conferences, meetings	high	low
participation in problem-solving task forces	high	low
advancement prospects of subordinates	high	low

Source: based on Kanter (2006).

and creates 'ineffective, desultory management and petty, dictatorial rules-minded managerial styles' (Kanter, 1997, p.135). Powerless managers often use 'oppressive' tactics, hold back colleagues, and punish others with whatever threats they can. This is not simply a consequence of bureaucracy; particular types of powerlessness are experienced by first-line supervisors, staff professionals, and senior executives, as Table 6.2 indicates.

Powerlessness is also generated by the complex web of embedded restrictions on the ability of individuals to pursue and realize goals (Gaventa, 1982; Clegg et al., 2006). The background and experience of many organizational actors often results in numerous forms of self-censorship and personal disempowerment. These range from beliefs, often born of bitter experience, about the inability to alter things (TINA – 'there is no alternative'), to general fear and concern about what will happen if they raise such issues (the 'Problem of Anticipated Consequences'). For those with little experience in successfully bringing about change (whether at school, in their personal lives, or in the organization), a resigned and fatalistic attitude is often a 'rational' response to avoid the pain and discomfort of dashed hopes and aspirations (Willis, 1977). The phenomenon Kanter attributes to bureaucracy in particular may also be rooted in structured inequalities in life experiences, opportunities and expectations both inside and outside the organization.

Table 6.2 Symptoms and sources of powerlessness

position	symptoms	sources
first line supervisors	Close, rules-minded supervision. Tendency to do things oneself, blocking subordinate development and information. Resistant, underproductive subordinates.	Routine, rules-minded jobs with little control over lines of supply. Limited lines of information. Limited advancement or involvement prospects for oneself or for subordinates.
staff professionals	Turf protection, information control. Retreat into professionalism. Conservative resistance to change.	Routine tasks seen by others as peripheral to 'real tasks' of line organization. Blocked careers. Easy replacement by outside experts.
senior executives	Focus on internal cutting, short-term results, punishing. Dictatorial top-down communications. Retreat to comfort of like-minded lieutenants.	Uncontrollable lines of supply because of environmental change. Limited or blocked lines of information from lower levels. Diminished lines of support due to challenges from public and special interest groups.

For those who remain more proactive, there are numerous ways in which they can suffer ongoing frustrations through 'organizational outflanking' (Mann, 1986). This phenomenon refers to the many ways in which those who attempt to put issues and concerns on the organizational agenda are prevented from doing so. Superiors may remain patronizing and aloof, conflicts and problems may be denied, the ability of critics to access resources or to raise and solve problems may be intentionally interfered with, others may be incited against individuals opening up issues, initiatives may be sabotaged, ignorance of the 'rules of the game' of agenda creation may hold people back, isolation can lead to being picked off, and so on. An awareness of these problems, and anticipation of the likely responses flowing from one's actions, can strengthen self-censorship.

Advocates of positive entrepreneurial politics often emphasize the importance of creativity and the exercise of initiative in addressing such challenges. Kotter, for example, stresses the significance of dramatic presentations and appeals to the 'heart of change', and one classic example is 'the glove story' (Kotter and Cohen, 2002).

The Glove Story

An engineer in a large American corporation was concerned that the company purchased a large number of safety gloves from several different suppliers, paying a range of prices for identical items. Despite his efforts to get this addressed, with potential for major cost savings, nobody would listen. After a while, he gained permission to access the boardroom prior to a meeting. He covered the boardroom table with a large pile of the gloves, all tagged with different suppliers, at different costs. He then stood by the table and waited. When the board members came in, they were shocked, but started to check the gloves. 'Is it right that we pay this amount for this glove, and a large amount more for this other glove?' 'Yep', replied the engineer. 'Is there a difference in quality?' 'Nope.' 'Then why do we do this?' The engineer just shrugged. After repeating this conversation with several board members, the board discussed the matter, and asked that the issue be addressed. The problem was solved.

What is Kotter's message? Communication is about grabbing people's attention, addressing emotions, packaging what one wants to say in a dramatic and appealing manner. While 'communication' flows easily off the tongue, effectively getting people's attention requires closer consideration of the 'heart of change'.

Source: based on Kotter and Cohen (2002).

There are many such inspirational stories. One motivational speaker explains how a manager with whom he worked was unable to persuade his manager that he did not have enough operators in his call centre to deal with the volume of business, but got no response. Finally, he went into his manager's office with a jug of water and a glass, put the glass on his manager's desk, poured from the jug until the water overflowed, and then said, 'This is what the conditions are like in my unit'. The motivational speaker commented, laughing, 'When I offered him this advice, I said don't sue me if you get fired.' Luckily, it worked. But the dangers of following such examples are real.

Hiding the hidden

The facilitator in a work redesign team in a large Australian industrial plant noted the conflict and disharmony that was severely disrupting the project. He gave a brief talk on the effects of power and powerlessness, and the role of implicit psychological contracts in affecting people's behaviour and concerns. The team acknowledged what was happening, and decided that they should write down their psychological contracts. One control room operator suggested that people would lie, and that everyone should write down instead what they thought each other's contracts were. The result was that no-one wrote anything, and the work redesign team continued to suffer from severe conflicts, albeit ones that tended to decline in significance over time. What does this say about a change agent's ability to bring such hidden tensions out into the open, and how this can done effectively?

Raising reasonable issues with senior managers, or in forums that appear to be ignoring or repressing them, can be difficult and dangerous. As one manager described, in relation to the 'real turf rules' in his organization, asking for clarity, or challenging one's bosses, can lead to a backlash if they feel threatened. These issues are not just personal but may be embedded in the 'unwritten ground rules' of the organization. Organizations have 'defensive routines' (Argyris, 1990), which are 'undiscussable', and the fact that they are undiscussable is also undiscussable. Getting issues onto the organizational agenda can be complex, frustrating and threatening, as well as challenging and career enhancing. In the face of these conditions, a cycle of powerlessness (beliefs, attitudes, and restricted abilities) is often created.

Overcoming powerlessness

To what extent do you feel powerless to address work or study problems that you face? How much of this is due to individuals or groups actively holding you back? To what degree do you think they are acting from a position of power, or from the kind of powerlessness identified by Kanter? How confident do you feel about being

Continued

able to overcome their opposition and constraints? To what extent is your degree of confidence due to present circumstances, or your past experiences? What can you do about it? If you plan to challenge existing custom or practice, do not neglect the traditional Turkish proverb, 'He who would tell the truth, should have one foot in the stirrup'.

Working the bureaucracy

Organization politics are triggered by a number of factors (see Chapter 8). Internal specialization and diversity creates occupational groups and departments with different skills, goals, values, beliefs and interests. A high level of interdependence means that cooperation is required from many different sources in order to get things done. In a rapidly changing external environment, the ability to obtain the active contribution of those diverse groups is essential for innovation. The entrepreneurial hero has to be able to mobilize and focus these groups to work the bureaucracy.

Why well-meaning efforts are thwarted

[C]hange experts have devised tactics over the years to help managers do a better job on everything from crafting a vision to rewarding employees for productive behaviour. Despite volumes of literature on planned change, legions of consultants, and the best efforts of corporate leaders, organizational change still appears to be a chaotic process. It is frequently mismanaged, beset by unexpected developments, and often largely unfulfilled. We stress the difficulty of change efforts to dispel well-intentioned attempts to portray 'change' as a discrete process, which when followed 'correctly' leads more or less inevitably to the new desired state [because] (1) Change is extraordinarily difficult, and the fact that it occurs successfully at all is something of a miracle. (2) Change is furthered, however, if and when an organization can strike a delicate balance among the key players in the process – change strategists, change implementers and change recipients – each group carries its own assumptions, agendas, and reactions. Unless these are considered both at the outset and during the unfolding of the change process, the most well-meaning efforts will be thwarted.

Source: from Kanter (1989, p.371).

Enterprising players of positive politics must creatively and proactively work in and with the political system of the organization. The successful implementation of major change means overcoming not only powerful vested interests, but also, as we have seen, the powerlessness that seems to impede many initiatives. The exercise of formal authority, successful initiatives to create 'strong cultures', or the pursuit of any other significant innovation, are unlikely to overcome opposition and inertia without active political networking. As Pfeffer (1992a, p.12) observes, 'unless and until we are willing to come to terms with organizational power and influence, and admit that the skills of getting things done are as important as the skills of figuring out what to do, our organizations will fall further and further behind'. This is, 'dancing with dissimilar partners without stepping on anyone's toes' (Kanter, 2003, p.20).

In this enterprise, broad-based relationships need to be established at three levels (Kotter, 1985):

1 managing peers and colleagues from different social backgrounds;
2 understanding and obtaining the support of senior management; and
3 motivating and directing those at lower organizational levels.

In the literature on project management structures, reference is often made to establishing senior level steering committees or stakeholder groups, middle level project or design teams, and lower level problem solving or issue groups (Wellins et al., 1991; Benders et al., 1995). Similarly, in research on change champions, the focus is frequently on top management strategic support and commitment (on 'patriarchs' and 'sponsors'), design and implementation teams or coalitions ('evangelists', 'drivers', 'change agents', 'visible' and 'invisible' project teams), and lower level adopters and resisters ('user champions', 'targets', 'subversives') (Geddes et al., 1990; Beatty and Lee, 1992; Davenport, 1993; Hutton, 1994). Technology management studies focus on global resource networks and local design networks that enrol technical and organizational actors (Clegg, 1989; Law and Callon, 1992).

In three international workshops with socio-technical change agents, it was found that activity at all three levels was crucial to the success of change projects (Badham, 1990). In the classic SAPPHO study of innovation, the presence of a senior level 'business innovator' was found to be the strongest predictor of success (Freeman, 1982). Beatty and Gordon (1991) confirm the importance of high level 'patriarchs' and 'godfathers' to advanced manufacturing technology applications. As the time of senior management is limited, and their change over often rapid, Beatty and Gordon (1991) argue that their main tasks occur at the 'genesis' stages of change. In implementing business process re-engineering, Hammer and Champy (2003, p.111) also stress the role of senior leadership:

Without strong, aggressive, committed and knowledgeable leadership there will be no one to persuade the barons running functional silos within the company to subordinate the interest of their functional areas to those of the processes that cross their boundaries. No one will be able to force changes in compensation and measurement systems, no one will be able to compel the human resources organization to redefine its job rating systems.

Senior managers may continue to play a crucial support role in these areas throughout a change project (Beatty and Gordon, 1991, p.93). Lower level evangelists, 'will need approval, empowerment and active support and often protection from top management to effectively promote [advanced manufacturing technologies] across organizational boundaries. Otherwise they may get bogged down in "turf wars"'. Studies of process re-engineering and total quality management have argued for the role of a senior management 'sponsor', 'someone who has the authority to legitimize the change' (Hutton, 1994, p.3):

> Ultimately it falls to the change leader or sponsor to create and maintain strong commitment and consensus among the executive team members with respect to the need and vision for change and the plans for creating radical improvement in strategic processes. Failure to achieve executive team consensus can prevent a business unit's process innovation efforts from ever getting off the ground, and failure to maintain commitment and consensus will diminish the degree of change that is achievable and delay progress and the realization of benefits (Hutton, 1994, p.181).

Stjernberg and Philips (1993) also emphasize legitimacy in their study of sociotechnical system projects. In their experience, 'resistance may come from superiors and peers as often as from subordinates. Moreover, this kind of resistance is more difficult to challenge and convert into support, since the change agent seldom has access to these external resisters' (Stjernberg and Philips 1993, p.1212). The difficult issue for change agents concerns dealing with attacks from outside their own departments. Middle level champions of organizational change are often at the mercy of such attacks, if a senior management coalition has not given legitimacy to initiatives by treating them as central to strategic goals. This external legitimation is central, as the existing culture is likely to be critical of change, as that is often the object of change.

The importance of middle management change activities is increasingly recognized. A Netherlands study reveals that what defines 'front runner' companies from the 'rest of the pack' is their more frequent use of cross-functional design and operation teams, and the degree to which they effectively delegate design and implementation responsibilities to these teams (Pennings et al., 1994, p.7). In their study of advanced manufacturing technology implementation, Beatty and Gordon (1991, p.86) argue that the roles of middle management change evangelists are more important than the senior 'business innovator' previously identified by the SAPPHO study. This is crucial, they argue, because the main project requirement is typically to 'see it through', sometimes over several years. Given the long, slow process of major change, the importance of a middle management evangelist is thus vital. In addition, multiskilled leaders are required for cross-functional projects, as they have the difficult task of mobilizing the 'visible' project team actively to run the project, and influencing the 'invisible' coalition on whose contribution project success depends (Geddes et al., 1990).

Develop 360-degree relationships

bosses (managing up):

- collect information about strengths, weaknesses, work styles and pressures
- honestly appraise your own skills and motives
- forge a relationship that matches these conditions
- relationships must be maintained by
  keeping your bosses informed; retaining a reputation for dependability and honesty and; using the time and resources of senior management selectively.

peers and colleagues (managing across):

- pay particular attention to good working relations across units or at a distance
- collect (update, monitor) detailed information about often fluid social relations
- understand the interdependent groups whose co-operation or compliance is required
- get to know the parties, their perspectives, and where there are likely to be conflicts
- obtaining the necessary power and influence and be willing to use it and
- plan activities answering such questions such as
  whose co-operation is necessary?; will they resist and why?; how strong are they?; can I reduce or overcome their resistance?

subordinates (managing down):

- account for individuals, their relationships, the social web they create and oocupy
- establish credibility, whatever your rank
- foster positive commitment, and productive conflict-resolution
- recognise their power over you (passive resistance, gossip, rumour etc)

Source: based on Kotter (1985).

Finally, at the level of lower middle management and the shopfloor, 'user champions' are important in training, providing assistance, and winning over 'converts'. For some, this function merges with middle management, as 'process owners' need to be identified that can accept responsibility for the project and act as lower level drivers of change (Davenport, 1993, p.182). This also involves the mobilization of enthusiasm and managing an increasing adopter/user role in change – a necessary transition in the move to self-regulating work structures. Friis (1988), for example, notes that in a number of computer system projects there was a move from a 'traditional user role' (no knowledge of design and computers), to an 'interested user role' (curiosity and interest awakening), to an 'analyzing user role' (wants to participate in analysis and influence change), to 'designing user role' (understands what is going on, builds prototypes, wants last word on potential to computerize), to 'evaluating user role' (considered as systems owner and wants to evaluate, test and modify, with 'experts' assisting). This is a change agency dynamic similar to the 'situational leadership' model of developing work teams (Blanchard and Peale, 1988), as higher level change agents move from a 'traditional analyst expert role' to 'collaborating expert role' to 'teaching and consultative expert role' in the change process. (Role taking and role switching are discussed further in Chapter 8.)

Just get on with the job

Do you just want to get on with the job and not worry about the politics? Does the idea of spending time playing political games and developing relationships seem too difficult and time consuming? Think of two change projects with which you have been involved, including one that went well, and one that went badly. In what ways do you think that the presence or absence of good working relationships at any of the three levels identified here were responsible for (i) how well the projects went, and (ii) how much you got out of them?

With major organizational change, particular sensitivity is needed towards those in different departments whose cooperation is necessary. Ongoing assessment and the development of good working relationships is essential. This requires particular skill and effort given that so many major initiatives involve working with people at a distance, through infrequent contacts, and often in rushed and pressured circumstances. The political entrepreneur may also need to be prepared, when appropriate, to go beyond communication, education and negotiation to include more subtle and forceful methods to overcome resistance. As Kotter (1985) notes, diversity creates a multitude of causes of resistance. It may occur because people have no time or resources, because they are limited in their abilities, because they have different assessments of the help that they are given, because they are unaware of what they need, because they do not trust us, or they are angry with us because they believe we have different interests at stake. The establishment of good working relationships is an essential part of discovering the source of opposition, minimizing it and finding solutions.

Playing positive politics

A dominant theme in the popular literature of office politics is the contrast between 'positive' and 'negative' politics. While recognizing the significance of power and politics, this distinction between productive and pathological forms of political behaviour has a long history (see the discussion in Chapter 2). In the 1970s, McClelland (1970;

1975) introduced the classic distinction between two such faces of power, exercised in pursuit of personal (bad) or institutional (good) ends. However, as with contemporary commentators on positive politics (Peters, Kotter, Kanter) McClelland was critical of what he called the American 'anti-leadership vaccine'. Through fear of the negative aspects of power, he argued, managers were in danger of losing their leadership capacity.

Fairness and honesty

Weldon Parish (writer) Priests shouldn't lie, Giovanni.

Father Giovanni Moretti (priest) There's no lying in poker, only bluffing, and God forgives bluffing.

Source: scene from *The Shadow Dancer* (2005, director Brad Mirman).

In contrast to traditional entrepreneurs, McClelland argued, successful leaders of large corporations are characterized not by a lower but a higher need for power. He called this need 'N-Pow', defined as a concern for influencing people, in contrast to N-Ach, the need for achievement (McClelland and Burnham, 1995, p.126). Leaders in large, complex organizations have to be able to mobilize others to carry out their wishes, rather than do everything themselves. Consequently, managers with high N-Pow tend to be more successful. However, he saw N-Pow as having two faces, one based on domination and the instrumental use of others, one grounded in influencing people to work together towards inspiring goals while treating people as ends in themselves.

The former, a 'personal' view of power, concerns defeating adversaries. The world is seen in terms of dominance and submission, a zero-sum game where 'if I win, you lose'. The imagery is that of the 'law of the jungle' in which the strongest survive by destroying their opponents, and others are treated as pawns in a world of conquest. The alternative 'socialized' face of power is characterized by a concern for group goals, for finding objectives that will inspire, for helping the group to formulate them, for providing members of the group with the means of achieving goals, and for giving group members the feeling of strength and competence that they need to work towards such goals. Group members are not pawns, but feel that they belong. Power is exercised for the benefit of others. Holding power is regarded with ambivalence, accompanied by doubts of personal strength, the realization that victories must be carefully planned in advance, and that every victory means a loss for someone. This is a concern with exercising influence for others, not over them.

Concern for the development of an ethical 'institutional' form of power has been taken up by recent advocates of 'ethical leadership' (Johns, 1995). The cover of *The Power of Ethical Management* (Blanchard and Peale, 1988), for example, exclaims, 'Integrity Pays! You Don't Have to Cheat to Win'. Blanchard and Peale emphasize the '5 Ps' of leadership:

purpose, pride, patience, persistence, and perspective. While emphasizing the 'power' of such leadership, the other 'P' – for politics – is notable by its absence. In the *Seven Habits of Highly Effective People*, Covey (1989) similarly focuses on the personal power of 'ethical' leadership, and it is difficult to challenge the benign nature of the seven habits he identifies:

- be proactive
- begin with the end in mind
- put first things first
- think win–win
- seek first to understand, then to be understood
- synergize and
- sharpen the saw.

Covey contrasts his approach to the manipulative and Machiavellian dimension of the 'personality ethic' promoted in the 1970s, and advocates a return to the principled 'character ethic'. However, looking at these seven habits as techniques, they can as readily be used by individuals or groups to dominate and to control others, as they can for Covey's stated purpose of uplifting and encouraging an alignment between individual and organizational principles. This is not Covey's purpose, and his introduction to 'principle based power' in *Principle Centred Leadership* (Covey, 1990), is further developed in *The Power Principle* where Lee (1997) defines the distinction between negative and positive politics more clearly. Once choice has been reached to use power and to shun powerlessness, Lee identifies three 'paths to power': *coercive* power, *utility* power, and *principle centred* power. Following a coercive path, leaders are obeyed because they can deploy unpleasant sanctions ('hard' or 'soft') for non-compliance. With utility power, compliance is based on exchange, on a trade, on negotiation. With principle centred power, compliance is based on respect for and belief in the leader. Coercive power means doing things *to* others. Utility power means doing things *with* others. Principle centred power means doing things *for* others.

Managing with power

In a study of 50 managers in high and low morale units, McClelland and Burnham (1995) found a higher than average need for power among managers in general, and a particularly high need among managers in the high morale units. Most importantly, however, they found in the high morale units that managers had a greater need for power than a desire to be liked (or N-Aff, the need for affiliation). Comparing 'affiliative' with 'personal power' and 'socialized power' managers, it was the affiliative managers that were least successful in generating high morale. Affiliative managers tended to make exceptions to rules to please people, which often antagonized others, and people did not have a clear sense of purpose or workplace rules. The 'socialized' or 'institutional' managers were the most successful, combining a high need for power with greater self-control and inhibition.

The 'institutional managers' play the influence game in a controlled way. They are empire builders and tend to create high morale as well as expand the organizations they head. They are more organization minded than other managers, they report that they like to work, they are willing to sacrifice some of their own self-interest for the welfare of the organization, and they have a keen sense of justice. It was as if they believed that everyone had to work hard, sacrifice for the organization, and get a just reward for the effort. This motivation cuts across the traditional 'authoritarian–democratic' leadership style framework. However, McClelland's research (1970) revealed that institutional managers made their subordinates feel strong and powerful rather than weak and powerless – the opposite of a traditional authoritarian leader. McClelland and Burnham (1995) also found that a majority of the better managers scored higher on democratic or coaching styles of management in comparison with the poorer performers adopting authoritarian and coercive styles.

This formulation of alternative forms of power continues a tradition started by Etzioni (1961) of distinguishing between the use of coercive, instrumental and normative forms of control. Where this perspective differs, however, is in the universal ethical claims being made for the normative 'principle centred' form. Like Blanchard (Hersey et al., 2007), Etzioni (1961) argues that different types of control have different effects on those being controlled, and that different leadership styles need to be aligned with the capabilities and motivation of the led. Lee (1997), however, dismisses such contingent thinking as it remains grounded in securing employee compliance. He contrasts this with the 'servant leader' (Greenleaf, 1977) model based on mutual trust and respect – in all circumstances.

Lee (1997) uses the following 'nurturing' metaphors to characterize the leadership task:

pathfinding accommodating the legitimate needs of stakeholders by clarifying vision, context, direction, location, goals, strategy, purpose, and pace

team building helping others to work together to create healthy, safe conditions for risk taking, helping others to become leaders, providing resources and being a resource, helping others move from dependence to independence to interdependence, helping others get things done, and getting out of the way

gardening working behind the scenes to create a culture that embodies core principles and values, determining how everyone works together, helping everyone agree on worthwhile purposes, creating enthusiasm and understanding in a critical mass of followers, identifying and removing obstacles, providing support, recognition and reward systems, procuring raw materials, pruning when necessary, planning for harvest.

In this perspective, 'To lead with honour and power challenges the best in us all; there is little room for the small-mindedness of parochial or gender-biased thinking and acting' (Lee, 1997, p.270). For anyone sceptical of such nurturing rhetoric, and in particular the metaphors of gardening and pruning, a recent critique of how one needs to guard against the view of 'human waste' implicit in such perspectives can be found in Bauman (2003).

A more pluralistic and less universally prescriptive view of positive politics is provided by Kanter (1983) and Kotter (1985). For Kotter, political entrepreneurs are involved in:

- creating visionary agendas and resource networks
- collecting and using information – political diagnosis, monitoring relationships, identifying directions of mutual interest
- establishing good working relationships, including different types of relationships with various groups, in the face of difficulties such as separation and time pressures
- building credibility and a reputation that saves time in dealings with colleagues and subordinates.

The picture of politics that Kanter (1983, p.179) gives of an 'integrative' organization in which such politics are played out is a remarkably rosy one, with little consideration given to any of the complexities of situational ethics:

Even though the system in innovating companies is more 'politicized' in one sense – with managers having to capture power that they are not directly given in order to get anything done – it is also more 'civil' at least on the surface. 'Opponents' are won over by persistent, persuasive arguments; open communication is used to resolve debates, not back-stabbing. Perhaps the very publicness and openness of the battlegrounds – if that word even seems appropriate – makes 'reason' prevail. It is hard for back-room bargaining or displays of unilateral power to occur when issues are debated in group settings. Public meetings require that concerns be translated into specific criticisms, each of which can then be countered by data or well-mounted arguments. And the heavy reliance on informal communication networks as a source of reputation places a check on dirty dealing. 'Bad press' would ensure that such a person gets frozen out. An innovating company, then, begins to substitute a control system based on debate among peers for one based on top-down authority.

'Positive' politics, Kanter argues, implies, 'campaigning, lobbying, bargaining, negotiating, caucusing, collaborating, and winning votes. That is, an idea must be sold, resources must be acquired or managed, and some variable numbers of other people must agree to changes in their own areas' (Kanter, 1983a, p.216). One company described it as a process to obtain 'buy in', 'preselling', 'sanity checks', and a log-rolling process of 'tin cupping' (Kanter, 1983a, p.157). This does not, she argues, have to involve domination, cutting others out, or monopolizing resources. Kotter (1985, p.3) also argues that politics in this form defeats the 'pathological aspects of modern organizations: the bureaucratic infighting, parochial politics, destructive power struggles and the like, which regularly reduce initiative, innovation, morale, and excellence in all kinds of organizations' (see Figure 6.1). Backstage politics, in contrast, involves backstabbing

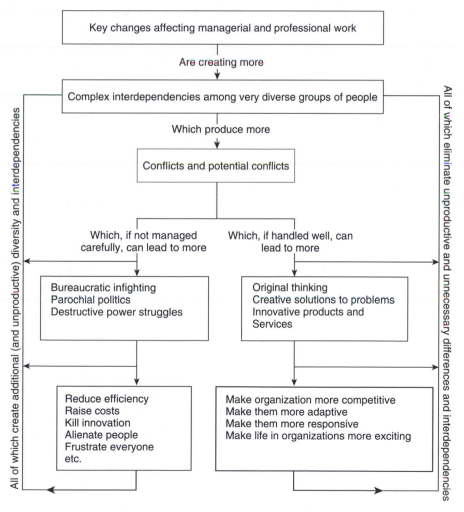

Figure 6.1 The challenge we now face. Reprinted with the permission of The Free Press, a Division of Simon and Schuster, from *Power and Influence: Beyond Formal Authority* by John P. Kotter. Copyright © 1985 by John P. Kotter.

to resolve debates, covert bargaining and displays of unilateral power, dirty dealing, and spreading rumours to destroy reputations. The entrepreneurial player of positive politics does not engage in such tactics.

Kanter and Kotter contrast the pragmatic and principled action orientation of their change masters and leaders with the entrenched ethics of task-focused managers, and the exaggerated and unhealthy optimism of those over-confident of their abilities and success. 'Naive' managers, they observe, assume that people want to cooperate, that unselfish motives are dominant, that people have warm and supportive relationships, and that differences are minimal, and relatively easy to overcome. 'Cynics' assume the inevitability of conflict, that selfish motives are dominant, and that relationships are predominantly adversarial. The problem with both approaches, however, lies in their inability to diagnose different situations. Neither can explain where and when cooperation or conflict will be found, because they always expect either cooperation and harmony, or bureaucratic infighting, respectively. Both positions overlook the array of issues and legitimate constituencies involved in organizational change. By adopting such a simplistic interpretation, these extreme views cannot tailor political solutions to the claims of a variety of stakeholders.

Consequently, Kanter and Kotter recommend a more balanced view. As Kanter observes, identifying 'confidence' lying at the heart of successful change, the confidence that she advocates is not 'over-confidence' but 'the sweet spot between arrogance and despair' (Kanter, 2005, p.13). It is a sweet spot that, as Kotter (1985) emphasizes, often proves to be beyond many people:

> Beyond the yellow brick road of naïveté and the muggers lane of cynicism, there is a narrow path, poorly lit, hard to find, and even harder to stay on once found. People who have the skill and the perseverance to take that path serve us in countless ways. We need more of these people. Many more.

Framebreaker, framemaker

The institutional imperative

In business school I was given no hint of the imperative's existence and I did not intuitively understand it when I entered the business world. I thought then that decent, intelligent, and experienced managers would automatically make rational business decisions. But I learned over time that isn't so. Instead, rationality frequently wilts when the institutional imperative comes into play.

Source: Warren Buffet, 1989, 'Letter to the Shareholders' cited in MacGregor Serven (2002, p.93).

Underlying support for positive politics is a broader entrepreneurial agenda, one that praises initiative, creativity and energy in breaking down established patterns of behaviour and ways of operating to bring about a new, and superior, order of things. Corporate entrepreneurial heroes are the harbingers of new products, processes and associated ways of doing and living. The politics they play in dismantling the old is justified, at least in part, by their claimed achievements in bringing about 'progress'.

One of the most frequent observations made in studies of the history of innovation, is the recurrent fact of such innovations being ignored or rejected by the very individuals, groups and institutions that appear to have most to gain from them. From tales of the machine gun being rejected by the military, to Xerox's invention of and subsequent failure to exploit the personal computer, the tale is repeated, an apparent 'march of folly' (Tuchman, 1990) being the rule rather than the exception. The first major challenge for entrepreneurial innovators is consequently seen as identifying and breaking down the established frames of reference which prevent the serious consideration and introduction of innovations.

Framing

The 'framing' of the world can be understood as selective and preferred ways of looking and understanding that are sometimes conscious and explicitly manipulated, but are also often tacit in nature and embedded in established forms of life. The idea that the world is structured by individuals, groups and institutions through the frames that they possess and deploy spans the disciplines of psychology, linguistics, marketing, social psychology, economics, innovation and business studies. It extends from the ways in which individuals have to select information in making sense of the world and decide how to act within it, through processes by which groups produce, negotiate and reproduce the shared 'definition of the situation' that allows them to cooperate, to the established routines, systems and technologies that define the character of organizational entities and units and systematically exclude alternative ways of operating and viewing the world (Orlikowski and Gash, 1994). In terms of major strategic reorientations, the focus is on the institutionalized paradigms or archetypes that shape fundamental assumptions about the relevant environment, desirable strategic directions, appropriate organizational design, and effective procedures and systems (Tushman and O'Reilly, 1997).

Innovation frames are the embedded assumptions, expectations, and knowledge that individuals have about technology, markets, and their organizational context. They include ideas of best practice, efficient production methods and, most importantly, what are perceived to be novel, feasible and valuable paths of innovation. Frames channel individuals and groups into particular innovation corridors, at the expense of others that are deemed impractical, irrelevant or excessively risky.

The breakdown of established frames is one of the hallmarks of the work of Kurt Lewin, whose contribution to the theory and practice of change management has recently been reappraised (Burnes, 2004). Lewin (1951) famously argued that it was necessary to 'unfreeze' the current situation before change implementation could begin. In classical organization development theory, this involves creating a 'psychological disturbance', through group facilitation and evidence gathering methods which put 'disconfirming' data and viewpoints onto the agenda (Badham et al., 2003). This also involves counselling and support for the painful personal transitions that people experience during organizational change (Bridges, 1991), such that initial responses of anger and denial, and subsequent lack of confidence, do not derail the process.

With regard to strategic change, Kanter (2004) introduces a time dimension to Lewin's 'unfreezing' process. In her analysis of the conditions required for successful corporate turnarounds, she emphasized the self-reproducing character of 'winning' and 'losing' streaks. In the face of organizational decline, the potential for turnarounds is held back, she argues, by deteriorating relationships, disappearing initiative, a culture of secrecy, denial and blame shifting, and scepticism about promises of change. Kanter emphasizes the need for creativity and persistence in navigating through three turnaround stages: first, facing facts and reinforcing responsibility; second, cultivating collaboration; and third, inspiring innovation and confidence (an alternative or supplementary phased approach to change to that of Kotter, 1995; see Chapter 8). While it is difficult to challenge such sensible advice, just how the stages are to be interpreted and sequenced in practice, and the specific actions that may be required, remain a matter for informed local management judgement. Analysts of strategic change are particularly concerned with the extent to which design and implementation should be carefully planned in advance, or allowed to emerge through circumstances and events. Moreover, what should be the balance between the mobilization of force and coercion, and the elicitation of participation and consent (Beer and Nohria, 2000)?

To bring about strategic change, it is often necessary to span two distinct domains, created by the old and the new frames of reference (Badham et al., 2003). The tensions which this can create are described by, for example, Abrahamson (2004) and Klein (2004) who focus on how leaders must be able to operate with 'multiple hats', and 'work the grain against the grain'. Klein sees change leaders working as 'insiders/outsiders', establishing credibility in terms of the old frame, while questioning established perspectives and arguing for their replacement. Abrahamson (2004) argues that change agents are involved in 'creative recombination', rather than the creative destruction identified by Schumpeter, using one element of the established frame against another, drawing on capabilities and successes in one area to challenge lack of capability and success in another.

Tushman and O'Reilly (1997) attribute the rigidity of innovation frames to what they call 'the success syndrome'; organizational size and age create cultural and structural inertia, reinforced by the complacency that comes from success in established markets.

Coercive persuasion and thought reform

As failed attempts at individual and organizational change show, changing attitudes and beliefs is complex and difficult. One of the founders of organization development methods for culture change, Edgar Schein, derived many of his ideas from interviews with American soldiers who had been indoctrinated by their captors during the Korean War. Schein (1961) coined the term 'coercive persuasion' to describe the process of thought reform that they suffered. Is this process similar to the methods that contemporary organizations use to 'rebrand' their cultures, and what political and ethical issues does this raise?

Coercive persuasion begins with the 'unfreezing' of established ideas, an intellectual process Schein describes as 'disconfirmation', creating initial intellectual upset by providing data that contradicts people's hopes or expectations. However, two further elements are necessary to create the initial conditions for change. First, the induction of guilt or survival anxiety. Second, the creation of psychological safety, or overcoming learning anxiety. The individual subject of thought reform must be made to believe that the disconfirming data provide a fundamental challenge to survival, or at least to the continued pursuit of their cherished ideals and ambitions. The anxiety this creates is an essential precondition for change, but may still only result in defensive behaviour. For initial unfreezing to occur, the individual needs to be provided with the psychological safety necessary to support them in the discomforting process of exploring new ways of thinking and behaving.

This unfreezing process provides the initial preconditions for change, but it does not guide the individual through the transition process of moving to a new way of framing the world. For this to occur, they must go through a complex process of what Schein termed 'cognitive re-definition', thinking through what new ideas mean to their traditional beliefs, values and judgements. This is a difficult and challenging task. In the coercive conditions in prison camps, this process is driven by the imitation of, or identification with, authoritarian role models. It is well known that, in such conditions, prisoners often come to imitate their guards, creating a 'negative' form of influential role modelling. The more 'positive' form involves authoritative mentors leading followers through a process of remodelling themselves in their image. An alternative method, and for Schein one that is more desirable and enduring in its influence, is 'scanning', which involves using trial and error learning, combined with deliberate and broad exposure to new ideas.

In order to 'refreeze' the individual's new ideas and behaviours, these must be, or be made to be, congruent with other behaviours, character and social influences. To avoid 'reversion', new forms of positive alignment need to be established.

Source: based on Schein (1996).

This is complemented by the investment of knowledge, skills and resources in 'dominant designs' in products and the processes involved in making them. Christensen (2000; Christensen and Overdorf, 2000) challenges management to explore the potential of 'disruptive' innovations that lie outside their innovation frame. Disruptive innovations concern inventing something new, whereas sustaining innovations merely improve existing systems and products. Sustaining innovations appear to be conservative, routine, mundane. But even incremental technological change can be challenging, involving as it often does the transformation of established mindsets, capabilities, responsibilities, relationships, hierarchies, and reward systems. As one engineer we spoke to commented, 'I had thought I was redesigning machines, but I now realize I was changing their jobs. It is more about people than things'.

A recurring concern in this field concerns how to preserve the organization structures and individual capabilities required to challenge current frames of reference, while exploiting existing capabilities, technologies, and markets (March, 1991). Tushman and O'Reilly (1997) suggest the creation of 'ambidextrous organizations', creating some project structures for incremental innovation and alternatives for breakthrough innovation. Christensen (2000) identifies three ways to institutionalize alternative resources, processes and values, by creating (internal) breakthrough project teams, by developing (external) spin-off organizations, and by buying in the capabilities through acquisition.

A key factor in creating structures and capabilities that challenge current frames concerns 'strategic anticipation' from the top of the organization (Nadler and Tushman, 1989). With the metaphor of 'punctuated equilibrium' to describe phases of relative stability and radical change, they emphasize the need for leaders to anticipate and drive radical innovations by 'bending' frames. The less effective alternative, of course, is to break those frames in reaction to disadvantageous conditions characterized by declining performance. Proactive change requires heroic leaders with the vision, energy, and enabling capabilities to make this happen (Nadler et al., 1995; Nadler, 1998).

In the context of strategic change management, therefore, entrepreneurial innovators have to be able to cope with tension and contradiction. Brown and Eisenhardt (1998) discuss working at 'the edge of chaos', and the need to develop strategies which, when interpreted through the lens of the existing frame, appear to be unpredictable, uncontrolled, and inefficient. Innovators thus have to be proactive, continuous, and diverse in their actions. This requires what Stacey (2007) describes as 'extraordinary management', or an ability to act in situations high in conflict and uncertainty. The heroic image arising from this discussion is the entrepreneurial leader as creative risk taker, able to challenge authority, and cope with uncertainty and contradiction. While respecting traditional ways of doing things, champions of innovation must also challenge those traditions. The entrepreneurial player of positive politics, consequently, has to work within as well as against the organization. This is less the bureaucracy-busting champion, with a secure vision of a new order, and more a flexible chameleon, who plays and challenges an unstable corporate game.

Studies of the processes through which innovations are diffused reinforce this image of the creative and flexible entrepreneur coping with uncertainty at the edge of chaos. For example, Rogers (1995) draws attention to the complex social and political processes involved in driving an innovation through the development, adoption, and implementation stages. Van de Ven et al. (1999) portray 'the innovation journey' as an untidy, iterative one driven by a fluid cast of characters who engage and disengage with the process over time, in contrast to the traditional rational–linear model of project management. Innovations frequently meet with resistance, and recent studies confirm the challenge of implementation, emphasizing the role of 'configurational intrapreneurs' (McLoughlin et al., 2000; Badham et al., 2003; McLoughlin and Badham, 2005). This is a messy process that often requires 'reinvention' (Rogers, 1995), 'reverse adaptation' (Leonard-Barton, 1995) and 'configuring' (Fleck, 1999).

According to Latour (1988), the political skills involved in weaving such socio-technical networks together require a '*Prince* for machines as well as machinations'. Drawing on studies of the history of technological innovation, an image emerges of 'heterogeneous engineers' weaving complex webs of social and technological elements to make innovation happen (Badham, 2005). In the work of Orlikowski (Orlikowski and Gash, 1994; Orlikowski, 1996) and others (Kamoche et al., 2002) this is a process of improvisation, as innovators deal with the uncertain nature of change, identifying, aligning and challenging alternative technological frames, welding the perspectives and interests of different groups who inevitably see innovation through different lenses. In Wenger's (1998) terms, this involves brokering multiple practices, acting as a 'bridging agent' between different social worlds, and participating in the 'technology brokering' (Hargadon, 2003) that is inevitably required in processes of 'recombinant innovation'.

Bust my frame

Think of an innovation in your own experience that met unexpected resistance from those working within the old frame? What kinds of arguments did they offer? What kinds of conditions frustrated this initiative? Did you provide ways in which those working with the old frame could identify with the innovation? Did you adapt the innovation to fit within their frame, or create new initiatives or structures to break down the frame? What worked and what didn't, and why? How did you cope with the uncertain and emergent nature of the innovation process? Do you see yourself playing positive politics in this process?

In this form, the romance of the entrepreneurial innovator is replayed yet again: in this case it is the romanticism of the 'marginal man' [*sic*] (Park, 1928), the creative outsider who is able to stand on the shoulders of multiple limited perspectives, and weld them into a new synthesis. This said, there is real, and continuing, disagreement over the degree to which the individual capabilities and 'heroism' of such brokers should be emphasized and glorified. To what degree do hero entrepreneurs who 'win out' do so because of the fortunes of circumstance and the availability of innovation elements (Hargadon and Sutton, 1997)? Should their solutions be celebrated as creating a triumphant success or merely imposing a particular partial resolution? However, the romantic imagery is never far from the surface. On the one hand, these views build on established 'sense-making' approaches to organizations (Weick, 2000), capturing the romance of the creative individual in the face of the iron cage of bureaucratic rationality, as well as the 'mindfulness' (Weick and Sutcliffe, 2001) of actors aware of the complexity and richness of organizational experience. On the other hand, they draw on and extend classical arguments for a more practical and realistic view of rational decision making (Cyert and March, 1983). They involve ironic praise for the pragmatic realists who acknowledge 'bounded rationality', work with the 'garbage can' nature of organizing and reorganizing (March and Olsen, 1983), initiate strategies of 'purposive muddling through' (Quinn, 1980), and deploy a playful 'technology of foolishness' (March, 1974; March, 2006) in the face of uncertain innovation processes.

Underlying such views of entrepreneurial frame breaking and the difficulties of bringing about the adoption of new frames are challenges to established images of innovation. The concept of a relatively stable world overthrown by heroic individuals does not reflect how innovation occurs in a period of continuous change. Rather than 'punctuated equilibrium' – periods of calm interrupted by major change – we see 'punctuated disequilibrium' (Page and Wiersema, 1992). Instability and renewal are commonplace, punctuated only by brief periods of apparent continuity. The ongoing activity of innovation is often more one of 'creative recombination' and 'collective entrepreneurship' (Andersen and Lundvall, 1988; Hargadon, 2003; Abrahamson, 2004) than paradigm-busting heroic entrepreneurs driving whirlwinds of creative destruction. Finally, innovation is also characterized by paradox and contradiction (March, 1991; Tushman and O'Reilly, 1997). The ability to cope with continuous change, to stand above the fray of competing perspectives and interests, to create new communities (and new 'collective wills') for change, to wrestle with paradox and contradiction, and establish alternative dynamic regimes of innovation, are all part of an established tradition of entrepreneurial heroism. As Elam (1993) notes, to remove such idealism from innovation is to overlook and undermine the social and moral forces that drive innovation. As Clegg et al. (2006) argue, this is to overlook the 'orchestration of power' on which innovation depends.

Conclusion

Brandy, cigars and human values

Lecturer So, have you addressed politics in your masters programme?

Manager Sure . . . we covered that in Ethics.

The argument for positive, productive politics would be diminished if this were to be reduced to a narrowly defined ethical question. Is this just an appeal to play the game according to a simple and fixed set of moral guidelines? This would be misleading. Of more interest are the issues surrounding how one decides what will count, for oneself and for others, in a given context, as a positive and moral stance. The additional concern of this chapter has been to draw from the deeper cultural roots of the concept of a positive politics, based on the values and beliefs of a culture of enterprise.

Underlying and legitimating corporate pursuit of profits and growth through change and innovation lies an entrepreneurial ethos that extends beyond the rational and the economic. For inheritors of the Schumpeterian imagination, this is a romantic quest, forging a collective will to build new 'kingdoms', and new communities. Not any kingdom or community, however, but regimes of innovation that foster a collaborative, and competitive, entrepreneurial spirit. It is this enthusiasm for an entrepreneurial spirit that underlies the exhortations of many contemporary champions of strategic innovation and change. Even deeper than this, however, lies an underlying faith in the value of ongoing organizational and self-transformation. From Covey's character ethic to Hamel's corporate rebels, from Weick's mindful improvisers to Nadler's heroic leaders, there is a romantic commitment to overthrowing established beliefs and prejudices, and striving to create a better world. Arguments for a 'positive politics' draw from this ethos, as the mobilization of collective power to overcome restrictive tradition and repressive authority.

As we saw in our outline of the entrepreneurial agenda, an established and influential view of entrepreneurial heroism provides us with a set of principles, strategies, and tactics for how to play such positive politics in contemporary organizations. If these are shorn of the simplistic evangelism of some of the cruder exponents of office politics, they can provide useful and thought provoking guidelines for the political entrepreneur.

In the next chapter, we will take a more critical look at the limitations and disadvantages of this viewpoint. Are bureaucratic traditions merely intransigent barriers to innovation and enterprise, and are their adherents solely self-interested defenders of outdated traditions unwilling to step outside their 'comfort zones'? Are there no dangers in a brave new world that engenders corruption, burnout, kitsch, and deep emotional manipulation as part of its innovation package? Does the heroic pursuit of the winning team and the all-conquering organization not have potentially undesirable side effects? The entrepreneurial hero tradition provides a useful critique of simple-minded rationality and adherence to formal organizational routines. But do the almost evangelical celebrations of heroic enterprising leaders and the 'cults of personality' and 'missionary management' sects go too far (Bunting, 2004)? What would a more balanced and reflective view of political entrepreneurship look like? It is, however, important, as we have argued in this chapter, not to throw out the useful and insightful pragmatist baby with the ideological bathwater.

Follow through

The seven skills of change masters: a leadership self-assessment

Many of the themes outlined in the entrepreneurial agenda are illustrated in Rosabeth Moss Kanter's (2006) 'seven skills' assessment. As individuals, or collaboratively in groups, using the bullet points as illustrations of each skill, assess your own and/or each others' skills. Rate your strength on each skill on a scale from 1 = weak to 5 = strong, then identify an example of 'best practice' under that heading from your recent experience and observations.

Skill 1 Tuning in to the environment: sensing needs and opportunities

- Becoming curious rather than reluctant about changes on the horizon.
- Monitor external environment for new ideas and imminent change.
- Notice emerging ideas and appetites before they become popular and well-known.
- Sense problems and weaknesses before they explode.
- Look to unexpected sources, both people and places, for ideas.
- Stay alert and mindful; avoid habitual behaviour, predictable routines.

Score   Best practice example

Skill 2 Kaleidoscope thinking: stimulating breakthrough ideas

- Seek new methods, new patterns, unconventional combinations or juxtapositions.
- Use humour and play to stimulate imagination, to look at old things in new ways.
- Surface and challenge common assumptions that are usually taken for granted.
- Break mental boundaries; use surprising ideas and insights from outside the usual fields.
- Brainstorm to enlarge options; get many people generating large quantities of ideas.
- Tap diversity of experience; encourage creative differences in behaviour and self-expression.

Score   Best practice example

Skill 3 Setting the theme: communicating inspiring visions

- Find big themes that can become big dreams awakening new aspirations.
- Communicate themes with clarity and pragmatism to drive action.
- Overcome inertia and get people excited about moving and doing.
- Articulate the vision in a dramatic, memorable way.
- Convey new visions diplomatically, with respect for predecessors and foundations.
- Find the personal passion to match your aspirations; show enthusiasm and conviction.

Score   Best practice example

Skill 4 Enlisting backers and supporters: getting buy-in, building coalitions

- Work personal networks to identify key influencers who could be champions.
- Garner support of power-holders – those with resources, information, or credibility.
- Live the rule of 'no surprises', pre-selling ideas before they are set in stone.
- Build a circle of advisers to provide feedback and 'sanity checks'.
- Widen the coalition, narrow opposition; move people from opposed to neutral to committed.
- Communicate personally; use all available media and keep communicating.

Score   Best practice example

Skill 5 Developing the dream: nurturing the working team

- Inspire people who will do the work to embrace the goals and build on them.
- Let go of full control; allow the team to take ownership of the tasks.
- Encourage a coherent identity for the team; help individuals feel included as members.
- Give the team time and space to focus, and protect them from distractions.
- Get the team the resources and support it needs; help the team solve problems.
- See to the care and feeding of the team's spirit and morale.

Score   Best practice example

Skill 6 Mastering the difficult middles: persisting and persevering

- Refuse to be derailed by obstacles; rather, look for ways around them.
- Be prepared to respond to unexpected opportunities or consequences.
- Access innovations and take directions not originally envisioned.
- Stay involved as a leader, cheer the team on, take action to break up logjams.
- Revisit assumptions; tune into the environment to make sure venture is still viable.
- Keep on going even when critics surface, using coalition members as defenders.

Score   Best practice example

Skill 7 Celebrating accomplishment: making everyone a hero

- Find milestones that provide occasions for celebration, even before the work is done.
- Credit people for their accomplishments and contributions; say thank you.
- Publicize successes widely to show the world the talent in your group.
- Use recognition-star making- to motivate and retain leaders and team members.
- Spread credit generously; don't be miserly because people are 'just doing their jobs'.
- Build special rewards and recognition into an incentive system for change.

Score   Best practice example

Your total score (between 7 and 35):   ☐

   This assessment is from Rosabeth Moss Kanter, *Leading with Confidence*, Global Leaders Network Seminar, Sydney, 26 September 2006: © HBR 617–495–6053.

Debrief

- What useful personal insights does this exercise reveal?
- What kinds of issues, if any, does this assessment of change agency capabilities *not* cover?

Organization politics at the movies: *Jamie's School Dinners*

In 2002, the celebrity chef Jamie Oliver tried to change the food being served in British schools, to create 'a better, cooler, cleverer, healthier nation'. A real-time documentary programme was produced, *Jamie's School Dinners* (Fresh One Productions). This follows Jamie's efforts through the following stages:

1 he pilots a new menu in two schools, in Greenwich and Durham, the latter having the reputation of being in the unhealthiest region in the country;
2 the new menus are 'rolled out' across other schools in the borough of Greenwich, which involves negotiating new contracts with suppliers;
3 Jamie lobbies the British government in an attempt to change the level of funding for meals provided by state schools.

Jamie did not have editorial control over the content (which is authentic), as it happened. The resulting documentary is both inspirational and salutary, presenting a dramatic and emotional picture of the complexity of the change process. As the change agent, or champion, Jamie moves from the rational, common-sense goal of producing healthy menus, to the realization that he is involved in 'brainwashing and retraining the bad habits of kids'.

Celebrity chef as change champion
As you watch the programme, consider the following questions:

Questions	Comments
The change: what is the current situation, and what is the desired situation?	
Who are the stakeholders: what will each gain, what will each lose?	

Jamie's tactics: what works and why?

Jamie's tactics: what doesn't work and why?

How does he alter his tactics in order to
strengthen his impact?

From Jamie's experience, what personal
attributes of the change agent contribute to
effectiveness?

And what personal attributes potentially reduce
that effectiveness?

How do Jamie's role and experience influence
his family and domestic life?

How do Jamie's family and domestic life
influence his change agency role?

What are the 'take home messages' for organizational change agents and leaders?

This programme can also be used to trigger a deeper discussion of the personal costs of being an 'entrepreneurial' change agent. The negatives include: the stresses and impositions that both Jamie and Nora impose on their families; the extent to which Jamie's energy, enthusiasm, likeability, and flexibility are compromised by egotism, concern with personal career, lack of consideration for others, and his manipulative behaviour. The mix of benefits and costs differs across different stakeholders, leading some to challenge Jamie's vision. Consequently, he is variously celebrated and abused by school pupils, kitchen staff, and the media. Whether or not this is a 'good cause' depends on who has the best narrative, or account, of the changes.

Debrief

This documentary can be read as the success story of a charismatic, forceful, and persistent change champion. But does Jamie Oliver possess Kanter's seven change agency skills, and are these important to his success? Does he have skills, capabilities, or an emotional profile that Kanter's model does not incorporate adequately? In particular, to what extent do you think that his success is attributable to the following:

- his ability to experiment, and to be open and reflective about his own ideas, actions, and initiatives

For example, as one of the kitchen ladies, Lesley, observes, 'He's like that, get your hands into it, isn't he?' Or as Jamie himself reflects on his conflicts with the head kitchen lady, Nora; after saying, 'I don't need this', he then adds a few moments later, 'But then she probably doesn't need me either.'

- his openness with regard to his own emotions and weaknesses

For example, Jamie comments, 'I don't feel comfortable, I'm out of my depth'; 'I don't know why I'm doing this really'; 'Makes me feel bad about myself, about food, about cooking'; 'I'm getting cocky'.

- his ability to apply time, energy and resources to the task as he successfully aligns his own interests with those of the public goal that he is pursuing

For example, using and developing his personal 'brand' as a friendly, socially-orientated chef, and using this documentary and other channels to spread his message.

7   The good, the bad, and the ugly

Chapter objectives

1 To consider the personal costs and benefits of 'winning' organizational politics.
2 To identify organizational conditions that encourage an instrumental and amoral Machiavellianism.
3 To explore the way in which the cultish nature of entrepreneurial evangelism can create personal and social problems.
4 To outline and discuss the stance of a critical and reflective political entrepreneur.

'Me, ambivalent?... Well, yes and no...'

An ugly game?

Is it possible to act with effectiveness and integrity? There are, as we have seen, imperatives to act politically. But what does playing this game do to us, the players? What effect does our success have on us, our families, society, and our environment? What kind of organizations have we created; and through our actions, what kind of organizations are we constantly recreating? What becomes of the 'losers' in this game? Are there attractive and ugly sides to politics, whether this takes the form of moral flexibility, or the pursuit of win–win solutions? In judging these issues, how do we go beyond discussion that offers only simple contrasts between 'positive' and 'negative' politics?

As we have seen, different commentators offer contrasting views of the nature and aims of organization political behaviour. Machiavelli offers a harshly realistic view of what is required in order to succeed, basing his advice on the way things actually are rather than on the way in which we think they should be: '[S]ince my intention is to say something that will prove of practical use to the enquirer, I have thought it proper to represent things as they are in real truth, rather than as they are imagined (Machiavelli, 1514, p.90). Flyvbjerg (1998) describes the consequences of this viewpoint as a 'strategies and tactics' approach to power, recognizing a complex and changing world, where enemies and allies are fickle and unpredictable, and where considered and decisive action is critical. But is there a danger for us as individuals in this approach, winning the game, but losing our souls, developing our reputation for managerial effectiveness, while abandoning our values, beliefs, and principles?

An alternative perspective, inspired by the work of the economist Joseph Schumpeter (1968; 1979), presents a more romantic view of individual and collective enterprise. The advice to change agents and innovators from this standpoint concerns the energetic search for creative solutions, overcoming bureaucratic inertia and other barriers to innovation, mobilizing the collective will for change and development. Machiavelli's bargain asks us to trade personal effectiveness for the loss of one's principles. However, this 'positive' view of organizational change offers a different bargain, in which we are invited to trade the successful defeat of barriers to innovation for the subordination of the individual to the collective, and the sacrifice of free time leading potentially to burnout and family collapse.

Recognizing such concerns, this chapter explores the contrasting imagery, disadvantages, and benefits of these perspectives. Here, we explore some of the personal consequences of adopting the strategies and tactics, and the political skills or expertise (see Chapter 9), that appear to be required in order to 'win' the turf game of organization politics. As Chapter 1 argued, these are aspects of work and organization that are often either overlooked, or actively repressed. When these issues are addressed, they are often reduced either to oversimplified moralizing (for example, 'thou shalt not'), or to short checklists of isolated guidance ('watch your back'). In other words, the management experience of organization politics is often reduced to a sterile or unappealing caricature.

The aim here is to develop a more realistic and nuanced perspective, raising some fundamental issues concerning the nature of the turf game and what it means to win, along with the implications for the players and their social context.

This treatment covers an aspect of organizational behaviour to which filmgoers and readers of fiction are routinely exposed. These cultural and media products represent organizations and those who work in them in a manner that displays greed, violence, treachery, soulless players who meet tragic ends, and the disregard of individuals and communities in the pursuit of self-interest (Hassard and Holliday, 1998). The concept of 'winning' reinforced by these portrayals is often narrow and destructive, a perspective that is both prevalent and plausible. The pervasiveness of this perspective may be explained, in part, by the cultural contradictions between an economizing business ethos, a romantic individualistic culture and an egalitarian political ethos (Bell, 1996).

Office space

In *Office Space* (1999, director Mike Judge), Joanna (played by Jennifer Aniston) works as a waitress at Chachki's, a fast food restaurant, while her male friends work in cubicles at the nearby computing company Initech. Joanna is criticized by her boss for not putting enough badges ('flair') on her uniform, not because she is formally 'required' to do so but because, as a committed employee selling the brand, she is expected to 'want' to; 'Customers can get a cheeseburger anywhere. They come to Chachki's for the atmosphere'. Her friends working in those cubicles at Initech are also desperately trying to display their commitment to the company in interviews with management consultants planning a downsizing, and the similarities between these apparently different working conditions are difficult to avoid.

Hollywood fiction? Clerical staff at Harvard University were asked to, 'Think of yourself as a trash can. Take everyone's little bits of anger all day, put it inside you, and at the end of the day, just pour it into the dumpster on your way out of the door' (Bunting, 2004, p.71).

We don't have to go to the movies to find such critical commentary. This is also expressed by organizational insiders. However, as March and Olsen (1983) argue, the 'rhetoric of administration' that describes and legitimates change usually sits alongside the 'rhetoric of realpolitik' which offers a more sceptical and cynical view. In many corporate culture change initiatives, the metaphor of organization as caring family and community is often invoked; Pfeffer and Sutton (2006) describe the corporation as community, arguing that distinctions between work and home are exaggerated. Nevertheless, this imagery often meets with cynicism, ambivalence, and game playing (Kunda, 1992; Casey, 1999). In many settings, organizational *mis*behaviour is more common than the expression of family and community values (Ackroyd and Thompson, 1999). That cynicism and ambivalence may also be directed towards the turf game, and the value attached to winning it (see Chapter 1).

The aim of this chapter, therefore, is to encourage reflection on these deeply embedded cultural issues. This reflective and critical perspective welcomes an entrepreneurial creativity which accepts rather than denies the ambiguity, uncertainty, and plurality of organizational values and practices. In other words, for personal and organizational effectiveness, it is surely necessary to accept and to work effectively with uncertainty, compromise, and competing viewpoints without lapsing into either orthodoxy or despair. As we shall see, however, there are a number of contemporary organizational trends and conditions that threaten to turn such a perspective into an instrumental and amoral Machiavellianism or a blinkered 'entrepreneurial evangelism'.

The new Machiavellians

> In the ostensible self, you really have as much of a man as usually figures in a novel or an obituary notice. But I am tremendously impressed now in retrospect by the realization of how little that frontage represented me, and just how little such frontages do represent the complexities of the intelligent contemporary. Behind it, yet struggling to disorganize and alter it, altogether, was a far more essential reality, a self less personal, less individualized, and broader in its references.
>
> It is just the existence and development of this more generalized self-behind-the-frontage that is making modern life so much more subtle and intricate to render, and so much more hopeful in its relations to the perplexities of the universe.
>
> *Source*: H.G. Wells, *The New Machiavelli* (1910, p.150).

For many contemporary management commentators, Machiavelli's sixteenth-century Florentine thinking has continuing universal relevance. This theme continues to pre-occupy researchers and theorists studying organizational power and its Machiavellian underpinnings (Clegg, 1989; Fleming and Spicer, 2005). Business texts continue to draw on Machiavelli's insights, and he would doubtless be delighted to learn that his advice continues to be applied. The list of recent publications based on his work is a long one. Here is a selection:

The New Machiavelli: Renaissance Realpolitik for Modern Managers (McAlpine, 1997)
A Child's Machiavelli: A Primer on Power (Hart, 1998)
The New Machiavelli: The Art of Politics in Business (McAlpine, 1999)
The New Prince: Machiavelli Updated for the Twenty-First Century (Morris, 2000)
Machiavelli, Marketing and Management (Harris et al., 2000)
Machiavelli on Modern Leadership: Why Machiavelli's Iron Rules Are as Timely and

Important Today as Five Centuries Ago (Ledeen, 2000)

The Corporate Prince: Machiavelli's Timeless Wisdom Adapted for the Modern CEO (Borger, 2002)

What Would Machiavelli Do?: The Ends Justify the Meanness (Bing, 2002)

The Modern Prince: What Leaders Need to Know (Lord, 2003)

As one would expect, the quality of these texts is variable (Galie and Bopst, 2006). These range from the lightweight and fun 'how to' guides to using and defeating 'dirty tricks' (Phipps and Gautrey, 2005), to deeper theoretical explorations of the personal and social dilemmas surrounding the 'dirty hands' problem (Harris et al., 2000). Our focus in this chapter lies primarily with the latter, and with the continuing relevance of an insightful tradition of critical reflection on the character of organizational leadership. Among many commentators who link leadership either with the concept of the Machiavellian 'character', or with the political strategies and tactics that Machiavelli recommended, there is a common concern: to what extent do contemporary organizational conditions and trends support these kinds of characters and behaviours? Are we currently encouraging a cadre of 'new Machiavellians', variously described as 'amoral chameleons' and 'narcissistic gameplayers'? As Chapter 4 argued, a degree of Machiavellian pragmatism is required in all managers, and especially in those who would implement or facilitate organizational change. If contemporary conditions are now such that more of this kind of behaviour is necessary, to manage change, to get things done, then we should perhaps be concerned with the potential personal costs and antisocial consequences of Machiavellian behaviour. As we will see, many of the traditional concerns about what has been called the Machiavellian personality have been addressed by contemporary critics of management, work, and organization.

High Machs in a lonely crowd

In their classic studies of the 'Machiavellian personality', Christie and Geiss (1970) argued that Machiavellian managers were becoming more prevalent and successful, due to increasing rates of organizational change, higher levels of uncertainty, and the spread of cosmopolitan urbanism. Following the development of what is now the most widely used index of Machiavellianism, the Mach IV personality assessment (see Chapter 9), Christie and Geiss conducted a series of studies into the character and activities of such individuals. Drawing on Machiavelli's works, this personality type was associated with:

- a lack of emotional involvement in interpersonal relationships; displaying a pragmatic and instrumental attention to the feelings and opinions of others
- a lack of concern with conventional morality; a utilitarian view of ethics, the situational use of lying, cheating and deceit

- a lack of gross psychopathology; holding an accurate evaluation of themselves and their needs
- low ideological commitment; focus on getting things done, flexible use of tactics to achieve their ends.

High Machs concentrate on winning, like to initiate and control social situations, manipulate more, win more often, are persuaded less, and persuade others more. Under controlled laboratory conditions, they are shown to be highly successful in negotiations involving face-to-face interactions in which improvisation is important, and emotional involvement is not so critical. Their cool, cognitive, situation-specific strategies make them less prone to distraction by personalities and feelings, and more focused on outcomes. Interestingly, as a result of their findings, Christie and Geiss changed their attitude towards their high Mach subjects, from criticism of their self-centred scheming, to an appreciation of their positive qualities:

- they do not use ingratiation as a tactic to make friends
- despite social pressure, they will not readily change their position just to fit the arguments and views of others
- they resist what they see as unjustified attempts to get them to lie or to cheat
- they adjust the amount of deceit and manipulation used to fit the situation
- they try to avoid being obviously manipulative
- their emotional distance can inspire admiration
- others tend to want them as partners
- high Machs are easier to schedule because they are more likely to turn up.

Medical Machiavellis

Christie and Merton (1958) uncovered the controversial nature of their Machiavellian research when they presented a research paper based on a study of medical students to a medical audience. One of their 21 slides addressed Machiavellianism, and the beliefs that one should not trust others completely, that it is wise to flatter important people, that there is a need to cut corners to get ahead, that one should only reveal the real reason for doing something if it is useful to do so. They had found that medical students were more likely to hold such beliefs than Washington lobbyists or business executives. The ensuing debate focused on this finding, with an emotive disagreement between the young urban medical dean, who praised students for their realistic attitudes, and an older rural dean, who condemned this situation as indicative of a failure to give adequate professional training to medical students.

Noting the attractive qualities of high Machs, Christie and Geiss were also concerned with the personal costs and limitations of the accompanying attitudes and behaviours. Their research followed the famous studies of the 'authoritarian personality' (see Adorno et al., 1950). That work, in turn, was inspired by the experience of totalitarian rule in both Nazi Germany and Stalin's Russia, in particular by the anxiety surrounding the apparent ease with which such autocratic leaders came to power, and the willingness of others to follow them.

This concern dates back to the 1950s, and to the work of David Riesman (1950). Riesman's book, *The Lonely Crowd*, argued that social change was affecting personality. In a society no longer at war, with basic material and technical challenges addressed, large bureaucracies created conditions in which the appearance of personal success was more important than actual performance. The ability to influence other people had become more significant than the ability to overcome technical problems. Riesman concluded that the modern character was moving from 'inner direction', in which personality is established early in life, and where guilt and shame are guiding motives, to 'outer direction', in which character is shaped by social experience and approval, and anxiety is a driving motive. In other words, organizational conditions were encouraging the rise of 'other directed' managers, who value manipulative skill above traditional craft skill. Riesman concluded that the inner compulsion or 'psychological gyroscope' that accompanied the then dominant Protestant work ethic was being replaced by an outer compulsion that focused on the opinions and desires of others. This concern would lead others to criticize the bland conformity of 'organization man' (Whyte, 1955) and the 'grey flannelled manager' (Ehrenreich, 1987). The focus on morality, it was argued, was being replaced by attention to morale; authority was replaced by manipulation. In his book *White Collar*, C. Wright Mills (1951, pp.233–4) described how the social engineering of 'cheerful robots' was becoming commonplace, as 'the Protestant work ethic, a work compulsion, is replaced by the conscious efforts of the personnel department to create morale'.

The narcissistic gamesman

As reputation replaces achievement, and the opinions of others become more influential than one's own, the stage is set for increasing mutual manipulation. During the 1970s, attention focused on how this intertwined with competitive individualism and careerism. In his book, *The Culture of Narcissism*, Lasch (1979) characterized the 'new managers' who appeared to have emerged as:

- anxious to get on with others
- organizers of their private lives to meet the demands of the corporation
- sellers of themselves, as if their own personalities were a commodity with market value

- possessors of a neurotic need for affection and reassurance and
- corruptible in values.

These 'narcissists' appear to have traits that contribute to success in the bureaucratic organization, placing a premium on the exploitation of interpersonal relationships, and discouraging the formation of deep personal attachments. Nevertheless, narcissists often had successful careers. Impression management comes naturally, serving the narcissist well in political and business organizations where effectiveness matters less than reputation. Beneath the surface of the 'cult of friendliness', Lasch argued, narcissistic managers exploit the quirks and pleasures of others for their own interests. The competitive status-seeker has to assume commanding positions in cocktail parties, recruit loyal retainers, avoid turning their back on enemies and, in the struggle for interpersonal advantage, use all the impression management and counter-manipulation tactics they can deploy. As a result 'competitive advantage through emotional manipulation increasingly shapes not only personal relations but relations at work as well' (Lasch, 1979, p.65).

Maccoby (1978) similarly argued that the successful modern manager was increasingly likely to be a 'gamesman'. In the past, management had been dominated by 'craftsmen', 'jungle fighters', and 'company men' (see Table 7.1). Those characters respectively matched the eras of early market economies, the rise of the industrial barons, and the subsequent bureaucratization of large organizations. But now, for Maccoby, with the development of increasingly dynamic, innovative, technology-based, global companies, it was the gamesman who had the upper hand. The gamesman was less interested in concrete results (like the craftsman), or in gaining power over others (the jungle fighter), or in the esteem of others (company man), and was more interested in making an impact, on winning, and on obtaining the subsequent rewards.

Table 7.1 Maccoby's corporate types

	craftsman	jungle fighter	company man	gamesman
meaning of competition	build the best; competition against self and materials	kill or be killed, dominate or be dominated	climb or fall; competition is the price for a secure position	win or lose, triumph or humiliation
source of energy	interest in work, goal of perfection, pleasure in building something better	lust for power, pleasure in crushing opponents, fear of annihilation	fear of failure, desire for approval of those in authority	the contest, new options, pleasure in controlling the play, to be the one at the top

Source: from Maccoby (1978, p.105).

From interviews with 250 senior managers, Maccoby described the gamesman as someone who loves change and wants to influence its course, likes calculated risks and is fascinated by new methods and techniques, and sees developing projects, human relations and his/her own career as a set of options and possibilities, as if they were moves in a game. The gamesman combines a complex set of tensions; cooperative but competitive, detached and playful but compulsively driven to succeed, a team player but an aspiring superstar, fair and unprejudiced but contemptuous of weakness. The goal is to be known as a winner, driven by fame and glory, the exhilaration of running teams, and gaining victories.

On the one hand, recognizing the gamesman's manipulative, and in many cases superficial, character, Maccoby's portrayal is a relatively attractive one. Here is an individual who is fair and open to new ideas, not hostile or vindictive, unbigoted, liberal and non-ideological. This gamesman appears to have advantages in a context that puts a premium on flexibility and dynamism. On the other hand, the surface, almost adolescent, qualities of the gamesman are seen by Maccoby as repressing an underlying set of problems. Gamesmen are dependent on others, but fear becoming trapped in the organizational web. Their limited capacity for social commitment and personal intimacy is further handicapped by the desire to maintain the illusion of limitless options. The gamesman does not, therefore, develop deep or intimate friendships. At their worst, gamesmen are unrealistic, manipulative, and compulsive workaholics, their hyperactivity concealing doubts over personal identity and purpose. The most compulsive players need competitive pressure to 'turn them on' and to energize them. Deprived of a challenge, they become bored and depressed. Life outside the game is meaningless. Retirement from the game also means depression and a loss of purpose. The desire for autonomy and the fear of being controlled can combine to create a mid-career uneasiness. Even the most successful gamesmen, Maccoby claims, experience self-contempt at performing for others rather than developing their own goals, unable to resolve the conflict between their desire for independence and their ambition to run the organizational team.

The narcissistic leader

In a more recent contribution to the study of leadership, Maccoby (2000) explores some of the characteristics, costs and benefits of 'narcissistic leaders', characters who stand somewhere between his own 'gamesman' and Lasch's 'narcissistic' personality. Drawing on Freud's distinction between 'erotic', 'obsessive' and 'narcissistic' character types, Maccoby identifies the narcissist as someone with an ability to impress and inspire others, but with the potential to be isolated and distrustful (and contrasts this with the other two types who like to love and be loved, or who are inner-directed, self-reliant and conscientious). Narcissists, in contrast, want to be admired, not loved, have vision and many followers, but are sensitive to criticism, lacking in empathy, and are poor listeners, with a distaste for mentoring and an intense desire to compete. Citing Jack Welch, he argues that productive narcissists are obsessive personalities who are able to convert other people to their point of view. For some this will appear as excessive egotism and evangelism. As one executive commented on his narcissistic chief executive, Larry Ellison, 'The difference between God and Larry is that God does not believe he is Larry'. Narcissistic personality weaknesses can lead to their owner's downfall. Maccoby cites Jan Carlzon of Scandinavian airlines (SAS) as an example of the weakness of not listening to others. Seeking to create an SAS organization with no fixed roles and only innovative plays, he gave the following dismissive response to one of his subordinates who argued for the value of military style forms of organization; 'Well, that may be true, if your goal is to shoot your customers'. Narcissistic leaders may also be unrealistic dreamers and paranoid about opposition. Maccoby praises their productiveness when they have a sense of perspective, humour and play, and recommends that they get trusty sidekicks, indoctrinate their organization, and get into analysis.

Source: based on Maccoby (2000).

While gamesmen may create successful projects and energize the organization for a time, in the long term they seem to lack the patience and commitment, to people and principles, necessary to sustain a dynamic organization. The fatal danger for the gamesman is, 'to be trapped in perpetual adolescence, never outgrowing the self-centred compulsion to score, never confronting their deep boredom with life when it is not a game, never developing a sense of meaning that requires more of them and allows others to trust them' (Maccoby, 1978, p.109). Younger gamesmen apparently fantasize about power and glory, and while their passion may be enough to motivate a project team, it may be inadequate to the task of directing a large corporation, lacking the endurance and corporate belief of the company man.

Ultimately, Maccoby argues, the gamesman lacks passion and compassion, and carries emotional self-protection against intense experiences. To bend their will to corporate goals, and to progress up the hierarchy, gamesmen require a degree of meanness and emotional stinginess, and they remain concerned with adapting themselves and with 'marketing' their personalities and achievements. This also means ignoring idealistic and courageous impulses that could jeopardize their careers. They do not develop a strong independent sense of self. They are inevitably detached from empathy and compassion where colleagues are concerned. Enthusiasm, rapid decisions, risk taking – all take place within the confines of the corporate game, detached from broader and deeper personal emotions and social contexts. The gamesman experiences guilt from a loss of self-respect, and a nagging sense of self-betrayal at the choice of career above

flexibility are potentially illusory, if personal freedom is equated with the ability to craft one's own meaningful work through mutual commitment and dependence, delayed gratification, and loyalty. Freedom from bureaucratic controls, however, has instead meant being cast adrift in a sea of insecurity, undermining the ability to establish a sustainable self, durable relationships, meaningful work, and a sense of identity. As Victor and Stephens (2004, p.481) argue, 'these high-velocity, high-commitment workplaces – flash in the pan collectives – offer no ongoing relationships, no safe haven, no personal space'.

Utilities at Cokemaking Oz

In an Australian cokemaking plant, an apparent bastion of Victorian-era industrial stability, anxieties were increasing due to what was seen as the regular pace of management changes. The plant was shifting from one initiative to another, with little regard for the impact on long-held traditions and ways of working.

In one part of the plant, Utilities, which had responsibility for managing the 'health' of the doors on the 'batteries', so that dangerous and expensive leaks of poisonous gases were avoided, managers and employees reacted and interacted differently with the change process. John, an operator on the batteries, joked that the goalposts moved so much at this company that 'they had wheels on'. For Diago, responsibility for managing the work of the team on the batteries with only minimal direction from supervisors meant that he felt far more stressed about work, such that he would think much more about it and often feel guilty. Diago was keen to leave and was looking for a job on the railways, which he saw as more secure and traditional.

For supervisors like Michael, the flexible new arrangements caused a degree of soul-searching. His role was to 'coach' and 'mentor' the battery teams to meet their targets and to act as a conduit between the teams and Albert, the manager. Though enthusiastic, he felt he was a supervisor without any real authority. The perceived lack of clarity in his role meant that he felt he was 'in no man's land: I know what they're [the employees] getting away with, but what do I do? I can't reprimand them'. This ambivalence affected him in other ways, too. In the past, as a union member, he felt he had been a 'protected species' but now, without either union protection or the traditional authority of a supervisor, he is 'forever aware that I have to cover my arse. I now have an expectation that someone down that road is going to f*** me over'.

Source: based on Badham and Down (2006).

As argued earlier, organizational conditions that combine instability and threat are likely to generate more Machiavellian responses. But as with all generalizations regarding social trends, the degree of change and its consequences should not be exaggerated. As Guest (2004) argues, claims (which are frequently overblown) regarding the exploitation of sub-contract labour have been met, in Europe, with protective legislation (Beck, 2000). Moreover, many organizational members prefer the autonomy that comes with being less dependent on the organization, revelling in new opportunities rather than being anxiously overwhelmed by threats. The contemporary workplace arguably comprises complex and shifting constellations of orientations to work, fluid power balances, and fluctuating configurations of trust and loyalty in the face of competitive and cooperative work relations. Yet such complexity and variety only adds to management uncertainties and challenges. The need for a flexible Machiavellian pragmatism (Chapter 4) is potentially heightened.

The development of novel forms of surveillance has also generated alarm. Cameras can help to prevent theft and other crimes, and contribute to safety. Closer performance monitoring can help to eliminate unfair and discriminatory working practices, as well as to improve customer service and working relationships. However, increased surveillance can have more insidious and negative implications. At the heart of methods for improving openness and transparency may lie a set of darker motives – the 'heart of darkness' described by Clegg et al. (2006). Surveillance now includes a much wider range of social and psychological forms of manipulation and control. Staff can now be subjected to '360 degree' surveillance, including detailed performance metrics, electronic monitoring, open-plan offices, and peer surveillance (Gabriel, 2005). Methods used by totalitarian programmes of 'thought reform' (Lifton, 1989) have been used in quasi-religious managerial programmes (Singer, 1995; Turnbull, 2001). McDonalds' counter staff are expected to display a programmed cheerfulness (Ritzer, 2006). Air hostesses are asked to think of passengers as guests in their own home. Hotel employees must be 'on brand' with regard to appearance and language to create the 'right' atmosphere. In other words, contemporary surveillance methods are used to manipulate and control thoughts and feelings as well as behaviour (Sewell and Barker, 2006).

Life in a corporate glass cage?

Camera lenses everywhere, ready to intrude into people's privacy, open plan offices and glass buildings, a quasi-religious obsession with 'transparency', audits, reviews, appraisals, feedbacks, lists and league tables, these suggest that the glass cage shares the chief quality of Foucault's Panopticon, that curious combination of Catholic obsession with the omnipotent eye of God and Protestant pre-occupation with clean efficiency. Like the Panopticon, the glass cage acts as a metaphor for the formidable machinery of contemporary surveillance, one which deploys all kinds of technologies, electronic, spatial, psychological and cultural. Never before have free citizens been spied upon by snooping governments, insurance companies,

Continued

employers and other prying organizations. Equally, however, never before have the snoopers been themselves targets of snooping. Transparency, the public's 'right to know' whether it applies to governments, state organizations, corporations, charities or the private lives of politicians or 'celebrities' has been elevated to a supreme value and the media have become its staunchest defenders. [T]he cardinal sins of today are hype, spin, dishonesty, manipulation, deception, fraud, ruses, trickery, scams, duplicity, cheating, lying, deceit, cons, corruption, and, above all, cover-ups.

[T]he glass cage also suggests that the modern employee is part of a cast exposed to the critical gaze of the customer with all the kicks, excitements and frustrations that this implies. It evokes vital elements of choice, exhibitionism and display which are entirely consistent with the narcissism of our times. The employee becomes part of the organizational brand on show, a brand whose glamorous image offers an instant face-lift to all who are part of it. Thus, exposure, with its thrills, horrors, and corresponding desires to protect privacy and create sheltered spaces, is the key to the experience in the glass cage, an experience not limited to employees, but to football managers, politicians and all other public figures when they euphemistically talk of the 'goldfish bowl' which magnifies the tiniest blemishes and exaggerates the smallest imperfections.

Source: from Gabriel (2006, p.3).

While it is unrealistic to exaggerate these trends, the dangers of intrusive control are real. Managers may be forced to play more intricate Machiavellian games, performing 'appropriately' to a wider group of clients, customers, superiors, and custodians of the new performance standards. With increased competition, inequalities of power, and lower levels of mutual trust and cooperation, the dynamics of domination and resistance around such controls can be expected to heighten and take new forms

---

Bait and switch

To discover what it is like for an American manager to be unemployed and job seeking, the social anthropologist Barbara Ehrenreich put herself in just this position. The experience turned out to be demeaning and depressing. Her experiences included *Wizard of Oz* dolls, personality tests, the manipulation of her curriculum vitae, and training to display oneself effectively to clients. The key ingredient of 'success' was the development of an uncritical and highly manipulative form of 'commercial self', with the attributes of a superficial Machiavellianism, and a loss of independence. She didn't get a job.

Source: based on Ehrenreich (2005).

(Fleming and Sewell, 2002). Is this likely to generate new forms of Machiavellian performance and gamesmanship, heightening the threats to personal security and development observed by Riesman, Maccoby, and Lasch?

Post-entrepreneurial cowboy and the cult of enterprise

> ### Convince yourself
>
> Morality becomes one's personal comfort zone in relation to the anticipated views of others. The measure of that comfort becomes a confidence in the casuistry necessary to persuade others that one's stories are plausible and one's choices reasonable. Rehearsals also encourage the most subtle form of hype, namely convincing oneself of one's own rectitude.
>
> *Source*: from Jackall (1988, p.189).

As we saw in the previous chapter, the Schumpeterian imagination is often blandly optimistic in its neglect of such dangers, celebrating the adoption of a creative entrepreneurial solution to all new developments. In the more evangelical proclamations of American advocates of this approach, described by one critic as a 'US Sloan Ranger' managerialism (Collins, 2003), the rhetoric of entrepreneurial heroism draws on 'Wild West' imagery (Leonard, 2004) in arguing for a proactive win–win solution to the challenges of innovation and change. Entrepreneurial heroes are uncritically portrayed as liberating figures, breaking down fossilized bureaucracies, sedimented organizational silos, and rigidly protected career enclaves, while ignoring the fact that such initiatives may also be creating new forms of instability, insecurity, and control. The Western-style enthusiasm is expressed in the imagery of 'new frontiers', 'shootouts', 'management in the OK Corral', and defeating 'masked raiders' (Leonard, 2004, pp.70–2). Varying forms of this cowboy rhetoric have also been identified as a key component of the inspirational message behind business process re-engineering (Grint, 1994) in addition to the 'wagon train' images of the 'journey' underpinning the rhetoric of organization development and culture change (Dunn, 1990).

This rhetoric has extended far beyond the limited confines of popular academic and management consulting commentary. Drawing on the experiences of British public sector management, several observers have pointed to the spread of a 'culture of enterprise' that puts all organizations and those who work in them on a Procrustean bed of entrepreneurialism. Taking upon themselves the heroic mantle of enterprise, promoters of this culture have created a 'one size fits all' model of the best practice organization. But, most importantly, they have also created a corresponding, and deeply intrusive, idea of a desirable 'one best' entrepreneurial personality.

Table 7.2 A culture of enterprise

Features of the entrepreneurial organization:

- *The creation of 'responsibilization' and 'autonomization'*
  making organizational units independent, but also responsible, deploying techniques such as audits, performance-related pay, devolved budgets, contracts
- *The cult of the customer*
  expectations, cultures, structures and reward systems are organized around the efficient satisfaction of customer demands, internal or external to the organization
- *A contract-like framework of obligations*
  strictly defined market relations or contractual frameworks, documenting defined functions, goals, and procedures that departments will set and monitoring of performance targets; this allows performance to be measured and units to be held responsible and accountable
- *A human resource management and development system*
  competency frameworks, psychometric testing, a new barrage of performance management and appraisal methods and structures, and contractual performance-based pay systems

Attributes of the entrepreneurial individual:

- *risk-taking*
- *self-reliance*
- *responsibility for self and actions*
- *achieving personal virtue through work*
- *rejection of romantic notion of work being separate from other spheres of social life*
- *antithetical to the demoralizing effect of technical instrumental rationality*

Source: based on Du Gay and Salaman (1982); Du Gay (1996; 2000; 2004).

Reminiscent of Young's (1958) classic satire on taking 'IQ' as a measure of self-worth in *The Rise of the Meritocracy*, critics of these developments point to the dangers associated with the authoritarian pursuit of such an ideal, particularly if it is accepted (Young, 1958). Surely, Young points out, when those judged 'inferior' by society truly believe it is because they *are* inferior, then the stage is set for the most authoritarian form of control imaginable. As emphasized by Du Gay (2000), the entrepreneur, in the contemporary ideal, is not one social category or identity amongst others, but the *only*, or at least, most important, category (see Table 7.2). A list of the qualities of the entrepreneurial ideal reveal how widely diffused and apparently 'common sense' such prescriptions are.

- In contrast to traditional bureaucratic ethics of adherence to procedure and repression of personal moral enthusiasms, the emphasis is market-oriented, proactive, empowered, and entrepreneurial.
- Individuals are expected to exercise discretion, take initiative, be charismatic, facilitating, teaching others to learn how to take responsibility for themselves, and fostering a sense of identification, commitment, and involvement amongst employees and with the organization within which they work.

- They are to be autonomous, productive, self regulating, responsible individuals, identifying with the goals of the organization, enhancing their own skills of self-development, and reflexively monitoring themselves in a way that combines self-understanding with self-control.
- For such an entrepreneurial personality, managing oneself, achieving business benefits, and attaining selfhood are one and the same thing, as one's career is managed such that work is not a painful obligation, or an instrumental occupation, but a route to self-development.

Microsoft UK

Microsoft director of people and culture in Britain complains that, 'We've had 13,000 applications in the last nine months, and we hired 14. We look for change agents, the best and the brightest'. As he continues to explain, however, what Microsoft looks for is not just cleverness; more important is the right kind of personality. 'If you aren't adaptable, it'll kill you here.' The problem is the 're-orgs', or reorganizations. In the past few months, 300 positions in the company have been 'touched', and 16 per cent of employees have moved jobs. People work there for an average of seven years at senior levels, and only three and a half years at junior levels. The company wants exemplary dedication for a short period of time. Management is 'always keeping an eye on the bottom 5 per cent – constantly testing them and asking, is it time for them to move on?'

Source: from Bunting (2004, p.97).

As Rose (1989) and others have argued, this has become a pervasive social ethic. We are encouraged to exercise self-regulation or control, supported by managers monitoring every aspect of our behaviour, in order to ensure that we are 'on brand' and serving the corporate good. Identifying similarities between programmes designed to inculcate such values, professional and religious movements, and self-help manuals, Rose (1989) draws on the work of radical philosopher Michel Foucault (see Chapter 9) in analysing the methods employed as intrusive 'technologies of the self'. They constitute sets of procedures, instructions and controls applied by individuals to themselves in the pursuit of goals that they have been persuaded are their own, but which are to a substantial degree imposed by self-interested organizations and the elites that control them. Rather than regulating behaviour through external systems of monitoring and control, these more intrusive controls and practices get inside the 'hearts and minds' of organizational members, to establish self-regulation. In C. Wright Mill's classic phrase, 'the whips are inside men' (Mills, 1951, p.234).

The story of emotional micro-management, and the stressful double binds that it can generate, is now part of the day-to-day life of managers in many organizations. As one manager at Orange (a British telecommunications company) observed:

> I see my values as aligned with Orange values. I don't hold myself up to being a saint, but I try to incorporate the brand values into everything I do. It's beginning to sound like a cult (Bunting, 2004, p.109).

Managers are encouraged to channel their efforts, energy, and emotions to the pursuit of a set of values encompassing customer care, pride in one's work, independence, and creativity. Yet, as the manager from Orange reflects, there is concern that this sounds like a cult.

This stereotype is emotive and challenging. However, the sharp contrast between conservative bureaucracy and dynamic enterprise is exaggerated and misleading. Bureaucratic structures perform many functions; restricting patronage, applying consistent rules and procedures, accumulating collective knowledge, providing order and stability (Adler and Borys, 1996; Stokes and Clegg, 2002; Leavitt, 2005). Where organizations depend on those functions for their survival (for example, where security and safety are priorities), appeals for the abandonment of bureaucracy may be questionable. Moreover, the methods, structures, ideas and values underpinning creativity and innovation are themselves often routine and bureaucratic in character. Management fads – total quality management, preventive maintenance, business process re-engineering – can be more aptly described as 'learning bureaucracy' (Adler, 1993) than a creative free-for-all, and can even impose strict rules, regulations, and procedures on those who use them. As some critical commentators have argued, this is not liberating, but an extension of more intimate forms of surveillance and emotional control which perpetuate rather than challenge traditional bureaucratic norms (Barker, 1993; Sewell, 1998).

The pressure for managers and employees to become more 'enterprising' have probably increased, but responses to these demands are uneven and complex. For example, in *Inf-Rail* (pseudonym for a French railway company), managers drew on their established corporate 'recipes' to equate enterprise with the company's ongoing concern with safety, technical superiority, and public service responsibilities (Bouguignon and Zarlowski, 2006). *Westland Bank* (a pseudonym for a British bank), under the banner of becoming more entrepreneurial, imposed new forms of regulation and standardization. While allowing greater autonomy and freedom in some areas, higher levels of peer surveillance and detailed work intensification were implemented in others (McCabe, 2006). In a French fashion company, *Beauty*, an intrusive culture of conformity was identified, but rather than being the outcome of internal corporate discipline and control, it appeared to be the result of a broader acceptance of a consumerist ethic of concern for the 'care of the self' (Dambrin and Lambert, 2006). At *Amway*, in contrast, a highly developed corporate ethos of independence and enterprise is apparent, yet under this banner the organization initiates a range of new forms of identity control, including influential processes of self-selection, as well as continuing cruder forms of direct regulation (Gross and Reifenscheidt, 2006; Salaman and Storey, 2006).

Underlying this variability are more complex notions of the form that the cult of enterprise takes and how it plays out in practice. While this questions any simple notions of a unitary 'culture of enterprise' transforming organizational life and sweeping all before it, the continuation of what some have described as 'initiative overload' is unlikely to abate. Managers and employees are likely to be faced with novel and more complex situations as new organizational forms intertwine with more traditional bureaucracies. Novel procedures and regulations, and new forms of performance management and reward systems, combine with established internal bureaucratic and external professional career paths. The pressures on 'enterprising' individuals to perform and succeed in such environments are likely to increase rather than to diminish.

Willing slaves?

Organizations are always working to capacity; there's no reserve because it's argued that it's too wasteful. People are working at such a level that it only takes one more thing – a personal crisis or work crisis [for them to snap] – there's no reserve. Some mission statements can be really crass, for example, 'Zero tolerance of defects'. People are expected to 'strive for excellence' rather than be good enough. A high proportion of the people coming to see us are on anti-depressants; they don't see much of their kids and they're bitterly resentful that they don't have more time at home (public health counsellor, quoted in Bunting, 2004, p.191).

What are the personal consequences of these developments? In their book, *The Second Shift*, Hochschild and Machung (1989) describe how women are increasingly forced into high pressure roles in the workplace *and* at home; in other words, they work a 'second shift'. This metaphor can be extended to the informal and emotional 'second shift' while at work. As one American worker replied to a question from his manager about what 'empowerment' meant to him, 'It means that now I have two jobs, not one. I have to do my work, and now I have to manage it as well'.

As a change agent in a large manufacturing company explained, 'It is all about whether you are going to put in that extra bit of effort to get things done.' But where is this effort to come from, and what are the effects? Most practical management advice identifies the need to put in more time, work smarter, devote more effort. Yet there is considerable evidence that managers are increasingly 'time poor'. In the face of downsizing and outsourcing, combined with enhanced performance monitoring, many managers are required to do more with less. The result is increasing work intensity, for which there is now significant evidence. One European survey reported that those who saw themselves working at 'very high speed' for all or almost all of the time rose from 17 to 25 per cent between 1991 and 1996. The negative effect of this phenomenon is heightened by a more pervasive sense of job insecurity. In 2001, the Organisation for Economic Co-operation and Development (OECD) reported that 41 per cent of British workers were unsure of their jobs, even if they performed well, while other studies in Britain revealed that the most dramatic increase in perceived job insecurity was among white collar workers. Work-related stress, depression, and anxiety account for 13.4 million lost working days per annum in Britain, more than any other work-related illness. The prevalence of self-reported stress more than doubled between 1990 and 2002, from 207,000 to 563,000. More than 20 per cent of British workers categorize their work as very or extremely stressful, and stress is cited as a problem by 36 per cent of professionals, 34 per cent of managers, and 22 per cent of skilled workers. Nearly a third of those earning over £20,000 a year have high levels of stress, three times the proportion of those with salaries below £10,000. It is estimated that stress costs British business over £400 million a year, and the World Health Organization estimates that stress will count for half of the ten most common medical problems in the world by 2020 (Bunting, 2004; Trinca and Fox, 2004).

As our 'entrepreneurial heroes' are expected to work harder and longer, and handle increased pressures, how will they cope? It may not be surprising that sales of personal organizers have grown rapidly (Abrahamson and Freedman, 2006), potentially due to attempts to find ways to manage time more effectively, and especially when one is required to undertake the proactive politicking required to 'get change done' in the current climate.

Multiplicity **and** *Click*

Escalating work pressures have become the subject of feature films.

The science fiction comedy *Mutiplicity* (1996, director Harold Ramis) chronicles the disasters that befall a building contractor who clones himself in order to keep his business, family, and friends happy. Symbolizing the conflicts that arise between our own multiple selves, the comedy (and tragedy) of the movie revolves around the tensions between the different clones.

In *Click* (2006, director Frank Coraci), an ambitious architect uses a 'fast-forward' magical remote control to rush through selected parts of his life in order to give him more time for his work. The movie illustrates some of the tragic consequences of being only 'half there' with the family, as attention is focused elsewhere, on job and career.

Are these stereotypes of the time-pressured manager exaggerated? Outside the movies, how can these kinds of pressures be handled effectively?

The employees at AMERCO (an American Fortune 500 company) are expected to have 'zero drag', which means a lack of external distraction from work (Hochschild, 1997). A partner, children, living far from work, outside interests – all of these earn debit points of 'drag' as they imply a lack of full commitment to the organization. As observed in the study by OECD in 2003, in America working hours have jumped dramatically in the last three decades with the average worker spending 199 more hours at work in 2000 than in 1973, and in Australia around 30 per cent of full time employees work more than 50 hours a week, twice as many as two decades ago. Managers and employees in Britain work much longer hours (Trinca and Fox, 2004, p.154). Between 1998 and 2003, for example, British workers put in an extra 0.7 hours a week on average, the number working over 48 hours has more than doubled since 1998, increasing from 10 per cent to 26 per cent, and those working more than 60 hours leapt by a third between 2000 and 2002, to one in six of all workers (Bunting, 2004).

Microsoft UK (continued)

The dedication that Microsoft UK requires from its workers is probably not sustainable, as employees lose momentum, or acquire family commitments. Work–life balance? 'What a stupid question', says Harvey, 'We hire very driven people who try to balance work–life over a life.' He refers us to the company's two-day Personal Excellence Programme, which inculcates a form of corporate philosophy: 'If you choose to have a family or play golf, you have to be honest about what kind of job you can do. Women look at how big those big jobs are, and take a choice.' That explains the 80–20 per cent split of men to women at the senior levels, but he insists that the 'senior ladies are getting through'. The average age of employees is 34, and most of those I met had no children. It's a two-way deal: employees know the score, and are paid handsomely (average salary is around £65,000, plus stock-options); in return they work hard.

Source: from Bunting (2004, p.124).

A soul at risk?

The new Machiavellians and the post-entrepreneurial cowboys, the conditions in which they operate, and the personal and organizational goals that they are expected to pursue, pose a set of challenges. But they are not ones that can be addressed by a return to traditional solutions and values. In the contemporary world, as Gergen (2000) argues, we are confronted, at work and at home, by what he calls 'microwave relationships', 'collage communities', and 'cardboard commitment'; in other words, we are potentially swamped by the need to handle multiple relationships, goals, and obligations. Pulled in different directions by competing demands at work as well as between work and

---

Principles into guidelines, ethics into etiquette

For those with the requisite discipline, sheer dogged perseverance, the agile flexibility, the tolerance for extreme ambiguity, the casuistic discernment that allows one to dispense with shopworn pieties, the habit of mind that perceives opportunities in others' and even one's own misfortunes, the brazen nerve that allows one to pretend that nothing is wrong even when the world is crumbling, and, above all, the ability to read the inner logic of events, to see and do what has to be done, the rewards of corporate success can be very great. Those who do succeed shape, in a decisive way, the moral rules-in-use that filter down through their organizations. The ethos that they fashion turns principles into guidelines, ethics into etiquette, values into tastes, personal responsibility into an adroitness at public relations, and notions of truth into credibility.

Source: from Jackall (1998, p.204).

---

family, the modern 'saturated' self is beset by ongoing ambivalence and angst as we strive to retain an integrated identity and, in Giddens's terms (1991, p.54), 'keep a coherent narrative going'.

Some commentators thus see in these trends a series of threats to the coherence of personal identity. Are we in danger of developing 'pastiche personalities'? Do we have to become adept at manipulating our multiple, fragmented and shifting relationships? Is the notion of 'self' under threat when confronted with competing views of who we are and what we should become? Organizations that seek to impose one particular view of who we are and should be may promise relief from this complexity, but ultimately cannot deliver. We seem to be increasingly involved in a reflexive form of 'serious play'. As Gergen (2000, p.7) observes, 'Under postmodern conditions, persons exist in a state of continuous construction and reconstruction; it is a world where anything goes that can be negotiated. Each reality of self gives way to reflexive questioning, irony and ultimately the playful probing of yet another reality. The centre fails to hold.'

That may appear to be an exaggerated claim, but it does address a widely recognized experience. As Kunda (1992) documents in his ethnography of the Tech organization, those who are subjected to 'strong culture' management programmes, instead of being converted to the new ethos, simply learn to present one 'self' to colleagues, and a different 'self' to bosses, mixing multiple messages and interpretations in the same ritualized meetings, becoming skilful players in displaying the right amounts and forms of commitment to different audiences. For Hochschild (1983), in her study of the 'emotional labour' of air hostesses, many organizational members are required to 'deep act' for their customers and colleagues, as commercialized training programmes and social pressures tell us how we should think, behave, and most importantly feel in work situations. How does one retain a meaningful and coherent understanding of one's self, she asks, as one's feelings become increasingly managed and commercialized? As Kondo (1990) illustrates in her study of Japanese company workers, these pressures have different effects and are used in different ways. The rhetoric, training, and practices that encouraged a view of the organization as a 'family' in the Japanese company she studied, were also used by employees to challenge the 'non-familial' use of people and inequalities of authority and reward. We may be more or less comfortable with such moralities and demands, using some, feeling guilty or repressed by others, and sidelining the rest. The key issue, however, is that we are forced to operate in organizations where others, as well as ourselves, are subject to such pressures and giving such performances.

These observations pose significant challenges for how we view the organizational self (Kunda, 1992). Classic models (still the stock in trade of management motivation theory and practice) include the 'economic' (Taylorist, motivated by instrumental rewards) and the 'social' (human relations, motivated by sense of belonging). These need to be complemented by a more 'complex' self (Schein, 1979), incorporating multiple roles and commitments (Redman and Snape, 2005). The result is a self that is more ambivalent, ironic, and fluctuating than is traditionally recognized or formally acknowledged.

While this view may appear contemporary, even post-modern, in character, it is grounded in traditional views of human nature. First, it builds on and extends Machiavelli's insights into people's fickle and contradictory nature, an issue discussed in Chapter 4. One-dimensional models of motivation, commitment and loyalty make way for a more complex view of reflective actors juggling a variety of competing commitments and views of who they are, how they should be, and how they must act. As Smelser (1998) argues, traditional one-dimensional rational models of the self are less appropriate when this ambivalent character is recognized. As Kunda (1992) found in Tech, Casey (1999) in Hephaestus, and Kondo (1990) in her Japanese family company, managers and employees are pulled between, on the one hand, support for and a desire to believe in 'strong culture' rhetoric and, on the other hand, an expressed cynicism and recognition of instrumentalism and inequality. Managers who are not aware of the ways in which their superiors, colleagues and subordinates are grappling with (or avoiding) such ambiguities are, arguably, not able to read or effectively influence others. Rather than viewing our colleagues as one-dimensional 'cultural dopes', it may be more realistic to see them as creatively wrestling with '360 degree ambivalence', love and hate towards, dependence on and control over, customers, superiors, colleagues, and subordinates.

Second, this perspective recognizes what social psychologists have observed about human nature in general, and what social scientists such as Giddens (1991) have long noted of social action; its inherently reflexive or reflective nature. On the one hand, our beliefs, values and identities are shaped by what others think about us, who we are and what we should be doing. We are performing for and seeking to enrol what

Mead (1967) describes as 'significant others'. In this sense, we take on identities and roles, and are pressured to conform. On the other hand, we are also reflective and critical beings, able to 'stand above' such demands and develop a particular stance towards them. We are inevitably, to a degree, 'distant' from the roles that we play. In the face of ambiguous and conflicting roles, audiences, and demands, we become what Goffman (1961) described as 'holding company' selves, tailoring our 'performance' to situational requirements. So long as we live in a world of plural organizations and institutions, we are inevitably confronted by multiple social demands, and are forced into a degree of juggling and gameplaying. In a sense we are all inevitably Machiavellian players, using our knowledge, tacit or otherwise, of how to perform and 'play the game' (Berger, 1991). A certain degree of 'ironic distance' (Hochschild, 1979) from our performances is a requirement as well as, from some points of view, a curse. For some, this condition is seen as exacerbated in the 'post-modern' era. Sinclair (2007), for example, has argued that contemporary leaders are not only forced to adopt and juggle multiple and fragmented identities, but they are encouraged to revel in this experience, albeit in ways that are shaped by corporate advertisers and leadership consultants.

You don't think that what is going on here isn't drama, do you?

In one of our own studies in a large Australian steelmaking plant, an action researcher introduces to a work design group an example of how some companies use 'playback theatre' to stimulate reflection on their processes and relationships. The group members are shown pictures of the Danish DeCapo group, who act out to corporate audiences the parts that they see being played in their workplace. Discussion then turns to the value of this use of drama. Joe, an electrician, responds earnestly and then with a smile; 'You don't mean to tell me that you think that what is going on here isn't drama, do you?' A few months later, a research colleague brings a video recorder into the maintenance work group meeting that he is observing. One of the team grabs the recorder and starts filming the group, and the researcher (who is indistinguishable from the others in his work overalls and manner) playing cards. Suddenly, one of the group, a shop floor operative who is attending drama classes and following a psychology degree at university, appears to become very aggressive, and leaps towards the camera yelling, 'What are you f****** doing?', before smiling. This is a world away from the card-playing workers portrayed in the post-World War Two British film *I'm All Right, Jack* (1959, director John Boulting), playing stereotyped 'us and them' roles with the middle-class managerial recruit. If this idea of performance, this sense of drama and irony, permeates even the most traditional, boring and dirty shopfloor environments, what does this say about how those seeking to influence such actors should 'read' their motives and behaviours?

What are the implications of this more reflective, multiple and ambivalent view of identity for traditional and contemporary concerns about the Machiavellian and entrepreneurial aspects of organization politics? As we have seen, unease about the character and fate of the 'New Machiavellian' is firmly established. Riesman was concerned about the lack of an 'internal gyroscope' to guide management actions. Whyte was critical of the inauthentic sociability of 'organization man'. Maccoby characterized the superficialities and pathologies of the 'gamesman'. Lasch was caustic in his condemnation of the self-defeating nature of the 'narcissist'. Sennett railed against 'the corrosion of character'. Studies of the presumed psychopathology of the Machiavellian personality continue (McHoskey et al., 1998).

The recurring theme revolves around the prospect of a meaningless and angst-ridden life of playing games, managing performances, and navigating the destructive and time-wasting organization politics. Should we therefore worry about the 'salvation of the soul', as organization politicians become 'servants to their careers, and strangers to themselves and others' (Maccoby, 1978, p.264)? Adopting a more reflective view of identity, however, the problem is not the soul-destroying character of instrumental game-playing, for as we have seen this is an inescapable aspect of the management role. Rather, it is the challenge of maintaining an identity that governs the game-playing and gives it meaning.

We each have some idea of who we 'really are', on which we base decisions concerning how to act when faced with choices. This potentially becomes a problem when we find ourselves moving from one role, community, and organization to another; colleague, boss, subordinate, change agent, worker, consumer, friend, partner. Which identity is most important, and which standards should we apply? Some critics of the trends we have discussed here argue for the importance of an inner-oriented authentic self, with a sense of coherence, direction, and integrity that is based on a relatively stable idea of who we really are. When we find that we have to play multiple roles, to be different things to different people, to play political games, does this threaten the integrity of our personality? Some critics evidently believe that it does pose such a threat (Holstein and Gubrium, 2000). However, many of us seem to be willing and happy to move from one setting and role to another without too many problems. Indeed, this behavioural flexibility can be regarded as a fundamental aspect of social (and political) skill, adapting to changing circumstances in appropriate, creative, and effective ways. In contrast, rigid attachment to a fixed set of behavioural norms is a social liability in complex and rapidly changing organizations. Consequently, this is not a simple contrast between inner-oriented authenticity and externally-focused superficiality. The danger is that a necessary degree of Machiavellian pragmatism may become an end in itself, where all that matters is the performance, without a guiding purpose or sense of achievement.

The belief that organizational conditions promote an all-consuming Machiavellianism lies behind the pessimism of many critics. Maccoby (1978, p.264), for example, praises the achievements of a limited number of 'managerial mutants' who 'are compassionate, idealistic, and courageous entrepreneurs who stimulate loyalty by their concern for others and their constant effort to understand and strengthen what is creative in others and their organizations'. He also argues that the ability to inspire loyalty and trust, and to use 'gamesmanship' to establish equity, democracy, and security, is compromised if corporate ownership is not based on the same principles. Without such support, even the idealistic manager is inevitably required to engage in manipulation and performance to get ahead, or to 'detach themselves from the contest if they want to pursue their heart' (Maccoby, 1978, p.265). Gabriel (2005; 2006) offers a postmodern version of the same pessimism. He describes how today's 'glass cages allow for more ambivalent and nuanced experiences, these stem from an emphasis on narcissistic display and exhibitionism but also from controls residing in ever-present and ever-more-subtle surveillance' (Gabriel, 2006, p.3). He contrasts this with his preferred ideal of the manager as citizen, as the basis for a constructive and meaningful stance towards corporate realpolitik. This image of the citizen, he argues, is one that balances rights and duties, engages with the views of others, and actively builds public communities, yet defers to the will of the majority. This concept is severely compromised, he concludes, by the dominant view of managers as careerist consumers who pay for what they want, pursue their own individual pleasure and advantage, and exit when things do not work out.

Consequently, there is widespread apprehension concerning the evangelical nature of the culture of enterprise, and the potential personal costs incurred by those who champion this perspective. Some of this concern is based on the authoritarian nature of advice that one should adhere to a one-dimensional entrepreneurial personality. Others criticize the attempted 'governance of the soul' and the 'commercialization of human feeling' through the promotion of corporate norms. A third strand of apprehension springs from reported increases in working hours and intensity, and the incidence of stress-related health problems. This combination of factors, it can be argued, leads to self-exploitation and potential self-destructiveness among those who push themselves and others in pursuit of the greater good. The problem thus lies, not with the endeavour to establish meaning and purpose for oneself to the benefit of the wider community, but with the uncritical acceptance of externally imposed expectations, and standards by which to judge ourselves and others. Is it inevitable that we sacrifice the values of public service, citizenship, collegiality, and corrupt our own sense of identity, in the pursuit of 'winning'?

The reflective political entrepreneur

> [T]he whole concept of effectiveness is inseparable from a mode of human existence in which the contrivance of means is in central part the manipulation of human beings

> into compliant patterns of behaviour; and it is by appeal to his own effectiveness in this respect that the manager claims authority within the manipulative mode.
>
> *Source*: from MacIntyre (1985, p.71).

Insider–outsider

We tend to live in a world of stereotypes based on our tendency to divide the world into good and evil, rational and irrational, and then side with one against the other. One does not have to be a fan of cognitive psychology to recognize resistance to living with uncertainty, ambiguity and ambivalence. As Festinger (1964) demonstrated, contrary evidence can even strengthen commitment to a deeply held belief. The cult of the entrepreneurial hero is unlikely to be shattered by pointing out that the world is more complex. When asked recently whether any of the confident leaders she celebrated exhibited a sense of irony, Kanter replied that she had 'not thought about it'. Equally clearly, those who see this cult as a doctrinaire managerialism that threatens values of liberalism, plurality and critical thought (Rose, 1989) are unlikely to be impressed by pointing to the inspirational use that can be made of some of the ideas and the value of some of the tactics recommended and capabilities developed. Our task here, in arguing for a crucial role for the political entrepreneur, is to go beyond such stereotypes, and we are not alone in this.

The field of organization studies now recognizes a range of typical responses to management initiatives designed to inspire enthusiasm. Some become 'bewitched' by this corporate propaganda, while others are 'bothered' by these transient superficial fads. The first response can trigger over-identification with 'the new way', while the latter invokes cynicism. A third category are 'bewildered' and ambivalent about the sincerity of such initiatives, accepting some components while doubting other aspects, but taking part in the masquerade of the new game of corporate commitment anyway (Badham and Down, 2006; Badham and McLoughlin, 2006). While this categorization is oversimplified, it captures a significant element of the organization context in which the political entrepreneur operates.

The political entrepreneur has to wrestle with the issues that this raises for anyone proactive in managing change. From the pinnacle of the organization, it is a simple matter to become enthusiastically committed to the rhetoric of 'new leadership', the removal of 'old inflexibilities', and the 'dinosaur' structures of bureaucracy and privilege, while stress and burnout increase, work intensification imposes new burdens on service delivery, personal relations deteriorate and are replaced by branded corporate images, and increased flexibility and insecurity threaten individual abilities to carve out a meaningful and satisfying work role and career. Support for political entrepreneurialism needs to be one that takes into account such dangers, at the same time as it encourages the adoption of a proactive stance towards addressing all such conditions. If confidence is really, as Kanter (2004, p.13) puts it, the 'sweet spot between arrogance and despair', then the confidence of the political entrepreneur has to distance itself from both the arrogance of much of the entrepreneurial tradition as well as the despair of some of its more pessimistic critics.

What does it mean to say that we are not alone in reaching this conclusion? There is a growing number of examples of political practice that goes beyond restricted stereotypes, involving attempts to grapple with how practice is to be understood. In her examination of 'tempered radicals' in large American corporations, for example, Meyerson (2001) concludes that many of us accept our multiple roles and conflicting identities, and do not identify solely with organizational goals and practices. The characters she describes as tempered radicals seek to enhance organizational performance as well as their own reputations and careers, including interests and concerns beyond work. This can involve, for example, concerns with sexual equality, multicultural diversity, and genuine empowerment. Tempered radicals thus maintain a degree of distance from organizational life, operating as an 'insider–outsider', or as 'outsiders within', who tap into their ambivalence towards the organization as a source of strength and vitality, rather than confusion and reluctance. As Trinca and Fox (2004) argue, this approach links with cultural changes that go beyond organizational boundaries, notably in the rise of what they call 'cultural creatives' who are concerned as much with environment and sustainability issues as with corporate growth.

From studies of middle managers in the public sector in Britain, Hoyle and Wallace (2005) have extended this perspective with what they describe as 'principled infidelity'.

We have them on the run

In their study of culture change in an Australian steelworks, Badham and McLoughlin (2006) describe how staff at different levels of the organization adopted varying styles of inside–outside engagement in addressing such tensions as part of a proactive stance towards bringing about change. At the end of the day, Garry, the plant manager, comes into the office of Ross, one of his subordinates, designated by him to work closely with the consultants implementing the new structural change programme at Steelmaking Oz. Ross complains about his day; 'We went out and interviewed all the people who they wanted us to interview. Then we get back to the office and find a fax describing all the questions we were expected to ask. What a farce.' Garry stands back and smiles; 'Great news. We have them on the run. They are making it up as they go along. This gives us more of a chance to shape the agenda.' They laugh, and go on their way. Next day, the shaping process begins again, in earnest, as the change is given a more participatory and culturally sensitive slant by the plant's managers than was intended by many of the programme developers and administrators.

In other words, managers act as mediators between the often contradictory policies that are handed down to them, and 'making things work' in their everyday context. The emphasis again lies with the adoption of a critical and proactive stance towards organizational initiatives and solutions, including simple exhortations to be more 'enterprising', without recourse to distanced cynicism.

Beyond two-dimensional views

How does the insider–outsider deal with organization politics? We have argued here and in previous chapters for a Machiavellian pragmatism, combined with the creative imagination that commentators such as Schumpeter have advocated. The popular interpretation of Machiavellian 'thuggery' offers a view of a ruthless war of all against all, justifying brutality and deceit in pursuit of self-interest. Entrepreneurial evangelism, a popular and uncritical celebration of creativity and enterprise, seeks to confine management energies to the pursuit of corporate innovation and performance, paying little attention to the potential costs imposed on those committed to this approach.

The practice and ethics of organization politics are handled inadequately by this popular two-dimensional view of negative and positive politics. For negative, read Machiavellian, but this view tends to neglect the realistic pragmatism and liberal morality that can underpin such a strategy. For positive, read a 'win–win', collaborative, and institutionalized approach, which in turn tends to overlook the autocratic illiberality of such a viewpoint in advocating 'one best way' and marginalizing alternative perspectives, trade-offs, and unanticipated consequences. In contrast, Figure 7.1 locates the perspective of the political entrepreneur as a third option, combining Machiavellian pragmatism and creative entrepreneurialism in a manner that avoids both thuggery and evangelism. In adopting this perspective, the political entrepreneur continues to face a number of challenges:

- there is a danger that flexible pragmatism, in its own right, may become more important than purpose and direction
- it remains necessary to cope with the cognitive and emotional dissonance that can arise in complex organizational settings characterized by ambivalence and multiple audiences (Badham and McLoughlin, 2006) and
- this requires a degree of reflexivity in relation to one's own narratives or accounts (see Chapter 9), and
- establishing a purposeful reputation and career, while recognizing both the constraints as well as opportunities which this can create.

In other words, we need to be critical, sceptical, and reflexive in relation to our own 'spin', our performances, our ongoing attempts at impression management.

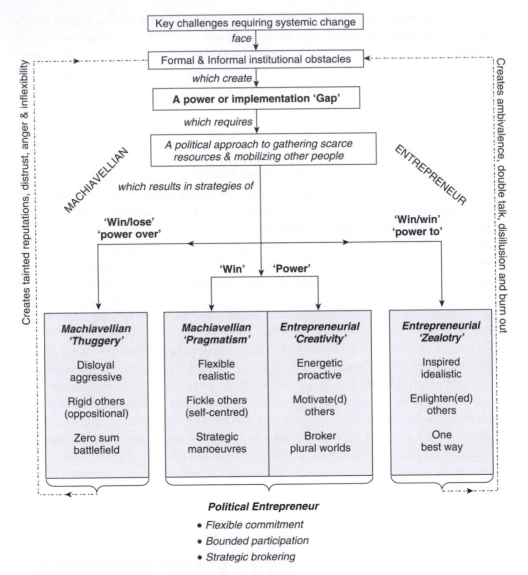

Figure 7.1 The political entrepreneur: a third power style.

Follow through

Mapping the political climate: stakeholder analysis as a Machiavellian tool

If you are involved in implementing, driving, influencing, or perhaps attempting to subvert a change initiative, then it is important to understand the political climate in the organization. That climate may be more or less sympathetic, or hostile. If it is sympathetic, then it may be useful to identify ways to maintain and strengthen support.

If it is hostile, steps to counter actual and potential threats and challenges may be required. One method for mapping this climate is *stakeholder analysis*. A stakeholder is anyone affected, directly or indirectly, by organizational change. Egan (1994) identifies nine categories of stakeholder.

- *Partners* who support your agenda.
- *Allies* those will support you, given encouragement.
- *Fellow travellers* passive supporters, perhaps committed to the agenda, but not to you.
- *Fencesitters* those whose allegiances are not clear.
- *Loose cannons* dangerous as they can vote against agendas in which they have no direct interest.
- *Opponents* players who oppose your agenda, but not you personally.
- *Adversaries* players who oppose both you and your agenda.
- *Bedfellows* those who support the agenda, but may not know or trust you.
- *The voiceless* stakeholders who will be affected by the agenda, but have little power to promote or oppose and who lack advocates.

Different stakeholders must be managed differently. Partners and allies need to be 'kept on side'. Opponents need to be converted. Adversaries have to be discredited and marginalized. Egan suggests that the needs of 'the voiceless' should also be addressed in case they are recruited by adversaries and used against the change agenda. To conduct a stakeholder analysis, first identify your change project or programme, then follow these steps:

1 Draw up a list of the stakeholders in the changes that you and colleagues are proposing. Assess their respective power to support or to block your proposals.
2 Establish what each *perceives* they will gain or lose if the changes go ahead. If you don't know their thinking, then you need to find this out. Their perceptions may be inaccurate, but that is where you must begin, if you want to alter them.
3 Use the planned benefits to strengthen support for the proposals among the 'winners'.
4 Identify ways to address the concerns of those who see themselves as 'losers', by altering the nature of the proposals, or by offering to mitigate losses in other ways.
5 Based on this analysis, design and implement a rolling stakeholder management plan to establish and maintain over time a supportive political climate, aware that the climate can change because of your actions, and through other events and circumstances.

It is interesting to consider how you are personally affected by using stakeholder analysis:

- Does this analysis encourage you to stereotype others as objects to be manipulated? What are the personal benefits and costs of this approach?

- Does stakeholder analysis suggest a manipulative war of all against all, or help to develop a more productive workplace? Would this encourage suspicion, distrust and deceit, or lead to an improved understanding of the views and motives of others?

Debrief

Stakeholder analysis has limitations and strengths:

Limitations

- Incomplete information concerning stakeholder perceptions and interests.
- Perceptions and interests are liable to change rapidly.
- Actions based on inaccurate analysis can be damaging.
- Analysis and understanding does not always mean that problems with particular stakeholders can be solved.

Strengths

- Need to be clear about friends, enemies, and neutrals.
- Essential that different stakeholder interests are addressed in appropriate ways.
- Forces consideration of the 'soft' factors concerning attitudes and interests.
- Deals in a structured, analytical way with the untidy organization politics.

Organization politics at the movies: *Dead Poets Society*

The film *Dead Poets Society* (1989, director Peter Weir) describes the experience of an innovative English teacher, John Keating (played by Robin Williams) who is employed by an extremely conservative and autocratic boys' school, Welton Academy. The school principles are tradition, honour, discipline, and excellence. For the boys, however, the principles of 'Hellton' are 'travesty, horror, decadence, and excrement'. Keating's methods for teaching English literature and poetry are unconventional. His aim is to inspire his students, to encourage them to think differently, and to challenge contemporary (1950s) norms of literary criticism. Keating stands on the classroom desks and shouts, and encourages the students to tear out of their texts an essay that he finds particularly offensive in its approach to assessing poetry. Keating is an innovator. As you watch the movie, consider the following:

- What methods and tactics does Keating use to inspire his pupils to think differently and to challenge their conformist behaviour?
- How would you assess the political climate facing Keating at Welton Academy?
- What are Keating's main successes and achievements as an innovator?
- And what are Keating's main mistakes and failures?
- How could Keating have acted differently in this context? What could he have done to develop a political climate more receptive to his nonconformist methods?

To what extent does your advice apply generally to innovators in bureaucratic settings?

Debrief

A competent and innovative teacher, Keating is politically naive, and an idealist whose lack of political awareness harms both himself and others. For his methods to have any chance of success, he would have to bring a more informed and creative approach to understanding and engaging the school politics. It is interesting to consider the tactics that he could have used to 'break the frame' of the traditional autocratic institution, moving with greater caution, building relationships, support, and a power base among his established and more senior academic colleagues. However, his main tactic is to build a narrow and fragile coalition of students around his ideas, ignoring the views and interests of his teaching colleagues. Keating is partly responsible for the suicide of one of his students, whose desire to become an actor he encourages, against the wishes of the boy's father. One member of his coalition betrays him, by exaggerating his actions, and Keating is fired. Would a more politically pragmatic, or more astutely entrepreneurial, Keating have been able to achieve more in these circumstances while doing less damage to himself and to those around him?

8 Power assisted steering: accounting and winning

Chapter objectives

1 To consider practical advice for change agents faced with organization politics.
2 To identify political approaches relevant to different stages of the change process.
3 To discuss the role of 'accounting' in presenting and legitimating political behaviour.
4 To develop a sustainable perspective on winning the turf game.

"Can everyone clearly fear me?"

Recipes for change

Advice on managing change tends to be straightforward, uncontentious, and consistent in what is advocated. In this chapter, we will first consider typical advice on implementation, and consider the limitations of this guidance in the context of a political perspective on change. We will then consider the implications for the role of change agents, particularly with regard to the use of political tactics to progress (and subvert) change.

Having explored positioning and accounting as aspects of political skill, we will finally develop a sustainable perspective on what it means to win, and to go on winning, the turf game.

Most practical management guidelines for effective change implementation offer a checklist of steps to follow. Collins (1998), among others, criticizes the prescriptive nature of this work for offering over-simplified 'n-step guides' or recipe style implementation lists. This criticism appears to be shared by many managers, who experience difficulty translating these 'recipes' into their organizational contexts (Buchanan et al., 1999). What are the problems with these recipes, and how can we both use and move beyond them?

Manager Can I just talk about the context here? In trying to create change in a healthcare environment, understanding the kind of political issues and being able to work with the political issues is absolutely critical. Because the politics largely defines what you can enact and you can't enact as change. When we first started, we had a typical linear–rational change methodology – the typical management consultancy approach – you follow step 7A, followed by step 7B. You set your terms of reference, then you analyse, then you redesign, then you pilot, then you implement. And after about three months of trying that, we had to chuck it out the window. The major reason for that was the methodology took no account of the political set-up and the political behaviour in the organization. We had to design a completely different methodology that took account of the politics of the organization. It was just so naive to assume that one could just go in and create some fabulous redesign for a new service, and just be able to implement it, if you had good planning. What it exposed was how deep and fundamental a lot of the political structures of the organization are, and how incredibly difficult those are to change.

In one widely cited recipe, Kotter (1995) offers an eight-step guide to change (Table 8.1). There are numerous such rational, linear models available. Ulrich (1998) presents a seven-step guide; Ward (1994) offers 13 implementation lessons; Eccles (1984) identifies 14 factors for successful change; Gustafson et al. (2003) list 18 predictors of successful change. From this perspective, effective change depends on clarity of objectives, good communications, appropriate leadership, and close monitoring and control to ensure that the initiative stays on target with respect to time and money. Ineffective change is blamed on poor leadership, unclear goals, tasks, milestones and budgets, and on poor control and communications – on failure to follow the recipe. The change agent thus needs two areas of expertise. First, with respect to the *content* of the changes being introduced (new information system, office building, payment system). Second, with respect to *controls*, understanding the stages of change, defining goals and tasks, monitoring progress, and

Table 8.1 Eight steps to transforming your organization

1 Establish a sense of urgency
  • Examine market and competitive realities
  • Identify and discuss crises, potential crises and major opportunities
2 Form a powerful guiding coalition
  • Assemble a group with enough power to lead the change effort
  • Encourage the group to work together as a team
3 Create a vision
  • Create a vision to help direct the change effort
  • Develop strategies for achieving that vision
4 Communicate the vision
  • Use every vehicle possible to communicate the new vision and strategies
  • Teach new behaviours by the example of the guiding coalition
5 Empower others to act on the vision
  • Get rid of obstacles to change
  • Change systems or structures that seriously undermine the vision
  • Encourage risk taking and non-traditional ideas, activities and actions
6 Plan for and create short-term wins
  • Plan for visible performance improvements
  • Create those improvements
  • Recognize and reward employees involved in the improvements
7 Consolidate improvements and produce more change
  • Use credibility to change systems, structures and policies that don't fit the vision
  • Hire, promote, and develop employees who can implement the vision
  • Reinvigorate the process with new projects, themes and change agents
8 Institutionalize new approaches
  • Articulate the connections between the new behaviour and corporate success
  • Develop the means to ensure leadership development and succession

Source: based on Kotter (1995).

taking remedial action to reduce and avoid deviations from plan. Most of this advice is formulaic, unremarkable, and common sense. Imagine advocating 'short term losses', 'lack vision', 'avoid training', 'be inflexible'.

These rational–linear models have one feature in common. They rely on the assumption that change unfolds in a tidy, logical sequence. Solutions are not identified until the problem has been clearly defined. The 'best' solution is not chosen until the options have been compared and evaluated. Implementation does not begin until there is agreement on the solution. Key actors each have clearly defined roles and responsibilities. Plans unfold more or less as specified. Implementation is closely monitored, and deviations from plan are corrected. The implementation process is bounded in terms of resources and time, with a clear completion date. The assumptions of rationality and linearity have attracted significant criticism, much of which has already been noted. Organizations rarely function in such a predictable manner, particularly with respect to strategic (major, messy, radical) change.

Kotter's recipe for change, and others like this, are difficult to apply in practice for several reasons. First, they identify an ideal agenda which management may not have the time and resources to address. Second, they are generic, with no guidance on how they can be translated into specific contexts. Third, the relationships between the ingredients, and the emphasis which each deserves, are not explored. Fourth, these approaches typically adopt the organization development (OD) viewpoint that conflict in an organization is caused by communication failures. Many OD interventions are designed to resolve conflict by creating forums for information-sharing, and the political dimension of change is overlooked.

Change processes are often untidy, iterative, and politicized (Pettigrew, 1985; Dawson, 2003). Tidy recipes are valuable in this respect, bringing order and structure to that complexity. Planning is easier when the dimensions of a problem can be plotted clearly. Decision making is more straightforward when information is presented in a manner that allows options to be assessed systematically. Communication is easier when goals and visions have been unambiguously stated. However, planning, decision making, and communicating are also socio-political processes. It is not 'the information' that counts as much as the players with their competing interpretations, values, interests and preferences. We therefore need to pay attention to the organizational context facing the change agent.

The context in which change agents operate varies from setting to setting, particularly with regard to political intensity. Figure 8.1 captures this variation by plotting the context on two dimensions. The vertical axis runs from 'challenged' at one extreme to 'accepted' at the other. Change initiatives that are understood and welcomed are likely to generate less conflict and political behaviour than ambiguous changes which are controversial and contested. The horizontal axis runs from 'marginal' to 'critical'. Change which is radical and rapid heightens uncertainty and conflict which are triggers for political action.

The change agent driving proposals which are critical to the organization, but which meet with broad acceptance, may be able to work quickly using representative (as opposed to all-inclusive) participation (quadrant 2). Change which is more marginal to the success of the business and which can be implemented at a more relaxed pace allows for extensive participation (quadrant 3). The lower half of the figure is the domain of traditional organization development, of 'truth, trust, love and collaboration' approaches to change.

Our concern, of course, lies mainly in the domain of power assisted steering. However, it is important to note that change which is politicized is not going to be driven exclusively by power–political behaviour. The conventional apparatus of project management, participation, communication, and organization development interventions, is still useful. A focus on the often overlooked political aspects of change implementation does not deny the relevance of more traditional methods and tools, but political behaviour is required in many contexts to complement those methods. Consequently, the change agent driving initiatives which are critical and challenged may have to resort

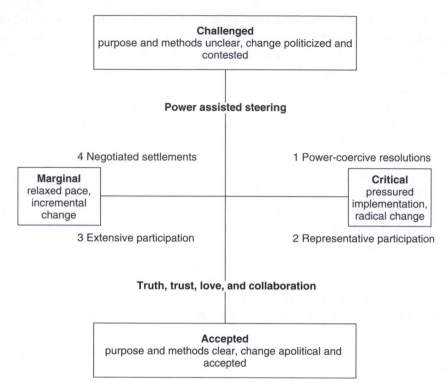

Figure 8.1 The change agency context.

to power–coercive solutions (quadrant 1). Dunphy and Stace (1990; Stace and Dunphy, 1994) argue from Australian evidence that major changes that are contentious, but which have to be introduced quickly, are more likely to succeed if management use a 'dictatorial transformation' approach. The problems with changes which are marginal, but are also challenged, may be resolved through negotiated settlements between advocates and opponents (quadrant 4).

Faced with an organizational context in which a greater or lesser degree of power assisted steering is required to advance the change agenda, Kotter's (1995) checklist, and others in that style, are at the same time incomplete, and informative. On the one hand, they lack a creative, reflective viewpoint. They cannot be 'followed' in a straightforward prescriptive sense. On the other hand, they can be used creatively to legitimate change and the steps involved, as tools to guide the implementation process, and as tactical weapons in the turf game. Despite what we know about the untidy backstage realities, change has to appear in public to be (and to have been) rational and linear. These are as much 'recipes for how change implementation should appear to be', as for how it should actually be managed.

Here is a paradoxical summary of practical advice for change agents concerning the use of rational–linear change implementation models:

- Beware simple recipes for effective change. These are not good reflections of actual change processes, and are not good guides for action, particularly political action.
- Embrace rational–linear accounts of change. These models show how the process should appear to be conducted, both during and after implementation. These are accurate guides to the 'politically correct' public representation of change.

Communication–consensus, or power–politics?

Conflict in an organization arises and can be resolved in different ways. Borum (1995) characterizes two perspectives, based on contrasting organizational assumptions, with different consequences for conflict resolution in practice.

The *communication–consensus model* is based on the following assumptions:

- the organization structure is relatively stable
- the elements (people, systems, technology) of the organization are well-integrated
- the elements in combination contribute to organizational operations
- efficiency and effectiveness are based on consensus around shared values and goals
- conflict and political behaviour are damaging and must be resolved.

These assumptions suggest a *communication strategy* for resolving conflict:

1 open up lines of communication
2 improve information base for parties involved, to change perceptions and attitudes
3 explore and settle differences of opinion
4 conflict resolved.

The *power–politics model* of organization is based on a different set of assumptions:

- the organization structure is subject to constant change
- the organization always contains disagreements and conflicts
- any element of the organization can contribute to disruption and change
- organizational functioning requires that some individuals impose control over others
- conflict and political behaviour are inevitable and must be managed.

Continued

These assumptions suggest a *political strategy* for resolving conflict:

1 assess and strengthen personal power position in relation to opponent or 'target'
2 deploy influencing tactics to change target's perceptions and attitudes
3 when that fails, use covert political tactics to undermine and neutralize target
4 personal and organizational objectives achieved.

Practice in most organizations spans and fluctuates across the continuum between these extremes. While conflict may often be resolved by improved communication, that strategy will be ineffective in other settings where political strategies will also be appropriate.

Source: based on Borum (1995).

Souls of fire: change agency and the politics of positioning

We are discussing the role of the change agent (singular) mainly for presentation purposes. While there may be an individual project lead, organizational change typically involves collective effort. Before exploring the political dimension of change agency, therefore, it is useful first to identify more clearly who those agents (plural) might be. This exploration will take us from the single change champion, through the notion of multiple interlocking roles, to a contemporary perspective on dispersed or distributed change leadership. We will then turn our attention to how those engaged in change agency can deal with the organization politics.

From his analysis of accounts of radical innovations, Schön (1963, p.84) identified a number of themes.

1 A new idea meets with indifference or active resistance, because it appears to counter established practice, and because it looks expensive and unworkable.
2 The new idea gets vigorous promotion, to sell and otherwise fight for the concept.
3 Advocates use personal networks rather than 'official' channels to disseminate the new idea, particularly in the early stages.
4 One individual emerges as 'champion of the idea'.

Schön regards it as a requirement that somebody is prepared to put themselves, 'on the line for an idea of doubtful success', and that, 'the new idea either finds a champion or dies'. Many commentators now use the term 'change champion'. Stjernberg and Philips (1993) refer instead to 'souls of fire', from the Swedish 'eldsjälar' meaning 'driven by burning enthusiasm'. But implementation is often a collective effort, and evidence suggests that, in some cases, change agency roles are widely dispersed across all organizational levels, with different individuals and groups assuming responsibility for parts of the process as it develops. In other words, in many cases, there may be large numbers of champions, souls of fire, or 'unsung heroes' helping to facilitate and implement change initiatives.

Following the theme of multiple change agents, Ottaway (1983) established the taxonomy shown in Table 8.2. This distinguishes change generators from implementers or adopters, identifying three or four 'sub-roles' under each of those main categories. Ottaway's taxonomy has a chronological flow, from change agents or initiators to users, noting that change is fluid, shifting over time as initiatives unfold, often in unanticipated ways.

Table 8.2 A change agents' taxonomy

Group	Category	Description
Change generators	**key change agents**	the primary initiator of an issue into a felt need – their methods and values dominate the process
	demonstrators	visibly show their support of the process of change set in motion by the key change agents – the first line of confrontation between agents and resisters
	patrons	have the task of generating financial and other public support for the change process
	defenders	defend the change process at grass roots, keep the issue alive, help work out the implications and consequences of proposals at the lowest levels
Change implementers	**external implementers**	brought in from outside to assist development of the change process
	external/internal implementers	brought in to help develop internal implementers, acting perhaps out of 'head office' in an advisory or training and development capacity
	internal implementers	responsible for implementing changes in their own groups, briefed to do this as a full time activity – may work with other categories of implementers
Change adopters	**early adopters**	first adopters of the change and thus the prototype for further adoption – high in commitment, change advocates, self-nominated, the link between implementers and other adopters
	maintainers	adopt change while retaining commitment to work roles, even while these are changing – if the maintainers don't change, there is no change
	users	get into the habit of working in the changed organization; if there are no users, there will be no change; at this level, most of us are change agents

Source: based on Ottaway (1983).

Adopting a similar perspective, Hutton (1994) identifies a 'cast of characters' including:

- *sponsors*, who legitimize and protect change initiatives
- *advocates*, who promote new ideas
- *change agents*, who are responsible for orchestrating implementation.

For Hutton the 'change agent' is anyone taking the lead, whether or not they are formally appointed to that role. From a hospital study, Brooks (1996) found that changes relied on the chief executive, a cadre of managers, and a diagonal slice of a dozen staff designated as 'networkers'. Denis et al. (2001) argue that change in organizations characterized by shared and ambiguous leadership, divergent objectives, and diffuse power (i.e., health care) depends on a 'leadership constellation', whose members play fluid and complementary roles. From studies of innovation processes, Van de Ven et al. (1999) challenge the stereotype of the lone creator with their finding that innovations depend on the contributions of many entrepreneurs engaging and disengaging with the process over time and in a variety of roles. Buchanan (2003) describes the re-engineering programme at Leicester Royal Infirmary in the 1990s as a 'dispersed responsibility' model of change.

In other words, change agency is often a *distributed* phenomenon, an observation echoed in recent commentary on distributed leadership (Bryman, 1996; Gronn, 2002a; Bennett et al., 2003). These domains are now often conflated in the concept of 'change leadership' (Nadler, 1998; Denis et al., 2001). Gronn (2002b) suggests that the defining feature of distributed leadership is 'concertive action', in which steps initiated by one individual are developed by others through the 'circulation of initiative'. Caldwell (2003; 2005) argues that the current fashion for empowerment in large part explains the development of such widely distributed change agency.

The static notion of the single change agent or champion does not always reflect the degree of involvement in many change processes. Change agency is emergent and fluid, and depends on the cast of characters. Those who 'take the lead' themselves change over time, as an initiative develops and matures, as other projects and actors come into play, as events deflect planned progress, and as responsibility changes hands. As change agency is a shifting set of complementary roles, political skill (see Chapter 9) is valuable to anyone who chooses to take such a role, whether formally or self-appointed.

Initiator, sponsor, implementer: what position or positions do you want to play, and with what types of change do you want to be involved? The problem is, it may be difficult to develop a fast-track, high-flying career by implementing at a relaxed pace minor and uncontroversial initiatives that have little impact. Career progression depends on high visibility and high impact (Rein et al., 2006). Consider Schön's requirement that somebody put themselves 'on the line'. Let us assume that one wishes to be perceived as effective, competent, credible, and successful. Positions in which one

'It's all right to do your regular work, Sanders, but haven't you caught on yet? The <u>big</u> money is in breakthroughs.'

© ScienceCartoonsPlus.com and Sidney Harris: reproduced with permission.

can take credit for successful outcomes are more desirable than those where the credit accumulates elsewhere. On the other hand, positions in which one is likely to attract blame for mistakes and failures are better avoided. Positioning can thus have a significant impact on reputation. This is an argument for positioning oneself in change agency roles that involve major, visible, high impact initiatives, but these are inevitably controversial and contested, politicized, and risky. The risks cover organizational outcomes, and the agent's reputation. The positions in which the risks are high, however, are often those where the potential rewards are high, too.

Positioning may not always be a simple matter of individual choice. The ability of change agents to switch roles depends on the substance and goals of the initiatives in hand, the formal position, power base and personal attributes of the individual, and the positions adopted by other players in the game at any one time. Positioning thus depends on circumstances, on an assessment of the context, and on the way in which events are unfolding. But even change agents trapped in formal positions can adopt strategies to distance themselves from a failing initiative by indicating, for example, lack of agreement with the way in which proposals are being advanced, or implementation is being progressed. Buchanan and Storey (1997) refer to this positioning and repositioning as 'role taking and role switching' (see Chapter 1, Table 1.1). The manner in which the players in the turf game position themselves in relation to change agendas, and the ways in which they take, define, and adjust those positions as change unfolds, is a component of political skill. Change agents must be able to shift their positions, to maximize personal influence and advantage, and to progress the change agenda for which they are responsible. As discussed earlier, this is not a simple argument for preserving self-interest, which is often regarded as categorically unethical. On the contrary, change agents with tarnished reputations and weakened credibility have limited opportunity to influence beneficial projects in future.

Practical advice concerning the positioning of the change agent thus includes:

- Position yourself in the domain of major, radical, significant, high impact, high visibility changes to maximize career advantage.
- Assess the balance of risks and rewards in this positioning strategy. Some high impact change may carry high personal and organizational risk.
- Select with care the change agency roles that you adopt in relation to particular initiatives, given the cast of other characters around you. These choices have implications for your developing reputation.
- Switch and redefine your roles as change unfolds, to achieve maximum organizational benefit and personal advantage, to preserve reputation and credibility.

The politics of change initiation

Most commentators have been concerned with the politics of change implementation. However, it is interesting also to consider the extent to which different approaches may be appropriate at different stages of the implementation life cycle, from initial conception of the idea, through launching the initiative, implementing or delivering the changes, and finally to completion. From a political perspective, it is helpful to remember that change initiatives also have an 'afterlife', a more or less protracted period during which stories circulate about the success (or failure) of the changes, and of the competence (or otherwise) of those responsible for initiating and implementing them.

Table 8.3 A phase model of political strategy and tactics

Phase	Political Strategies/Tactics
initiation	the politics of project presentation, issue-selling, justifying
launch	the politics of project definition, recruiting support, coalition building
delivery	the politics of driving, steering, keeping momentum, blocking resistance
completion	the politics of termination and withdrawal, reporting back, moving on
afterlife	the politics of representation, tales and myths of problems and success

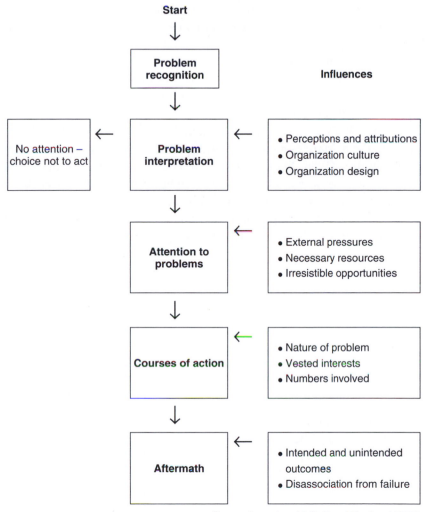

Figure 8.2 contents:

Start
↓
Problem recognition
↓

Influences

No attention – choice not to act ← **Problem interpretation** ←
- Perceptions and attributions
- Organization culture
- Organization design

↓

Attention to problems ←
- External pressures
- Necessary resources
- Irresistible opportunities

↓

Courses of action ←
- Nature of problem
- Vested interests
- Numbers involved

↓

Aftermath ←
- Intended and unintended outcomes
- Disassociation from failure

Source: based on McCall and Kaplan (1990).

Figure 8.2 Phases of management decision making.

Table 8.3 suggests in outline how the political strategies and tactics of change agency may need to shift in emphasis at different stages.

What tactics are helpful in getting a change proposal off the ground? McCall and Kaplan (1990) model the phases of management decision making (Figure 8.2), arguing that problems have to be recognized as such, and interpreted as significant, in order to attract attention. The factors influencing problem interpretation include the perceptions and attributions of those involved, organization design and culture, the availability of resources, external pressures, and the promise of irresistible opportunities. A problem gets little or no attention when those in positions of influence do not recognize the issue as important, or where the causes of this problem are attributed to other factors, which may be beyond their control. Issues can also be sidelined when the solution is perceived to benefit only some other (competing) group or function, or where those key decision makers have already decided that resources need to be deployed to higher priority tasks, or believe that the opportunities in this case are minimal.

A key political task at the initiation stage is to make sure that the issues figure prominently on a management agenda which is likely to be crowded with other competing initiatives. March and Olsen (1983, p.292) refer to this as the 'organization of attention'. Dutton (1988; Dutton et al., 2001) refers to this as marketing ideas, as orchestrating impressions, and as 'issue-selling'. Any organization, therefore, is 'a market-place for ideas', each competing with each other for attention, endorsement, and resources. Kanter (1983a) previously argued that change agents compete for 'capital' in three markets; the knowledge market for ideas, the economic market for resources, and the political market for support. Ideas do not appear on the management agenda simply because they are 'obvious' or even where they are backed by evidence. Ideas rise to prominence by the efforts of their advocates to 'market' or to sell those issues to colleagues. While some issue-selling methods are public and visible, others take place backstage and are less easy to identify.

Researcher Can you give me some examples?

Manager The first year of the re-engineering programme, we had a situation where we had a directors group who are all the senior managers of the organization, and they met every week. There was this huge programme, fifty people seconded full time, nearly 100 projects, and yet if you looked at what those senior managers spent their time doing, you'd think re-engineering wasn't happening. OK, there were all sorts of horrendous things going on. There was a financial crisis. There was somebody potentially doing a [sabotage] job in the operating theatres. There was a winter bed crisis. There was an impending industrial dispute over staff salaries. And this meant that senior managers were all engaged in things that were very urgent, but not necessarily important. So you have this huge programme, and to judge from what senior managers were doing, you might not even have known it was happening. So it was a question of how to engage those people with the change process at the same time.

Dutton and colleagues describe several techniques for manipulating senior management perceptions, agendas, decisions, and actions. In Chapter 3, we explored the ethics of the case of 'Sam and Bob'. Bob was given the 'best new project' funding following his successful lobbying campaign, while Sam did nothing to 'sell' his ideas. According to one set of commentators (Cavanagh et al., 1981), tactics such as these introduce 'irrelevant differences' between competing proposals and can therefore be regarded as unfair and unethical. While 'manipulation' is indeed often used as a negative term, suggesting devious, disreputable behaviour, Dutton argues that managers who are not prepared to use such methods are likely to find (as did Sam) that their good ideas do not attract attention, and are not pursued, while other competing issues and initiatives find support and resources.

The techniques identified in Dutton et al.'s (2001) research are summarized in Table 8.4, which identifies three main categorizes of 'moves'. *Packaging moves* concern ways in which ideas can be 'wrapped' to make them more appealing, more urgent, more acceptable, and include presentation tactics and bundling tactics. *Involvement moves* concern ways in which relationships and structures can be exploited to build support for ideas. *Process* moves concern preparation, timing, and degree of formality in issue selling.

The skills of the change architect: coalition building tactics

- concentrate on team creation as well as team building
- 'clear' your investment with a senior manager
- secure appropriate blessings from other relevant managers
- create 'cheerleaders' for your project
- engage in horse-trading if appropriate
- formalize coalitions, with committees or steering groups.

Source: based on Kanter (1983a).

Sonenshein (2006) develops a similar approach to 'issue crafting', which involves the manipulation of public language to make issues appear to be more legitimate, urgent, and trustworthy for the audience. Issues are crafted through embellishing (emphasizing particular features), subtracting (playing down parts of the argument) and through consistency (we all share the same values and goals). These tactics can rely either on a normative perspective (fairness, obligation, values, do the right thing) or on an economic perspective (objective, rational, commercial, business oriented). In Sonenshein's study, the most common issue-crafting tactics involved economic embellishing and normative subtracting, in other words emphasizing commercial gain and paying less attention to values.

Practical advice concerning the politics of change initiation thus includes:

- Be ready to use a combination of conventional and political tactics to progress the change agenda, depending on context and on the development phase of the initiative.

Table 8.4 Issue-selling moves and tactics

Packaging moves

Presenting
- using the logic of the business plan, 'running the numbers', using lots of figures and charts, conveying a logical and coherent structure, emphasizing bottom-line impacts
- continuous proposal making, raising issues many times over a period, prepare the target to better 'hear' a full proposal
- making changes appear incremental, by 'chunking' ideas into components to make them more palatable to potential targets

Bundling
- tying issues to profitability, market share, organizational image
- tying issues to the concerns of key constituents

Involvement moves
- targets of involvement; knowing who to involve and when
- involving senior management in supporting ideas
- clearing the idea with your immediate superior
- involving colleagues and other departments in supporting ideas
- involving outsiders, like consultants, to gain credibility
- customizing issue-selling to stakeholders
- using formal committees and task forces to legitimize issues
- creating a task force with a diverse membership

Process moves

Formality
- deciding appropriate degree of formality in issue-selling

Preparation
- collecting background information on context before selling, preparing people to support an idea when the time comes
- understanding social relationships, organizational networks, and strategic goals and priorities

Timing
- being persistent through a lengthy issue-selling process
- sensing when to hold back and when to move forward, based on level of support
- involving relevant others at an early stage

Source: based on Dutton et al. (2001).

- Orchestrate the impressions and understandings of others, particularly in the early stages of implementation, through agenda management and issue-selling tactics.
- Sell your ideas through a combination of packaging, involvement, and process moves.
- Recognize that while some may regard issue-selling tactics as unethical, these methods are often necessary to promote good ideas in settings where there are many other ideas competing for attention and resources.

The politics of change implementation

How should change agents approach the political dimension of their role when it comes to implementation? How can political tactics best be deployed effectively to shape the nature, direction, and outcomes of change? How can change agents balance the delivery progress of a change agenda with the interests of the organization, and with personal reputation and career aspirations? There is no shortage of general advice on the use of power and political tactics, a tradition that dates from Machiavelli (1514) and *The Prince* (see Chapter 4), through *Princessa: Machiavelli for Women* (Rubin, 1997; see   Chapter 5). Change agents can be regarded as contemporary 'Princessas' and 'Princes'. However, the mainstream literature of power and politics does not speak directly to the work of organizational change agents, and most commentary on change management either ignores power and politics, or advises change agents that this is territory to avoid. In this section, we will focus on political advice that has been directed at management in general, as well as change agents.

Researcher What do you see as the advantages to the individual of being able to use political behaviour?

Manager The key advantage, I think, is that you can more successfully achieve the outcomes that you personally are looking for in the process. I think there is an ability to understand the visible and invisible parts of the organization, and I think the skilled political operator is able to tap into those invisible aspects far more easily. So they will be exposed to a different series of information sources and they'll be able to get information to different people far more easily.

The other advantage I think is that you can disproportionately attract attention and support if you martial your campaign well. And I think if you can tap in to the sympathies people have for a particular function, or the fact that other senior managers have worked in that function in the past, and use your network of people, you can actually seek to develop quite a strong case for protecting or developing your part of the organization.

Arguing that getting things done is at least as important as deciding what to do in the first place, Pfeffer (1992a, p.27) sets out a 'seven point plan' for the effective exercise of organizational power and influence, and thus for implementing change:

1 decide your goals
2 diagnose patterns of interdependence, focusing on those who are influential
3 establish their views of your goals
4 identify their power bases

5 identify the bases of your own power and influence
6 determine effective strategies and tactics for the situation
7 choose a course of action.

Egan (1994) offers further advice on choosing a political strategy, starting with 'the practice of positive politics'; in other words, the change agent should have a legitimate, institution-building agenda. This reflects a positive, desirable, 'facilitative' view of power (Clegg, 1989) in which the function of political activity is to 'shepherd' issues through the organizational maze. The change agent should in Egan's view welcome competing agendas, conduct a stakeholder analysis, and plan a political campaign as follows:

- learn the name of the game in your organization; how are politics played here?
- get to know the playing field, the informal organization, the communication networks
- identify the key players (not always obvious) and their main interests
- get organized; enlist your supporters early; form powerful alliances and coalitions
- use informal networks to gather intelligence, and to send unobtrusive messages
- develop relations with those who you know will support you
- know who owes you favours, and call these in when necessary
- balance overt and covert action
- know when to go public and when to work behind the scenes
- learn how to use trade-offs; maximize flexibility without becoming 'slippery'
- use drama and theatre, sparingly; use stirring gestures that don't cheapen the agenda.

There is a lot of advice similar to this in circulation. Martin and Sims (1964, pp.218–19) summarized many of these ideas some decades ago. They asked:

How can power be used most effectively? What are some of the political stratagems which the administrator must employ if he is to carry out his [*sic*] responsibilities and further his career? This is an area that has been carefully avoided by both students and practitioners of business – as if there were something shady about it. But facts are facts, and closing our eyes to them will not change them. Besides, if they are important facts, they should be brought into the open for examination.

Martin and Sims (1964, p.218) also observed that, 'though we glorify ambition in the abstract, we frown on its practice and are distressed by the steps which must be taken if ambition is to be translated into actual development. Thus when power is coupled with ambition, we shy away and try to pretend that neither exists'. From their study of the biographies of 'well-known leaders of history', including Rockefeller and Ford, combined with interviews with contemporary executives, Martin and Sims identified

Table 8.5 Common political tactics

taking counsel	Able executives are cautious about how they seek and receive ideas.
alliances	The executive system in a firm is composed of sponsorship and protégé relationships.
manoeuvrability	Wise executives maintain their flexibility, never committing themselves to any one position or programme.
communication	It is not good strategy to communicate everything one knows. It may be advantageous to withhold information or to time its release.
compromising	Executives should accept compromise with tongues in their cheeks. Although appearing to alter a view, they should continue to press towards a clear-cut set of goals.
negative timing	Action is initiated, but implementation is slow; the executive is considering and studying the problem, the difficulties that are to be overcome, the implications that must be dealt with.
self-dramatization	Dramatists select and arrange aspects of reality in order to arouse emotions, convince, and persuade others to change their views.
confidence	Executives must act decisively. Once a decision is taken, executives who maintain the impression of knowing what they are doing, even if they do not, are both using and increasing their power simultaneously.
always the boss	Personal relations with subordinates are sometimes considered the mark of a good executive. However, an atmosphere of friendship interferes with operational efficiency and limits the manager's power.

Source: based on Martin and Sims (1964).

the nine tactics shown in Table 8.5. A decade later, *Harvard Business Review* carried an article on 'power and the ambitious executive', by McMurry (1973, pp.140 and 145) who argued that:

> The methods of holding top-management power in a company strike many people as devious and Machiavellian. They involve calculated alliances, compromises, and 'deals' – and often they fly in the face of practices advocated by experts on organizational behaviour. . . . Such strategies are not always noble and high minded. But neither are they naive. From the selfish standpoint of the beleaguered and harassed executive, they have one primary merit: they enhance his [*sic*] chances of survival.

McMurry's (1973) advice was similar to that offered earlier by Martin and Sims (1964), adding passive resistance as a tactic, emphasizing the need to be ruthless when expedient, but otherwise repeating familiar advice concerning selective communications, impression management, maintaining flexibility, and avoiding friendships with subordinates.

Dealing with 'the influence process between specialist and executives', Pettigrew (1974) lists ten 'defensive tactics' with which managers can more or less tactfully ignore the potentially unwelcome advice of their advisers:

 1 straight rejection
 2 'bottom drawer' it
 3 mobilize political support against the specialist
 4 the 'nitty gritty' tactic, criticizing detail to frustrate and annoy the specialist
 5 the emotional tactic, to induce guilt in the specialist
 6 'but in the future', things will be different, so your recommendations won't apply
 7 the invisible man, avoiding all personal contact with the specialist
 8 'further investigation is required', to create delay
 9 the scapegoat, who will make implementation impossible
10 deflection, onto issues where the specialist is less well-informed

Pettigrew (1985) offers interesting advice on the use of structural methods, in addition to political tactics that are based on personal behaviour. His suggestions for manipulating structures and processes to shift the focus of attention includes setting up management development initiatives to challenge existing thinking, redesigning administrative mechanisms, career paths and reward systems, creating task forces around issues and problems, promoting and changing the responsibilities of key individuals (role models), and replacing those who leave (creative retirals) with supporters. Pettigrew also advises the change agent to fragment grand visions into manageable segments, to exercise patience and perseverance, and when necessary to back off and wait until the timing is more appropriate.

Subversion tactics

From studies of long-term change involving information systems, Keen (1981) describes the counter-implementation tactics often used to block initiatives. He also identifies how such tactics can themselves be blocked, with counter-counter-implementation tactics. Rather than treating counter-implementation as negative, Keen observes that, as many innovations are 'dumb ideas', proactive attempts to subvert implementation are often desirable.

Counter-implementation tactics

- divert resources to other projects, to slow down this one
- dissipate the energies of key players, so they have less time for this project
- exploit inertia, using moves based on 'the need' for delays
- have vague and complex goals

- avoid the 'organizational' issues; we can deal with the 'people problems ' (which will sink the project) at a later stage
- question the champion's credibility and legitimacy to minimize their influence
- use the 'great idea, let's do it properly' tactic, by adding more people to the project group, making the aims more ambitious, and making it harder to reach agreement
- never disagree in public, as all of the above can be achieved while consistently appearing to offer visible support.

Counter-counter-implementation tactics

- establish clear goals and direction
- use simple phased programming
- seek out and respond proactively to resistance
- rely on face-to-face contacts
- create a prior 'felt need' for the initiative
- if necessary, exploit or create a crisis
- co-opt early support from those directly affected by the change
- create a powerful planning committee or steering group
- every major project needs a 'fixer', or 'wheeler–dealer' with the prestige, visibility, and legitimacy to facilitate, deter, and negotiate effectively.

Source: based on Keen (1981), Bardach (1977), and Grover et al. (1988).

Pfeffer (1992a, p.273) also demonstrates how organizational design can be used in power plays. He notes that, 'Power is built by ensuring that you control as much territory as possible, and this control is obtained by placing your allies in key positions and by expanding the activities over which you have formal responsibility'. Pfeffer (1992a, p.207) offers further advice on interpersonal influence. Affecting the way in which decisions are viewed early in the process can be critical in influencing the outcome, particularly where a 'social consensus' for an initiative or a direction can be demonstrated. Pfeffer refers to this as 'the principle of social proof'; as individuals, we are more likely to accept a view when we believe that it is shared with others (Cialdini and Sagarin, 2005, calls this 'social validation'). Pfeffer emphasizes the effect of physical attractiveness, positive association, flattery and working through friends and acquaintances to influence third parties, and advocates the controlled use of emotion as an influence tactic. He also emphasizes the importance of careful timing:

- It is sometimes appropriate to move first, particularly when, once started, it will be difficult to stop.
- Use deliberate and accidental delay; call for further study, while the advocates get tired of waiting and give up, backers move on to other projects, deadlines and windows of opportunity are consequently missed.

- Play the waiting game. Make others wait for you, thus demonstrating your power and emphasizing your importance.
- Use deadlines to signal urgency and importance, and to counter delaying tactics. Always favour the side that has the momentum.
- Manipulate the order of consideration. Committees often choose the good candidate or proposal that follows a run of weak contenders. Launch two proposals and let the weaker get trashed first, so that the second looks stronger by comparison, and the group may not want to trash the proposer twice; by the time the second proposal comes up, there is less time for debate. Stop an issue by not putting it on the agenda.
- Choose propitious moments. Other events and coincidences can create 'ripeness'. So, find circumstances in which particular proposals will find and attract attention.

This discussion of the politics of change implementation would be incomplete without consideration of the problems of resistance to change. Markus (1983) identifies four theories of resistance, each with different underpinning assumptions, and implications for practice:

people-focused explanations, which blame individuals, personalities, attitudes, values, preferences;

systems-focused explanations, which assume the fault lies with process and equipment design and operating characteristics, such as complexity, user-friendliness, adaptability;

organization-focused explanations, which focus on resistance generated by changes to roles, ways of working, social interaction, status differentials, and the allocation of responsibilities;

politics-focused explanations, where the cause of resistance lies with the redistribution of power, the 'ownership' of and patterns of access to information and decision making and the exercise of influence.

From these four broad sets of considerations, the 'political variant' has greater explanatory power, Markus (1983) argues, although when looking for solutions to resistance, changing the people (literally, or through training), and fixing design problems, are easier to achieve. Organizational and political causes of resistance to change are more common, but are more complex to address, unless the problems can be anticipated and resolved in advance. Eccles (1984), identifies thirteen sources of resistance (Table 8.6).

Eccles (1984) also identifies a hierarchy of five anti-resistance techniques:

1 Convince your critics of the selfless nature of your proposals. If they can be brought on side without having to pay them a price, then that is a cost-effective approach.
2 Demonstrate that the behaviour you want will have a track to the top, and that it is in their interests to climb aboard.

Rules to remember

Robbins (2005) offers the following political advice.

1 *Frame your arguments in terms of organizational goals*
Robbins argues that self-interest must be camouflaged, couching arguments in terms of benefits to the organization. Open displays of self-interest will limit one's career.

2 *Develop the right image*
Learn to project the appropriate image in terms of the organization culture, its goals, values, modes of dress, style of leadership, who to avoid, whether or not to take risks, and so on. Style is as important as substance in the context of performance reviews.

3 *Gain control of organizational resources*
Resources that are scarce and important, including knowledge and expertise, make the holder more valuable to the organization, and therefore more powerful and influential.

4 *Make yourself appear indispensable*
Power is enhanced by appearing to be indispensable. You don't actually have to be indispensable as long as key individuals believe that you are.

5 *Be visible*
Ensure that others know about your achievements, by highlighting your successes and having influential others do this for you, too. Lobby for projects that will increase your visibility.

6 *Develop powerful allies*
Decisions are often made in favour of those who have the most support, so cultivate influential contacts (who can also be a source of information) at all organizational levels.

7 *Avoid 'tainted' colleagues*
Every organization has people whose performance, loyalty, and status are questioned, and your effectiveness may also be questioned if you become associated with them.

8 *Support your boss*
It is useful not to annoy or to undermine the person responsible for evaluating your performance. It is more valuable to support your boss and to make them look good.

Source: based on Robbins (2005, pp.609–10).

Table 8.6   Sources of resistance to change

ignorance	failure to understand the problem
comparison	the solution is disliked as an alternative is preferred
disbelief	feeling that the proposed solution will not work
loss	change has unacceptable personal costs
inadequacy	the rewards from change are not sufficient
anxiety	fear of being unable to cope in the new situation
demolition	change threatens destruction of existing social networks
power cut	sources of influence and control will be eroded
contamination	new values and practices are repellent
inhibition	willingness to change is low
mistrust	motives for change are considered suspicious
alienation	alternative interests valued more highly than new proposals
frustration	change will reduce power and career opportunities

Source: based on Eccles (1984).

3 Buy their support, or flatter them – as with the British health minister who, when asked how he would get the support of complaining doctors for the creation of the National Health Service replied, 'we will stuff their mouths with gold'. That worked.
4 Marginalize your critics and use their skills for the benefit of the rest of the organization. They can be 'exited' later if they remain a nuisance.
5 Neutralize or 'exit' them. Termination may be the only effective way to neutralize.

Tactics for blocking interference

wait them out	they should eventually go away
wear them down	keep pushing and arguing, be persistent
appeal to higher authority	you'd better agree because they do
invite them in	ask them to join the party
send emissaries	have friends in whom they trust talk to them
display support	have 'your' people present and active at key meetings
reduce the stakes	make concessions in areas that are particularly damaging
warn them off	let them know that top management will notice their dissent
and remember	only afterwards does an innovation look like the right thing to have done all along

Source: based on Kanter (1983a).

The advice in this section on the politics of change implementation has several interesting characteristics. One finds the same guidance restated in similar ways by different authors. We also seem to be repeating the 'recipe-based approach' criticized in the previous section. Change cannot be managed with a checklist. Political behaviour cannot be planned and implemented from checklists of tactics. While recognizing this limitation, Table 8.7 repeats the same style, and summarizes the main dimensions of this advice for planning a political strategy, with regard to context, positioning, relationships, and tactics. These are all ongoing methods for building and maintaining credibility, reputation, and influence in the organization. As discussed in Chapter 9, the appropriate and effective use of these methods is a component of the change agency role, a characteristic of political skill, a key dimension of what we will describe as political expertise.

Practical advice with regard to the politics of change implementation thus includes:

- Stakeholder analysis is an old but still valuable tool for surveying the organization's political landscape.
- From the above checklists, the change agent should seek to develop a wide behaviour repertoire of political strategies (overall approaches) and tactics (specific methods).
- Develop political sensitivity to detect when other players are using these strategies and tactics against you. Keep your political 'antennae' switched on.
- Accept that, on occasion, ruthless tactics may be required to deal with resistance.
- Pay particular attention to context, positioning, relationships, and tactics, and to how these relate and contribute to the pursuit of your agendas and objectives.

Accounting: the politics of completion and afterlife

As many small children and criminals will know, it is often possible to win praise and avoid punishment, in spite of the circumstances, by being able to tell a good story. The plausible and compelling account can be an extremely powerful influence tactic. In national politics such tactics are suspect, labelled as 'spin'. However, the ability to construct a credible account is valuable in many management contexts, and is a key component of the political skill of the change agent, involving the calculated use of language and imagery.

> We exercise power and influence, when we do it successfully, through the subtle use of language, symbols, ceremonies, and settings that make people feel good about what they are doing. A friend once remarked that it is management's job to make people do what they need or have to do in order to make the organization prosper. In a similar fashion, it is the job of people interested in wielding power and influence to cause others to feel good about doing what we want done. This involves the exercise of symbolic management (Pfeffer, 1992a, p.279).

Table 8.7   Planning a political strategy

Organizational context

- make sure that you have a positive, legitimate, organization performance-enhancing agenda
- get 'clearance' for your initiative from a senior manager or sponsor
- establish control of scarce and important resources, including information
- learn how politics are played around here, what works, who are the 'sponsors' and 'protégés'
- do a stakeholder analysis, identify key players' needs and interests

Personal positioning

- it helps if you have a cause which colleagues will want to support
- look and act powerful, successful and decisive, radiate self-confidence, project the image, constantly create the impression of someone who knows clearly what they are doing and why
- develop your communication skills, in persuasion, influencing, selling, self-dramatization
- why reveal everything; it is often advantageous to withhold information or to time its release
- highlight successes and achievements, be visible, choose visible projects, appear indispensable

Exploiting relationships

- enlist supporters, distance yourself from those with dubious reputations
- form a coalition with a powerful voice, recruit 'votes' if you have to, establish alliances with known power-brokers, develop and exploit your networks
- formalize your coalition when appropriate by creating a steering group, a committee, a task force
- do favours, then call these in when necessary to support your agenda
- barter, negotiate, trade; only compromise on minor issues while pressing for your goal

Tactical planning

- balance your open and public actions with covert 'backstage' activity
- decide when to push fast, and when to hold back and delay
- use 'negative timing' to create delays; there are key issues to analyse, difficulties to overcome, problems to solve, implications to consider
- neutralize interference by wearing them down, waiting them out, inviting them in, using third parties, trade and compromise, displays of overwhelming support, and threat
- never commit yourself fully to any given position; maintain flexibility, and room to manoeuvre.

Our reputation is based on what others know about us, which is in turn based in part on what we tell them. Reputation, as argued in Chapter 2, is one source of power for the change agent, conferring influence and freedom to manoeuvre. The concept of reputation equates with what Wight (1978) calls 'prestige', a concept around which he notes there is much confusion. Wight (1978, p.97) defines prestige as 'the halo around power', as 'the influence derived from power', and as 'the recognition by other people of your strength'. Noting the ambiguities in this term, Wight (1978, p.99) comments:

> Thus prestige, like honour, is an ambiguous term. It may mean deliberately refraining from exercising your power because you prefer the advantages of not having

done so; and in this sense it comes very near to being magnanimity, which as Burke said is not seldom the truest wisdom in politics. Or it may mean forcing other people to admit your power on every occasion; and in this sense it is simply an extreme policy of asserting your 'honour' and interests ... one is 'power based upon reputation', and the other is 'reputation based upon power'.

We then explored the links between reputation and accounting in Chapter 3; accounts can be used to explain, justify, defend, and promote the actions of the change agent. This is a 'language game', and language usage that is appropriate in one context may be wholly inappropriate in another setting. Equally, the same terms may be decoded to mean quite different things in different contexts. Consequently, Burns (1961, p.262) refers to the 'dual code', moral and linguistic, surrounding the use of political behaviour. In other words, the moral legitimacy of action is a relative matter, depending on the context and the goals being pursued. Which is the better story? The critical account which presents your actions as abhorrent, reprehensible, damaging, and unethical? Or the glowing portrait which portrays your behaviour as appropriate, professional, beneficial – and ethical? What can be presented as legitimate in one context may be unacceptable in another. Burns points to the discrepancies between the public and private terminologies describing political games. Players can be represented as *collaborators* in a common enterprise, while at the same time being *rivals* for rewards, resources and progression. Both attributes – collaboration and competition – are socially valued. However, there is a clear distinction between issues that are discussable *backstage*, and what can be aired and admitted in *public*.

March and Olsen (1983) also draw attention to this dual linguistic and moral code in their distinction between what they describe as the *rhetoric of administration* and the *rhetoric of realpolitik*. The rhetoric of administration concerns structures, procedures, efficiency, effectiveness, planning, economy, and management control. The rhetoric of realpolitik concerns power struggles, competing interests, dominance, and political control. March and Olsen (1983, p.291) argue that these twin rhetorics work in parallel in the 'ritual of reorganization':

On the one hand, a commitment to administrative purity is made tolerable by an appreciation of realpolitik, much as a commitment to personal purity is made tolerable by an appreciation of human weakness. At the same time, a commitment to realpolitik rhetoric is made consistent with human hopes by a faith in the imaginability of improvement through human intelligence. It should not be surprising to find that both rhetorics survive and thrive, and that both find expression in the symbols of reorganization.

March and Olsen (1983, p.288) also note that the interpretation and reception of proposals for change can alter through time. They argue that 'persistent repetition of similar ideas and similar arguments over a relatively long period of time appears to make some difference. Persistence both increases the likelihood that a proposal will be current at an opportune time and creates a diffuse climate of availability and legitimacy for it. Recommendations that produce a storm at one time are later accepted without opposition.'

Does this once again turn the management of change in general, and accounting for the behaviour of the change agent in particular, into a game of impression management, in which illusion and form are more significant than substance and achievement? Must organizational change merely follow cultural norms in sustaining the cosmetic of rationality, even when this is not an accurate representation of events? March and Olsen (1983, p.290) ask if the ritual of reorganization is simply, 'a tactic for creating an illusion of progress where none exists'. Their defensive response draws from an analysis of government changes in America in the twentieth century, but remains relevant to contemporary organizational settings:

> Any effective deceit is testimony to a belief deeply enough held to warrant the costs of hypocrisy. If we observe that everyone says the same thing while doing different things, we are observing something important about the political system, and the beliefs on which it rests. Virtuous words sustain the meaning and importance of virtue, even among sinners. To view the symbols of politics as intentional efforts by sophisticated actors to deceive the innocent is likely to exaggerate the extent to which things as fundamental as optimism that mankind can direct and control its environment for the better can be manipulated arbitrarily as a tactic. Leaders need reassurance too. More generally, organization and reorganization, like much action, are tied to the discovery, clarification, and elaboration of meaning as well as to immediate action or decision making.

Evidence for a dual linguistic code, or twin rhetorics, is no platform for simple manipulation with false information and other deceits. The accounts given by politicians and change agents often reflect their beliefs, which are often deeply held. We are assuming in our account in this book that change agents want to make a difference, to have a positive impact on the organizations in which they work. And as we have tried to show, efficacy in that regard involves a combination of skills and abilities, one of which is the ability to provide, when asked or challenged, a plausible account of their actions, a good story.

Pfeffer's (1992a) observation that decisions must appear rational is fundamental. He notes that, with complex, multidimensional issues, rational analysis rarely helps us to choose the best option. Decision quality is difficult to assess, and so is rarely pursued. There is almost always scope for suggesting criteria and presenting information selectively in ways that favour one's preferred position. Is it unseemly to be 'caught out' doing this kind of thing? Well, Pfeffer suggests that you could hire an external consultant, and rely on their impartial (but carefully briefed) judgement.

Read (1992) outlines a model of how we construct accounts for our actions, when we are challenged. The central feature of an acceptable account is *coherence*, the extent to which it 'hangs together' in the perception of the audience. The construction of a 'good' account must consider both the circumstances of the case, and the perspectives of those constituents whom the account is designed to sway. Read emphasizes the role of goals, and the primary goal is to construct an account that will be believed and honoured. The problem is that the secondary goals of truthful representation, and avoidance of blame, may often conflict. The person constructing the account must decide which goals take precedence:

> If our primary goal is truth, then our focus is to develop the most accurate account possible. However, if our primary goal is to justify or excuse our behaviour we must focus on how to do this. And, if in constructing such an account, we must be less than faithful to the facts, we must ensure that the reproacher does not find out ... this suggests that often we may be quite concerned with what the reproacher knows so that we can know whether and how the facts constrain us (Read, 1992, p.5).

Read identifies four major types of accounts, with different implications for how the account is constructed (Table 8.8). The main consideration when constructing an account is the perspective of the person delivering the challenge. How much do they already know? What is their current interpretation? What are their beliefs and perceptions about how society and organizations work? For Read (1992, p.9) the account construction process must consider:

- the kind of account we wish to construct
- our desire to have the account honoured

Table 8.8 The construction of accounts

Category	Construction
The excuse	Admit the damaging behaviour, claiming that you are not responsible; negative consequences were unforeseen, you were under pressure at the time, the damage was actually caused by something, or someone, else.
The justification	Admit responsibility but claim the behaviour was justified in context; no harm was done, or positive outweigh negative consequences.
The concession	Admit to the offence, expressing apologies and remorse, and offer restitution; through this approach also seek to deflect censure and blame.
The refusal	Deny that the damaging behaviour ever happened; claim that the challenger's version or perception of events is inaccurate; deny that the challenger has any right of reproach, because they are not involved, or suffered no personal damage.

Source: based on Read (1992).

- what we know of the facts of the case
- what the challenger knows, or is likely to learn, of the facts
- the reproacher's beliefs about social and physical causality
- our own beliefs about social and physical causality.

The aim is to, 'evaluate the account we construct from the perspective of the challenger so that we can judge the likelihood that the account will be honoured' (Read, 1992, p.9). The more coherent the challenger judges our account to be, the more likely it is to be honoured or accepted. The point is, it does not much matter how convincing the person presenting the account believes it to be; what matters is how compelling the audience judges it to be. Bies and Sitkin (1992) thus argue that our goals when we offer excuses to others include making our behaviour intelligible and warranted. The adequacy of the account, and the sincerity of the communicator are also key factors, according to Bies and Sitkin, in determining whether our account will be accepted.

Practical advice for change agents with regard to accounting thus includes:

- Be sensitive to the moral and linguistic codes of your organization; know what is acceptable and legitimate, in terms of behaviour and language in different settings.
- Be attuned to the different codes and values of different groups, departments, sections and occupational sub-groups in the organization.
- Recognize that the representation of political behaviour as reasonable in context is a critical dimension of your political skill, and the political skill of others, too.
- Be prepared to provide coherent, sincere and compelling accounts to justify political behaviour in the change process, taking into consideration how such accounts will be interpreted and judged by your audience.
- Recognize that accounts may not always be entirely faithful to the facts as you understand them, but that this is not a licence for deceit for its own sake.

A winning perspective

The moral maze

Bureaucracy poses for managers an intricate set of moral mazes that are paradigmatic of the quandaries of public life in our social order. Within this framework, the puzzle for many individual managers becomes: How does one act in such a world and maintain a sense of personal integrity? (Jackall, 1988, pp.193–4).

We have described organization politics as a game, a turf game, involving a competition of ideas, and particularly ideas concerning desirable, beneficial, advantageous organizational change. The prizes for winning this game include praise and recognition, status and reputation, intrinsic satisfaction and material rewards, and increased power and influence. Winning, however, also involves beating the competition, creating losers. If that is what winning means, then how can it be acceptable to play this game at all? The answer to this question depends on the perspective that we bring to the concept of 'winning'.

As noted previously, checklists of advice are of limited use on their own. That guidance reveals the rich variety of political behaviour and the range of interacting factors involved in organizational change. But how should change agents implement this advice? In particular, how can change agents address Jackall's (1988) puzzle concerning the 'moral maze' in which most managers find themselves? An appropriate frame of reference is required, to guide practice in this regard. Such a perspective is missing from the change management literature as well as from commentary on organization politics. The term 'perspective' refers to a set of considerations, or convictions, which inform the change agent's decisions and actions. At least seven considerations (no particular order) emerge from this discussion.

1 *Reality is illusory*
   Constructing convincing and acceptable accounts of our actions is particularly important when political behaviour is concerned. Reality is socially constructed; and organizational reality is what we define it to be. From this point of view, 'political' is a category of behaviour used by players in the turf game for different purposes. The ability to represent 'your' behaviour as non-political while accusing 'me' of politicking can be a critical skill, in establishing legitimacy for some actions while delegitimating others. This position leads to accusations of 'all form without substance'. However, this aspect of organizational life is inescapable, and establishing legitimacy for ideas that we sincerely believe to be right could also be regarded as a moral imperative. How will political actions be regarded and assessed? What form of accounts will be appropriate if challenged? Can political behaviour be represented as reasonable in context? Is it possible to weave a cloak of defensibility? Dealing effectively with these issues is central to the change agent's reputation and influence, which must be considered here in a broad social sense, and not merely in relation to a narrow group of current constituents. A concern with personal reputation is a factor triggering and sustaining political behaviour, and is also a factor restraining such action.

2 *Game on*
   The turf game involves continuing exchange, not single plays. The cast of characters can be large and fluid, depending on the flow of events and outcomes. This is a dynamic game of action and response, of anticipating how others will react to one's position and tactics, and of then behaving accordingly. Players are not always well informed about each other or about plans and intentions. This is a game played often in mist. Some moves are substantial, some are symbolic, but all can

be significant. There are no time limits, and there is always a rematch. Winning and losing, therefore, are not final outcomes, but transient states in an ongoing competition. Winning often means simply winning this time around.

3 *The credibility factor*

This is a game of credentials, in which reputations are important assets and power bases. The credibility of players is crucial; will individuals keep to their goals and promises? Are their threats and actions credible? As a change agent, what do you want a reputation *for*? A reputation that involves dealing with the difficult issues, and difficult people, and making beneficial things happen, gives the possessor increased influence, enhanced career prospects, and greater ability to obtain resources and support for change. Winning in this context thus has personal advantages, but also gives the organization a more powerful asset for driving current and future change initiatives.

4 *In context*

Political behaviour is one category of change implementation behaviour. The concept of power assisted steering implies that organizational change has motive forces behind it other than political goals and aspirations. To win in this context merely implies an effective combination of political and conventional tactics, to achieve the outcomes that one believes to be desirable. Conventional change management methods (project management, participation, communication, organization development, planned change) still apply. But what is the political climate, the political temperature? What approaches will work in this context given past experience, current stakeholders, and future aspirations?

5 *Situational ethic*

As Chapter 3 argued, it is difficult to apply normative ethical principles to political behaviour in organizational contexts. Given the conflicts of obligation that arise, there is often more than one reasonable conclusion to political dilemmas, depending on how considerations and criteria are weighed and balanced. Decisions are often based on an informed judgement of what is possible, what is acceptable, what is justifiable, and what is defensible. 'Merely accounting' may be seen as a cosmetic position. However, if one truly believes in the benefits of a change agenda, is it ethical willingly (if reluctantly) to lose to the competition's superior political tactics? Or is it unethical not to counter those tactics?

6 *The reflective practitioner*

Schön (1983) argues that the decisions and actions of the reflective practitioner are informed by a considered combination of theory, evidence, and personal experience. New situations are conceptualized as unique, but in the light of relevant theoretical frameworks and experience. Decisions are thus based on a combination of knowledge and conceptualization of the context, managerial judgement, and creativity. In this view, practice is improvisatory, and sometimes experimental. The change agent is a *bicoleur*, using whatever resources are to hand, including opportunity, luck and accidents of good timing. This sometimes involves the use of complicating strategies, with multidimensional, multifaceted approaches, to deal with different stakeholder constituencies and to confuse and block interference and subversion from different sources. The reflective practitioner is also self-conscious, self-aware and self-critical, learning from experience, and from mistakes. This type of self-monitoring is particularly valuable in a context where the boundaries of acceptable behaviour are approached, and in some instances crossed, in the pursuit of change agendas.

7 *Risky shift*

The change agency role is not an easy one. Major initiatives render the change agent more visible, and more vulnerable. The role requires a behaviour repertoire that extends into various forms of Machiavellian actions, as well as other managerial styles. This involves a conscious switch from one position in relation to change to another, to reduce risk and maximize personal advantage. It also requires energy and commitment, perhaps even passion, as well as creativity. It involves the acceptance of risk to career. The penalties for error can be high, while the rewards for success are sometimes intangible if significant. This can be more of a lifestyle than a job. Without energy, commitment, and stamina the change agent is likely to struggle. It is this particular combination of characteristics that renders the label *political entrepreneur* particularly apt in these circumstances.

The concept of 'winning' has several connotations. Change creates winners and losers. The strategies and tactics explored here can be used to increase the probability that one belongs more often to the former group. In the context of conflicts of interests, or the competition of ideas, or clashes of wills, political tactics can be deployed in order to win. But in the context of reputation, the notion of winning assumes a broader and subtly different significance. This may mean achieving and holding the position to which one aspires. This may also mean deliberately choosing to concede or to lose in the interests of longer term personal, interpersonal, and organizational goals. In other words, 'winning' is a socially constructed outcome, depending on what one wants to achieve, depending on how one wants to be seen. This may involve actions to which one may not want to admit publicly. Jackall (1988, p.196) eloquently describes the advantages, ambiguities and costs of 'winning' the turf game:

On the other hand, winning carries with it the knowledge of others' envy and the fear that one's defeated opponents are lying in wait for an opportunity to turn the tables. One adopts then a stance of public humility, of self-effacing modesty that helps disguise whatever sense of triumph one might feel. Moreover, winning, say, on a policy dispute carries the burden of implementation, sometimes involving those whom one has defeated. One must then simultaneously protect one's flanks and employ whatever wiles are necessary to secure requisite cooperation. Here the disarming social grace that is a principal aspect of desirable managerial style can be particularly useful in making disingenuousness seem like 'straight arrow' behaviour. Finally, winning sometimes requires the willingness to move decisively against others, even though this might mean undermining their organizational careers. These may be neighbours on the same block, members of the same religious communion, long-time work colleagues, or, more rarely, members of the same club. They may be good, even excellent, employees. In short, managerial effectiveness and others' perceptions of one's leadership depend on the willingness to battle for the prestige that comes from dominance and to make whatever moral accommodation such struggles demand. In the work world, those who adhere either to secular democratic precepts as guides or, even more, to an ethic of brotherly love, run the risk of faltering in those struggles. But those who abandon the ethics of caritas and hone themselves to do what has to be done must accept the peculiar emotional aridity that is one price of organizational striving and, especially, of victory.

Ultimately, 'winning' means achieving what one believes to be right, and most of us are prepared to fight (metaphorically) to that end. This perspective is intended as a broad guide for the change agent, for the political entrepreneur, in establishing a personal sense of integrity, in acting to establish and to develop their own reputation, in defining their own understanding of what it means to 'win the turf game'.

Follow through

Issue-selling: moves and tactics

The following questionnaire identifies a number of issue-selling techniques. You may find it interesting to consider how common these techniques are, in your experience, and to compare your assessment with that of colleagues.

How often are these issue-selling methods used by managers in your experience? (tick box)	never	rare	sometimes	often	very often
1 using the logic of the business plan, 'running the numbers', using lots of figures and charts, conveying a logical and coherent structure, emphasizing bottom-line impacts	❏	❏	❏	❏	❏
2 continuous proposal making, raising issues many times over a period, prepare the target to better 'hear' a full proposal	❏	❏	❏	❏	❏
3 making changes appear incremental, by 'chunking' ideas into components to make them more palatable to potential targets	❏	❏	❏	❏	❏
4 tying issues to performance targets, activity levels, to community image	❏	❏	❏	❏	❏
5 tying issues to the concerns of key constituents	❏	❏	❏	❏	❏

How often are these issue-selling methods used by managers in your experience? (tick box)	never	rare	sometimes	often	very often
6 targeting – knowing who to involve and when	❑	❑	❑	❑	❑
7 involving senior management in supporting ideas	❑	❑	❑	❑	❑
8 clearing ideas first with senior management opinion leaders	❑	❑	❑	❑	❑
9 involving colleagues and other departments in support of ideas	❑	❑	❑	❑	❑
10 involving outsiders, such as management consultants, to gain credibility	❑	❑	❑	❑	❑
11 customizing issue-selling methods to the key stakeholder	❑	❑	❑	❑	❑
12 using formal committees and task forces to legitimize issues	❑	❑	❑	❑	❑
13 creating a task force with a diverse membership	❑	❑	❑	❑	❑
14 deciding the appropriate degree of formality when issue-selling	❑	❑	❑	❑	❑
15 collecting background information on context before selling, preparing people to support an idea when the time comes	❑	❑	❑	❑	❑
16 exploiting social relationships, organizational norms, and strategic priorities	❑	❑	❑	❑	❑
17 being persistent through a lengthy issue-selling process	❑	❑	❑	❑	❑
18 sensing when to hold back and when to move forward, based on level of support	❑	❑	❑	❑	❑
19 involving relevant others at an early stage	❑	❑	❑	❑	❑

Scoring

	never	rare	sometimes	often	very often
Score this diagnostic using this scale	1	2	3	4	5

This will give you a result between 19 and 95. So what?

Low score 35 or less. Either there is not a lot of issue-selling behaviour in your organization. Or, for some reason you don't witness the issue-selling that goes on.

High score 75 or more. Either, this is far too high, and senior management should seek to reduce the volume of issue-selling, and consequently the number of issues demanding attention at any given time. Or, you witness a lot of behaviour that can be interpreted as issue-selling, and this is a sign of a dynamic, innovative organization.

Moderate score Around 60. Clearly there is some issue-selling taking place in this organization. Is this appropriate? Or does this reflect only a moderate level of energy and enthusiasm for innovation and change?

- In your judgement, is the use of these techniques acceptable?
- In your experience, are these techniques used in your organization successfully to identify and effectively focus senior management attention on priority issues?
- In your experience, are these techniques used in your organization to focus Board attention on initiatives of interest to their advocates, but of dubious corporate benefit?

Source: based on Dutton et al. (2001).

Debrief

The items in the questionnaire describe three different categories of issue-selling technique, concerning packaging moves, involvement moves, and process moves:

Packaging moves

Items one to five are known as packaging moves because they concern the different ways in which ideas can be 'wrapped' to make them more appealing, more urgent, more acceptable. Items one to three are known as *presentation* tactics, while items four and five are called *bundling* tactics.

Involvement moves

Items 6 to 13 are known as involvement moves because they concern the various ways in which social relationships and structures can be adjusted and exploited to build support for ideas and initiatives, involving senior personnel, colleagues, outsiders, and key stakeholders.

Process moves

Items 14 to 19 are known as process moves because they concern issues of formality, preparation and timing in issue-selling; should a formal or informal setting be used when influencing a target group, what 'groundwork' is required in advance of selling, deciding how quickly, or slowly, to move.

Organization politics at the movies: *Contact*

The movie *Contact* (1997, director Robert Zemeckis) is based on the novel by Carl Sagan, about Eleanor (Ellie) Arroway (played by Jodie Foster) and her passion for astronomy, and in particular her obsession with the search for extraterrestrial intelligence (SETI). As a child, she scans the short wave radio spectrum contacting people around the country, asking her father, 'Could we talk to the moon? Could we talk to Jupiter? Do you think there's people on other planets?'

The analysis suggested here is based on three short clips from the first half of the movie, identified here in terms of the relevant DVD tracks. The first segment lasts for 15 minutes, and establishes the context. The second segment lasts 10 minutes, and the third segment lasts another 15 minutes. It is useful to pause the movie for discussion after each of these segments. The overall aims of this analysis are:

1 to identify examples of organization political skill
2 to identify illustrations of organization political naivety and ineptitude
3 to relate the thesis of this movie to the practice of organization politics.

The adult astronomer Dr Ellie Arroway works on the SETI project at the radio telescope array in Arecibo, Puerto Rico, listening for radio signals from other planets. A previous colleague, Dr David Drumlin (Tom Skerritt) is the newly appointed Head of the National Science Foundation (NSF). He criticizes Ellie's efforts, regarding her work as 'professional suicide'. Faced with budget restrictions, his view is that they should, 'stop wasting time on this nonsense', and 'stop wasting money on pie in the sky abstractions'. Drumlin cancels Ellie's project, without warning or consultation, but she gets funding from a mysterious private backer, and leases time at a government-owned telescope array in New Mexico.

We will join the movie 40 minutes into the action. After four years in New Mexico, without results, Ellie is told by her blind colleague, Kent Clark, that Drumlin and the NSF have again decided to terminate her project by not renewing her lease. 'We're a joke to them. They want us out. They don't want the high priestess of the desert using their telescopes any more.' This time she has three months' notice to quit. Before working through the following sequence of clips, if time and circumstances allow, watch 30 seconds of track 5, showing David Drumlin and Ellie Arroway meeting in the roadway beside his jeep. This identifies the two main characters whose actions form the focus of the following analysis, and also establishes their (hostile) relationship.

Open with Drumlin's jeep coming up the hill.

End with Ellie muttering 'Asshole'.

1 'Holy shit': track 11 (15 minutes)
Open with a shot of the planet. The first five minutes establishes context. Focus on the behaviours of Ellie Arroway and David Drumlin.
End with Drumlin giving the presentation as 'leader of the team'.

Told that she has only three months left, Ellie picks up a signal. The camera swings from the telescope array, to a close-up of her face, to her eyes, as she realizes what she is hearing. 'Holy shit', she cries. She and her team verify the authenticity of the signal and its deep space source, Vega. 'Who we going to call now?' asks Fisher. 'Everybody' replies Ellie.

Cut to the mayhem outside the New Mexico facility with cameramen and journalists jostling for position and information. Cut to two choppers sweeping in low across the desert at high speed, landing right in front of the main building. The men who jump out are in suits, accompanied by armed soldiers. The group includes Dr David Drumlin, and Senator Michael Kitz (James Woods), National Security Adviser. Kitz asks, 'Where's the girl?' From the point at which we join the movie, through to the scene in the White House, observe in particular the following behaviour:

a   What organization political skills does Drumlin display?
b   What organization political mistakes does Ellie make?
c   What advice would you give to Ellie?

2 What am I doing here?: track 19 (10 minutes)

Open with Ellie asking, 'What am I doing here?' on her secret backer's plane.
End with Ellie asking, 'Where can I get a great dress?'

Ellie's team discovers that the alien signal includes a massive volume of obscure technical data. At this point, Ellie's secret backer reveals himself, explaining how he has monitored her career and why he chose to provide her with funding. But he has discovered where in the signal the Vegans have located the 'primer' that enables the message to be fully decoded. With this breakthrough information, Ellie finds herself back in the White House. After her presentation, a former boyfriend (Palmer Joss, played by Matthew McConaughey) appears. He is a theologian and Presidential Adviser. Ellie is surprised by his presence.

Watching this sequence, observe again the following behaviour:

a   What organization political skills does Drumlin display?
b   What organization political mistakes does Ellie make?
c   How could Ellie have handled this more effectively?

3 Only one occupant: track 22 (15 minutes)

Open with 'Ellie you were right'.
Close with Drumlin's speech.

Even with the primer, Ellie and her team are not at first able to decipher the alien technical information. Finally, they establish that they have been sent instructions to build a space transport, to journey to the signal's source. However, the vessel can only carry one occupant. Who should it be? A selection committee is formed, including scholars, scientists, philosophers and theologians (and Palmer Joss, the ex-boyfriend). International applications are invited. Ellie is an obvious choice. Drumlin declares that he is a candidate, too.

Watching this sequence, what can we add to what has already been observed:

a   What further political mistakes does Ellie make?
b   How else should she have behaved differently?

It is helpful to bring together the three sets of observations concerning the skills displayed by Drumlin, the mistakes that Ellie has made, and the advice that could be offered to Ellie to help her to develop her political skills. Looking at the advice for Ellie that this discussion has generated, it can then be instructive to consider the following two key questions:

a   Is this advice limited to actors in a Hollywood science fiction movie, or does it apply to change agents and project team leaders in general?
b   To what extent does that advice apply to a male project team leader?

4 Integrity loses, deceit wins

This third clip from the movie (track 22) ends with Drumlin making this short speech to Ellie:

> I know you must think this is all very unfair. Maybe that's an understatement. What you don't know is, I agree. I wish the world was a place where fair was the bottom line, where the kind of idealism you showed at the hearing was rewarded, without taken advantage of. Unfortunately, we don't live in that world.

The thesis of the movie, up to this point, could be expressed as 'integrity loses, deceit wins'. Ellie answered the selection committee's questions honestly, and consequently was not chosen to pilot the alien craft. Drumlin told the committee what they wanted to hear, and he was their unanimous choice.

To what extent does this argument generalize to organizations in the real world, to our workplaces, to our behaviour?

Debrief: Contact

What political skills does Drumlin display?

- He has made sure that he is present for this momentous event.
- He is dressed appropriately for the occasion.
- He presents himself as an 'insider', like the key players.
- He does not introduce Ellie or her team to the other members of his group.
- He knows the names and understands the roles of the key players.
- He takes the vacant role of translator between scientists and lay people.
- He appears credible to both groups, plays both sides as appropriate.
- His physical positioning puts him at the centre of the action.
- He adopts leadership behaviours, giving 'casual' instructions to Ellie and her team.
- He always appears cool, calm, collected and in control.
- He is in control of the organizational processes here.
- He has prearranged (through the Presidential Aide, Rachel Constantine, played by Angela Basset) his role as 'leader' of the team presenting to the media.

- He is prepared to tell others, particularly power brokers and decision makers, exactly what they want and expect to hear, in order to achieve his objectives.

What political mistakes does Ellie make? (1)

- She has a 'little girl lost' image.
- She plays a 'one move' chess game, not thinking ahead.
- She acts on impulse.
- She had no plan for handling this event.
- Too open, too honest, too trusting.
- Too emotionally engaged.
- Her behaviour is passive, offering no challenge to Drumlin's interference.
- She puts her project before the needs of the people with whom she has to deal.
- She is disorganized.
- She has no understanding of how she is perceived by the power brokers.
- She has no understanding of the impact she is having on others.
- She shows no deference to the power brokers.
- She ignores the protocol of the situation.
- She tries to tell the power brokers their job.
- Lack of an appropriate degree of paranoia.
- She clearly has not learned from past experience with Drumlin and his colleagues.

What political mistakes does Ellie make? (2)

- She holds all the cards, the odds are all in her favour, yet she still loses control.
- She speaks of 'we' instead of 'I'.
- She is still too emotional.
- Her responses to the interjections of others are emotional.
- She is defensive and argumentative.
- She is easily diverted, loses focus.
- She has not prepared this presentation adequately.
- She has not anticipated the reactions to what she has to reveal.
- She has not considered the pace or sequence with which to release this information.
- She has done no audience research.
- She allows Drumlin to talk over her without challenge.
- She allows Drumlin to give her instructions during her presentation.
- She does not clearly 'sell' the ideas that she wishes to convey at this stage.
- She thus allows significant doubts to be expressed.
- She trusts her former boyfriend, Palmer Joss, and agrees to meet him while he is a member of the Selection Committee, and she is a candidate.

Advising Ellie

- Lose the 'little girl lost' image.
- Get a haircut and some smart new clothes; look and sound like 'them'.
- Stop with the nervous hand wringing.
- Get breathing and voice projection lessons; drop the husky voice and nervous cough.
- Plan, predict, anticipate.
- Think big, talk the talk, see the bigger picture.
- Do your homework.
- Lose the arrogance, scorn and disrespect for 'outsiders'.
- Back off from the emotional inputs and responses.
- Be less trusting, even (especially?) of those who you consider to be friends.
- Be paranoid. Be very paranoid.
- If you don't have the political and organizational skills, consider buying them in.
- Tailor your presentation content to your audience.
- Face the audience when you present, and do not turn your back.
- Choose your position in the room; do not be sidelined.
- Adopt a non-adversarial style.
- Network, make friends, recruit allies.
- Get to know the power brokers, their names, their roles, their needs and interests.
- Withhold 'core' information when appropriate.
- Time the release of your information with care.

Most, if not all, of this advice is generic in its application to 'real world' change agents and project leaders, and it is not difficult to translate this advice between the sexes.

9 Political expertise: why you need it, and how to develop it

Chapter objectives

1 To consider the argument that political skills will become increasingly significant for management in general and change agents in particular.
2 To identify the factors that trigger organization politics.
3 To explore Michel Foucault's perspective on power and politics.
4 To examine the nature of political expertise in the context of change agency, and how such expertise can be developed.

"We already have quite a few people who know how to divide. So, essentially, we're now looking for people who know how to conquer."

© Mike Shapiro. Reproduced with permission.

Has the ground moved?

In this chapter, we first consider why organization politics are significant for the change agent, given current organizational trends, and the factors that trigger political behaviour. Reinforcing this argument, we explore Foucault's perspective on the pervasive nature of power. Finally, we explore the concept of political expertise and how it can be developed.

As Chapter 7 argued, for many commentators, the character of organizations in the twenty-first century is quite different from that of the second half of the twentieth century. Bureaucracy and hierarchy have given way to empowered, multiskilled teamwork, and rigid procedures have been abandoned in favour of creativity, speed, and flexibility of response. Change, innovation, revolution, and discontinuity are the norm; stability, evolution and consistency imply commercial suicide (Christensen and Overdorf, 2000; Hammer, 2004). The concept of organization is an anachronism in a world of partnerships, joint ventures, networks, and other forms of interorganizational collaboration (Pettigrew and Fenton, 2000). Previously stable coalitions and interest groups are replaced with transient alliances. Traditional position power is of limited use in this context, and other modes of interpersonal influence are necessary. As career ladders are dismantled, and individual performance is difficult to measure, the appearance of success becomes just as significant. The competition of ideas becomes an even hotter contest for promotion and status. Political and other interpersonal skills appear to be at a premium in such settings (Semadar et al., 2006)

Have organization politics really become more prevalent? It is tempting to think that, in the mid-twentieth century, as socio-technical systems thinking and the organization development movement were under construction, the political climate was less volatile, less hostile. Neither of those movements recognized a political dimension to their work design and organizational problem solving methods. This relative tranquillity does not characterize organizational research and management experience today, as a glance at the literature or a search of websites dealing with 'office politics' reveals.

Implementing change in a politically hostile context is problematic. Buchanan (2003) explores how political agendas influenced the goals and methods of a major change programme in a British hospital, concluding that the change agent requires a combination of skills including political awareness and the use of tailored influence tactics. Badham et al. (1997) discuss how action researchers had to adopt differently politicized change strategies in each of three companies involved in an Australian project to implement team-based cells. Gollop and Ketley (2007) describe the influence tactics used to involve clinical staff in health service improvements, including direct appeal, demonstrating new methods, shaming individuals by exposing them to the superior performance of colleagues who have adopted new methods, bribery, and the avoidance of management jargon. Change agents may often have to cope with multiple demands including ambitious performance targets, tight deadlines, intrusive management controls, recalcitrant staff, counter-implementation tactics, and a rapidly shifting and unpredictable environment.

If the climate has become more turbulent, then change agents may indeed require political skills to a higher degree. However, the stereotype of the 'flat and fluid' post-modern organization is probably overdrawn (many organizations do not possess those features), and the political dimension is probably a permanent landmark on the organizational terrain. Despite such qualifications, several factors may have heightened awareness of political agendas. The scope and pace of change appear to have widened. One study suggests that most organizations undergo major changes on average every three years, interspersed with constant minor changes (Whittington and Mayer, 2002). This pattern of change, and the ongoing search for novel techniques (Leseure et al., 2004), may have increased concern with the complex pluralistic politics of multiple constituencies, particularly when dealing with radical organization redesign.

Observing that managers now operate in 'fast-paced, turbulent work contexts, fuelled with ambiguity through organization downsizing, restructuring and redesign, technological change, and mergers and acquisitions', Perrewé et al. (2000, p.115) argue that executive stress has become a major problem. Stress may be relieved through holidays, exercise, and relaxation. Perrewé and colleagues suggest, however, that the development of political skill can also be an antidote to workplace stress, by enhancing interpersonal control, and by increasing the ability to cope more confidently with potentially stressful situations. However, as discussed in Chapter 7, some of the management ambivalence towards organization politics may result from an appraisal of the personal costs of 'winning'.

This view of a politicized future is inconsistent with some recent thinking about management trends. Handy (1997) argues that organizations should be seen as communities, and that employees should be treated as citizens. Pfeffer and Sutton (2006) argue that the workplace is no different from family and community settings. Both of those commentaries support the view that commercial success depends on consistency of values, identity, and purpose. In the light of the argument of this book, however, such a viewpoint is naive, perhaps dangerous. Naive, because it ignores the nature and implications of organizational structures, power inequalities, and political agendas. Dangerous, because it ignores the potential benefits of tension, conflict and political behaviour. Dangerous, because this perspective puts ideological constraints in the path of those who would resist, challenge, and otherwise seek to subvert an organization's practices and goals, when they believe these to be misguided or flawed. Dangerous, because it hinders discussion of the need to act politically, and how to cope with the personal costs as well as the benefits of acting in this way. The harmonious community of citizens, pursuing aims and activities without question, with presumed benefit to all, is unlikely to be an effective or successful venture.

In sum, the contemporary change agent appears to be faced with multiple constituencies, stakeholders, and perceptions, and with change agendas which are complex, multi-layered, pressured, contested, politicized, and shaped by changing management fashions. After we have examined the triggers of political behaviour in more detail, we will turn our attention to the nature of the skill or expertise that may be required to deal with such a politicized environment, and to how that expertise can be developed.

Personal, decisional, and structural triggers

What factors encourage and intensify political behaviour? There seem to be four main and related sets of triggers: *personal* characteristics, *decision* characteristics, *structural* characteristics, and of course *organizational change* (Chanlat, 1997).

Personal characteristics

We do not have to assume innate self-interest, or a drive for power, in order to find explanations for political behaviour at an individual level (as Klein, 1988, suggests). As Schön (1963) argues (see Chapter 1), change is often driven by a 'champion', who is motivated by personal values and beliefs which can extend to passionate commitment. That commitment may be attached to a new corporate strategy or structure, to a shift in organization culture, to the redesign of work, to a new payment system, and so on. Individuals with strong convictions can be expected to use their skills in persuasion and influence, and other methods. These political tactics may become more extreme to the extent that challenge and resistance are regarded as unwarranted, ill-founded, or perhaps motivated by personal agendas irrelevant to organizational processes and outcomes.

Political behaviour is the natural consequence of ambition and the desire for career advancement. The more ambitious you are, the more likely you are to argue and lobby for your ideas, your innovations, your projects. Organization populations usually contain a proportion of ambitious individuals whose ideas naturally and necessarily compete with each other. Tension and conflict are central features of all organizations, and while interpersonal conflict ('I don't like you') can become hostile and damaging, conflict of ideas ('I don't like your proposals') is healthy and desirable. As we have seen, on its own the 'reasoned case' is a weak weapon in the conflict of ideas. A range of other political techniques is helpful in recruiting allies, marginalizing opponents, forming coalitions, selling issues, and focusing sustained attention on your idea, agenda or project.

These behaviours are encouraged by organizational recruitment, appraisal, training and promotion policies. When did you last see a recruitment advertisement asking for people without drive, ambition, or fresh ideas? How many favourable appraisals rely on the appraisee having no performance improvement suggestions of their own to offer? Who got promoted because they were lacking in drive and creativity? (Of course, individuals are on occasion favourably appraised and promoted for lacking these features. But usually these are moves in someone else's political game, which is not made public.)

Political behaviour can also be triggered by the desire for retribution and revenge. Where we have been the targets of political tactics, reciprocity may appear to be a satisfying option. This can become extremely damaging, to the players and to the organization. However, the survey results presented in Chapter 1 suggest that many managers enjoy the power play. This is a game played (usually) by consenting adults. Losing is not a disaster; that experience can improve awareness and skill, and losing can be an invitation to, or an excuse for, a rematch.

Decision characteristics

Decisions vary on the extent to which they are structured, or unstructured. Structured decisions are 'programmable', and can be resolved using known decision rules. Deciding how many kilometres you can drive before you need to stop to buy more petrol is a structured, programmable decision. Unstructured decisions are unprogrammable, and cannot be resolved using decision rules. Examples of unprogrammable decisions include:

- how should the role of the human resource management function be developed?
- would it be more appropriate to use a total quality management or a process redesign approach to address cost overruns and employee morale problems?
- which of these three different lines of product innovation should we pursue?

Routine, day-to-day operational decisions tend to be more structured. Significant strategic decisions tend to be unstructured. To complicate matters, unstructured decisions often have to be made in the face of change and uncertainty. Who knows what size the organization will be in five years' time, or what the composition of the workforce will be? What are the main factors affecting product quality and employee morale, and can we be sure that quality management or process redesign will actually address those factors? How can the balance of costs and benefits of restructuring be assessed? Who knows what innovations the competition will launch? Who knows what developments will or will not take place in information technology hardware and software – and prices – over the next two years?

The number of management decisions that can be reached unambiguously on the basis of information, analysis, and logical reasoning, is limited. Strategic decisions are value laden. Information and analysis may point in particular directions, but information alone is usually inadequate to resolve an unstructured problem. In these circumstances, one expects reasonable people to disagree. It cannot be undesirable that two managers, say, with different past experiences and current preferences, argue the merits of work redesign and process re-engineering solutions. That debate is normal and valuable. Put another way, 'When two people always agree, one of them is unnecessary' (Pfeffer and Sutton, 2006, p.31).

Certain factors heighten the politicization of issues and decisions (Pfeffer, 1992a), including:

- the involvement of large numbers of people
- decisions involving interdepartmental coordination
- decisions about promotions and transfers
- decisions about resource allocation
- decisions at higher organizational levels
- interdependence between parties who have different views
- scarcity of resources
- disagreement on goals
- importance of the issue.

Pfeffer (1992a, p.37) notes that 'power is more important in major decisions, such as those made at higher organizational levels and those that involve crucial issues like reorganization and budget allocations; for domains in which performance is more difficult to assess such as staff rather than line production operations; and in instances in which there is likely to be uncertainty and disagreement'.

However, we are not talking just about the value of information sharing and open discussion. We are dealing with the possible deployment of a range of other political tactics (such as issue-selling; see Chapter 8) to recruit support, deflect resistance, and win the debate. The outcomes of the turf game concern individual reputation and career progress, and the status of sections, departments and occupational groups. Organizations are not debating societies with a set of polite and structured rules. To win the competition of ideas, skilled players typically do whatever they can, within the constraints imposed by social norms, organization culture, and considerations of personal reputation, to ensure that their ideas prevail.

Political behaviour thus follows from the numerical superiority of unstructured decisions over structured ones. It is also a consequence of the tendency for informed and interested parties to disagree with each other, partly on the interpretation of information and analyses, and partly because they are likely to hold differing beliefs, values and preferences.

Structural characteristics

Lencioni (2006) argues that 'silos' are the main source of damaging turf wars and organization politics. As organizations grow, functions and departments emerge, each specializing in their own activities; purchasing, production, marketing, distribution, accounting, human resource management. This horizontal differentiation creates legitimate independent interest groups – silos – with competing goals and priorities. They are also likely to make competing calls on the organization's resources, particularly in the context of generating innovative and creative initiatives for change and development in their respective areas. The concept of organization as united and harmonious community in pursuit of shared goals is an idealistic fiction of management literature and corporate publicity. Klein (1988) points out that, while scarce resources can trigger political behaviour, political tactics can in turn make resources scarce for others, reinforcing the inevitability of politics. Vertical and horizontal differentiation creates the need to control and coordinate the work of others, and generate resistance from those in subordinate positions. In addition, as complex network and partnership structures develop, the need to obtain information, cooperation, support, and compliance from those over whom one has no management authority becomes more significant, putting an even higher premium on political and influencing skills. Political behaviour is thus an inevitable result of structural differentiation (Johnson and Gill, 1993).

Organizational change

Change threatens to push individuals out of their 'comfort zones', as well as jeopardizing existing practices and routines, status hierarchies, information flows, resource allocations, and power bases. In addition, change proposals often generate disputes concerning objectives and the best way to achieve them. It is predictable that those who believe that they will lose, in some regard, or who feel that there are better ways to achieve the same or better results, are likely to put up a fight, initially by presenting a reasoned critical case, and by presenting what they believe to be more effective options. If those voices are not heard, or when those counter-proposals fail, some will abandon the challenge and 'go with the flow'. However, it is also predictable that, where the stakes are high and the issues are important, some detractors are likely to continue their resistance through more covert, political means. Organizational change, therefore, is a further trigger and intensifier of political behaviour.

These four sets of interrelated factors present a powerful combination. Political behaviour in organizational settings is a naturally occurring phenomenon, resistant to management attempts to stifle or eradicate it. Rather than attempt to 'manage away' organization politics, the more appropriate response is to manage this dimension of the management role in general, and of the change agency role in particular.

Foucault and the pervasive nature of power

No contemporary treatment of power is complete without reference to the work of the French philosopher and historian, Michel Foucault, who died in 1984. Foucault was concerned with the development of the human sciences since the eighteenth century, and with the evolution of forms of discipline and control. His best known writings deal with prisons, punishment, and the evolution of sexuality (Foucault, 1977; 1979). As a homosexual in France in the mid-twentieth century, Foucault was no stranger to prison life. While his work is not directly concerned with the politics of organizational change, his analysis offers novel insights.

As we argued earlier, popular notions of social and organizational power have two main features. First, power is generally regarded in *negative* terms. Power corrupts, political behaviour is counter-productive. Second, power is typically regarded and defined as *episodic* in nature. Power is a resource possessed by some individuals who exercise it over others through social interaction. We have sought in this book to challenge and extend these notions. We have argued that power and political behaviour, in organizational change, cannot realistically be regarded in a wholly negative light, and that political behaviour is inevitable, necessary and desirable. We have also demonstrated how power inequalities are embedded in social and organization structures. Power can be exercised through ongoing 'non-decision making' and through 'mobilization of bias' as well as in face-to-face episodes of interpersonal influence. Foucault also argues for the productive and pervasive aspects of power, but his work brings radical and fresh conceptualization and force to these arguments.

Foucault's writing style often makes severe demands on the reader. One is therefore drawn either to 'edited highlights' (Rabinow, 1984), or to the extensive 'secondary' literature produced by his interpreters (Burrell, 1988; Clegg, 1989; McKinlay and Starkey, 1998). Much of this secondary literature adopts a style at least as opaque as the original, and interpreters tend to disagree over 'what Foucault said'. In addition, Foucault produced a vast and related body of work that resists fragmentation into 'topics', such as a narrow focus on power. A brief treatment, such as this, is open to accusations of oversimplification.

Two concepts are central to Foucault's notions of power: *bio-power*, and *disciplinary power*. Bio-power operates through establishing and defining what is normal or abnormal, and thus what is socially deviant or acceptable in thought and behaviour. Bio-power is targeted at society as a whole, and is achieved through a variety of *discursive practices*: talk, writing, debate, argument, representation. The media thus play a significant role in sustaining and altering what we conceive as socially normal and deviant. Bio-power exercises control over us through 'constituting the normal', and operates through our individual cognition and understanding. Assuming you accept without challenge the 'constitution of the normal', as this is currently represented, bio-power assumes a self-disciplining role as far as your thinking and behaviour are concerned. No powerful superior managerial or supervisory figure is necessary to keep you under control. This is a long way from an 'episodic' conception of power, but reinforces the need to question the 'constitution of the normal', rather than tacitly accept current and taken-for-granted definitions and representations.

Disciplinary power operates through the construction of social and organizational routine, and is targeted at individuals and groups. Foucault thus regards power as a set of techniques whose effects are achieved through *disciplinary practices*. Disciplinary practices are simply the tools of surveillance and assessment used to control and regiment individuals, to render us docile and compliant. The social and organizational control of the individual, from this perspective, relies on a 'micro-physics' of cultural practice. This involves practical, sometimes taken-for-granted, techniques of discipline, surveillance and coercion. The techniques or mechanisms which achieve compliance include (Hiley, 1987, p.351):

- the ways in which the allocation of physical space (in a prison, office or factory) establishes homogeneity and uniformity, establishes individual and collective identity, locates the individual in terms of rank or status, and fixes the individual in a network of social relations
- the control of behaviour through timetables, regimentation, standardization of work routines, repetitive activities
- the 'composition of forces' in which individuals become elements in larger aggregates, member of the team, part of the assembly line, and so on
- the use of job ladders and career systems, with their attendant future promises of reward, to encourage consent to organizational demands (e.g., Savage, 1998).

Resistance to such disciplinary practices merely demonstrates and reinforces the necessity for discipline. One does not have to visit prisons to witness these mechanisms in use. They are evident in schools, hospitals, factories, banks, insurance companies, and in universities. We would perhaps not normally regard office layouts, timetables, career ladders, and work allocations, for example, as manifestations of power. However, these practices clearly shape – and discipline – our day-to-day activity and interactions, and are critical elements in the 'field of force relations' controlling and regimenting us, helping to guarantee our compliance with social and organizational norms and expectations.

We are confronted daily with this 'web of power', this 'field of force relations', which is created and recreated by the cultural practices which we act out and to which we, typically, submit. As Hardy and Clegg (1996, p.637) observe, 'we are also prisoners in a web of power that we have helped to create'. Those practical and specific institutional, organizational practices condition our thought processes; we accept much of those disciplinary practices as natural, and therefore do not question them. These disciplinary practices are thus a positive basis for social and organizational order.

The creation and maintenance of disciplinary practices, in Foucault's perspective, are not processes driven by the plans and intentions of specific individuals. Power here is not equated either with domination by the powerful, or with capitalist exploitation of the working class. (However, it is still possible to argue that disciplinary power can be of value to managers in an organizational context, particularly when it comes to exacting willing compliance with managerial instructions.) The 'field of force relations' is not stable, and is not an inevitable consequence of social or organizational structure. It is instead a shifting network of alliances. Points of resistance and fissure can 'open up' at many points in this network, as old alliances fracture, as individuals regroup, and as new alliances are formed. In other words, this is a conceptualization of power which emphasizes the shifting and inherently unstable networks and alliances in organizations, and across society as a whole (Clegg, 1989, p.154). In this respect, Foucault's concern with the strategic deployment of power and political tactics is similar to that of Machiavelli.

Foucault's paradigm of disciplinary technology (based on Jeremy Bentham) is the *panopticon*. The panopticon is an architectural structure, a prison, whose cells range around a central watchtower from which the cells' occupants can be surveyed by a single, unseen, observer. Imagine you are an occupant of one of the cells. You are constantly and regularly subject to surveillance, from which you cannot hide or escape. You do not know when you are being observed, but the certainty of surveillance from the watchtower is always with you. How will that knowledge influence your behaviour? You must constantly behave as if you are being watched. You become 'self-surveying'. Your obedience is thus assured. As with the operation of bio-power, the structure of the panopticon encourages self-discipline. Here again we see the power of normality and routine in controlling individual behaviour, rather than episodic power. The panopticon can be regarded in two ways. First, this is a practical demonstration of disciplinary architecture. Second, and more significantly, the panopticon is a metaphor for the field of force relations, disciplinary power and bio-power, tacitly influencing and constantly controlling our behaviour through our own self-monitoring.

This perspective raises one central question, much debated. Are we trapped in this shifting web of cultural practices? Or, having demystified and understood it, are we capable of 'breaking free', and of transcending or redesigning the web? Foucault uses the expression 'power/knowledge' to address this question. This is a difficult concept to explain in brief; the point is that power and knowledge are inextricably intertwined. The construction and representation of knowledge in society (including knowledge of what is normal and what is deviant) is dependent on the exercise of power. Therefore, 'knowledge is not the antidote of power' (Hardy and Clegg, 1996, p.695). The generation of more knowledge simply opens further opportunities for the exercise of power, for the control and manipulation of others. Knowledge is not emancipatory in this perspective, but simply a vehicle for perpetuating, albeit in a dynamic and shifting form, the web of power to which we are subject. Foucault's position is contrasted with more traditional notions of power in Table 9.1.

In this brief overview, we appear to have reached some depressing conclusions. We are surrounded by a pervasive web of power. Improved knowledge of power relations is not emancipatory. There is little we can do about this. We may be able to open up 'points of resistance' and change the details, but the field of force relations will in essence prevail.

It is useful to recall that Foucault's is but one, radical–alternative, perspective on social and organizational power relations. The value of a perspective depends in part on the purpose with which one approaches and adopts it. If you are a social philosopher and historian with a critical interest in the social and political order, then Foucault's perspective is challenging and enlightening. If you are a manager trying to drive a change initiative, then Foucault's views may sound like an esoteric distraction. An episodic concept of power and power relations, therefore, still has relevance and value to those engaged in day-to-day social interaction and interpersonal influence. But this is to enter into a fruitless debate about 'which perspective is correct?'. Power is a contested concept around which a number of contrasting perspectives have developed. There is, therefore,

Table 9.1   Foucault versus traditional concepts of power

traditional concept of power	Foucault's concept of power
power is possessed, is accumulated, is vested in the individual	power is pervasive, is a totality, is reflected in concrete practices
power is in the hands of social and organizational elites; resistance is futile	power is to be found in the micro-physics of social life; power depends on resistance
we are subject to the domination of those who are more powerful than we are	we construct our own web of power in accepting current definitions of normality
power is destructive, denies, represses, prevents, corrupts	power is productive, contributes to social order, which is flexible and shifting
power is episodic, visible, is observable in action, is deployed intermittently, is absent except when exercised	power is present in its absence, discreet, operating through taken-for-granted daily routines and modes of living
knowledge of power sources and relationships is emancipatory, can help us overcome domination	knowledge maintains and extends the web of power, creating further opportunities for domination

as Chapter 2 also argued, value in being able to view this complex and slippery notion from different angles, and to be aware of and be able to draw on the strengths and limitations of different perspectives.

What, then, is the particular relevance of Foucault's position to the contemporary political entrepreneur? First, this perspective forces us to look with a critical and sceptical eye at so-called radical change, and to identify underlying continuities in organization structures and power relations. 'Radical' change may often be a representation, a cosmetic, concealing deep structural continuity despite the rhetoric, and despite the new labels suggesting that major upheavals and transformations are afoot. Second, it reminds us that the change driver is part of the field of force relations, changed as well as changing, subject to the influences of power as well as deploying power–political strategies. Third, this is a further reminder that local points of resistance to change can be expected to emerge, and to be exploited.

Foucault's stance forces us to pay attention to the myriad of mundane, transparent, taken-for-granted, daily routines that constantly shape our thinking and behaviour, and that of others. Knowledge may not be emancipatory, but it can be useful. The turf game involves understanding and anticipating the interests and moves of other stakeholders. A broad knowledge of the forces acting on their thinking and behaviour is invaluable. As Foucault makes clear, the field of force relations is unstable and shifting, and is amenable to challenge and dispute. Knowledge thus opens opportunities to 'fight back' against power. Finding and opening up appropriate points of resistance to power can be achieved proactively. Foucault offers us not simply 'consciousness raising', with respect to the pervasiveness of power, but also an analytical framework, which suggests creative options for action.

Foucault would dismiss the notion of 'triggers' of political behaviour as irrelevant. Our behaviour constitutes the field of force relations of which we are a part. Our apparently humdrum activities reflect and maintain the power of the disciplinary practices to which we are subject, particularly in organizational contexts. Political behaviour does not require to be 'triggered'. As observed in Chapter 1, Zaleznik (1997) distinguishes between 'real work' and 'psychopolitics'. 'Real work' is sane, legitimate, productive. 'Political preoccupations' are unhealthy, diverting, illegitimate. From Foucault's perspective, this distinction is meaningless. Real work and psychopolitics are each inextricably implicated in the other; real work is political behaviour which is real work.

Another implication of Foucault's perspective concerns the extent to which we as individuals are active in our own domination, through our uncritical acceptance of taken-for-granted practices, and of current definitions of what is normal and acceptable, and what is not, in our society. Foucault thus encourages a critical, questioning stance towards what we might otherwise regard as 'normal' or 'routine'. We have elsewhere in this book explored what it might mean to argue that the political entrepreneur should act in an ethical manner. One of Foucault's aims was to demonstrate that, while social institutions and organizational practices may appear neutral, their political role in controlling and regimenting individuals is often obscured. Foucault's perspective thus serves to remove that obscurity, opening such practices to challenge and resistance.

Savvy and street smarts: the development of political expertise

---

Political skill

Political skill is: 'an interpersonal style construct that combines social astuteness with the ability to relate well, and otherwise demonstrate situationally appropriate behaviour in a disarmingly charming and engaging manner that inspires confidence, trust, sincerity, and genuineness' (Ferris et al., 2000, p.30).

What is 'political skill', and how can it be developed? Ferris et al. (2005) call this 'savvy and street smarts'. In this section, we establish that political skill cannot be seen as a discrete set of capabilities, but rather as an integral component of the management role in general and of change agency in particular. We will also argue that the concept of *expertise* is more appropriate than the notion of skill in this context. However, as most commentators use the term skill when exploring these issues, we will begin the discussion with this term.

There is no shortage of advice on political tactics, and it might be expected that the concept of political skill would now also be well developed. However, this issue has been largely ignored, leading Butcher and Clarke (1999) to describe organization politics as 'the missing discipline' in management development which focuses instead on collaboration, openness, and trust. The survey findings in Chapter 1 showed 80 per cent of managers reporting that they had no education or training in this area. Most of the research and commentary on attributes of effective change agents has ignored political skill.

Is political skill simply a facet of social and interpersonal skill? Ferris et al. (2005) offer the bizarre argument that political skill is distinct from social skill because the latter does not involve deliberate manipulation for personal ends. This is hardly a valid observation, as all social exchanges involve some form of manipulation (you ask the questions, I provide the answers) or social interaction would not work. All interpersonal behaviours can be attributed with political intent, even where the actors involved interpret their behaviours differently.

While clearly there is overlap (as with influencing tactics), political skill (which itself is a socially constructed concept) may be distinguished more clearly from social skill with reference to the behaviour repertoire that is perceived to be involved in organization politics, and to the nature of the judgements leading to the use of political tactics. The behaviour repertoire involves the creative use of tactics such as image building, information games, scapegoating, alliances, networking, compromise, rule games, positioning, and 'dirty tricks'. Decisions concerning whether and how to use political tactics rely on judgements concerning contextual warrant, credible accounting, and reputational impact. The conduct and maintenance of harmonious and effective interpersonal relationships, the domain of social skill, thus appear quite different from the domain of political skill when viewed through the lenses of behaviour repertoire and decision criteria.

The competent change agent

Considering the attributes of the effective change agent, it is difficult to escape from competency lists. McBer, a consultancy organization, developed a competency model of the successful change agent, summarized in Table 9.2 (Cripe, 1993), emphasizing a combination of interpersonal, diagnostic, initiation, and organizational skills.

From a Birmingham University study of public sector change leaders, Wooldridge and Wallace (2002) identify the 'nine habits of successful change leaders', summarized in Table 9.3, emphasizing the role of external relationships as well as internal management.

Hutton (1994) contrasts the desirable and undesirable attributes of change agents (Table 9.4). These frameworks (and there are many similar profiles in the literature) do not address organization politics. Hutton (1994, p.16) argues that the change agent should be, 'able to recognize and deal with office politics without becoming involved in the politics'. Just how this feat is to be achieved – addressing politics without involvement in politics – is not explained, and the political dimension is omitted from the self-assessment checklist which follows Hutton's discussion of those attributes. Hutton (1994, p.252) also notes that this job 'is not for everyone', as it can be demanding, tiring, lonely, and

Table 9.2   The McBer competency model for successful change agents

interpersonal skills

- able to express empathy
- have positive expectations of people
- display genuineness

diagnostic skills

- knowledge of the principles of individual and organization development
- able to collect meaningful data through interviews, surveys and observation
- able to draw conclusions from complex data and make accurate diagnoses

initiation skills

- able to influence and market skills, and persuade internal customers to use services
- able to present in a concise, interesting, and informative way
- able to manage group dynamics
- problem solving and planning skills, to help improve goal setting and performance

organization skills

- designing adult learning and organization development exercises
- administering resources such as personnel, materials, schedules and training sites

Source: based on Cripe (1993).

Table 9.3   Nine habits of successful change leaders

1	Focus staff on strategic objectives, ensuring that they are aware of why they are being asked to work in a particular way.
2	Listen to staff, to identify the issues that have to be resolved if the organization is to achieve its objectives.
3	Listen to members of the community, and work outside the boundaries of the organization, engaging the public as partners in delivering outcomes.
4	Prioritize professional development; change leadership must have legitimacy in the professional culture if it is to be accepted.
5	Work with leaders of local services; forward-looking organizations are building partnerships with others to establish seamless services across their boundaries.
6	Prioritize the achievement of results; change leaders who display consistency of purpose, rather than using success simply to promote their careers.
7	Use information to overcome barriers. Develop an open culture, discussing and exploring issues rather than hiding them and leaving them unsaid.
8	Use project-based working to create a climate in which individuals and teams can contribute to performance improvement.
9	Tell the story creatively and incessantly, using inspirational imagery, to help staff make sense of the complex, multi-layered nature of change.

Source: based on Wooldridge and Wallace (2002).

Table 9.4 Desirable and undesirable attributes of the change agent

desirable	undesirable
believes that this is the right thing to do	sees this job as a stepping stone in career
patient, persistent	impatient, lacking persistence
honest, trustworthy, reliable	devious, unreliable, untrustworthy
positive and enthusiastic	unable to convey enthusiasm
confident but not arrogant	has high need for praise and recognition
good observer and listener	poor listener, insensitive to others' feelings
flexible and resourceful	inflexible, arrogant, cold, unapproachable
not easily intimidated	moral putty, changes view to fit context
good sense of humour	status-conscious
willing to accept risks and challenges	risk averse, protective of image and career
recognizes and deals with office politics	political and manipulative
prefers an inclusive cooperative style	prefers a secretive, adversarial style

Source: based on Hutton (1994).

risky, as well as satisfying. Furthermore, while the role usually presents opportunities 'to make a difference', the rewards are often intangible, and recognition may not always be forthcoming, either.

Skilled political actors

Echoing the competency lists for effective change agents, a number of studies have produced profiles of skilled political actors. For example, from their study of the views of chief executives, middle managers, and first line supervisors, Allen et al. (1979) conclude that the effective organizational politician is articulate, sensitive, socially adept, competent, popular, extroverted, self-confident, aggressive, ambitious, devious, intelligent, and logical. This reads like a list of the characteristics of effective leaders from research in the mid-twentieth century, with the exception perhaps of 'aggressive' and 'devious' (see, for example, Stogdill, 1948 and 1974). However, the different groups in this research had contrasting views. Chief executives felt that political actors had to be articulate and sensitive. Managers, on the other hand, felt that they should be socially adept. The most effective political actors in the perception of supervisors, however, were popular and aggressive.

Voss (1992) lists the following attributes as necessary to 'play the game' of office politics:

- focus on the job to build your credit
- skills of observation and listening
- identify the opinion leaders, the fence-sitters

- judge personalities and interests
- develop unobtrusive partnerships based on reciprocity
- avoid the blatant use of power
- negotiation skills, and know when to push, when to concede
- ability to make the boss look good
- don't alienate superiors, don't say no
- develop loyal and competent subordinates (who make you look good)
- patience.

Voss notes that developing political 'antennae' and building a reputation can take a considerable amount of time, hence his final remark concerning patience.

Continuing the theme of competency profiles, Butcher and Clarke (2001) discuss the attributes of 'the constructive politician' in terms of conceptual understanding (intellectual grasp), personal understanding (clarity of goals), awareness (of political context) and interpersonal skills (handling relationships). This model is summarized in Table 9.5. Butcher and Clarke (2001) argue that the process of developing effective political skills can involve a lengthy, difficult, and personal journey, reflecting the 'seasoning process' through which women have been found to develop political skill (Mainiero, 1994a; see Chapter 5).

Researchers studying perceptions of organization politics from a positivist perspective (see the discussion in Chapter 2) have also sought to develop a model of political skill. This approach is concerned first with establishing a stable and valid measure of political skill, and then with correlating this construct with other variables. Once again, this is based on an academic literature review rather than on conversations with managers who are actually engaged in organization politics. However, the resultant model identifies four dimensions measured using a political skills inventory with 18 Likert-scaled items (Ferris et al., 2005 and 2007; Brouer et al., 2006). This is summarized in Table 9.6. Studies using university students and staff as participants, with this and similar measures, produced the following conclusions:

- political skill measured with this inventory correlates moderately with measures of self-monitoring and emotional intelligence
- those who score high on political skill display less anxiety, and are less likely to perceive stressful events as threatening
- political skill is not correlated with general mental ability (i.e., intelligence)
- political skill is a predictor of both job performance and of subordinate evaluations of leadership ability
- the dimension of political skill related most strongly and positively to performance rating is social astuteness.

There are at least three problems with this perspective. First, in identifying only four components of political skill, this represents a superficial view of the depth and breadth

Table 9.5   Capabilities of the constructive politician

---

conceptual understanding

- power and politics: evaluating the complexity of the influence process and the role of motives
- relationships: evaluating the different barriers for organizational relationships
- political mechanisms: recognizing the value of lobbying, stealth and the adherence to formal procedure
- pockets of good practice: appreciating the value of establishing worthwhile causes to stimulate organization change

self-understanding

- clarity: about balancing personal and organizational motives
- managerial irreverence: a healthy scepticism about the limits to what is possible in formal organizations

awareness

- stakeholder knowledge: knowing the agendas and motivations of key players
- organizational knowledge: knowing who makes key decisions and how they are made
- business environment knowledge: knowing the critical organization issues

interpersonal skills

- persuasive presentation: developing collaborative outcomes through personal enthusiasm, suggestion, logical connections and the disclosure of motives
- productive challenge: causing others to analyse their assumptions
- reading others: ongoing observation and evaluation of the motives and actions of others.

Source: based on Butcher and Clarke (2001, pp.95–6).

of the expertise and creativity required to operate effectively in this domain. Missing from this account are issues concerning ability to assess the organizational context, to understand 'the game', to build power bases and sources, to integrate conventional with political tactics, to appreciate the significance of positioning and role switching, planning political strategy, the management of favours and compromises and trade-offs, the selective use of information, the use of advisers and advice, avoiding commitment to maintain room to manoeuvre, creating and exploiting organization structures, issue-selling, accounting, and careful timing, for example. However defined, political skill is a multidimensional construct. The dimensions identified by Ferris et al. (2005) do not appear to capture the richness of this domain.

A second problem concerns the use of self-rated items, e.g., 'I pay close attention to facial expressions', and 'I know a lot of important people', to measure aspects of political skill such as social astuteness and networking, respectively. While this approach may be consistent with the methods used in positivist research, it is almost certainly not consistent with the way in which most managers understand, observe, use, and are

Table 9.6 Dimensions of political skill

dimension	definition	sample inventory items
social astuteness	attuned observers, good interpreters of behaviour, self-aware, sensitive to others, clever	I understand people very well. I pay close attention to people's facial expressions.
interpersonal influence	subtle and convincing style, calibrate actions to the situation, to the 'target', be flexible	I am able to make most people feel comfortable and at ease around me. I am good at getting people to like me.
networking ability	adept at using networks, develop friendships and build alliances easily, skilled in negotiation and conflict resolution	I spend a lot of time and effort at work networking with others. At work, I know a lot of important people and am well connected.
apparent sincerity	appear honest and open, and to have integrity, authenticity, sincerity, genuineness, no ulterior motives	It is important that people believe I am sincere in what I say and do. I try to show a genuine interest in other people.

Source: based on Ferris et al. (2005 and 2007).

affected by political skill in practice. In addition, those are items which could be used to measure generic social skills. Describing people with high political skill, Ferris et al. (2005, p.128) claim that:

> Politically skilled individuals convey a sense of personal security and calm self-confidence that attracts others and gives them a feeling of comfort. This self-confidence never goes too far so as to be perceived as arrogance but is always properly measured to be a positive attribute. Therefore, although self-confident, those high in political skill are not self-absorbed (although they are self-aware) because their focus is outward toward others, not inward and self-centred. . . . We suggest that people high in political skill not only know precisely what to do in different social situations at work but how to do it in a manner that disguises any ulterior, self-serving motives and appears to be sincere.

Although this characterization sounds plausible, it appears to be based mainly on supposition, as the authors report no observations of, or interviews with, skilled organization politicians, or indeed interviews with observers of such characters. Consequently, these sweeping generalizations may be inaccurate. Some skilled politicians may be arrogant and self-centred, but are clever enough not to display those traits when to do so could be damaging. It is also possible that skilled politicians often do not know precisely how to act, and use a risky combination of improvisation, experiment and, as noted in the Preface to this book, *bricolage*.

The third problem with this approach is that political skill, however defined, is divorced from the wider organizational context. Political skill is surely an integral component of the conduct of management in general, and of change agency in particular. To isolate the concept of political skill in terms of discrete individual attributes is of limited value. The concept of skill may not therefore be the best tool with which to explore this area.

Buchanan and Boddy (1992) argue that the concept of *expertise* is more appropriate. Competency frameworks tend to identify lists of discrete skills, capabilities, and other attributes, and the accompanying measures often assume that we are addressing well-defined problems using clearly identifiable competencies, in pursuit of known (or knowable) solutions. The concept of expertise, in contrast, captures the diagnostic and judgemental capabilities required to deal with less well-bounded situations, where 'correct' solutions are difficult to identify, and where as Provis (2004) observes, there may be more than one reasonable solution to a problem. Summarizing research in this area, Buchanan and Boddy (1992, pp.118–20) identify seven characteristics of experts and expertise:

1 *Experts excel in their own domain.* Based on long experience, expertise is often domain-specific, and is not always transferable to other contexts. The expert surgeon will not necessarily be a highly effective change agent.
2 *Experts work with large and meaningful patterns.* Chess masters recall clusters of pieces and sequences of moves rather than information about individual pieces and tactics. Experts organize their knowledge base more effectively, observing patterns in the detail, taking 'the helicopter perspective'.
3 *Experts solve problems faster and with fewer errors.* Skill becomes automatic with practice. Attention to pattern rather than detail allows solutions to be identified more quickly. Perceived patterns can trigger ideas for solutions and actions, again reducing the need for time-consuming information gathering and analysis.
4 *Experts have better memories.* The automatic nature of skill frees up memory space, and information subjected to patterning or 'chunking' is more easily stored and recalled than the details. Experts do not have greater capacity; they use what is available more efficiently.
5 *Experts use deeper and more principled conceptualizations.* The conceptual categories used by experts are less superficial and based more on principles and theories; novices tend to rely more on the surface details of problems.
6 *Experts spend more time qualitatively analysing problems.* Novices plunge directly into problem solving, while experts stand back and try to understand the problem first, building a mental representation from which to infer relationships and define the situation. While experts may be slower in the initial stages of problem solving, they still solve problems faster overall.
7 *Experts have strong self-monitoring skills.* Experts ask more questions, are more aware of when they have made an error, why they have not understood, when they need

to check their solutions. Self-knowledge makes experts better able to assess the difficulty of the situation they face.

Expertise thus involves a combination of abilities to organize, process, use, and reflect on knowledge effectively, and is not simply based on the possession of superior knowledge or a collection of discrete competencies.

The political entrepreneur

One argument of this book might seem to be that the savvy, street smart, cunning, manipulative Machiavellian manager will enjoy more career success than ethically constrained colleagues. Chapter 1 claimed that the change agent who is not prepared to act politically will fail. Chapter 4 demonstrated that Machiavellian pragmatism was central to personal and organizational effectiveness. Reinforcing the discussion in Chapter 7, this chapter has also argued that current organizational trends put political skills at a premium. However, the evidence does not support the argument that the 'high Mach' manager (Christie and Geiss, 1970) is more successful (see the self-assessment at the end of this chapter). To make this argument clear, we must distinguish between the high Mach manager or change agent who behaves consistently in the manner that a high score implies, regardless of context, and the high Mach who only uses those behaviours and tactics when the situation requires, when that approach will probably be effective in achieving desired personal and organizational outcomes, and where the impact on personal reputation is likely to be either neutral or positive. In short, there is a crucial difference between being high Mach all the time, and being high Mach, pragmatically, when necessity commands.

Gemmill and Heisler (1972) found that high Mach managers suffered higher job strain, lower job satisfaction, and experienced less control over their organizational surroundings. A high Mach orientation was not linked with upward mobility. They offer a number of explanations:

A final reason that managers with greater Machiavellian orientations may report more job strain and less job satisfaction arises from the degree to which the organization in which they are employed provides the situational characteristics, outlined by Christie, which are required for the saliency of Machiavellian behavior: (1) opportunity for improvisation in the sense that rewards or outcomes are not tied to objectively defined performance but can be influenced by the manner in which the situation is handled, (2) opportunity for face-to-face interaction, and (3) potential for emotional arousal. To the extent that a large, bureaucratic organization preprograms actions, utilizes standardized rules for allocating rewards, and operates with a norm of impersonality, these situational characteristics would be minimized. When these characteristics are minimized, managers with greater Machiavellian orientations should do no better than managers with lower

Machiavellian orientations in terms of achieving desired outcomes. The findings of this study with respect to positional mobility are consistent with this expectation (Gemmill and Heisler, 1972, p.60).

In a bureaucratic structure, high Mach managers are frustrated by the lack of opportunity to manipulate and control events and outcomes. As discussed earlier, however, the stable, rule-bound bureaucracy is not the only organizational form found today. The flat, flexible, fast, and fluid organization offers considerable scope for emotional arousal, for direct social interaction, for improvisation. In other words, those organizational trends appear to create the conditions in which Machiavellian managers thrive. Nevertheless, Graham (1996) found that project managers with high Mach scores did not have more successful careers, measured by salary, than their low-scoring colleagues. One explanation lies with the Machiavellian behaviour repertoire. Managerial success involves using that repertoire in a flexible manner, according to circumstances. Any manager acting consistently in a Machiavellian manner is less likely to be effective than one who tailors their methods to the context.

The stereotype of the politically skilled change agent arising from the discussion in this chapter is not the caricature of the Machiavellian, but includes competencies, a behaviour repertoire, and also the creative, self-critical, diagnostic, and judgemental perspective captured by the term expertise. Deciding how to act in particular circumstances is not a matter of reading off a checklist, but of informed improvisation. Knowledge of the context and of the other players must lead to a creative choice of strategy and tactics. It may be helpful, therefore, to shift the language away from organization politicians and political skill.

The term *political entrepreneur* (Laver, 1997) captures more effectively the nature of the *political expertise* that is required to deal with this dimension of the change agency role. Change agency is not, of course, an exclusively political activity, but political expertise is a key component of the behaviour repertoire. Why use the term political entrepreneur? As discussed in the Preface, 'political activist' suggests a role that is national, visible, and ruthless, while 'political operator' implies self-serving deviousness. Political entrepreneur has the advantage of highlighting the risk-taking and creative dimensions of the role of the change agent, and also captures the personal commitment to, even passion for, change.

The term political entrepreneur suggests more than a behaviour repertoire, referring also to a perspective that integrates political strategies and tactics with an innovative, reflective, self-monitoring approach to how those behaviours should be deployed. This also captures 'the winning perspective' discussed in Chapter 8, where 'winning' was defined as achieving outcomes that one believes to be right and appropriate in organizational terms, not simply beating the opposition for personal satisfaction. To highlight the nature of this perspective, the first edition of this book contrasted the four perspectives on politics summarized in Table 9.7; the 'puritan' who avoids politics, the 'street fighter' who plays for fun, the 'sports commentator' who watches but does not play, and the 'political entrepreneur'.

Table 9.7 Perspectives on organization politics

puritan	does not get involved at any level because politics means 'dirty tricks', and is unethical and damaging
street fighter	the 'pure politician' for whom playing the game, to win, by whatever means, is the end in itself – and is enjoyed
sports commentator	understands the game and can pass appropriate comment and judgement, but does not become personally involved in the play
political entrepreneur	adopts a creative, committed, reflective, risk-taking approach, balancing conventional methods with political tactics when the circumstances render this necessary, appropriate, and defensible

---

Confessions of a change agent: why did I do it?

- I wanted a job to look forward to in the morning, and not want to leave in the evening.
- I saw it as a great opportunity to learn. I get charged up with more learning. I need that. I needed to get my hands dirty.
- It gave me a chance to show my capabilities. It is a very tiring and frustrating job. On the other hand, it gives you a great opportunity to excel.
- I am a risk taker. I need some excitement and power-play while at work.
- I believe that the only way to meet the challenges of the external business environment is to offer the customer what they really want.
- It gave me an opportunity to work with some highly motivated and committed individuals. Together we were able to make it happen.
- I have thick skin. I realized that I was going to make some enemies during the change process – as well as some very influential and powerful friends.
- I was able to accept the challenge due to the stage of my personal lifestyle (boyfriend overseas, dog at home). I sacrificed my spare time for the company – and for the financial and non-financial rewards.
- Even though I was an inexperienced change agent, I was confident that I had skills, knowledge and attributes to make it happen. Or that I could find an expert (internal or external) to assist me to make it happen.
- If I would fail, I could still work with [this organization] – or elsewhere, because I am tolerant of ambiguity.

Source: answer given by a female Finnish manager, working and studying in Australia, when asked why she had accepted a particularly difficult and demanding change agency role.

The consequence of this analysis is that, to be an effective change agent, one has to adopt the perspective of the political entrepreneur. Other perspectives may bring short term success and rewards, but are likely to fail in the medium to long term with regard to making things happen, getting things done, and building a credible, sustainable reputation as a change agent. The attributes of the political entrepreneur are summarized in Table 9.8.

Table 9.8 adopts the presentation style of other commentators in this field, but it should be recognized that such a fragmented list does not adequately capture the integrated nature of this combination of competencies, behaviours, and perspective.

Table 9.8 Attributes of the political entrepreneur

intellectually equipped	recognizes the value of competing approaches to understanding power and politics in the organization
power sensitive	understands the sources and bases of power, and also how power is embedded in organization structures and systems, as well as in routine, everyday practice
power builder	able to develop power bases through accumulating and exploiting appropriate resources and expertise
behaviour repertoire	has a behaviour repertoire that includes a range of interpersonal skills, such as impression management, conversation control, and influencing techniques
skill and will	has a behaviour repertoire that includes a range of political strategies and tactics, and a readiness to use these
creativity in context	able to deploy that behaviour repertoire creatively and appropriately to fit the context, in a style that can be described as 'intuitive artistry'
trigger sensitive	understands the combination of factors which warrant political behaviour in particular settings, and those which suggest that other approaches would be more appropriate
diagnostic capability	able to read the shifting politics of the organization, and the changing motives and moves of other stakeholders
positioning	taking and switching roles appropriately, to maximize personal advantage, to address opposition, and to drive the change agenda – to 'take the space'
plays the long game	understands the trade-offs in the turf game, and is able to calculate (perhaps intuitively) when it is appropriate to lose a play in the game in order to achieve advantage later
credible accounting	able and willing to construct plausible accounts of behaviour when challenged, to defend political methods
reputation builder	able to construct a reputation as a skilled political player, and to sustain and develop that reputation consistently, based on ongoing critical reflection on experience

Can such political expertise be developed? Ahearn et al. (2004) and Brouer et al. (2006) argue that although political skill is partly innate, it can be improved through training and experience. The management development agenda seems to have three main components. First, the skills and knowledge required to implement change effectively. These appear to be extensive, but most are generic management competences whose significance is increased in a change agency context. Second, the behaviour repertoire. The political entrepreneur has to be able to engage the politics of the organization and the change process. Using political strategies and Machiavellian tactics does not require a change in personality, but rather an extended, appropriate, and creatively deployed behaviour repertoire.

An understanding of organization politics seems to be part of the taken-for-granted 'recipe knowledge' of most experienced managers. The third, and most significant, element in the management development agenda thus concerns a reflexive perspective on the role, using knowledge and experience in a creative, improvisatory, contextually appropriate and self-critical manner. The change agent must be concerned with the relationships between a warrant for political behaviour, the outcomes, the need for appropriate accounting, and the implications for reputation. Can such a perspective be learned or trained? Schön (1983) argued that this was how professionals, tacitly, already operated.

There are many 'offline' and 'online' methods for developing political expertise. Offline, books such as this stimulate awareness, provide terminology, generate discussion and reflection through case analysis, offer self-assessments and other diagnostic tools, and develop a conceptual framework and decision criteria for sustainable decision making in politicized contexts. The acquisition and development of political skill, however, as most commentators have observed, and for those to whom these behaviours do not come naturally, must depend on online methods, on the job, through experience, through 'getting one's hands dirty' (Provis, 2004). The experience of leading, managing, or facilitating change is developmental in several dimensions, including political expertise. Buchanan (1999) describes how involvement in a whole-hospital re-engineering programme contributed significantly to the personal and career development of many of those who worked in and with the re-engineering teams or 'laboratories' as they were known. This experience can lift the individual from a narrow functional role and expose them to organization-wide issues and processes, to external perspectives, to novel change implementation methodologies and tools, and to organization politics. That exposure can dramatically enhance the individual's career aspirations as well as widening their career opportunities.

In summary, it is more helpful to think in terms of a perspective, an outlook, a way of viewing and using organization politics, than it is to consider competency lists. As Hutton (1994) argues, there is no one single profile for the effective change agent, or for the political entrepreneur. A perspective can be brought to bear on a situation in a number of different ways, with different consequences for action. But those different approaches may each be reasonable, and effective, in the circumstances.

A loss of innocence

Our intention has been to expose to wider scrutiny the role of political behaviour in relation to organizational change and innovation. The fluid, unpredictable, 'high velocity' organizational context is now taken for granted. This has meant the replacement of stable organization hierarchy and position power with shifting networks and coalitions where expert and referent power become more useful. Position power is today further weakened by the deeply unfashionable nature of autocratic management. As we have argued, political expertise appears to be at a premium in this context.

Evil bastards and dirty tricks

However, it is often suggested to us that some readers find offensive the argument of this book, some of the language quoted, the nature of the incident reports in Chapter 3, examples of political strategies and tactics, and perhaps even some of the cartoons used as illustrations. Are we in danger of creating a surface impression of concern with 'evil bastards' who play 'dirty tricks' (cartoon, Chapter 1)? It is not our intention to offend, but rather to present the reality of organization politics as it is experienced by practising managers, as supported by research, to offer insights into the nature of the turf game, and also to develop a working perspective on a key dimension of the change management role.

It has also been our intention to confront commentators who regard organization politics in negative terms. The authors' nightmare is that someone else will publish their argument first. With trepidation, as the manuscript for the first edition of this book was nearing completion, we acquired a copy of *Confronting Company Politics* (Stone, 1997). Stone, a psychologist and change consultant, argues that political behaviour has a single cause, in an individual's attempts to protect their ego. Stone advocates a single response: shut down the politicking. Despite a case woven with existential philosophy, Stone's argument is oversimplified and unrealistic. It ignores the complexities of organizational life, and marginalizes the positive contributions of political behaviour. The denial of organization politics can drive discussion underground, silencing critics and stifling challenge. This position serves the interests of the 'evil bastards' by placing them beyond polite discussion and professional debate.

We trust that readers will look below the surface impression and find an argument here that links political expertise to professional, competent, legitimate, constructive, positive, and ethical management behaviour in general, and to change agency behaviour in particular. We have argued that the change driver should be a self-critical and reflective *political entrepreneur*. This perspective involves a committed, creative, risk-taking approach to deciding appropriate action, in a given context. This perspective has also been described as 'intuitive artistry'. While politics and dirty tricks may well sometimes be equated, we suggest that there is nothing illegitimate or evil about our central argument.

Beyond the interpersonal

As we have seen, political expertise is often identified as a sub-category of social and interpersonal skill. There is substance in that viewpoint, which parts of this book have perhaps reinforced. We have dealt, for example, with issues such as conversation control, impression management, influencing techniques, and various approaches to management and leadership style. These are all topics that find space on interpersonal skills development courses. However, we have tried to demonstrate that this categorization is misleading. Political expertise involves elements that include, but go some considerable distance beyond what are commonly understood to be interpersonal skills, as shown in Table 9.8.

A loss of innocence

Just before our first edition went into production, one of us visited a hospital which was running a major transformation project. The change agents were not experienced managers, but were recruited from across the organization; pharmacy manager, ward nurse, radiographer, medical secretary. The discussion turned from the change initiatives to their experiences and personal learning, and to the skills which they had acquired in their new roles. One of them summed up the discussion with the expression, 'a loss of innocence'. Implementing change in this hospital involved identifying key players and opinion leaders, finding ways to influence or to recruit them, to co-opt their support, or to find ways around their resistance. Their change approach was in part reliant on systematic, rational, analytical techniques of process mapping and redesign, performance improvements and organization development. But the change game, they quickly discovered, was also a turf game.

Most if not all experienced managers will probably recognize the issues and arguments of this book, as would those hospital change agents. Political behaviour is a widely experienced phenomenon. However, it is not so widely discussed or analysed openly in organizational settings, where it remains a taboo subject. The discussion found in the literature is either remote from the practical concerns of organizational change, or offers oversimplified and unrealistic advice. Some managers may thus feel unnecessarily guilty about playing the turf game to achieve desired results, in career and organizational terms.

This 'loss of innocence' is critical. Honest self-reflection on one's political tactics and accounts brings them directly into conscious awareness, making them available for analysis, critical judgement, and improvement. Avoidance of this reflection and self-knowledge, in an attempt to remain 'squeaky clean' by avoiding organization politics, courts the risk of self-deception. Such an avoidance strategy also puts one at risk of being sidelined by more competent players. This further risks the criticism that one is unskilled and unprofessional in being unable to deal with those players. The choice for some, therefore, may lie between loss of innocence or loss of the change agenda to the street fighters, saboteurs and subversives.

The argument of this book is that the change agent who is not politically skilled will fail. For those who believe that political behaviour is invariably damaging and should be avoided, developing a successful management career will probably be difficult. For those who believe that involvement in the turf game is unethical, the experience of change implementation is likely to be a frustrating one, with that frustration escalating along with the significance of the changes in hand. Honest self-appraisal is more daring, and more rewarding.

In the domain of practical action, management is a contact sport. If you don't want to get bruised, don't play. And as Frankel (2004) points out, if you don't play, you can't win. There is little to be gained by complaining about the turf game, its players, its tricks, its strategies, its tactics and its potential damage. Criticism of organization politics is likely to have as much impact as complaints about the British weather. Political behaviour can be managed, but it cannot be managed away. We hope that we have shown that there is much to be gained by understanding and engaging with the turf game. Managing change can be a demanding and exhausting role, but it is also developmental and rewarding. The political is a key aspect, which can also be demanding. But we also know that some managers find positive challenge and reward in the turf game, and this may be particularly related to successful organization development and change as well as to personal career success.

Our concluding advice for change agents, therefore, is to recognize the hypocrisy, shed the innocence, abandon the guilt, play the turf game, aim to win on one's own terms, and enjoy.

Follow through

Are you too soft to be a manager?

It should be borne in mind that there is nothing more difficult to handle, more doubtful of success, and more dangerous to carry through than initiating changes in a state's constitution. The innovator makes enemies of all those who prospered under the old order, and only lukewarm support is forthcoming from those who would prosper under the new. Their support is lukewarm partly from fear of their adversaries, who have the existing laws on their side, and partly because men are generally incredulous, never really trusting new things unless they have tested them by experience. In consequence, whenever those who oppose the changes can do so, they attack vigorously, and the defence made by others is only lukewarm. So both the innovator and his friends come to grief (Machiavelli, 1514, p.51).

This is one of the most well-known quotations from Machiavelli, whose sixteenth-century ideas on national political strategy and tactics still divide opinion. For the change agent, the question which Machiavelli asks is: how far are you prepared to go to achieve your objectives? Machiavelli put moral scruples at a discount, regarding them as a handicap. Research in this area was inspired by Christie and Geiss (1970), and they designed an assessment of an individual's Machiavellian tendencies. Their questionnaire is known as the Mach IV*, because it went through a number of development iterations, and identifies whether the respondent is 'High Mach' or 'Low Mach', or somewhere in between.

The Mach IV questionnaire

Please read each of the following statements carefully, and put a tick at the point on the scale which most closely represents your own attitude. Please score these statements honestly, and not in relation to what you feel might be an 'ideal' or 'correct' response.

	strongly agree	agree	neutral	disagree	strongly disagree
1 The best way to handle people is to tell them what they want to hear.	5	4	3	2	1
2 When you ask someone to do something for you, it is best to give the real reasons for wanting it rather than giving reasons which might carry more weight.	1	2	3	4	5
3 Anyone who completely trusts anyone else is asking for trouble.	5	4	3	2	1
4 It is hard to get ahead without cutting corners here and there.	5	4	3	2	1
5 Honesty is the best policy in all cases.	1	2	3	4	5
6 It is safest to assume that all people have a vicious streak and it will come out when they are given a chance.	5	4	3	2	1
7 Never tell anyone the real reason you did something unless it is useful to do so.	5	4	3	2	1
8 One should take action only when sure it is morally right.	1	2	3	4	5
9 It is wise to flatter important people.	5	4	3	2	1

*The Mach IV questionnaire and scoring guide are reprinted from *Studies in Machiavellianism,* by Richard Christie and Florence L. Geiss, Academic Press, New York. Copyright (1970), with permission from Elsevier.

	strongly agree	agree	neutral	disagree	strongly disagree
10 All in all, it is better to be humble and honest than important and dishonest.	☐ 1	☐ 2	☐ 3	☐ 4	☐ 5
11 Barnum was very wrong when he said there's a sucker born every minute.	☐ 1	☐ 2	☐ 3	☐ 4	☐ 5
12 People suffering from incurable diseases should have the choice of being put painlessly to death.	☐ 5	☐ 4	☐ 3	☐ 2	☐ 1
13 It is possible to be good in all respects.	☐ 1	☐ 2	☐ 3	☐ 4	☐ 5
14 Most people are basically good and kind.	☐ 1	☐ 2	☐ 3	☐ 4	☐ 5
15 There is no excuse for lying to someone else.	☐ 1	☐ 2	☐ 3	☐ 4	☐ 5
16 Most people forget more easily the death of their father than the loss of their property.	☐ 5	☐ 4	☐ 3	☐ 2	☐ 1
17 Most people who get ahead in the world lead clean, moral lives.	☐ 1	☐ 2	☐ 3	☐ 4	☐ 5
18 Generally speaking, people won't work hard unless they are forced to do so.	☐ 5	☐ 4	☐ 3	☐ 2	☐ 1
19 The biggest difference between most criminals and other people is that criminals are stupid enough to get caught.	☐ 5	☐ 4	☐ 3	☐ 2	☐ 1
20 Most people are brave.	☐ 1	☐ 2	☐ 3	☐ 4	☐ 5

Calculate your score by adding the numbers beside the boxes that you ticked.

Score =   ☐

Your score on this self-assessment will lie somewhere between 20 and 100.

A moderate score – neither high nor low – is 60. Consider yourself a Low Mach if you have a score of 45 or lower. Consider yourself a High Mach if you have a score of 75 or above.

The typical High Mach personality is someone adept at manipulating others for their own purposes. This involves the following features:

- lack of emotional involvement in interpersonal relationships
- cool and distant
- treats people as objects to be manipulated
- lack of concern for traditional morality
- deceit considered to be utilitarian rather than reprehensible
- low ideological commitment
- lack of adherence to inflexible ideals
- focus on maintaining power.

The main differences between High Mach and Low Mach individuals include (based on Graham, 1996, p.69):

High Machs	Low Machs
are resistant to social influence	are susceptible to social influence
focus on the task, not easily distracted	focus on the person, distracted by interaction
treat people as thinking objects	treat people as individuals
pursue the goal	interested in the process
resist appeals based on values and beliefs	accept appeals based on values and beliefs
good at improvising discussion and strategy at same time	not good at improvising discussion and strategy at the same time
confess less often to lying	confess more often to lying
initiate and control structure	accept and follow structure

How do you feel about your score? Is this an accurate reflection of your true personality? Do you think you would like to be more Machiavellian, or less, and why?

If you were appointing someone to manage a major organizational change, which would be more desirable, a Low Mach or a High Mach individual?

Debrief

Are you too soft to be a manager?   Must the effective change agent be a High Machiavellian? Is a warrant for introducing change also a warrant for cunning, devious, manipulative, underhand behaviour? This cannot be the case. Ferris et al. (1992), exploring how political factors affect promotion decisions, note that the 'pure organizational politician' will hit an early promotion ceiling through inability to display a balance between 'political savvy' on the one hand and 'solid past performance and demonstrated ability' on the other. Like all managers, the change agent must be aware of the impact actions may have on reputation.

The central argument here concerns the extent to which change agents must develop a behaviour repertoire, whether these tactics are labelled 'dirty tricks', 'office politics', 'Machiavellian' or not. Just as national politicians can justify their actions with the claim, *raison d'état* (for the good of the state), so change agents acting as political entrepreneurs can justify their behaviour in terms of benefit to the organization.

Christie and Geiss (1970) claim that the Mach IV score is an accurate predictor of how we behave with other people; whether we become emotionally involved, or whether we simply use others to suit our own ends. Studies have shown that men are more Machiavellian than women, and that doctors and psychiatrists have higher scores than people in more 'passive' professions such as accountancy and research and development. Although 'Machiavellian' is an insult, Christie and Geiss observed that Machiavellians have several positive attributes, identified in Chapter 7.

We need, therefore, to adopt a more balanced perspective on Machiavellian thinking, and implications for management practice, than most of the commentary on Machiavelli allows. Based on discussions that we have had with numerous management groups about these issues, Table 9.9 tries to answer some of the main questions which this approach can raise.

Organization politics at the movies: *Thirteen Days*

Based on a true story, this movie can be used as a major case study to explore issues influencing the strategic management decision-making process. It portrays the politicized nature of this process through the manner in which the key characters, their motives, their perceptions, their personal interests, and their relationships with each other intertwine to deliver the outcome. But the narrative also locates organization politics in the context of other factors which combine to influence strategic decisions.

The movie *Thirteen Days* (2002, directors David Self and Roger Donaldson) is a dramatized account of the Cuban Missile Crisis which almost triggered nuclear war between America and Russia in October 1962. The action focuses on those whose interactions, influence attempts, and decisions shape the manner in which this problem is resolved. The narrative unfolds through the eyes of Kenny O'Donnell (played by Kevin Costner), aide to President John F. Kennedy. The critical decisions in this case concern how to respond to the discovery (from airborne reconnaissance) that Russia has deployed nuclear missiles on the island of Cuba, off the Florida coast. This is an unacceptable security threat, and America wants the missiles withdrawn. The outcome of some American responses to this threat, however, could be a nuclear holocaust. Influencing these decisions is a close-knit group of advisers, all male. Women appear briefly in background nurturing and emotional support roles, particularly O'Donnell's wife and family. The male dress code is strict, with formal office wear for most occasions, jackets buttoned at almost all times.

Table 9.9 Machiavellian FAQs

So, do we all need to become Machiavellians now?	**No**. But as a change driver, you may need to use those behaviours in some circumstances.
Are you telling me I have to change my personality?	**No**. But do you want to consider widening your behaviour repertoire of political tactics?
Are some organizations 'politics free'?	**No**. But some are more political than others; change makes politics more intense and visible.
Will it not be chaos when everyone is a skilled political player?	**No**. Skilled players have a more interesting 'high performance' game – and this is a team game as well as one-on-one; that's not chaos.
Can management control and stop political behaviour?	**No**. This is a naturally occurring phenomenon, an inevitable aspect of organizational reality.
Should management try to control and stop political behaviour?	**Not necessarily**. Natural social controls usually shut down the 'political activists' who are causing damage by their blatant behaviour.
My organization has a management code of conduct. Should I ignore that?	**Yes, sometimes**. No set of rules can deal with every situation. Use the contents of your code as guidelines, not as inflexible requirements.
Surely politics is always damaging?	**No**. Dealing effectively with political issues can bring several personal and organizational benefits, particularly to the change process.
Do I have to abandon the values of trust and openness in communications and relationships generally?	**Absolutely not**. Constant changes may have made people resistant to further organizational changes, and these social values become even more important. But – do a stakeholder analysis; are you going to manage all your stakeholders with the same approach?
It has to be unethical to get directly involved in political games, even in major organizational change?	**No**. If you are a change driver, you could be seen as unprofessional and incompetent if you ignore the political issues blocking an organizationally beneficial project.
Will I be accused of inconsistency if I am open and honest today, and devious and Machiavellian tomorrow?	**No**. You have to use the management approach that is consistent with your diagnosis of the situation. What is inconsistent about that?

The director and writer, David Self, researched memoirs, literature, journalistic accounts, declassified CIA documents and White House tapes, as well as speaking to participants including Ted Sorenson (White House Counsel), Robert McNamara (Secretary of Defence) William B. Ecker (Navy Air Commander) and Dino Brugioni (CIA photo interpreter). He also draws from the account written by the President's brother, Robert Kennedy (1968). The White House, oval office, cabinet room and President's desk were recreated in detail.

The central thesis of *Thirteen Days* is that strategic decisions are not single events based on a rational consideration of the evidence, but are embedded in a complex organizational process influenced by contextual, temporal, social, political, and emotional factors, as well as by a range of overt and covert influencing tactics. As you watch the movie, identify how those causal factors, singly and in combination, lead from the problem, the initial condition, to finally explaining the desired outcome, by completing the following table (hints in brackets):

initial condition	causal factors		outcome
	contextual	(physical setting)	
	temporal	(timing, pacing of events)	
	processual	(sequence of events)	
Russian missiles deployed on the island of Cuba	social	(key people and their interactions)	Russia withdraws its missiles from Cuba
	emotional	(feelings and their intensity)	
	political	(the backstage action)	
	behavioural	(actions of key individuals)	

Debrief: Thirteen Days

The event sequence of the film revolves around the key decision maker, John F. Kennedy, and a range of decision influencers whose respective views on appropriate actions differ markedly. The action unfolds over 12 days of continuous meetings in the White House cabinet room and nearby offices. There is limited contact with families and outsiders. We see the housebound wife contrasted with male power plays in 'the boys' room' of strategic decision making. America wants Russia to remove its missiles from Cuba immediately, and also wants to avoid war. If American action is slow, Russia will move more missiles to Cuba and consolidate their installation. America introduces a quarantine. On 24 October, Russian cargo ships sail towards the naval blockade. They stop short. Is Russia backing down? Or have the ships stopped to pick up Soviet submarine escorts? A rapid response to this new situation is required. Delay could send inappropriate signals about American intentions. A wrong decision reached in haste could have disastrous consequences. While some decisions can be taken in a considered manner, others have to be made rapidly with incomplete and ambiguous information, in the face of internal disagreements. Information becomes available in a fragmentary manner, as Kennedy and his associates are faced not with a single decision but with a constant stream of interrelated judgements.

Rejecting military options, and making an appropriate judgement about which of two inconsistent Russian messages to reply to, Kennedy and his team make the 'correct' decisions, the Russians withdraw their missiles, and war is averted. Your analysis of causal factors, explaining the outcome, should look something like this:

initial condition	causal factors		outcome
	contextual	relative isolation of cabinet room	
	temporal	rapid pace of uncertain events	
	processual	12 days of meetings and decisions	
Russian missiles deployed on the island of Cuba	**social**	hawks and doves, cliques and collusions	Russia withdraws its missiles from Cuba
	emotional	high tension and anxiety	
	political	'backstaging' to avoid a 'sting'	
	behavioural	competing recommendations advanced	

Social factors, in the pattern of group dynamics, also contribute to decision outcomes. Kennedy has the ultimate leadership role, considering information and balancing views before selecting courses of action. However, information about Russian intentions is open to multiple interpretations, and there are difficulties in anticipating Russian responses to American actions. Kennedy is the target of a series of influence attempts, as his advisers forcefully advocate their positions. These advisers include his brother Robert, his aide O'Donnell, other members of his administration, bureaucrats, and senior military commanders (the 'hawks' advocating military action). These advisers form cliques and collude to advance their preferred options. They challenge the views of others. They make public statements giving the media access to their internal debate, thus bringing external pressure to bear on other players. Some (notably Adlai Stevenson) are deliberately used to deal with awkward confrontations.

Emotional and 'backstage' political factors also shape decision outcomes. Judgements are reached not through an objective assessment of evidence, but in a tense and highly charged emotional atmosphere. Issues of national security clash with the desire to avoid nuclear war, and differences in views also reflect personality clashes. In addition to rational and emotional appeal, one attempt to influence Kennedy is based on a complicated 'sting'.

The military hawks advocate a course of action as imperative, emphasizing that there are no other credible options. The recommendation at the heart of this 'sting' has a high (if not certain) probability of failure, which is concealed from Kennedy, while it is admitted that, naturally, there are risks. The 'sting' is that the failure of the recommended action will predetermine subsequent decisions, constraining Kennedy's room for manoeuvre. It is the subsequent 'forced' decisions which the hawks want to achieve. One role for a supportive adviser, therefore, is to stand back from immediate pressures, and to consider motives, outcomes, and options. O'Donnell is alert to this 'sting'. He telephones navy close reconnaissance pilots personally to tell them what to say if shot at (that is, to lie, by claiming they did not encounter enemy fire), to avoid giving the hawks their rationale for military intervention. (In a similar manner, the young queen *Elizabeth* in the film by Shekhar Kapur, 1998, is successfully 'stung' by traitorous courtiers when advised to invade Scotland, an enterprise doomed to failure. Her adviser Walsingham saves her from further misfortunes. See Organization politics at the movies, Chapter 5.)

Thirteen Days is faithful to Allison's (1969; 1971) seminal analysis. Seeking to explain those events, and to apply that understanding to subsequent Vietnam war policy, Allison contrasts three models of decision making; the rational policy, organizational process, and bureaucratic politics models. He observes that, while public and academic orthodoxy may place major decisions above politics, an understanding of such decisions is incomplete without a knowledge of 'bargaining games', and of how decision influencers will be advantaged or disadvantaged by particular choices. He also observes that decisions do not arise as discrete issues, and that players are confronted with many simultaneous, emergent and competing issues. Therefore, 'each player is forced to fix upon his issues for that day, fight them on their own terms, and rush on to the next' (Allison, 1969, p.708). The resulting 'collage' of decisions and actions is contingent on the nature of the emergent issues and the pace at which the game is played. Decision outcomes are not the result of a rational, linear analysis of evidence, but of a series of time-dependent influence attempts, power plays, negotiations and manipulations. Allison (1969, p.707) describes the game of bureaucratic politics:

> Men [*sic*] share power. Men differ concerning what must be done. The differences matter. This milieu necessitates that policy be resolved by politics. What the nation does is sometimes the result of the triumph of one group over others. . . . What moves the chess pieces is not simply the reasons which support a course of action, nor the routines of organizations which enact an alternative, but the power and skill of proponents and opponents of the action in question.

Thirteen Days takes the viewer inside these complex and politicized decision processes, moving with the cast of characters as they confront and deal with the emerging issues, and as they confront and attempt to influence other players. The notion that management decisions and actions are more dependent on influence and political process than on rational analysis is now widely accepted (Pettigrew, 1973 and 1985; Pfeffer, 1992a; Dawson, 1994 and 1996). *Thirteen Days* provides a valuable complement to the traditional lecture room coverage of management decision making, as well as a potentially fruitful source of debate. For further commentary on this movie, see Buchanan and Huczynski (2004).

References

Abrahamson, E. (2004) *Change Without Pain: How Managers Can Overcome Initiative Overload, Organizational Chaos, and Employee Burnout*. Boston, MA: Harvard Business School Press.

Abrahamson, E. and Freedman, D.H. (2006) *A Perfect Mess: The Hidden Benefits of Disorder*. New York: Little, Brown & Co.

Ackroyd, S. and Thompson, P. (1999) *Organizational Misbehaviour*. London: Sage Publications.

Adler, P. (1993) 'The learning bureaucracy: New United Motors Manufacturing Inc.', in B. M. Staw and L.L. Cummings (eds), *Research in Organizational Behaviour*. Greenwich, CT: JAI Press. pp.111–94.

Adler, P. and Borys, B. (1996) 'Two types of bureaucracy: enabling and coercive', *Administrative Science Quarterly*, 41(1): 61–89.

Adorno, T.W., Frenkel-Brunswik, E., Levinson, D.J. and Sanford, R.N. (1950) *The Authoritarian Personality: Studies in Prejudice*. London: W.W. Norton & Co.

Ahearn, K.K., Ferris, G.R., Hochwarter, W.A., Douglas, C. and Ammeter, A.P. (2004) 'Leader political skill and team performance', *Journal of Management*, 30(3): 309–27.

Allen, R.W., Madison, D.L., Porter, L.W., Renwick, P.A. and Mayes, B.T. (1979) 'Organizational politics: tactics and characteristics of its actors', *California Management Review*, 22(1): 77–83.

Allison, G.T. (1969) 'Conceptual models and the Cuban missile crisis', *The American Political Science Review*, LXIII(3): 689–718.

Allison, G.T. (1971) *The Essence of Decision: Explaining the Cuban Missile Crisis*. Boston, MA: Little, Brown & Co.

Alvesson, M. and Willmott, H. (2002) 'Identity regulation as organizational control: producing the appropriate individual', *Journal of Management Studies*, 39(5): 619–40.

Andersen, E.S. and Lundvall, B.A. (1988) 'Small national systems of innovation facing technological revolutions: an analytical framework', in C. Freeman and B.A. Lundvall (eds), *Small Countries Facing the Technological Revolution*. London: Francis Pinter. pp.9–36.

Argyris, C. (1985) *Strategy, Change and Defensive Routines*. Boston, MA: Pitman Publishing.

Argyris, C. (1990) *Overcoming Organizational Defenses: Facilitating Organizational Learning*. Needham, MA: Allyn and Bacon.

Arkin, A. (2004) 'The fairer sex', *People Management*, 10(20): 40–42.

Arroba, T. and James, K. (1988) 'Are politics palatable to women managers? How women can make wise moves at work', *Women in Management Review*, 3(3): 123–30.

Astley, W.G. and Sachdeva, P.S. (1984) 'Structural sources of intraorganizational power: a theoretical synthesis', *Academy of Management Review*, 9(1): 104–13.

Axelrod, A. (2000) *Elizabeth I CEO: Strategic Lessons From The Leader Who Built An Empire*. New Jersey: Prentice Hall.

Babcock, L. and Laschever, S. (2003) *Women Don't Ask: Negotiation and the Gender Divide*. Princeton, NJ: Princeton University Press.

Bacharach, S.B. and Lawler, E.J. (1981) *Power and Politics in Organizations: The Social Psychology of Conflict, Coalitions, and Bargaining*. San Francisco: Jossey-Bass.

Bacharach, S.B. and Lawler, E.J. (1998) 'Political alignments in organizations: contextualization, mobilization, and coordination', in R.M. Kramer and M.A. Neale (eds), *Power and Influence in Organizations*. Thousand Oaks: Sage Publications. pp.67–88.

Bachrach, P. and Baratz, M.S. (1962) 'The two faces of power', *American Political Science Review*, 56: 947–52.

Bachrach, P. and Baratz, M.S. (1970) *Power and Poverty*. London: Oxford University Press.

Badham, R. (1986) *Theories of Industrial Society*. London: Croom Helm.

Badham, R. (1990) *Circuits of Change: Report on Workshops with Sociotechnical Change Agents in Denmark, the Netherlands and the UK*. Wollongong: University of Wollongong.

Badham, R. (2005) 'Technology and the transformation of work', in S. Ackroyd, R. Batt and P. Thompson (eds), *Handbook of Work and Organization*. Oxford: Oxford University Press. pp.115–38.

Badham, R. and Down, S. (2006) 'A (bi)polar night of icy darkness?: ambiguity and ambivalence in the rationalization of the organizational self', Sydney: Macquarie University Working Paper Series.

Badham, R. and McLoughlin, I. (2006) 'Ambivalence and engagement: irony and cultural change in late modern organizations', *International Journal of Knowledge, Culture and Change Management*, 5(4): 133–44.

Badham, R., Couchman, P. and McLoughlin, I. (1997) 'Implementing vulnerable socio-technical change projects', in I. McLoughlin and M. Harris (eds), *Innovation, Organizational Change and Technology*. London: International Thomson. pp.146–69.

Badham, R., Garrety, K., Morrigan, V., Zanko, M. and Dawson, P. (2003) 'Designer deviance: enterprise and deviance in culture change programmes', *Organization*, 10(4): 707–30.

Bardach, E. (1977) *The Implementation Game: What Happens After a Bill Becomes a Law*. Cambridge, MA: MIT Press.

Barker, J.R. (1993) 'Tightening the iron cage: concertive control in self-managing teams', *Administrative Science Quarterly*, 38(3): 408–37.

Barnard, C. (1968) *The Functions of the Executive*. Cambridge, MA: Harvard University Press.

Bauman, Z. (2003) *Wasted Lives: Modernity and its Outcasts*. Cambridge: Polity Press.

Beatty, C.A. and Gordon, J.R.M. (1991) 'Preaching the gospel: the evangelists of new technology', *California Management Review*, 33(3): 73–94.

Beatty, C.A. and Lee, G.L. (1992) 'Leadership among middle managers – an exploration in the context of technological change', *Human Relations*, 45(1): 957–89.

Beck, U. (2000) *The Brave New World of Work*. Cambridge: Polity Press.

Beer, M. and Nohria, N. (eds) (2000) *Breaking the Code of Change*, Boston, MA: Harvard Business School Press.

Bell, D. (1996) *The Cultural Contradictions of Capitalism*. New York: Harper Collins.

Benders, J., De Hann, J. and Bennett, D. (1995) *The Symbiosis of Work and Technology*. London: Francis Pinter.

Benfari, R.C., Wilkinson, H.E. and Orth, C.D. (1986) 'The effective use of power', *Business Horizons*, 29: 12–16.

Bennett, N., Wise, C. and Woods, P. (2003) *Distributed Leadership*. Nottingham: National College for School Leadership.

Bennis, W.G. (1984) 'Transformative power and leadership', in T.J. Sergiovanni and J.E. Corbally (eds), *Leadership and Organizational Culture: New Perspectives on Administrative Theory and Practice*. Urbana: University of Illinois Press.

Bennis, W.G. and Nanus, B. (1985) *Leaders: The Strategies for Taking Charge*. New York: Harper & Row.

Berger, P.L. (1991) *Invitation to Sociology: A Humanistic Perspective*. London: Penguin Books.

Berle, A.A. and Means, G.C. (1935) *The Modern Corporation and Private Property*. New York: Macmillan.

Bies, R.S. and Sitkin, S.B. (1992) 'Explanation as legitimation: excuse-making in organizations', in M.L. McLaughlin, M.J. Cody and S.J. Read (eds), *Explaining One's Self to Others: Reason-Giving in a Social Context*. Hillsdale, NJ: Lawrence Erlbaum. pp.183–98.

Bing, S. (2002) *What Would Machiavelli Do?: The Ends Justify the Meanness*. New York: Collins.

Blanchard, K. and Peale, N.V. (1988) *The Power of Ethical Management*. New York: William Morrow.

Bondanella, P. and Musa, M. (1979) *The Portable Machiavelli*. Harmondsworth: Penguin Books.

Borger, H. (2002) *The Corporate Prince: Machiavelli's Timeless Wisdom Adapted for the Modern CEO*. Bloomington, IN: First Books Library.

Borum, F. (1995) *Organization, Power and Change*. Copenhagen: Handelshøjskolens Forlag.

Bouguignon, A. and Zarlowski, P. (2006) 'Change in performance management practices and identity: a case study', paper presented at the European Group for Organization Studies Colloquium, Bergen, Norway, July.

Brandon, R. and Seldman, M. (2004) *Survival of the Savvy: High-Integrity Political Tactics for Career and Company Success*. New York: Free Press.

Brass, D.J. and Burkhardt, M.E. (1993) 'Potential power and power use: an investigation of structure and behaviour', *Academy of Management Journal*, 36(3): 441–70.

Bridges, W. (1991) *Managing Transitions: Making the Most of Change*. New York: Perseus Publishing.

Brooks, I. (1996) 'Leadership of a cultural change process', *Leadership and Organization Development Journal*, 17(5): 31–7.

Brouer, R.L., Ferris, G.R., Hochwarter, W.A., Laird, M.D. and Gilmore, D.C. (2006) 'The strain-related reactions to perceptions of organizational politics as a workplace stressor: political skill as a neutralizer', in E. Vigoda and A. Drory (eds), *Handbook of Organizational Politics*. Thousand Oaks, CA: Sage Publications. pp.187–206.

Brown, S.L. and Eisenhardt, K.M. (1998) *Competing on the Edge: Strategy as Structured Chaos*. Boston, MA: Harvard Business School Press.

Brubaker, R. (1984) *The Limits of Rationality: An Essay on the Social and Moral Thought of Max Weber*. London: Allen and Unwin.

Brunsson, N. (2002) *The Organization of Hypocrisy: Talk, Decisions and Actions in Organizations*. Stockholm: Copenhagen Business School.

Bryman, A. (1996) 'Leadership in organizations', in S.R. Clegg, C. Hardy and W.R. Nord (eds), *Handbook of Organization Studies*. London: Sage Publications. pp.276–92.

Buchanan, D.A. (1999) 'The logic of political action: an experiment with the epistemology of the particular', *British Journal of Management*, 10 (special conference issue): 73–88.

Buchanan, D. (2003) 'Demands, instabilities, manipulations, careers: the lived experience of driving change', *Human Relations*, 56(6): 663–84.

Buchanan, D.A. (2007) 'You stab my back, I'll stab yours: management experience and perceptions of organization politics', *British Journal of Management*, 18.

Buchanan, D. and Badham, R. (1999a) *Power, Politics and Organizational Change: Winning the Turf Game*. London: Sage Publications.

Buchanan, D. and Badham, R. (1999b) 'Politics and organizational change: the lived experience', *Human Relations*, 52(5): 609–29.

Buchanan, D.A. and Boddy, D. (1992) *The Expertise of the Change Agent: Public Performance and Backstage Activity*. Hemel Hempstead: Prentice Hall.

Buchanan, D. and Huczynski, A. (2004) 'Images of influence: *Twelve Angry Men* and *Thirteen Days*', *Journal of Management Inquiry*, 13(4): 312–23.

Buchanan, D. and Storey, J. (1997) 'Role taking and role switching in organizational change: the four pluralities', in I. McLoughlin and M. Harris (eds), *Innovation, Organizational Change and Technology*. London: International Thomson. pp.127–45.

Buchanan, D., Claydon, T. and Doyle, M. (1999) 'Organization development and change: the legacy of the nineties', *Human Resource Management*, 9(2): 20–37.

Buchanan, D., Fitzgerald, L., Rashid, A., Horder, C., Ferlie, E., Addicott, R. and Baeza, J. (2005) 'Improvement stories, hypercomplexity, pure plays, and hybrids: roles in change in the professional network organization', paper presented at the British Academy of Management Annual Conference, University of Oxford, September.

Buhler, P. (1994) 'Navigating the waters of organizational politics', *Supervision*, 55(9): 24–26.

Bunting, M. (2004) *Willing Slaves: How the Overwork Culture is Ruling Our Lives*. New York: Harper Collins.

Burch, G. (2005) *The Way of the Dog: The Art of Making Success Inevitable*. London: Capstone Publishing.

Burnes, B. (2004) 'Kurt Lewin and the planned approach to change: a re-appraisal', *Journal of Management Studies*, 41(6): 977–1002.

Burns, T. (1961) 'Micropolitics: mechanisms of institutional change', *Administrative Science Quarterly*, 55: 257–81.

Burrell, G. (1988) 'Modernism, postmodernism and organizational analysis: the contribution of Michel Foucault', *Organization Studies*, 9(2): 221–35.

Butcher, D. and Clarke, M. (1999) 'Organizational politics: the missing discipline of management?' *Industrial and Commercial Training*, 31(1): 9–12.

Butcher, D. and Clarke, M. (2001) *Smart Management: Using Politics in Organizations*. Houndmills, Basingstoke: Palgrave.

Butcher, D. and Clarke, M. (2003) 'Redefining managerial work: smart politics', *Management Decision*, 41(5): 477–87.

Byrne, R.W. (1996) 'Machiavellian intelligence', *Evolutionary Anthropology Issues, News and Reviews*, 5(5): 172–80.

Byrne, R.W. and Whiten, A. (1988) *Machiavellian Intelligence: Social Expertise and the Evolution of Intellect in Monkeys, Apes and Humans*. Oxford: Clarendon Press.

Caldwell, R. (2003) 'Models of change agency: a fourfold classification', *British Journal of Management*, 14(2): 131–42.

Caldwell, R. (2005) *Agency and Change: Rethinking Change Agency in Organizations*. Abingdon: Routledge.

Calhoon, R.P. (1969) 'Nicolo Machiavelli and the 20th century administrator', *Academy of Management Journal*, 12(2): 205–12.

Casey, C. (1999) 'Come, join our family: discipline and integration in corporate organizational culture', *Human Relations*, 52(2): 155–78.

Cavanagh, G.F., Moberg, D.J. and Velasquez, M. (1981) 'The ethics of organizational politics', *Academy of Management Review*, 6(3): 363–74.

Chandler, A.D. (1993) *The Visible Hand: The Managerial Revolution in American Business*. Cambridge, MA: Belknap Press.

Chanlat, J.-F. (1997) 'Conflict and politics', in A. Sorge and M. Warner (eds), *Handbook of Organizational Behaviour*. London: International Thomson. pp.472–80.

Christensen, C.M. (2000) *The Innovator's Dilemma: When New Technologies Cause Great Firms to Fail*. New York: Harper Collins.

Christensen, C.M. and Overdorf, M. (2000) 'Meeting the challenge of disruptive change', *Harvard Business Review*, 78(2): 66–76.

Christie, R. and Geiss, F.L. (1970) *Studies in Machiavellianism*. New York: Academic Press.

Christie, R. and Merton, R.K. (1958) 'Procedures for the sociological study of the values climate of medical schools', *Journal of Medical Education*, 33(2): 125–53.

Cialdini, R.B. (2001) *Influence: Science and Practice*. Boston, MA: Allyn and Bacon. (fourth edn.)

Cialdini, R.B. and Sagarin, B.J. (2005) 'Principles of interpersonal influence', in T.C. Brock and M.C. Green (eds), *Persuasion: Psychological Insights and Perspectives*. Thousand Oaks: Sage Publications. pp.143–69.

Clegg, C. (1993) 'Social Systems that Marginalize the Psychological and Organizational Aspects of Information', *Behaviour and Information Technology*, 12(5): 261–6.

Clegg, S.R. (1989) *Frameworks of Power*. London: Sage Publications.

Clegg, S.R., Courpasson, D. and Phillips, N. (2006) *Power and Organizations*. London: Sage Publications.

Coates, J.F. (1994) 'Organizational politics: a key to personal success', *Employment Relations Today*, 21(3): 259–62.

Cobb, A.T. (1986) 'Political diagnosis: applications in organizational development', *Academy of Management Review*, 11(3): 482–96.

Collett, P. (2004) 'Show and tell', *People Management*, 10(8): 34–5.

Collin, A. (1996) 'Re-thinking the relationship between theory and practice: practitioners as map-readers, map-makers – or jazz players?', *British Journal of Guidance and Counselling*, 24(1): 67–81.

Collins, D. (1998) *Organizational Change: Sociological Perspectives*. London: Routledge.

Collins, D. (2003) 'Re-imagining change', *Tamara: The Journal of Critical Postmodern Organization Science*, 2(4): 4–11.

Collins, J. (2001) *Good to Great: Why Some Companies Make the Leap and Others Don't*. New York: Harper Collins.

Conklin, W. (1993) 'Playing the game of corporate politics', *Communication World*, 10(9): 26–9.

Covey, S. (1990) *Principle Centred Leadership*. New York: Simon and Schuster.

Covey, S.R. (1989) *The Seven Habits of Highly Effective People: Restoring the Character Ethic*. New York: Simon and Schuster.

Covey, S.R. (2004) *The Eighth Habit: From Effectiveness to Greatness*. New York: Simon and Schuster.

Cripe, E.J. (1993) 'How to get top notch agents of change', *Training and Development*, 47(12): 52–7.

Cross, R.L., Parise, S. and Weiss, L.M. (2007) 'The role of networks in organizational change', *McKinsey Quarterly*, April: 1–11.

Crozier, M. (1973) 'The problem of power', *Social Research*, 40(2): 211–28.

Cyert, R.M. and March, J.G. (1983) *A Behavioral Theory of the Firm*. New Jersey: Prentice Hall.

Dahl, R.A. (1957) 'The concept of power', *Behavioural Science*, 2: 201–15.

Dalton, M. (1959) *Men Who Manage*. New York: Wiley.

Dambrin, C. and Lambert, C. (2006) 'Be yourself or rather be your brand: care of the self as a control tool in a cosmetics firm', paper presented at the European Group for Organization Studies Conference, Bergen, Norway.

Davenport, T.H. (1993) *Process Innovation: Re-engineering Work Through Information Technology*. Boston MA: Harvard Business School Press.

Dawson, P. (1994) *Organizational Change: A Processual Approach*. London: Paul Chapman Publishing.

Dawson, P. (1996) *Technology and Quality: Change in the Workplace*. London: International Thomson.

Dawson, P. (2003) *Reshaping Change: A Processual Approach*. London: Routledge.

DeLuca, J.R. (1999) *Political Savvy: Systematic Approaches to Leadership Behind-the-Scenes*. Berwyn, PA: Evergreen Business Group.

Denis, J.-L., Lamothe, L. and Langley, A. (2001) 'The dynamics of collective leadership and strategic change in pluralistic organizations', *Academy of Management Journal*, 44(4): 809–37.

Department of Health (2002) *Code of Conduct for NHS Managers*. London: Department of Health.

Dick, P. (2005) 'Dirty work designations: how police officers account for their use of coercive force', *Human Relations*, 58(11): 1363–90.

Dobson, M.S. and Dobson, D.S. (2001) *Enlightened Office Politics: Understanding, Coping with, and Winning the Game – Without Losing Your Soul*. New York: AmACOM (American Management Association).

Drory, A. (1993) 'Perceived political climate and job attitudes', *Organization Studies*, 14(1): 59–71.

Drory, A. and Romm, T. (1988) 'Politics in organization and its perception within the organization', *Organization Studies*, 9(2): 165–79.

Drory, A. and Romm, T. (1990) 'The definition of organizational politics: a review', *Human Relations*, 43(11): 1133–54.

Du Gay, P. (1996) *Consumption and Identity at Work*. London: Sage Publications.

Du Gay, P. (2000) *In Praise of Bureaucracy: Weber, Organization, Ethics*. London: Sage Publications.

Du Gay, P. (2004) 'Against 'Enterprise' (but not against 'enterprise', for that would make no sense)', *Organization*, 11(1): 37–57.

Du Gay, P. and Salaman, G. (1982) 'The culture of the customer', *Journal of Management Studies*, 29(5): 615–33.

DuBrin, A. (1990) *Winning Office Politics*. Englewood Cliffs, NJ: Prentice Hall.

Dunn, S. (1990) 'Root Metaphor in the Old and New Industrial Relations', *British Journal of Industrial Relations*, 28(1): 1–31.

Dunphy, D.C. and Stace, D.A. (1990) *Under New Management: Australian Organizations in Transition*. Sydney: McGraw-Hill.

Dutton, J.E. (1988) 'Understanding strategic agenda building and its implications for managing change', in L. Pondy, R.J. Boland and H. Thomas (eds), *Managing Ambiguity and Change*. Chichester: Wiley. pp.127–55.

Dutton, J.E., Ashford, S.J., O'Neill, R.M. and Lawrence, K.A. (2001) 'Moves that matter: issue selling and organizational change', *Academy of Management Journal*, 44(4): 716–36.

Eagly, A.H. (2005) 'Achieving relational authenticity in leadership: does gender matter?' *The Leadership Quarterly*, 16: 459–74.

Eccles, T. (1984) *Succeeding with Change: Implementing Action-Driven Strategies*. London: McGraw-Hill.

Egan, G. (1994) *Working the Shadow Side: A Guide to Positive Behind-the-Scenes Management*. San Francisco: Jossey-Bass.

Ehrenreich, B. (1987) *Hearts of Men: American Dreams and the Flight from Commitment*. New York: Anchor.

Ehrenreich, B. (2005) *Bait and Switch: The (Futile) Pursuit of the American Dream*. New York: Metropolitan Books.

Eisenhardt, K.M. and Bourgeois, L.J. (1988) 'Politics of strategic decision making in high-velocity environments: towards a mid-range theory', *Academy of Management Journal*, 31(4): 737–70.

Elam, M. (1993) *Innovation as the Craft of Combination: Perspectives on Technology and Economy in the Spirit of Schumpeter*. Linköping: Department of Technology and Social Change Tema T.

Etzioni, A. (1961) *Complex Organizations: A Sociological Reader*. New York: Holt, Rinehart and Winston.

Falco, M.J.E. (2004) *Feminist Interpretations of Niccolo Machiavelli*. University Park, PA: Pennsylvania University Press.

Feldman, D. and Klitch, N. (1991) 'Impression management and career strategies', in K. Giacalone and P. Rosenfeld (eds), *Applied Impression Management: How Image Making Affects Managerial Decisions*. London: Sage Publications. pp.67–80.

Ferris, G.R. and Kacmar, K.M. (1992) 'Perceptions of organizational politics', *Journal of Management*, 18(1): 93–116.

Ferris, G.R. and King, T.R. (1991) 'Politics in human resources decisions: a walk on the dark side', *Organizational Dynamics*, 20(2): 59–71.

Ferris, G.R., Buckley, M.R. and Allen, G.M. (1992) 'Promotion systems in organizations', *Human Resource Planning*, 15(3): 47–68.

Ferris, G.R., Frink, D.D., Galang, M.C., Zhou, J., Kacmar, M. and Howard, J.L. (1996) 'Perceptions of organizational politics: prediction, stress-related implications, and outcomes', *Human Relations*, 49(2): 233–66.

Ferris, G.R., Perrewé, P.L., Anthony, W.P. and Gilmore, D.C. (2000) 'Political skill at work', *Organizational Dynamics*, 28(4): 25–37.

Ferris, G.R., Adams, G., Kolodinsky, R.W., Hochwarter, W.A. and Ammeter, A.P. (2002a) 'Perceptions of organizational politics: theory and research directions', *Research in Multi-Level Issues Volume 1: The Many Faces of Multi-Level Issues*: 179–254.

Ferris, G.R., Hochwarter, W.A., Douglas, C., Blass, F.R., Kolodinsky, R.W. and Treadway, D.C. (2002b) 'Social influence processes in organizations and human resource systems', *Research in Personnel and Human Resources Management: Volume 21*: 65–127.

Ferris, G.R., Treadway, D.C., Kolodinsky, R.W., Hochwarter, W.A., Kacmar, C.J., Douglas, C. and Frink, D.D. (2005) 'Development and validation of the Political Skill Inventory', *Journal of Management*, 31(1): 126–52.

Ferris, G.R., Treadway, D.C., Perrewé, P.L., Brouer, R.L., Douglas, C. and Lux, S. (2007) 'Political skill in organizations', *Journal of Management*, 33(3): 290–320.

Festinger, L. (1964) *When Prophecy Fails: A Social and Psychological Study*. New York: Harper Collins.

Fiorina, C. (2006) *Tough Choices: A Memoir*. London and Boston: Nicholas Brealey Publishing.

Fitzgerald, L., Ferlie, E., Wood, M. and Hawkins, C. (1999) 'Evidence into practice?: an exploratory analysis of the interpretation of evidence', in A. Mark and S. Dopson (eds), *Organizational Behaviour in Health Care: The Research Agenda*. London: Macmillan. pp.189–206.

Fleck, J. (1999) 'Learning by trying: the implementation of configurational technology', in D. Mackenzie and J. Wacjman (eds), *The Social Shaping of Technology*. Milton Keynes: The Open University Press. pp.244–58.

Fleming, P. and Sewell, G. (2002) 'Looking for the good soldier, Švejk: alternative modalities of resistance in the contemporary workplace', *Sociology*, 36(4): 857–73.

Fleming, P. and Spicer, A. (2005) 'Stewart Clegg: towards a Machiavellian organization theory', *The Sociological Review*, 53(supplement 1): 95–105.

Flyvbjerg, B. (1998) *Rationality and Power: Democracy in Practice*. Chicago: University of Chicago Press.

Foucault, M. (1977) *Discipline and Punish: The Birth of the Prison*. Harmondsworth: Penguin Books.

Foucault, M. (1979) *The History of Sexuality: Volume 1*. Harmondsworth: Penguin Books.

Frankel, L.P. (2004) *Nice Girls Don't Get The Corner Office: Unconscious Mistakes Women Make That Sabotage Their Careers*. New York: Warner Business Books.

Freeman, C. (1982) *Economics of Innovation*. Harmondsworth: Penguin Books.

French, J.R.P. and Raven, B. (1958) 'The bases of social power', in D. Cartwright (ed.), *Studies in Social Power*. Ann Arbor, MI: Institute for Social Research.

French, W.L. and Bell, C.H. (1999) *Organization Development: Behavioural Science Interventions for Organization Improvement*. Englewood Cliffs, NJ: Prentice Hall International. (sixth edn.)

Friis, S. (1988) 'Action research on systems development: case study of changing actor roles', *ACM Computers and Society*, 18(1): 123–38.

Fritzsche, D.J., Huo, Y.P., Sugai, S., Tsai, S.D.-H., Kim, C.S. and Becker, H. (1995) 'Exploring the ethical behaviour of managers: a comparative study of four countries', *Asia Pacific Journal of Management*, 12(2): 37–61.

Frost, P.J. and Egri, C.P. (1991) 'The political process of innovation', in L.L. Cummings and B.M. Staw (eds), *Research in Organizational Behaviour, Volume 13*. Greenwich, CT: JAI Press. pp.229–95.

Gabriel, Y. (2002) 'Essai: on paragrammatic uses of organizational theory – a provocation', *Organization Studies*, 23(1): 133–51.

Gabriel, Y. (2005) 'Glass cages and glass palaces: images of organization in image-conscious times', *Organization*, 12(1): 9–27.

Gabriel, Y. (2006) 'Spectacles of resistance and resistance of spectacles', paper presented at the Academy of Management Conference, Critical Management Workshop on Resistance, Atlanta, GA.

Galbraith, J.K. (1974) *The New Industrial State*. Harmondsworth: Penguin Books.

Galie, P.G. and Bopst, C. (2006) 'Machiavelli and modern business: realist thought in contemporary corporate leadership manuals', *Journal of Business Ethics*, 65(3): 235–50.

Gandz, J. and Murray, V.V. (1980) 'The experience of workplace politics', *Academy of Management Journal*, 23(2): 237–51.

Gardner, W.L. (1992) 'Lessons in organizational dramaturgy: the art of impression management', *Organizational Dynamics*, 21(1): 33–46.

Gaventa, J. (1982) *Power and Powerlessness: Quiescence and Rebellion in an Appalachian Valley*. Oxford: Clarendon Press.

Geddes, M., Hastings, C. and Briner, W. (1990) *Project Leadership*. London: Gower Publishing Ltd.

Gemmill, G.R. and Heisler, W.J. (1972) 'Machiavellianism as a factor in managerial job strain, job satisfaction and upward mobility', *Academy of Management Journal*, 15(1): 51–62.

Gergen, K. (2000) *The Saturated Self: Dilemmas of Identity in Contemporary Life*. New York: Basic Books.

Giddens, A. (1991) *Modernity and Self-Identity*. Cambridge: Polity Press.

Gilligan, C. (1982) *In a Different Voice*. Cambridge, MA: Harvard University Press.

Ginzberg, A. and Abrahamson, E. (1991) 'Champions of change and strategic shifts: the role of internal and external change advocates', *Journal of Management Studies*, 28(2): 173–90.

Glick, P., Lameiras, M., Fiske, S.T., Eckes, T., Masser, B., Volpato, C., Manganelli, A.M., Pek, J.C., Huang, L.L., Sakalli-Ugurlu, N., Rodriguez Castro, Y., Pereira, M.L., Willemsen, T.M., Brunner, A., Six-Materna, I. and Wells, R. (2004) 'Bad but bold: ambivalent attitudes toward men predict gender inequality in 16 countries', *Journal of Personality and Social Psychology*, 86(5): 713–28.

Goffman, E. (1959) *The Presentation of Self in Everyday Life*. New York: Doubleday Anchor.

Goffman, E. (1961) *Encounters: Two Studies in the Sociology of Interaction*. London: Macmillan.

Gollop, R. and Ketley, D. (2007) 'Shades of resistance: understanding and addressing scepticism', in D.A. Buchanan, L. Fitzgerald and D. Ketley (eds), *The Sustainability and Spread of Organizational Change: Modernizing Healthcare*. London: Routledge. pp.85–102.

Graham, J.H. (1996) 'Machiavellian project managers: do they perform better?', *International Journal of Project Management*, 14(2): 67–74.

Gray, J.L. and Starke, F.A. (1984) *Organizational Behaviour: Concepts and Applications*. Columbus OH: Merrill Publishing.

Greenleaf, R.K. (1977) *Servant Leadership: A Journey into the Nature of Legitimate Power and Greatness*. New York: Paulist Press.

Greiner, L.E. and Schein, V.E. (1988) *Power and Organization Development: Mobilizing Power to Implement Change*. Reading, MA: Addison Wesley.

Griffin, G. (1991) *Machiavelli on Management: Playing and Winning the Corporate Power Game*. New York: Praeger.

Griffin, G. and Parker, C. (2003) *Games Companies Play: An Insider's Guide to Surviving Politics*. Oxford: Capstone Publishing.

Grint, K. (1994) 'Reengineering history: social resonances and business process re-engineering', *Organization*, 1(1): 179–201.

Gronn, P. (2002a) 'Distributed leadership as a unit of analysis', *Leadership Quarterly*, 13(4): 423–51.

Gronn, P. (2002b) 'Distributed leadership', in K. Leithwood, P. Hallinger, K. Seashore-Louis et al. (eds), *Second International Handbook of Educational Leadership and Administration*. Dordrecht: Kluwer. pp.653–96.

Gross, C. and Reifenscheidt, N. (2006) 'Self-made men or ready-made men: enterprising selves as regulated identities', paper presented at the European Group for Organization Studies Conference, Bergen, Norway.

Grover, V., Lederer, A.L. and Sabherwal, R. (1988) 'Recognizing the politics of MIS', *Information and Management*, 14: 145–56.

Guest, D. (2004) 'Flexible employment contracts, the psychological contract and employee outcomes: an analysis and review of the evidence', *International Journal of Management Reviews*, 5/6(1): 1–19.

Gustafson, D.H., Sainfort, F., Eichler, M., Adams, L., Bisognano, M. and Steudel, H. (2003) 'Developing and testing a model to predict outcomes of organizational change', *Health Services Research*, 38(2): 751–76.

Hamel, G. (2000) *Leading the Revolution*. Boston, MA: Harvard Business School Press.

Hammer, M. (2004) 'Deep change: how operational innovation can transform your company', *Harvard Business Review*, 82(4): 84–93.

Hammer, M. and Champy, J. (2003) *Re-engineering the Corporation: A Manifesto for Business Revolution*. London: Nicholas Brealey Publishing.

Hampshire, S. (1989) *Innocence and Experience*. London: Penguin Books.

Handy, C. (1997) 'The citizen corporation', *Harvard Business Review*, 75(5): 26–7.

Hardy, C. (1985) 'The nature of unobtrusive power', *Journal of Management Studies*, 22(4): 384–99.

Hardy, C. (ed.) (1995) *Power and Politics in Organizations*. Aldershot: Dartmouth Publishing.

Hardy, C. (1996) 'Understanding power: bringing about strategic change', *British Journal of Management*, 7 (special conference issue): 3–16.

Hardy, C. and Clegg, S.R. (1996) 'Some dare call it power', in S.R. Clegg, C.Hardy and W.R. Nord (eds), *Handbook of Organization Studies*. London: Sage Publications. pp.622–41.

Hardy, C. and O'Sullivan, L. (1988) 'The power behind empowerment: implications for research and practice', *Human Relations*, 51(4): 451–83.

Hargadon, A. (2003) *How Breakthroughs Happen: The Surprising Truth About How Companies Innovate*. Boston, MA: Harvard Business School Press.

Hargadon, A. and Sutton, R.I. (1997) 'Technology brokering and innovation in a product development firm', *Administrative Science Quarterly*, 42(4): 716–49.

Harrell-Cook, G., Ferris, G.R. and Dulebohn, J.H. (1999) 'Political behaviors as moderators of the perceptions of organizational politics – work outcomes relationships', *Journal of Organizational Behaviour*, 20(7): 1093–105.

Harris, J. (1990) 'Ethical values of individuals at different levels of the organizational hierarchy of a single firm', *Journal of Business Ethics*, 9(9): 741–50.

Harris, P., Lock, A. and Rees, P. (2000) *Machiavelli, Marketing and Management*. London: Routledge.

Harrison, E.F. (1987) *The Management Decision-Making Process*. Boston, MA: Houghton Mifflin.

Hart, C. (1998) *A Child's Machiavelli: A Primer on Power*. New York: Studio.

Hartley, J., Benington, J. and Binns, P. (1997) 'Researching the roles of internal agents of change in the management of organizational change', *British Journal of Management*, 8(1): 61–73.

Hassard, J. and Holliday, R. (eds) (1998) *Organization Representation: Work and Organization in Popular Culture*. London: Sage Publications.

Hawley, C. (2001) *100+ Tactics for Office Politics*. New York: Barrons.

Hersey, P., Blancard, K.H. and Johnson, D.E. (2007) *Management of Organizational Behavior: Leading Human Resources*. New Jersey: Prentice Hall.

Hewlett, S.A. (2002) 'Executive women and the myth of having it all', *Harvard Business Review*, 80(4): 66–73.

Hickson, D.J., Hinings, C.R., Lee, C.A., Schneck, R.E. and Pennings, J.M. (1971) 'A strategic contingencies theory of intra-organizational power', *Administrative Science Quarterly*, 16(2): 216–29.

Higgins, S.O.L. and Gilberd, P. (2000) *Leadership Secrets of Elizabeth I*. Cambridge MA: Perseus Publishing.

Hiley, D.R. (1987) 'Power and values in corporate life', *Journal of Business Ethics*, 6(5): 343–53.

Hite, S. (2000) *Sex and Business*. London: Financial Times Prentice Hall.

Hobbes, T. (1651) Leviathan. Harmondsworth: Penguin 1982.

Hochschild, A.R. (1979) 'Emotion work, feeling rules and social structures', *American Journal of Sociology*, 85(3): 551–75.

Hochschild, A.R. (1983) *The Managed Heart: Commercialization of Human Feeling*. Berkeley, CA: University of California Press.

Hochschild, A.R. (1997) *The Time Bind: When Work Becomes Home and Home Becomes Work*. New York: Henry Holt and Co.

Hochschild, A.R. and Machung, A. (1989) *The Second Shift*. New York: Avon Books.

Holden, M. (2003) *The Use and Abuse of Office Politics: How to Survive and Thrive in the Corporate Jungle*. Sydney: Allen and Unwin.

Holstein, J.A. and Gubrium, J.F. (2000) *The Self We Live By: Narrative Identity in a Postmodern World*. New York: Oxford University Press.

Hope, K. (2006) 'Style gains substance', *People Management*, 23 February, 18–19.

Hoyle, E. and Wallace, M. (2005) *Educational Leadership: Ambiguity, Professionals and Managerialism*. London: Sage Publications.

Huczynski, A. (2003) *Influencing Within Organizations: Getting In, Rising Up and Moving On*. London: Routledge. (second edn.)

Hughes, E.C. (1958) *Men and Their Work*. Westport, CT: Greenwood Press.

Hutton, D.W. (1994) *The Change Agent's Handbook: A Survival Guide for Quality Improvement Champions*. Milwaukee, WI: ASQC Quality Press.

Jackall, R. (1988) *Moral Mazes: The World of Corporate Managers*. New York: Oxford University Press.

Johns, T. (1995) 'Don't be afraid of the moral maze', *People Management*, 1(20): 32–4.

Johnson, P. and Gill, J. (1993) *Management Control and Organizational Behaviour*. London: Paul Chapman.

Kacmar, K.M. and Carlson, D.S. (1997) 'Further validation of the perceptions of politics scale (POPS): a multiple sample investigation', *Journal of Management*, 23(5): 627–58.

Kacmar, K.M. and Ferris, G.R. (1991) 'Perceptions of organizational politics scale (POPS): development and construct validation', *Educational and Psychological Measurement*, 51(1): 193–205.

Kakabadse, A. and Parker, C. (1984) *Power, Politics and Organizations: A Behavioural Science View*. Chichester: Wiley & Sons.

Kamoche, K.N., Pina e Cunha, M. and Vieira da Cunha, J. (eds) (2002) *Organizational Improvisation*. London and New York: Routledge.

Kanter, R.M. (1979) 'Power failure in management circuits', *Harvard Business Review*, 57(4): 65–75.

Kanter, R.M. (1983a) *The Change Masters: Corporate Entrepreneurs at Work*. London: George Allen & Unwin.

Kanter, R.M. (1983b) *Men and Women of the Corporation*. New York: Basic Books.

Kanter, R.M. (1989) *When Giants Learn to Dance: Mastering The Challenges of Strategy, Management, and Careers in the 1990s*. London: Unwin.

Kanter, R.M. (1997) *Rosabeth Moss Kanter on the Frontiers of Management*. Boston, MA: Harvard Business School Press.

Kanter, R.M. (2004) *Confidence: How Winning Streaks and Losing Streaks Begin and End*. London: Random House.

Kanter, R.M. (2005) *Commitment and Community: Communes and Utopias in Sociological Perspective*. Cambridge, MA: Harvard University Press.

Kanter, R.M. (2006) 'Leading with Confidence', paper presented at the Global Leaders Network Seminar, Sydney.

Kanter, R.M., Stein, B.A. and Jick, T.D. (2003) *The Challenge of Organizational Change: How People Experience It and Manage It*. New York: Free Press.

Keen, P.G.W. (1981) 'Information systems and organizational change', *Communications of the ACM*, 24(1): 24–33.

Kennedy, R.F. (1968) *Thirteen Days: The Cuban Missile Crisis October 1962*. London: Macmillan.

Kim, W.C. and Mauborgne, R. (2003) 'Tipping point leadership', *Harvard Business Review*, 81(4): 60–9.

Kipnis, D., Schmidt, S.M., Swaffin-Smith, C. and Wilkinson, I. (1984) 'Patterns of managerial influence: shotgun managers, tacticians, and bystanders', *Organizational Dynamics*, 12(3): 58–67.

Klein, J. (2004) *True Change: How Outsiders on the Inside Get Things Done in Organizations*. San Francisco, CA: Jossey-Bass.

Klein, J.I. (1988) 'The myth of the corporate political jungle: politicization as a political strategy', *Journal of Management Studies*, 25(1): 1–12.

Knights, D. and Murray, F. (1994) *Managers Divided*. Aldershot: Gower.

Kondo, D.C. (1990) *Crafting Selves: Power, Gender, and Discourses of Identity in a Japanese Workplace*. Chicago, IL: University of Chicago Press.

Kotter, J. and Cohen, D. (2002) *The Heart of Change: Real Life-Stories of How People Change Their Organizations*. Harvard: Harvard University Press.

Kotter, J.P. (1985) *Power and Influence: Beyond Formal Authority*. New York: Free Press.

Kotter, J.P. (1995) 'Leading change: why transformation efforts fail', *Harvard Business Review*, 73(2): 59–67.

Kotter, J.P. (1999) 'What effective general managers really do', *Harvard Business Review*, 77(2): 145–59.

Kramer, R.M. (2006) 'The great intimidators', *Harvard Business Review*, 84(2): 88–96.

Kumar, P. and Ghadially, R. (1989) 'Organizational politics and its effects on members of an organization', *Human Relations*, 42(2): 305–14.

Kumar, K. and Thibodeaux, M. (1990) 'Organizational politics and planned organizational change', *Group and Organizational Studies*, 15(4): 357–65.

Kunda, G. (1992) *Engineering Culture: Control and Commitment in a High-Tech Corporation*. Philadelphia: Templeton University Press.

Laborde, G.Z. (1987) *Influencing With Integrity: Management Skills for Communication and Negotiation*. Bethel, CT: Crown House Publishing.

Lasch, C. (1979) *The Culture of Narcissism: American Life in an Age of Diminishing Expectations*. New York: W.W. Norton & Co.

Latour, B. (1988) 'How to write *The Prince* for machines as well as for machinations', in B. Elliott (ed.). *The Control of Technology*. Edinburgh: Edinburgh University Press. pp.20–43.

Laver, M. (1997) *Private Desires, Political Action: An Invitation to the Politics of Rational Choice*. London: Sage Publications.

Law, J. and Callon, M. (1992) 'The life and death of an aircraft: a network analysis of technical change', in W. Bijker and J. Law (eds), *Shaping Technology/Building Society: Studies in Sociotechnical Change*. Cambridge, MA: MIT Press. pp.21–52.

Leary, M.R., Knight, P.D. and Barnes, B.D. (1986) 'Ethical ideologies of the Machiavellian', *Personality and Social Psychology Bulletin*, 12(1): 75–80.

Leavitt, H.J. (2005) *Top Down: Why Hierarchies Are Here to Stay and How to Manage Them More Effectively*. Boston, MA: Harvard Business School Press.

Ledeen, M. (2000) *Machiavelli on Modern Leadership: Why Machiavelli's Iron Rules are as Timely and Important Today*. New York: St Martins Press.

Lee, B. (1992) *Savvy: Thirty Days to a Different Perspective*. Knoxville, TN: Alliance Press.

Lee, B. (1997) *The Power Principle: Influence with Honor*. New York: Simon and Schuster.

Lencioni, P. (2006) *Silos, Politics and Turf Wars*. San Francisco, CA: Jossey-Bass.

Leonard, P. (2004) 'Westerns, weddings and web-weavers: reading gender as genre in organizational theory', *Gender, Work and Organization*, 11(1): 74–94.

Leonard-Barton, D. (1995) *Wellsprings of Knowledge: Building and Sustaining the Sources of Innovation*. Boston, MA: Harvard Business School Press.

Leseure, M., Birdi, K., Bauer, J., Denyer, D. and Neely, A. (2004) *Adoption of Promising Practice: A Systematic Review of the Literature*. London: Advanced Institute of Management Research.

Lewin, K. (ed.) (1951) *Field Theory in Social Science: Selected Theoretical Papers by Kurt Lewin*. London: Tavistock Publications. (UK edition published 1952, edited by Dorwin Cartwright)

Lifton, R.J. (1989) *Thought Reform and the Psychology of Totalism: A Study of 'Brainwashing' in China*. Chapel Hill: University of North Carolina Press.

Linde, C. (1993) *Life Stories: The Creation of Coherence*. New York: Oxford University Press.

Lord, C. (2003) *The Modern Prince: What Leaders Need to Know*. New Haven, CT: Yale University Press.

Lukes, S. (2006) *Power: A Radical View*. London: Palgrave Macmillan. (second edn.)

McAdams, D.P. (1997) *The Stories We Live By: Personal Myths and the Making of the Self*. New York: The Guilford Press.

McAdams, D.P. (2005) *The Redemptive Self: Stories Americans Live By*. New York: Oxford University Press.

McAlpine, A. (1997) *The New Machiavelli: Renaissance Realpolitik For Modern Managers*. London: Aurum Press.

McCabe, D. (2006) 'The house of the dead: strategic and operational limits to the enterprise self', paper presented at the European Group for Organization Studies Conference, Bergen, Norway.

McCall, M.W. and Kaplan, R.E. (1990) *Whatever it Takes: The Realities of Managerial Decision Making*. Englewood Cliffs, NJ: Prentice Hall. (second edn.)

McCarty, J. (2004) *Bullets Over Hollywood: The American Gangster Picture from the Silents to "The Sopranos"*. Cambridge, MA: Da Capo Press.

McClelland, D.C. (1970) 'The two faces of power', *Journal of International Affairs*, 24(1): 29–47.

McClelland, D.C. (1975) *Power: The Inner Experience*. New York: Irvington.

McClelland, D.C. and Burnham, D.H. (1995) 'Power is the great motivator', *Harvard Business Review*, 73(1): 126–39 (first published 1976).

McGregor, D.M. (1960) *The Human Side of Enterprise*. New York: McGraw-Hill.

MacGregor Serven, L.B. (2002) *The End of Office Politics as Usual: A Complete Strategy for Creating a More Productive and Profitable Organization*. New York: AmACOM.

McHoskey, J.W., Worzel, W. and Szyarto, C. (1998) 'Machiavellianism and psychopathology', *Journal of Personality and Social Psychology*, 74(1): 192–210.

MacIntyre, A.C. (1985) *After Virtue: A Study in Moral Theory*. London: Duckworth.

MacIntyre, M.G. (2005) *Secrets to Winning at Office Politics: How to Achieve Your Goals and Increase Your Influence at Work*. New York: St Martins Press.

McKinlay, A. and Starkey, K. (eds) (1998) *Foucault, Management and Organization Theory*. London: Sage Publications.

McLaughlin, M.L., Cody, M.J. and Read, S.J. (1992) *Explaining One's Self to Others: Reason-Giving in a Social Context*. Hillsdale, NJ: Lawrence Erlbaum Associates.

McLoughlin, I. and Badham, R. (2005) 'Political process perspectives on organization and technological change', *Human Relations*, 58(7): 827–45.

McLoughlin, I., Badham, R. and Couchman, P. (2000) 'Rethinking politics and process in technological change', *Technology Analysis and Strategic Management*, 12(1): 17–39.

McMurry, R.N. (1973) 'Power and the ambitious executive', *Harvard Business Review*, 51(6): 140–45.

Maccoby, M. (1978) *The Gamesman: Winning and Losing the Career Game*. New York: Bantam.

Maccoby, M. (2000) 'Narcissistic leaders', *Harvard Business Review*, 78(1): 68–77.

Machiavelli, N. (1514) *The Prince*. (George Bull, trans.) London: Penguin Books 1961.

Machiavelli, N. (1531) *The Discourses*. (Leslie Walker, trans.) Harmondsworth: Penguin Classics 1984.

Madison, D.L., Allen, R.W., Porter, L.W., Renwick, P.A. and Mayes, B.T. (1980) 'Organizational politics: an exploration of managers' perceptions', *Human Relations*, 33(2): 79–100.

Maidique, M.A. (1980) 'Entrepreneurs, champions and technological innovation', *Sloan Management Review*, 21(2): 59–76.

Mainiero, L.A. (1994a) 'On breaking the glass ceiling: the political seasoning of powerful women executives', *Organizational Dynamics*, 22(4): 5–20.

Mainiero, L.A. (1994b) 'Getting anointed for advancement: the case for executive women', *Academy of Management Executive*, 8(2): 53–67.

Mangham, I. (1979) *The Politics of Organizational Change*. Westport, CT: Greenwood Press.

Mann, M. (1986) *The Source of Social Power Volume 1: A History of Power from the Beginning to AD 1760*. Cambridge: Cambridge University Press.

Mann, S. (1995) 'Politics and power in organizations; why women lose out', *Leadership and Organization Development Journal*, 16(2): 9–15.

March, J.G. (1974) *Leadership and Ambiguity: The American College President*. New Jersey: McGraw-Hill.

March, J.G. (1991) 'Exploration and exploitation in organizational learning', *Organization Science*, 2(1): 71–87.

March, J.G. (2006) 'Rationality, foolishness, and adaptive intelligence', *Strategic Management Journal*, 27(3): 201–14.

March, J.G. and Olsen, J.P. (1983) 'Organizing political life: what administrative reorganization tells us about government', *American Political Science Review*, 77(2): 281–96.

Markus, M.L. (1983) 'Power, politics and MIS implementation', *Communications of the ACM*, 26(6): 430–44.

Martin, N.H. and Sims, J.H. (1964) 'Power tactics', in H.J. Leavitt and L.R. Pondy (eds), *Readings in Managerial Psychology*. Chicago and London: The University of Chicago Press. pp.217–25.

Maslyn, J.M., Farmer, S.M. and Fedor, D.B. (1996) 'Failed upward influence attempts: predicting the nature of subordinate persistence in pursuit of organizational goals', *Group and Organization Management*, 21(4): 461–80.

Matejka, K., Ashworth, D.N. and Dodd-McCue, D. (1985) 'More power to ya!' *Management Quarterly*, 26: 33–4.

Mayes, B.T. and Allen, R.W. (1977) 'Toward a definition of organizational politics', *Academy of Management Review*, 2: 672–8.

Mead, G.H. (1967) *Mind, Self, and Society: From the Standpoint of a Social Behaviorist*. Chicago, IL: University of Chicago Press.

Metcalf, H.C. and Urwick, L. (eds) (1940) *Dynamic Administration: The Collected Papers of Mary Parker Follett*. New York: Harper and Brothers.

Meyerson, D.E. (2001) *Tempered Radicals: How People Use Difference to Inspire Change at Work*. Boston, MA: Harvard Business School Press.

Mills, C.W. (1951) *White Collar: The American Middle Classes*. New York: Oxford University Press.

Mintzberg, H. (1977) 'The manager's job: folklore and fact', *Harvard Business Review*, 55(44): 49–61.

Mintzberg, H. (1983) *Power in and Around Organizations*. New Jersey: Prentice Hall.

Morris, D. (2000) *The New Prince: Machiavelli Updated for the Twenty-First Century*. New York: Renaissance Books.

Nadler, D. (1998) *Champions of Change: How CEOs and Their Companies Are Mastering the Skills of Radical Change*. San Francisco: Jossey-Bass.

Nadler, D.A. and Tushman, M.L. (1989) 'Organizational frame bending: principles for managing reorientation', *Academy of Management Executive*, 3(3): 194–204.

Nadler, D.A., Shaw, R.B. and Walton, A.E. (1995) *Discontinuous Change: Leading Organizational Transformation*. San Francisco, CA: Jossey-Bass.

Nonaka, I. and Takeuchi, H. (1995) *The Knowledge Creating Company: How Japanese Companies Create the Dynamics of Innovation*. New York: Oxford University Press.

Nye, J. (2002) 'The new Rome meets the new barbarians', *The Economist*, 362(8265): 23–5.

Oakley, J. (2000) 'Gender-based barriers to senior management positions: understanding the scarcity of female CEOs', *Journal of Business Ethics*, 27(4): 321–34.

O'Connor, E.S. (1995) 'Paradoxes of participation: textual analysis and organizational change', *Organization Studies*, 16(5): 769–803.

Orlikowski, W.J. (1996) 'Improvising organizational transformation over time: a situated change perspective', *Information Systems Research*, 7(1): 63–92.

Orlikowski, W. and Gash, D.C. (1994) 'Technological frames: making sense of information technology in organizations', *ACM Transactions on Information Systems*, 2(2): 174–207.

Ottaway, R.N. (1983) 'The change agent: a taxonomy in relation to the change process', *Human Relations*, 36(4): 361–92.

Oxford English Dictionary, www.askoxford.com.

Page, R.A. and Wiersema, M.F. (1992) 'Entrepreneurial strategies and radical innovation: a punctuated disequilibrium approach', *The Journal of High Technology Management Research*, 3(1): 65–81.

Palmer, I., Dunford, R. and Aking, G. (2005) *Managing Organizational Change: A Multiple Perspectives Approach*. New York: McGraw-Hill.

Park, R.E. (1928) 'Human migration and the marginal man', *The American Journal of Sociology*, 33(6): 881–93.

Paul, Annie M. (1999) *One Mean Renaissance Man*, http://www.salon.com/books/it/1999/09/13/machiavelli, pp. 1–4.

Peled, A. (1999) 'Politicking for success: the missing skill', *Leadership and Organizational Change*, 21(1): 20–9.

Pennings, J.M., Cobbenhagen, J. and Hertog, F.D. (1994) 'Core competencies and organizational innovativeness', Maastricht: Working Paper 1994–035, United Nations University-MERIT.

Perrewé, P.L. and Nelson, D.L. (2004) 'Gender and career success: the facilitative role of political skill', *Organizational Dynamics*, 33(4): 366–78.

Perrewé, P.L., Ferris, G.R., Frink, D.D. and Anthony, W.P. (2000) 'Political skill: an antidote for workplace stressors', *Academy of Management Executive*, 14(3): 115–23.

Peters, T. (1994) 'Interview', *Independent on Sunday*, 15 May.

Pettigrew, A.M. (1973) *The Politics of Organizational Decision-Making*. London: Tavistock Publications.

Pettigrew, A.M. (1974) 'The influence process between specialists and executives', *Personnel Review*, 3(1): 24–30.

Pettigrew, A.M. (1977) 'Strategy formulation as a political process', *International Studies of Management and Organization*, 7(2): 78–87.

Pettigrew, A.M. (1985) *The Awakening Giant: Continuity and Change in ICI*. Oxford: Basil Blackwell.

Pettigrew, A.M. (1987) 'Context and action in the transformation of the firm', *Journal of Management Studies*, 24(6): 649–70.

Pettigrew, A.M. (ed.) (1988) *The Management of Strategic Change*. Oxford: Basil Blackwell.

Pettigrew, A.M. and Fenton, E.M. (eds) (2000) *The Innovating Organization*. London: Sage Publications.

Pettigrew, A.M. and McNulty, T. (1995) 'Power and influence in and around the boardroom', *Human Relations*, 48(8): 845–73.

Pettigrew, A.M., Ferlie, E. and McKee, L. (1992) *Shaping Strategic Change: Making Change in Large Organizations – The Case of the National Health Service*. London: Sage Publications.

Pfeffer, J. (1992a) *Managing With Power: Politics and Influence in Organization*. Boston, MA: Harvard Business School Press.

Pfeffer, J. (1992b) 'Understanding power in organizations', *California Management Review*, 34(2): 29–50.

Pfeffer, J. and Sutton, R.I. (2006) *Hard Facts, Dangerous Half-Truths, and Total Nonsense: Profiting from Evidence-Based Management*. Boston, MA: Harvard Business School Press.

Phipps, M. and Gautrey, C. (2005) *21 Dirty Tricks at Work: How to Win at Office Politics*. Oxford: Capstone Publishing.

Pinchot, G. (1985) *Intrapreneuring: Why You Don't Have to Leave the Corporation to Become an Entrepreneur*. New York: Harper & Row.

Pitkin, F.H. (1984) *Fortune is a Woman*. Berkeley and San Francisco: University of California Press.

Provis, C. (2004) *Ethics and Organisational Politics*. Cheltenham, UK: Edward Elgar Publishing Limited.

Provis, C. (2005) 'Dirty hands and loyalty in organizational politics', *Business Ethics Quarterly*, 15(2): 283–98.

Punch, M. (1996) *Dirty Business: Exploring Corporate Misconduct*. London: Sage Publications.

Quinn, J.B. (1980) 'Managing strategic change', *Sloan Management Review*, 21(4): 3–20.

Rabinow, P. (ed.) (1984) *The Foucault Reader*, London: Penguin Books.

Rankin, I. (1995) *Blood Hunt*. London: Headline/Orion Books.

Read, S.J. (1992) 'Constructing accounts: the role of explanatory coherence', in M.L. McLaughlin, M.J. Cody and S.J. Read (eds), *Explaining One's Self to Others: Reason-Giving in a Social Context*. Hillsdale, New Jersey: Lawrence Erlbaum Associates. pp.3–19.

Redman, T. and Snape, E. (2005) 'Unpacking commitments: multiple loyalties and employee behaviours', *Journal of Management Studies*, 42(2): 301–28.

Reed, M. (1989) *The Sociology of Management*. London: Harvester Wheatsheaf.

Rees, D. (2004) *Women in the Boardroom: A Bird's Eye View*. London: Chartered Institute for Personnel and Development.

Rein, I.J., Kotler, P., Stoller, M.R. and Hamlin, M. (2006) *High Visibility: Transforming Your Personal and Professional Brand*. New York: McGraw-Hill Publishing Co. (third edn.)

Riesman, D. (1950) *The Lonely Crowd: A Study of the Changing American Character*. New Haven, CT: Yale University Press.

Riley, P. (1983) 'A structurationist account of political culture', *Administrative Science Quarterly*, 28(3): 414–37.

Ritzer, G. (ed.) (2006) *McDonaldization: The Reader*. Thousand Oaks, CA: Pine Forge Press. (second edn.)

Robbins, S.P. (2005) *Organizational Behaviour*. Englewood Cliffs, NJ: Prentice Hall. (eleventh edn.)

Rogers, E. (1995) *The Diffusion of Innovation*. New York: Free Press. (fourth edn.)

Rose, N. (1989) *Governing the Soul*. London: Routledge.

Rosenfeld, P., Giacalone, R.A. and Riordan, C.A. (1995) *Impression Management in Organizations: Theory, Measurement, Practice*. London: Routledge.

Rousseau, J.J. (1762) *The Social Contract or Principles of Political Right*. (M. Cranston, trans.) Harmondsworth: Penguin Books (1968 edition).

Rozakis, L. and Rozakis, B. (1998) *The Complete Idiot's Guide to Office Politics*. New York: Macmillan.

Rubin, H. (1997) *Princessa: Machiavelli for Women*. London: Bloomsbury Publishing.

Russell, B. (1938) *A New Social Analysis*. London: George Allen & Unwin.

Ryan, M.K. and Haslam, S.A. (2005) 'The glass cliff: evidence that women are over-represented in precarious leadership positions', *British Journal of Management*, 16(2): 81–90.

Ryan, M.K. and Haslam, S.A. (2007) 'The glass cliff: exploring the dynamics surrounding the appointment of women to precarious leadership positions', *Academy of Management Review*, 32(2): 549–72.

Salaman, G. and Storey, J. (2006) 'Understanding enterprise', paper presented at the European Group for Organization Studies Conference, Bergen, Norway.

Salmon, R. and Salmon, W. (1999) *Office Politics for the Utterly Confused*. New York: McGraw-Hill.

Savage, M. (1998) 'Discipline, surveillance and the 'career': employment on the Great Western Railway 1833–1914', in A. McKinlay and K. Starkey (eds), *Foucault, Management and Organization Theory*. London: Sage Publications. pp.65–92.

Schein, E. (1996) 'Kurt Lewin's change theory in the field and in the classroom: notes toward a model of managed learning', *Systemic Practice and Action Research*, 9(9): 27–47.

Schein, E.H. (1961) *Coercive Persuasion: A Socio-psychological Analysis of the Brainwashing of American Civilian Prisoners by the Chinese Communists*. New York: W.W. Norton & Co.

Schein, E.H. (1979) *Organizational Psychology*. New York: Prentice Hall.

Schilit, W.K. (1986) 'An examination of individual differences as moderators of upward influence activity in strategic decisions', *Human Relations*, 39(10): 933–53.

Schön, D.A. (1963) 'Champions for radical new inventions', *Harvard Business Review*, 41(2): 77–86.

Schön, D.A. (1983) *The Reflective Practitioner: How Professionals Think in Action*. New York: Basic Books.

Schrijvers, J.P.M. (2004) *The Way of the Rat: A Survival Guide to Office Politics*. London: Cyan Books.

Schumpeter, J. (1968) *The Theory of Economic Development*. Cambridge, MA: Harvard University Press.

Schumpeter, J. (1979) *Capitalism, Socialism and Democracy*. London: Allen and Unwin.

Scott-Morgan, P. (1995) *The Unwritten Rules of the Game*. New York: McGraw-Hill.

Selznick, P. (1957) *Leadership in Administration*. New York: Harper & Row.

Semadar, A., Robins, G. and Ferris, G.R. (2006) 'Comparing the validity of multiple social effectiveness constructs in the prediction of managerial job performance', *Journal of Organizational Behaviour*, 27(4): 443–61.

Sennett, R. (1998) *The Corrosion of Character: The Personal Consequences of Work in the New Capitalism*. New York: W.W. Norton & Co.

Sewell, G. (1998) 'The discipline of teams: the control of team-based industrial work through electronic and peer surveillance', *Administrative Science Quarterly*, 43(2): 397–428.

Sewell, G. and Barker, J.R. (2006) 'Coercion versus care: using irony to make sense of organizational surveillance', *Academy of Management Review*, 31(4): 934–61.

Shaw, B. (2004) 'Hollywood ethics: developing ethical issues Hollywood style', *Journal of Business Ethics*, 49(2): 167–77.

Shulman, D. (2006) *From Hire to Liar: The Role of Deception in the Workplace*. New York: ILR Press.

Sinclair, A. (2007) *Leadership for the Disillusioned: Moving Beyond Myths and Heroes to Leading That Liberates*. Melbourne: Allen and Unwin.

Singer Dopson, M.D. (2001) *Enlightened Office Politics: Understanding, Coping with, and Winning the Game – Without Losing Your Soul*. New York: AmACOM.

Singer, M.T. (1995) *Cults in our Midst: The Hidden Menace in Our Everyday Lives*. San Francisco, CA: Jossey-Bass.

Singh, V. and Vinnicombe, S. (2005) *The Female FTSE Report 2005*. Cranfield: Cranfield University School of Management.

Singh, V., Kumra, S. and Vinnicombe, S. (2002) 'Gender and impression management: playing the promotion game', *Journal of Business Ethics*, 37(1): 77–89.

Skinner, Q. (1981) *Machiavelli*. Oxford: Oxford University Press.

Smelser, N.J. (1998) 'The rational and the ambivalent in the social sciences: 1997 presidential address', *American Sociological Review*, 63(1): 1–16.

Smith, A. (1776) *An Inquiry into the Nature and Causes of the Wealth of Nations*. Harmondsworth: Penguin 1982.

Sonenshein, S. (2006) 'Crafting social issues at work', *Academy of Management Journal*, 49(6): 1158–72.

Stace, D.A. and Dunphy, D. (1994) *Beyond the Boundaries: Leading and Re-creating the Successful Enterprise*. Sydney: McGraw-Hill.

Stacey, R. (2007) *Strategic Management and Organizational Dynamics*. New Jersey: Prentice Hall. (fifth edn.)

Starkey, D. (2001) *Elizabeth: Apprenticeship*. London: Vintage.

Stewart, R. (1963) *The Reality of Management*. London: Pan/Heinemann.

Stjernberg, T. and Philips, A. (1993) 'Organizational innovations in a long-term perspective: legitimacy and souls-of-fire as critical factors of change and viability', *Human Relations*, 46(10): 1193–221.

Stogdill, R.M. (1948) 'Personal factors associated with leadership', *Journal of Psychology*, 25: 35–71.

Stogdill, R.M. (1974) *Handbook of Leadership: A Survey of Theory and Research*. New York: Free Press.

Stokes, J. and Clegg, S.R. (2002) 'Once upon a time in a bureaucracy: power and public sector management', *Organization*, 9(2): 225–47.

Stone, B. (1997) *Confronting Company Politics*. Houndmills, Hampshire: Macmillan Business.

Swan, J. and Scarbrough, H. (2005) 'The politics of networked innovation', *Human Relations*, 58(7): 913–43.

Tannen, D. (1990) *You Just Don't Understand: Women and Men in Conversation*. New York: William Morrow.

Tannen, D. (1995) 'The power of talk: who gets heard and why', *Harvard Business Review*, 73(5): 138–48.

Thompkins, J.M. (1990) 'Politics: the illegitimate discipline', *Management Decision*, 28(4): 23–8.

Trinca, H. and Fox, C. (2004) *Better than Sex: How a Whole Generation Got Hooked on Work*. Sydney: Random House.

Tuchman, B. (1990) *The March of Folly*. New York: Abacus.

Turnbull, S. (2001) 'Quasi-religious experiences in a corporate change programme: the roles of conversion and the confessional in corporate evangelism', paper presented at the Critical Management Studies conference, University of Manchester.

Turner, R. (1987) *The Anthropology of Performance*. New York: PAJ Publications.

Tushman, M.L. and O'Reilly, C.A. (1997) *Winning through Innovation: A Practical Guide to Leading Organizational Change and Renewal*. Boston, MA: Harvard Business School Press.

Ulrich, D. (1998) 'A new mandate for human resources', *Harvard Business Review*, 76(1): 124–34.

Valle, M. and Perrewé, P.L. (2000) 'Do politics perceptions relate to political behaviours?: tests of an implicit assumption and expanded model', *Human Relations*, 53(3): 359–86.

Van de Ven, A.H., Polley, D.E., Garud, R. and Venkataraman, S. (1999) *The Innovation Journey*. New York and Oxford: Oxford University Press.

Van Maanen, J. (1980) 'Beyond account: the personal impact of police shootings', *American Academy of Political and Social Science*, 452: 145–56.

Veblen, T. (1958) *The Theory of Business Enterprise*. New York: Mentor Books.

Velasquez, M., Moberg, D.J. and Cavanagh, G.F. (1983) 'Organizational statesmanship and dirty politics: ethical guidelines for the organizational politician', *Organizational Dynamics*, 12(2): 65–80.

Victor, B. and Stephens, C. (2004) 'The dark side of the new organizational forms: an editorial essay', *Organization Science*, 5(4): 479–82.

Vigoda, E. (2003) *Developments in Organizational Politics: How Political Dynamics Affect Employee Performance in Modern Work Sites*. Cheltenham, UK: Edward Elgar Publishing Limited.

Vigoda-Gadot, E. and Kapun, D. (2005) 'Perceptions of politics and perceived performance in public and private organizations: a test of one model across two sectors', *Policy and Politics*, 33(2): 251–76.

Von Zugbach, R. (1995) *The Winning Manager: Coming Out on Top in the Organization Game*. London: Souvenir Press.

Voss, B. (1992) 'Office politics: a player's guide', *Sales and Marketing Management*, 144(12): 46–52.

Voyer, J.J. (1994) 'Coercive organizational politics and organizational outcomes: an interpretive study', *Organization Science*, 5(1): 72–85.

Wallace, P.G. (1990) 'Power in practice', *Australian Health Review*, 13(1): 55–62.

Ward, M. (1994) *Why Your Corporate Culture Change Isn't Working*. Aldershot: Gower.

Watson, T.J. (1994) *In Search of Management: Culture, Chaos and Control in Managerial Work*. London: Routledge.

Webb, M.S. (2006) 'Why boys get better gifts – and higher salaries', *The Sunday Times, Money*, 1 January, 3.9.

Weber, M. (1919) *Politics as a Vocation* (D. Owen and T.B. Strong, trans.) London: Hackett. (2004 edn.)

Weick, K.E. (2000) *Making Sense of the Organization*. Oxford: Blackwell.

Weick, K.E. and Sutcliffe, K.M. (2001) *Managing the Unexpected: Assuring High-Performance in an Age of Complexity*. San Francisco, CA: Jossey-Bass.

Wellins, R.S., Byham, W.C. and Wilson, J.M. (1991) *Empowered Teams: Creating Self-Directed Work Groups that Improve Quality, Productivity and Participation*. San Francisco, CA: Jossey-Bass.

Wells, H.G. (1910) *The New Machiavelli*. London: Penguin Classics. (2005 edition.)

Wenger, E. (1998) *Communities of Practice: Learning, Meaning and Identity*. Cambridge: Cambridge University Press.

Whittington, R. and Mayer, M. (2002) *Organizing for Success in the Twenty-First Century: A Starting Point for Change*. London: Chartered Institute of Personnel and Development.

Whyte, W.H. (1955) *The Organization Man*. Harmondsworth, Middlesex: Penguin Books.

Wickenberg, J. and Kylén, S. (2004) 'How frequent is organizational political behaviour?' Göteborg: Fenix Program, Chalmers University of Technology.

Wight, M. (1978) *Power Politics*. Harmondsworth: Penguin Books.

Willis, P.E. (1977) *Learning to Labour: How Working Class Kids Get Working Class Jobs*. London: Saxon House.

Wilson, F. (2002) *Organizational Behaviour and Gender*. Aldershot: Ashgate. (second edn.)

Wolfe, R.L. (1997) *Office Politics: Positive Results from Fair Practices*. Menlo Park, CA: Crisp Publications.

Wood, K.G. (2001) *Don't Sabotage Your Success: Make Office Politics Work*. Oakland, CA: Enlightened Concepts Publishing.

Wooldridge, E. and Wallace, L. (2002) 'Modern times: public sector modernization', *People Management*, 8(7): 28–30.

Yeung, R. (2003) *The Ultimate Career Success Workbook*. London: Kogan Page.

Young, M. (1958) *The Rise of the Meritocracy*. Harmondsworth, Middlesex: Penguin Books.

Zaleznik, A. (1997) 'Real work', *Harvard Business Review*, 75(6): 53–63.

Author index

Subject index